Post-trauma and the Recovery Governance of Cultural Heritage

Toshiyuki Kono · Junko Okahashi
Editors

Post-trauma and the Recovery Governance of Cultural Heritage

Springer

Editors
Toshiyuki Kono
Graduate School of Law
Kyushu University
Fukuoka, Japan

Junko Okahashi
Faculty of Liberal Arts
University of the Sacred Heart
Tokyo, Japan

ISBN 978-981-19-6040-6 ISBN 978-981-19-6041-3 (eBook)
https://doi.org/10.1007/978-981-19-6041-3

This Springer imprint is published by the registered company Springer Nature Singapore Pte Ltd.
The registered company address is: 152 Beach Road, #21-01/04 Gateway East, Singapore 189721, Singapore

Contents

Editors and Contributors

About the Editors

Toshiyuki Kono is Director, executive vice president, and distinguished professor of Kyushu University, Japan. He was born in Osaka, Japan, in 1958. After graduating from the Faculty of Law, Kyoto University, he went on to obtain his LL.M. from the Graduate School of Law, Kyoto University. He is a specialist in private international law, international civil procedure law, and international cultural heritage law. He was a member of UNESCO's Expert Groups for the drafting of the Convention for the Safeguarding of the Intangible Cultural Heritage (2003) and the Convention on the Protection and Promotion of the Diversity of Cultural Expressions (2005). He was appointed as a member of the Executive Committee of the International Council on Monuments and Sites (ICOMOS) in 2011. After working as vice president, he was elected as the 8th president of ICOMOS in 2017. As the former president, he continues as an honorary president of ICOMOS. He is the series editor of Springer's book series Perspectives in Law, Business, and Innovation.

Junko Okahashi is currently an associate professor in international cultural cooperation at the University of the Sacred Heart, Tokyo, Japan. She holds a Ph.D. in Arts and Sciences (Area Studies) from the University of Tokyo. As a staff member and program specialist of UNESCO from 2002 to 2011, she assisted states parties to the Convention concerning the Protection of the World Cultural and Natural Heritage. She continued to advocate for the implementation of their cultural heritage policies, in particular through formulating World Heritage site management plans in Asia and activating the process of World Heritage periodic reporting in Africa. Her research quest in cultural heritage policies and the theory/philosophy of conservation is sought through a combination of document-based work and fieldwork. She investigates the correlation and compatibility between multilateral governance of international norms related to cultural heritage (World Heritage, import and export of cultural properties, intangible cultural heritage, cultural diversity, historic urban landscapes) and case-specific on-site conditions, in an attempt to harmonize local needs and international orientations.

Contributors

Kealy Loughlin School of Architecture, University College Dublin, Dublin, Ireland

Kono Toshiyuki Kyushu University, Fukuoka, Japan

Marchand Trevor H. J. Social Anthropology, School of Oriental and African Studies, London, UK

Mukai Junko Rimo Associates, Naha City, Okinawa, Japan

Nishi Kazuhiko Agency for Cultural Affairs, Tokyo, Japan

Okahashi Junko University of the Sacred Heart, Tokyo, Japan

Tanaka Eisuke Research Faculty of Media and Communication, Hokkaido University, Sapporo, Japan

Yamada Hiroki Research Institute of Cultural Properties, Teikyo University, Fuefuki city, Japan

Yatsunami Ren Kyushu University, Fukuoka, Japan

Part I
Limits of International Framework for the Post-trauma Recovery of Cultural Heritage

Chapter 1
Introduction

Toshiyuki Kono

Various stakeholders such as international organizations, NGOs, national governments, and experts, developed the concepts and methods of governance of cultural heritage throughout the twentieth century. Mainly to prevent the destruction of cultural heritage in the armed conflict, UNESCO and some leading NGOs developed international legal frameworks and collaborative activities on a global scale. On the other hand, there seem to be much fewer tools to cope with post-traumatic situations. The Convention for the Protection of the World Natural and Cultural Heritage may be the sole existing legal framework to cope with post-traumatic situations of cultural heritage. However, the "Kathmandu Valley" as a World Heritage property in Nepal, which the Gorkha Earthquake damaged in 2015, raises many issues related to the effectiveness of the World Heritage system, although various domestic and foreign stakeholders made many efforts after the earthquake. Part I of this volume illustrates the limits of the current international legal frameworks for the governance of cultural heritage and the management of post-disaster situations.

Toshiyuki Kono Distinguished professor, Kyushu University, Japan. Toshiyuki Kono was born in Osaka, Japan, in 1958. After graduating from the Faculty of Law, Kyoto University, he went on to obtain his LL.M. from the Graduate School of Law, Kyoto University. He is a specialist in private international law, international civil procedure law, and international cultural heritage law. He was a member of UNESCO's Expert Groups for the drafting of the Convention for the Safeguarding of the Intangible Cultural Heritage (2003) and the Convention on the Protection and Promotion of the Diversity of Cultural Expressions (2005). He was appointed as a member of the Executive Committee of the International Council on Monuments and Sites (ICOMOS) in 2011. After working as vice president, he was elected as the 8th president of ICOMOS in 2017. As the former president, he continues as an honorary president of ICOMOS. He is the series editor of Springer's book series Perspectives in Law, Business and Innovation.

T. Kono (✉)
Kyushu University, Fukuoka, Japan
e-mail: konoto@law.kyushu-u.ac.jp

T. Kono and J. Okahashi (eds.), *Post-Trauma and the Recovery Governance of Cultural Heritage*, https://doi.org/10.1007/978-981-19-6041-3_1

Chapter 2
Questioning the Adaptability of Global Governance in the Safeguarding of Cultural Heritage in Post-trauma Situations

Toshiyuki Kono

Abstract Existing international frameworks to protect the cultural heritage and those to prevent from disasters are insufficient to cope with recovering from such situations where cultural heritage was damaged or lost. In the context of the governance for the protection of cultural heritage, especially from legal perspectives, it is essential to arrange special case studies.

Keywords Conventions · UNESCO · Sendai Framework · ICOMOS · ICCROM · Global governance

2.1 International Cultural Heritage Law and the Post-trauma Situation

The protection of cultural heritage first became an international legal concern when Emmer Vattel discussed it in his book *Le Droit des Gens* (1758). The adoption of the legal form as a system for the protection of cultural heritage began with General Directive No. 100 (1863), signed by President Lincoln during the American Civil War. This document, known as the Lieber Code after its drafter, was the starting point for the position that churches, hospitals, libraries, museums, works of art, and collections should be treated with respect and as exceptions from a humanitarian point of view. This position was followed up by the Hague Convention with respect to the Laws and Customs of War on Land (1899, 1907) and the Geneva Convention (Convention IV) (1949). In contrast to this development of general international law, the Treaty on the Protection of Artistic and Scientific Institutions and Historic Monuments (Roerich Pact), a regional agreement among the nations of the Americas, was established in 1935 as international law specific to cultural heritage. However, it was not until the establishment of UNESCO in 1945 that it began to develop globally. UNESCO has so far established the Convention for the Protection of Cultural Property in the Event of Armed Conflict (the Hague Convention), its Protocol I (1954),

T. Kono (✉)
Kyushu University, Fukuoka, Japan
e-mail: konoto@law.kyushu-u.ac.jp

T. Kono and J. Okahashi (eds.), *Post-Trauma and the Recovery Governance of Cultural Heritage*, https://doi.org/10.1007/978-981-19-6041-3_2

and Protocol II (1999), the Convention on the Means of Prohibiting and Preventing the Illicit Import, Export, and Transfer of Ownership of Cultural Property (1970), the Convention on the Protection of the World Cultural and Natural Heritage (1972), the Convention for the Protection of the Underwater Heritage (2001), and the Convention for the Safeguarding of the Intangible Cultural Heritage (2003), comprising a total of five cultural heritage-related conventions. While the Hague Convention is a wartime law, the other four conventions are mechanisms for protecting cultural heritage in peacetime. They differ in that they are specific to certain categories of cultural heritage (movable property, immovable property, underwater heritage, and intangible heritage). Since they also differ in their protection methods, it is necessary to look at the functions and limitations of each treaty in the post-trauma context.

First, the 1970 Convention which copes with stolen or illegally exported cultural properties is primarily concerned with upstream and downstream regulation of the art market, focusing on the economic value of the cultural property, and does not explicitly address theft or export in response to disaster or war damage. In the case of the Underwater Heritage Convention, a typical example of an activity that the Convention seeks to prevent is the destruction of sunken ships for treasure hunting. To prevent this, the Convention requires preserving underwater cultural heritage *in situ* and prohibiting its movement. Underwater cultural heritage could be damaged by landslides on the seabed or destroyed by mines, but the Convention does not provide a mechanism to deal with such situations.

In the case of intangible cultural heritage, a violent act or natural disaster may cause damage to the person or community that holds the intangible cultural heritage. In such cases, the community's intangible cultural heritage would be registered on the List of Intangible Cultural Heritage in Need of Urgent Safeguarding. The Intergovernmental Committee would provide budgetary support for its protection. In reality, however, no such case has yet been registered on this list.[1] On the other hand, since the inception of the World Heritage Convention, there have been several cases of properties that have become World Heritage sites after being damaged or damaged after becoming World Heritage sites. For example, there are cases where properties were reconstructed after their destruction before becoming World Heritage Sites (e.g., the Old Town of Warsaw and Mostar). In some cases, simultaneous inscription on the World Heritage List and the List of the World Heritage in danger was used as leverage for reconstruction after an earthquake (e.g., Arge Bam). More recently, a World Heritage site was deliberately blown up (e.g., Palmyra), destroyed by an earthquake (e.g., Kathmandu), and damaged by fire (e.g., Notre-Dame de Paris). Financial and technical assistance may be provided through international cooperation, but this does not apply to movable property housed in the damaged buildings.

The Hague Convention (still Protocol I concerns restrictions on the movement and returns of movable cultural property) and Protocol II of 1999 apply to both buildings and collections. For example, the Biblioteca Nazionale Centrale di Firenze, one of the 17 items on the list[2] for "enhanced protection" introduced by Protocol II is an example

[1] https://ich.unesco.org/en/lists#2019.

[2] http://www.unesco.org/new/index.php?id=135808.

that includes both buildings and collections. However, both the Hague Convention and Protocol II apply only in the event of armed conflict. Furthermore, the "enhanced protection" of Protocol II, introduced to correct the institutional weaknesses of the Hague Convention, as mentioned above, lists only 17 cases. There is much to be done in terms of the effectiveness of the treaty regime.

Of the existing UNESCO conventions related to cultural heritage, the World Heritage Convention seems to be the only one that has worked from the perspective of recovery in post-traumatic situations. However, it is challenging to do anything about it if it is lost before inscribing on the World Heritage List. For example, the Declaration on the Intentional Destruction of Cultural Heritage, adopted by the UNESCO General Conference in 2003 in response to the bombing of the two Bamiyan Buddhas (before the inscription of Bamiyan Valley on the World Heritage List), suggests the limitations of the five cultural heritage-related conventions.

Practically only the World Heritage Convention has contributed to the reconstruction and recovery of cultural heritage in post-traumatic situations. The normative debate over damaged or destroyed world cultural heritage was on whether it retains "outstanding and universal value" or meets the authenticity and integrity requirements. The discussions were expert-centered.

In recent years, people have become increasingly aware of the impact of climate change[3] on cultural heritage, not to mention the intentional destruction of World Heritage sites and large-scale natural disasters such as earthquakes and typhoons. Hence, more dialogues between experts and citizens would be necessary.

2.2 International Framework for Disaster Prevention and Mitigation and Cultural Heritage

In the wake of the Great East Japan Earthquake, an international framework for disaster prevention and mitigation has been compiled as the Sendai Framework (2015–2030). The Sendai Framework includes a small number of provisions related to cultural heritage.[4]

Article 5 stresses that it is urgent and critical to anticipate, plan for and reduce disaster risk in order to more effectively protect...., cultural heritage..., and thus strengthen their resilience.[5] Article 24(d) emphasizes to systematically evaluate, record, share and publicly account for disaster losses and understand.... cultural

[3] A major expert meeting on cultural heritage and climate change was held by ICOMOS, UNESCO and IPCC at the end of 2021 IPCC-LIII(bis)/INF. 4.

[4] https://www.undrr.org/theme/cultural-heritage.

[5] (5) It is urgent and critical to anticipate, plan for and reduce disaster risk in order to more effectively protect persons, communities and countries, their livelihoods, health, cultural heritage, socioeconomic assets and ecosystems, and thus strengthen their resilience.

heritage impacts.[6] Furthermore, Article 30(d) recommends investments in disaster risk reduction, achieving resilience to protect and support the protection of cultural and collecting institutions and other sites of culturally relevant organizations, museums, and other sites of historical, cultural, and religious interests.[7]

In response to the Sendai Framework, UNESCO has submitted a report[8] on its activities in 2019 as a part of the 2019 Global Assessment Report on Disaster Risk Reduction (GAR),[9] which refers to three specific programs. These three programs are the Geoparks International Geoscience and Geoparks Programme (IGGP), the Man and the Biosphere Programme (MAB), and the World Heritage Convention.[10] UNESCO's implementation of the Sendai Framework may be limited to World Heritage sites concerning cultural heritage. As mentioned above, the World Heritage Convention is the only cultural heritage-related treaty that can be useful for coping with post-traumatic situations. If the Sendai Framework is also limited to World Heritage sites,[11] cultural heritage other than World Heritage sites is omitted from the ambit of international agreements on either side.[12]

From the perspective of international arrangements, there seems to be no framework that addresses the issues of cultural heritage, recovery, and reconstruction head-on, except for the World Heritage Convention. On the other hand, international organizations such as UNESCO, ICOMOS,[13] Blue Shield International,[14] and

[6] Understanding Disaster Risk (priority 1) (24) (d) To systematically evaluate, record, share and publicly account for disaster losses and understand the economic, social, health, education, environmental and cultural heritage impacts, as appropriate, in the context of event-specific hazard-exposure and vulnerability information.

[7] Investing in disaster risk reduction for resilience (priority 3) (30) (d) To *protect or support* the protection of cultural and collecting institutions and other sites of historical, cultural heritage and religious interest.

[8] Pavlova, I. et al. (2019), UNESCO designated sites–natural and cultural heritage sites as platforms for awareness raising. Contributing Paper to GAR 2019. https://www.undrr.org/publication/unesco-designated-sites-natural-and-cultural-heritage-sites-platforms-awareness-raising.

[9] https://www.undrr.org/publication/global-assessment-report-disaster-risk-reduction-2019.

[10] https://www.undrr.org/publication/unesco-designated-sites-natural-and-cultural-heritage-sites-platforms-awareness-raising.

[11] The UNDRR has also covered Kathmandu after the earthquake (e.g., https://www.undrr.org/news/building-kathmandu-back-better), but I get the impression that awareness of the issue from the perspective of cultural heritage protection is weak.

[12] Japan, a country prone to frequent disasters, has responded by "operating" the subsidy system to protect cultural properties (see the Nishi paper in this project). However, in FY2021, the National Center for Cultural Properties Disaster Prevention was established within the National Institutes for Cultural Heritage. https://ch-drm.nich.go.jp/ This is an important initiative to strengthen the horizontal cooperation of rescue activities that have been conducted in various regions to rescue movable cultural properties and books damaged by the disaster and to collaborate with the Heritage Manager System of the Japan Institute of Architects and Building Engineers (JIABE). Establishing this center could be positioned as Japan's effective response to the Sendai Framework.

[13] https://www.icomos.org/en/focus/reconstruction.

[14] https://theblueshield.org/.

ICCROM[15] organized specific projects such as international conferences and case studies. Recommendations for World Heritage Recovery and Reconstruction adopted in 2018 (the Warsaw Recommendation) support conducting case studies. In response to this expectation, ICOMOS and ICCROM jointly organized a project where country reports were collected and put together.[16] However, there have still been few projects and results conducted from the legal system's perspective, which is why individual case studies seem essential.

2.3 Conclusion

Existing international frameworks for the protection of cultural heritage and those for the prevention from disasters are not well designed to cope with such situations where cultural heritage is damaged or lost. Therefore, it is crucial to arrange a particular case study in the context of governance to protect cultural heritage, especially from a legal perspective.[17]

References

ICOMOS/ICCROM. (2021). Analysis of case studies in recovery and reconstruction. *Case studies, Vols. 1 and 2*. https://openarchive.icomos.org/id/eprint/2447/

Kono, T. (2020). International law and cultural heritage–from the viewpoint of museums and damages/disasters. *Hakubutsukan Kenkyu, Museum Studies*, *55*(8, 627), 2–3. (In Japanese)

Toshiyuki Kono Distinguished professor, Kyushu University, Japan. Toshiyuki Kono was born in Osaka, Japan, in 1958. After graduating from the Faculty of Law, Kyoto University, he went on to obtain his LL.M. from the Graduate School of Law, Kyoto University. He is a specialist in private international law, international civil procedure law, and international cultural heritage law. He was a member of UNESCO's Expert Groups for the drafting of the Convention for the Safeguarding of the Intangible Cultural Heritage (2003) and the Convention on the Protection and Promotion of the Diversity of Cultural Expressions (2005). He was appointed as a member of the Executive Committee of the International Council on Monuments and Sites (ICOMOS) in 2011. After working as vice president, he was elected as the 8th president of ICOMOS in 2017. As the former president, he continues as an honorary president of ICOMOS. He is the series editor of Springer's book series Perspectives in Law, Business and Innovation.

---

[15] https://www.iccrom.org/section/disaster-resilient-heritage/disaster-risk-management-cultural-heritage.

[16] ICOMOS/ICCROM (2021), Analysis of Case Studies in Recovery and Reconstruction, Case Studies, Vols. 1 and 2. http://openarchive.icomos.org/id/eprint/2447/.

[17] Kono (2020), p.3.

Chapter 3
Governance Challenges in Nepal After the Gorkha Earthquake, in Light of the World Heritage Convention

Hiroki Yamada

Abstract This chapter focuses on the issues in the restoration of the historic buildings in the "Kathmandu Valley" World Heritage property in Nepal damaged by the Gorkha Earthquake in 2015. It can be a good example to discuss the effectiveness of the World Heritage system based on the goals of the World Heritage Convention, including the organizational structures and procedures written in the Operational Guidelines for the implementation of the World Heritage Convention as a framework for international cooperation for the protection of precious cultural heritage. The Gorkha Earthquake led to a critical situation for cultural heritage. It exposed the immaturity of the cultural heritage protection systems in Nepal, but historically the disaster also improved the protection system. Undoubtedly, various domestic and foreign stakeholders made many efforts after the earthquake. However, some restoration projects did not follow the Operational Guidelines and did not seem adequately implemented. This chapter considers the effectiveness of the World Heritage system and the domestic system in Nepal for protecting cultural heritage after summarizing its institutional and operational issues.

Keywords Governance · Nepal · World Heritage · Operational guidelines · Reconstruction · Authenticity

---

H. Yamada (✉)
Research Institute of Cultural Properties, Teikyo University, Fuefuki city, Japan
e-mail: yamada.hiroki.xn@teikyo-u.ac.jp

T. Kono and J. Okahashi (eds.), *Post-Trauma and the Recovery Governance of Cultural Heritage*, https://doi.org/10.1007/978-981-19-6041-3_3

3.1 Introduction

The World Heritage Convention[1] (after this, referred to as Convention) aims to protect the cultural and natural heritage of Outstanding Universal Value[2] (after this, referred to as OUV) to humanity within an international framework. This chapter will focus on the cultural heritage protection system based on this framework (after this, referred to as the World Heritage system). It includes the domestic and international organization structures and procedures following "the Operational Guidelines for the implementation of the World Heritage Convention" (after this referred to as the Operational Guidelines) and brand images of the World Heritage for the local and foreign people. As of June 2022, 897 cultural properties[3] have been inscribed on the World Heritage List (After this, referred as to WHL) and are managed under the World Heritage system.

The World Cultural Heritage property of the "Kathmandu Valley"[4] (after this, referred to as KVWHP) suffered damage to a vast number of historic buildings in the Gorkha Earthquake, a major earthquake of magnitude M7.8 on 25 April 2015 with its epicenter in the Gorkha region of central Nepal and its aftershocks (after this referred to as the "Gorkha Earthquake"). More than seven years after the disaster, reconstruction works continue until now. In general, during recovery from a disaster, the inadequacies of the cultural heritage protection system and various problems are more likely to be exposed than during ordinary situations. In countries developing cultural heritage protection systems, these problems tend to be even more complicated. It has been pointed out in the discussion of the World Heritage Committee that the restoration of the damaged cultural heritage of KVWHP had not been proceeding properly.[5] The problems in the recovery process were mainly due to the extensive damage caused by the earthquake. However, it was also a result of the inadequacy of the cultural heritage protection system even before the disaster.

---

[1] UNESCO (1972) Convention Concerning the Protection of the World Cultural and Natural Heritage, adopted by the 17th Session of the General Conference of UNESCO on 16 November 1972, entered into force on 17 December 1975. https://whc.unesco.org/en/conventiontext/. Accessed 20 May 2022.

[2] Outstanding Universal Value means cultural and/or natural significance which is so exceptional as to transcend national boundaries and to be of common importance for present and future generations of all humanity. (The Operational Guidelines (2021), Paragraph 49).

[3] There are 936 cultural heritage sites, including the number of Mixed heritage sites on the World Heritage List (June 2022).

[4] In order to distinguish between the Kathmandu Valley as a geographical feature and the "Kathmandu Valley" as a World Heritage Site, the Kathmandu Valley listed as a World Heritage Site will be referred to as KVWHP.

[5] For example, it pointed out paragraph 8 in Decision: 42 COM 7B.12(2018) "*Also considers that the potential and ascertained threats to the OUV of the property are so considerable that the recovery process needs to be made more effective, and that the scale and scope of the disaster and the response required goes well beyond the capacity and resources of the Department of Archaeology of Nepal (DoA), and also considers that much greater input, collaboration and coordination of support is needed from the international community*".

There were problems in the legal system, operation, and the administration's capacity to restore historic buildings and preserve historic settlements. At every World Heritage Committee session since the Gorkha Earthquake, the World Heritage Centre prepared draft decisions to inscribe KVWHP on the List of World Heritage in Danger (After this, referred as to LWHD). It aimed to support the restoration of the damaged cultural heritage of KVWHP and strengthen the domestic protection system with international assistance. However, at each session, the World Heritage Committee overturned the draft decisions due to opposition from Nepal and some Committee members,[6] who were selected from the State Parties. The restoration of the damaged historic buildings has still been underway without fundamental strengthening of the domestic cultural heritage protection system, and the serious deterioration of the property's architectural and town-planning coherence has continued.[7] This situation can be seen as part of the malfunctioning of the World Heritage system as a legal framework for international cooperation for cultural heritage held by Nepal and other countries.

With this background, this chapter reviews international and domestic systems for protecting the cultural heritage of KVWHP, considering the issues of the conservation and reconstruction of damaged historic buildings of KVWHP.

3.2 The World Heritage Convention and the Kathmandu Valley

This clause summarizes the structure of the World Heritage system and the outline of KVWHP.

3.2.1 The World Heritage Convention

This section summarizes the Convention, the World Heritage Committee as an intergovernmental committee to implement the Convention, and the contents of the Operational Guidelines.

3.2.1.1 The Role of the World Heritage Convention

The World Heritage Convention was adopted in 1972 as a result of the international campaign launched by UNESCO in 1964, including the international cooperation project to rescue Nubian sites, involving the Abu Simbel Temple, from the threat of

[6] There are 21 Committee members selected considering the balance among the regions.

[7] For example, World Heritage Committee (2017) 41.COM/7B.95. Paragraph 5 mentioned it.

submergence caused by the construction of the Aswan High Dam. As of 2022, 194 countries have ratified the Convention. The preamble[8] of the Convention states that:

> Noting that the cultural heritage and the natural heritage are increasingly threatened with destruction[…],
>
> Considering that protection of this heritage at the national level often remains incomplete because of the scale of the resources which it requires and of the insufficient economic, scientific, and technological resources of the country where the property to be protected is situated,
>
> Considering […] need to be preserved as part of the world heritage of mankind as a whole,
>
> Considering that it is essential for this purpose to adopt new provisions in the form of a convention establishing an effective system […],

These show the idea of protecting the World Heritage properties with international cooperation. On the other hand, the protection of World Heritage properties is principally the duty of each State Party.[9] The protection depends on the legal systems of each State Party and its operation by the State Party. Article 6 of the Convention states that:

> Whilst fully respecting the sovereignty of the States on whose territory the cultural and natural heritage […] without prejudice to property right provided by national legislation,
>
> The States Parties undertake […] to give their help in the identification, protection, conservation […] if the States on whose territory it is situated so request.

It means that international assistance through the World Heritage Committee will be provided only at the requests of States Parties.[10]

3.2.1.2 The Role of the World Heritage Committee

The World Heritage Committee[11] is responsible for implementing the Convention and has held its regular sessions 44 times from 1977 to the present (June 2022). The Committee is composed of 21 members selected among the State Parties to the Convention.[12] In each session of the Committee, they deliberate on the World Heritage properties, such as the state of conservation of properties on the WHL and nominated properties for inscribing the List. Whenever a situation or action may

---

[8] UNESCO (1972) Convention Concerning the Protection of the World Cultural and Natural Heritage. UNESCO, p.1–2.

[9] Ibid., Article 4 states, "*Each State Party to this Convention recognizes that the duty of ensuring the identification, protection, conservation, presentation and transmission to future generations of the cultural and natural heritage referred to in Articles 1 and 2 and situated on its territory, belongs primarily to that State*".

[10] Ibid., Article 13.

[11] Ibid., Article 8 described the World Heritage Committee as "*An Intergovernmental Committee for the Protection of the Cultural and Natural Heritage of Outstanding Universal Value*".

[12] Ibid., Article 8.

affect the OUV of a property, the World Heritage Committee deliberates on the conservation of the property, with the reports on the State of Conservation submitted by the State Parties holding the property and the views of Advisory Bodies. The World Heritage Centre, which is the Secretariat of the Committee,[13] collects the information necessary for the deliberations and prepares the agenda. KVWHP, severely damaged by the Gorkha Earthquake in 2015, has been the subject of consideration on its State of Conservation at each World Heritage Committee session since the earthquake.

3.2.1.3 The Role of the Operational Guidelines

Operational Guidelines described the specific methods and procedures for protecting World Heritage properties. The State Parties with properties inscribed on the WHL are required to protect their properties per the Operational Guidelines. Unlike the Convention, the Operational Guidelines is a document subject to revision according to the circumstances of the time. The first version of the Operational Guidelines, prepared in 1977, contained only 28 paragraphs.[14] Today, it is much more comprehensive, with 290 paragraphs in 2021. The Operational Guidelines require States Parties to inform the Committee, through the World Heritage Centre, of their intention to undertake or to authorize in an area protected under the Convention major restorations or new constructions which may affect the OUV of the property.[15]

3.2.1.4 The Role of the List of World Heritage in Danger

The List of World Heritage in Danger (LWHD) is the list of the properties inscribed in the WHL that need the major operations for conservation or international assistance under the Convention, or properties threatened by serious and specific dangers, such as earthquakes.[16]

If a property is faced with specific and proven imminent danger (Ascertained Danger),[17] such as "serious deterioration of materials" and "serious deterioration of architectural or town-planning coherence" caused by the Gorkha Earthquake, or if the property is faced with threats which could have deleterious effects on its inherent characteristics (Potential Danger),[18] such as "lack of conservation policy",

[13] Operational Guidelines (2021), paragraph 3c.

[14] World Heritage Committee (1977) CC-77/CONF.001/8. (https://whc.unesco.org/archive/opguide77a.pdf) Accessed 20 June 2022.

[15] Operational Guidelines (2021), paragraph 172.

[16] Ibid., paragraph 177.

[17] Ibid., paragraph 179, (a).

[18] Ibid., paragraph 179, (b).

the property may be inscribed on the LWHD following the procedure described in the Operational Guidelines.[19] The Committee shall allocate a specific, significant portion of the World Heritage Fund to financing of possible assistance to World Heritage properties inscribed on the LWHD.[20] This assistance may be significant for the State Parties, especially losing protection systems under critical situations, such as after international conflicts or grave natural disasters, which may affect the OUV of the property.

As the procedure, the State Party first prepares a report on the State of Conservation and submits it to the World Heritage Committee. Then, after reviewing it by the World Heritage Centre and the Advisory Bodies to the World Heritage Committee, it was discussed in the World Heritage Committee session. If a property would be faced serious situation, the Committee may decide whether the World Heritage Centre be authorized to take the necessary action to ascertain, in consultation with the State Party concerned, including the Reactive Monitoring Mission[21] that dispatch experts from ICOMOS[22] or/and ICCROM[23] to accurately assess the situation on the site. The Committee deliberates on the information obtained in this way.[24] The Committee examines the information available and decides on the inscription of a property on the LWHD, following two-thirds of the Committee members present and voting. The Committee will then define the programme of corrective action and propose it to the State Party concerned for immediate implementation.[25] Inscription on the LWHD is the final step in this process.

A property shall be removed from the WHL if the property has deteriorated to the extent that it has lost the OUV which determined its inclusion in the WHL.[26] The Committee will try to avoid such a situation by consulting with the State Party concerned and developing remedial measures. However, if, for example, the restoration work carried out has substantially impaired the OUV of the property, the Committee may, through its deliberations of the Committee, unavoidably decide to remove the property from the WHL or exclude only the area in question.[27]

[19] Ibid., paragraphs 183–191.

[20] Ibid., paragraph 189.

[21] Reactive Monitoring means the reporting by the Secretariat, other sectors of UNESCO, and the Advisory Bodies to the Committee on the state of conservation of specific World Heritage properties that are under threat. (Operational Guidelines (2021), paragraph 169). Operational Guidelines (2021), paragraph 176. e) explains the Reactive Monitoring Mission.

[22] International Council on Monuments and Sites (ICOMOS).

[23] The International Centre for the Study of the Preservation and Restoration of Cultural Property (ICCROM).

[24] Operational Guidelines (2021), paragraph 179.

[25] Ibid., paragraph 186.

[26] Ibid., paragraph 192.

[27] In 2017, Bagrati Cathedral was excluded from the World Heritage property of Bagrati Cathedral and Gelati Monastery in Georgia.

3.2.2 *"Kathmandu Valley" as a World Heritage Property*

This section summarizes the status of KVWHP and the protection system strengthened through the Convention.

3.2.2.1 Overview of the World Heritage Property of "Kathmandu Valley"

KVWHP was inscribed on the WHL shortly after the establishment, consisting of seven Monument Zones. These are widely distributed in the Kathmandu Valley, with three urban centers containing the royal palaces, temples, and public spaces of the three kingdoms of the Newars, who flourished during the Malla period (thirteenth-eighteenth centuries). These three are Hanuman Dhoka Durbar Square, Patan Durbar Square, and Bhaktapur Durbar Square. The remaining four are the temple complexes of Changunarayan, Swayambhu, Pashupati, and Boudhanath (Fig. 3.1). Each Monument Zone has the boundary of the property[28] and the buffer zone.[29] The boundary includes historic buildings mainly owned by public and religious organizations, such as royal palaces and temples identified as specific components of KVWHP. The buffer zones of KVWHP include a strip of urban fabric surrounding the Monument Zones and many other historic temples, monasteries, and privately owned traditional houses that are not listed as components of KVWHP. KVWHP has a value not only as a single monument identified as a component but also as a historic urban landscape consisting of multiple historic buildings. The historic buildings and urban fabric are used as living heritage that includes both tangible and intangible heritage by the community during Hindu and Buddhist festivals and daily practices. KVWHP is the pride and daily life of the Newari people living in the Kathmandu Valley and is a significant source of income from tourism.

3.2.2.2 Efforts to Strengthen the Protection System for World Heritage Properties

The beginning of the protection of KVWHP was the UNESCO-funded plan[30] for the conservation of cultural heritage, which was applied as an official government policy in 1977. This plan became the basis for the framework of protection since its inscription on the WHL in 1979. However, as mentioned earlier, the Operational Guidelines in the early stage were not detailed and did not guide the establishment

[28] It was called the core zone at that time of inscription on the List in 1979.

[29] The spatial area surrounding the boundary for effective protection of the property.

[30] Sekler et al. (1977) Master Plan for the Conservation of the Cultural Heritage in the Kathmandu Valley. UNESCO, UNDP.

Fig. 3.1 Locations and images of 7 Monument Zones of KVWHP (1 ~ 4, 6, 7 taken in Sep. 2015, 5 taken in June 2016) (© TNRICP)

of a Management Plan for each property. In 1992, the World Heritage Committee began discussing the state of conservation of KVWHP because the impact of urban development had become an issue and KVWHP were losing traditional townscape created by the fusion of Hinduism and Buddhism. After the discussion for a decade, the World Heritage Committee inscribed KVWHP on the LWHD in 2003. In conjunction with this decision, the World Heritage Committee adopted to formulate an Integrated Management Framework (after this referred to as IMF).[31] In 2007, the Government of Nepal and the Department of Archaeology of the Ministry of Culture, Tourism and Civil Aviation (after this referred to as DoA) established IMF with financial and technical support from the World Heritage Centre.

Through the development of the IMF, DoA and international experts reviewed the protection system for KVWHP and delineated the property's boundary and buffer zone, which had not been determined at the time, as Protected Monument Zone (after this, referred to as PMZ). In addition, the World Heritage Committee required government leaders and city planning departments to improve Acts and by-laws.[32] IMF also clarified that DoA has the primary authority to coordinate conservation activities at the PMZs, whereas previously, each city administration or

[31] Department of Archaeology (2007) Integrated Management Framework.

[32] National Federation of UNESCO Associations in JAPAN (2008) World Heritage Annual Report. p. 38 (in Japanese).

religious organization had independent jurisdiction over each PMZ.[33] It established the on-site management representative (site manager) in each PMZ. The protection system of KVWHP seemed to be strengthened by its inscription on the LWHD and international support from 2003 to 2007.

3.3 The Domestic Legal System for Cultural Heritage in Nepal

As mentioned above, the protection and conservation of each World Cultural Heritage property is the responsibility of each State Party, and its legal protection depends on the domestic legal system. This clause summarizes the domestic legal system in Nepal regarding the protection of cultural heritage related to KVWHP.

The Reactive Monitoring Mission Report[34] for KVWHP, conducted in 2019, states that the relevant national laws and regulations for cultural heritage protection include the Ancient Monuments Preservation Act (1956), the Guthi Corporation Act (1976), the Pashupati Area Development Trust Act (1987), the National Building Code (after this referred to as NBC) (1994) in heritage areas, the building by-laws,[35] and the Town Development Act (1988). These laws and regulations can be divided into two categories:

(1) The legal system mainly concerned with protecting individual historic monuments such as temples and royal palaces, and
(2) The legal system mainly concerned with conserving historic settlements, such as traditional houses and historic townscapes.

Although the names of Nepalese laws add the effective year according to Bikram Sambat (BS), in this text, the Gregorian Date (AD) is used to facilitate the readers' understanding (Table 3.1).

---

[33] Shrestha (2016) *Swayambhu: A World Heritage Destination*. OCHSPA, p. 110–129.

[34] Wijesuriya and Forbes(2019) Report on the Joint World Heritage Centre/ICOMOS/ICCROM Reactive Monitoring Mission to the World Heritage Property of the Kathmandu Valley (Nepal, C 121bis). p. 14.

[35] Kathmandu Valley Town Develop Committee (2007) Kathmandu Upatyakā Bhitrakā Nagarapālikā Ra Nagaronmukha Gā.Bi.Sa. Harumā Garine Nirmāna Sambadhi Māpadanda, Kāthamandau Nagar Bikāsa Samiti, Ministry of Physical Planning & Works, Government of Nepal, 2063B.S. (in Nepali) However, each municipality, such as Bhaktapur and Patan, has formulated its building by-laws.

Table 3.1 Chronicle of the legal system for the protection of cultural heritage in Nepal

International	Domestic
• World Heritage Convention (1972) • Beginning of the World Heritage List (1978)	• Establishing of the Department of Archaeology (1952) • The Ancient Monument Preservation Act (1956) • Establishing of the Guthi Sansthan (1964) • The Local Administration Act (1971) • The Guthi Corporation Act (1976)
Inscription of the "Kathmandu Valley" on the World Heritage List (1979)	
• Nara Document on Authenticity (1994)	• The Pashupati Area Development Trust Act (1987) • Town Development Act (1988) • Kathmandu Valley Development Authority Act (1988) • Ancient Monuments Preservation Rules (1989) • National Building Code (1994) • Building Act (1998)
Inscription of the "Kathmandu Valley" on the List of World Heritage Sites in Danger (2003)	
• Requirement of the Management Plan for each property on the World Heritage List, Major Revision of Operational Guidelines (2005) • Integrated Management Framework (2007)	• Building By-laws of municipality which has jurisdiction of the Protected Monument Zone. building by-laws in Bhaktapur (2003) • Building Rule (2009)
The Gorkha Earthquake (2015)	
• Requirement of Heritage Impact Assessment, adding 118bis. on the Operational Guidelines (2019)	• Basic Guidelines for the Conservation and Reconstruction of Earthquake Damaged Heritage (2015) • Basic Construction By-laws for Settlement Development Urban Planning and Building Construction (2015) • Revising the general building by-laws (2016) • The Local Government Operation Act (2017)

3.3.1 The Legal System for the Protection of Individual Historic Monuments

3.3.1.1 The Ancient Monument Preservation Act

The most important law relating to the protection of cultural heritage in Nepal is the Ancient Monument Preservation Act (1956), which is under the jurisdiction of DoA and mainly concerns the authority to grant permits for the restoration and maintenance of cultural heritage. The objects to be protected under this law are "Ancient Monument", "Archaeological Object", "Curio (modern handicrafts not exceeding hundred years of age) ", etc. "Ancient Monument" means temple, monument, house, abbey, cupola, monastery, *stupa, Bihar*[36] etc. which have their importance above one hundred years.[37] Ancient Monuments are categorized as public or private in terms of ownership, and classified in three categories as international importance, national importance, and local importance.[38] In addition, the area around the ancient monuments and other sites can be declared as a Protected Monument Zone (PMZ).[39] Permission from DoA is required for any event, construction, or building activity within a PMZ. The Ancient Monument Preservation Act states that DoA has the authority to permit the restoration and maintenance of the ancient monuments of Nepal.[40] Ownership of the ancient public monuments shall be vested in DoA. DoA shall conserve, maintain, and renovate them.[41] For privately-owned historic buildings within a PMZ, the conservation, maintenance, and renovation will be carried out by the parties concerned and at the discretion of DoA. For those outside the PMZ, it is stipulated that the local government or related parties shall carry out the conservation works following the instructions of DoA.

The provisions related to restoration and reconstruction are essential to ensure appropriate restoration of the damaged historic buildings. The Ancient Monument Preservation Act states that the restoration of historic buildings (ancient monuments) listed in the inventory and the construction, repair, renovation, and reconstruction within PMZs shall be carried out with approval from DoA. If an owner applies to municipalities for the building permit with the drawing of planned buildings in the PMZ, municipalities must obtain the approval of DoA under the Act before accepting the drawing. After reviewing the drawings received from the municipality, DoA may approve, reject, or instruct to revise the drawings. Furthermore, if the construction of houses or other structures in the PMZ does not follow the approved drawings, DoA can stop the project. In this way, DoA has the authority to grant permits for historic buildings. If DoA disapproves, the construction cannot be carried out. The Ancient Monuments Preservation Rules (1989)

---

[36] Bihar means Vihara (विहार), the Sanskrit term for a Buddhist monastery.

[37] Ancient Monument Preservation Act (1956), 2(a).

[38] Ibid., 3A.

[39] The Ancient Monument Preservation Act (1956) describes it as Preserved Monument Area in English. However, the seven Monument Zones of the Kathmandu Valley World Heritage property declared as PMZs have been gazetted under the provisions of this Act.

[40] Ibid., Article 3(6), *"Anyone who, on his/her own land within the Protected Monument Zone, is willing to construct a new house or building or to repair, alter or reconstruct a house or building so as to make changes on its original shape, shall have to construct, repair, alter or reconstruct it as is matching the style of the area and as is inconsonance with the standard prescribed by the Department of Archaeology"*.

[41] Ibid., 3B. *"Most public antiquities refer to buildings and archaeological sites related to the royal palace"*.

show details of the committee structure and other regulations following the Ancient Monument Preservation Act.[42]

To complement the existing legal system, DoA has also formulated the Basic Guidelines for the Conservation and Reconstruction of Earthquake Damaged Heritage (2015) and the Manual on Preservation and Reconstruction of Earthquake Damaged Monuments (2016) to facilitate appropriate conservation and restoration after the disaster. Although these guidelines are not legally binding, they encourage proper conservation and restoration by ancient monument owners and provide a basis for guidance by DoA.

3.3.1.2 The Local Government Operation Act

Among numerous articles of the Local Government Operation Act (2017), article 9 has provisions associated with the declaration of any area within a municipality or rural municipality.[43] The provincial government and the local government can declare the area found important from historical, archeological, arts, and cultural points of view as a "cultural or touristic zone" by defining its boundary. The Provincial government can formulate a unique program and budget allocation to conserve and protect such zones. As per this Act, the local government can fix the property taxes (property tax, service tax, land tax, Etc.) within its boundary and monitor the construction, renovation, and repair works as per prevailing building by-laws and National Building Code (NBC). In addition, the local government has to protect, develop and enhance local language, culture, and arts and crafts by regulating and monitoring festivals, rituals, and museum conservation.

3.3.1.3 The Local Administration Act

Article 9(6) of the Local Administration Act (1971) mentions that the Chief District Officer, who is under the Ministry of Home Affairs, shall maintain the records of public waterspouts, springs, ponds, lakes, rest houses, pilgrims' houses, temples, caves, monasteries, mosques Etc. within the district. Moreover, Chief District Officer can enforce their maintenance through the concerned municipality or Guthi Corporation if those structures are dilapidated or destroyed in the absence of their owner.

The local government is also responsible for the on-site management of the component parts. In the case of the Hanuman Dhoka Durbar Square, the Hanuman Dhoka Durbar Museum Development Committee, the joint committee of DoA and the Kathmandu Metropolitan City (KMC), is responsible for the day-to-day

[42] Ibid., Article 21.

[43] "*Gaupalika*" in Nepalese.

maintenance and management of the palace, while the KMC works strongly cooperated with DoA.

Tourism is a significant industry for Nepal, accounting for 7.8% of the national GDP (2017 yearly).[44] Before the new coronavirus pandemic, the local governments collect entrance fees to KVWHP. In Bhaktapur, the entrance fee is not only used to subsidize the restoration of historic buildings and incentives for townscape conservation but also to build and operate the municipal colleges and hospital,[45] making it a massive source of income for the municipality that owns the World Heritage property.

Following the abolition of the monarchy on 28 May 2008 and the enactment of the new constitution on 15 September 2015, Nepal gradually transitioned to a federal system. The mayoral elections were held in 2017, the first local elections in 20 years. The promulgation of the new constitution has led to a shift in authority from the central government to local governments. Shortly, the role of local governments will become even more critical in protecting cultural heritage, especially historic private buildings in the historic settlements, and it is expected that their measures will have a more direct impact.

3.3.1.4 The Guthi Corporation Act

The Guthi Corporation Act (1976) was enacted to operate the Rajguthi, which had been under the jurisdiction of the Government of Nepal, under a new legal corporation called Guthi Corporation (Guthi Sansthan). From the perspective of cultural heritage protection, this is a law of the maintenance and operation of historic buildings, which are public facilities such as temples, monasteries, rest houses, etc., located mainly in urban areas and settlements. These public facilities have been historically maintained and managed by Guthis, a religious and customary management organization that enshrines them, since before the establishment of the Ancient Monument Preservation Act (1956). According to the Guthi Corporation Act, "Guthi" means and includes a Guthi (trust) endowed by any philanthropist through relinquishment of his or her title to movable or immovable property or any other income-yielding property or fund for the operation or maintenance of any shrine and other institution or for the operation of any festival. The land pledged for these management expenses is called Guthi land.[46] In 1964, the Guthi Corporation was established as a government agency to manage and administer the rituals on the

---

[44] World Travel & Tourism Council (2018) Travel & Tourism Economic Impact. p. 1.

[45] Yamada (2017) Prospects for the Establishment of a Preservation System for Historic Settlements, in Technical Assistance Project for the Protection of Cultural Heritage Affected by the Earthquake in Nepal. National Research Institute for Cultural Properties, Tokyo, p. 44–49.

[46] Shakya (2013) The Management System of Communal Space of Courtyard-style Settlement in the Historic City of Nepal: a case study of the old residential area of Patan, the Doctoral Dissertation of Kyoto University p. 11.

Guthi land, manage the offerings made to the temple, and protect the buildings, ornaments, etc., under the Guthi Corporation Act.

3.3.1.5 Pashupati Area Development Trust Act and Organization Registration Act

In addition to the legal tools mentioned above, there are a few more site-specific acts and rules governing PMZ. The Pashupati Area Development Trust Act (1987) applies to the PMZ of Pashupati, which is also one of the Monument Zones of KVWHP and an important Hindu holy site. The Act provides a trust to protect, maintain, and develop it. The trust established a council to make arrangements, manage donations, etc., and plan and develop the district for worship per festivals and traditional religious rites and ceremonies at all temples in the district, including the Pashupatinath Temple.[47] The trust has designated the Prime Minister as its patron[48] and the Minister of Culture, Tourism and Civil Aviation as the head of the trust.[49] There are Boudhanath Area Development Committee under the Development Committee Act in PMZ of Boudhanath, and the Federation of Swayambhu Management and Conservation (FSMC) under the Organization Registration Act in PMZ in Swayambhu.

The Ancient Monument Preservation Act (1956) is the most significant among all these acts. Numerous recommendations from UNESCO from time to time also govern KVWHP. When KVWHP was inscribed on the LWHD in 2003, following the advice from international experts sent to the site, the government of Nepal prepared the Integrated Management Framework (IMF)[50] in 2007. Building by-laws for construction, renovation, and conservation of private houses within PMZs of KVWHP were also formulated in the same year, for instance, building by-laws for Boudhanath PMZ (2007) and Bhaktapur Durbar Square PMZ (2007).

3.3.2 The Legal System for the Protection of Historic Settlements

3.3.2.1 The Legal System for New Individual Buildings

Regulations on new individual buildings are mainly based on the Building Act (1998) and Building Rule (2009) established by the government. While municipalities and rural municipalities own building permits, the Department of Urban

---

[47] Pashupati District Development Trust Act (1987), Article 10.

[48] Ibid., Article 5.

[49] Ibid., Article 7.

[50] It is considered as the Management Plan of KVWHP.

Development and Building Construction (DUDBC) and the Urban Development and Building Construction Office provide technical guidances. In the Building Act, article 10, the Ministry of Urban Development (after this referred to as MOUD) set the obligation to comply with the National Building Code (NBC) (1994). NBC includes various standards based on structure type, etc., and most of NBCs are based on the Indian standards. After the Gorkha Earthquake, NBCs were revised to take more seismic performance into account. For example, the reinforced concrete structure standard was strengthened by increasing the cross-sectional area of reinforced concrete columns. Before the Gorkha Earthquake of 2015, only a few municipalities implemented NBCs, but the MOUD made it mandatory for all municipalities in post-earthquake construction. In other words, traditional structures that could be built before the NBC are prohibited in present.

3.3.2.2 The Legal System for Urban Planning

The first legal system for the conservation of historic settlements (including historic cities) is the Town Development Act (1988). This law relates to formulating town planning to carry out the reconstruction, expansion, and development of existing cities, not only historic settlements, and includes regulations of land use zones and demolition of unauthorized buildings. The law authorizes the establishment of a Town Development Committee to carry out urban planning in specific areas,[51] which may, from time to time, regulate, control, or prohibit acts and activities within the urban planning area as necessary, with clear public notice, and may regulate the possession and use of places of archaeological, religious, or historical importance, and may regulate the construction and demolition of buildings of any kind in historic sites.[52,53] It can regulate the construction and demolition of all kinds of buildings, prevent actions that affect the beauty of nature and landscape, and control traffic there.[54] The Kathmandu Valley Town Development Authority initially had the authority to regulate the area in the Kathmandu Valley under the Kathmandu Valley Development Act. However, in principle, each municipality in the Kathmandu Valley has the authority to regulate under the Local Government Operation Act (2017).

MOUD is drafting a new Urban Development Act now (in June 2022) to supersede the earlier the Town Development Act (1988) and the Kathmandu Valley Development Authority Act (1988).

---

[51] Town Development Act (1988), Article 4.

[52] Ibid., Article 9.1.1. To enjoy and use agricultural land, natural heritage, flora, forest, fauna, archaeological, religious, and historical sites as well as cultivated and barren land and immovable property.

[53] Ibid., Article 11.1.3 To prepare necessary project and to implement it in town planning area for proper development and conservation of religious, cultural, and historical heritage subject to prevailing law of Nepal on ancient monument.

[54] Ibid., Articles 9 and 10.

3.3.2.3 Building By-Laws

Though municipalities give the final building permit for individual house construction (addition, renovation, or retrofitting), KVWHP is governed by the regulations of DoA. However, in some cases, the municipal building by-laws (e.g., Bhaktapur municipality) include those regulations associated with KVWHP.

The Gorkha Earthquake in 2015 destroyed many buildings in the historic settlements in the Kathmandu Valley and outside. Most of them were in rural municipalities that had been Village Development Committees (after this, referred to as VDC). They did not have building by-laws to regulate new construction, as a simple application used to be adequate to build houses. The new constitution of Nepal in 2015 transformed the country into a federal system, with earlier municipalities becoming local governments. Also, the local area restructuring in 2017 has converted earlier VDCs either into new municipalities or added to the existing municipal boundary.[55] Those newly formed and old municipalities with the addition of historic settlements in their new boundary could not formulate building by-laws and could not control post-earthquake reconstruction of private houses in the historic settlements. As a result, individual inhabitants started reconstructing their collapsed/damaged houses on an ad-hoc basis, destroying the townscape and building characters of the historic settlements.

Acknowledging these issues of historic settlements, the MOUD came up with new building by-laws in 2015, after the earthquake. These general building by-laws apply to all newly formed municipalities, which have yet to formulate their building by-laws. As these general building by-laws do not have provisions for regulating building construction in historic settlements, the issue of conservation was unsolved. In 2016, the MOUD revised the general building by-laws and added article '14a' associated with all heritage settlements and provisions for construction in historic settlements. At present, most of the newly formed municipalities are following this regulation, even old municipalities like Lalitpur Metropolitan City which had their building by-laws for regulating the old municipal boundary. However, some municipalities which adopted these general building by-laws for historic settlements slightly modified them to suit their local contexts.

These building by-laws have provisions for declaring "heritage settlement" for the first time. To become a heritage settlement, it should have at least four different attributes: (a) should have 50 or more houses, (b) generally established 100 years before, (c) settlement should have chaityas, temples, rest houses, and "*Sattal*" (public houses), well, sunken waterspout, pond etc. built using local arts and architecture, (d) should have social institutions like "Guthi" to regulate traditional

[55] By 2017, the country had 293 municipalities, only 58 a decade ago. For instance, Khokana, which was earlier VDC, was included in the Karyabinayak municipality. Furthermore, Karyabinayak municipality was added to Lalitpur Metropolitan City at the time of local area restructuring.

festivals, rituals, and prayer. In addition to provisions for building construction. So far, one historic settlement outside the Kathmandu valley (Bidur Municipality) declared its settlement as "heritage settlement".

3.4 Damage and Recovery from the Gorkha Earthquake

The Gorkha Earthquake caused extensive damage to the historic buildings, including ancient monuments and traditional private houses in the PMZs of KVWHP. Restoration is still underway after seven years. This section summarizes an overview of the damage caused by the Gorkha Earthquake and the restoration process.

3.4.1 Overview of Damage Caused by the Gorkha Earthquake

On 25 April 2015, the Gorkha Earthquake occurred. 8,979 people lost their lives, and 22,309 were injured,[56] 498,852 buildings were fully collapsed or beyond repairs, and 256,697 buildings were partially damaged, in a wide area, including the capital city of Kathmandu.[57] The earthquake also caused extensive damage to cultural heritage, not only to historic buildings but also to movable cultural heritage (e.g., Buddha statues) and intangible cultural heritage (e.g., rituals). According to DoA, which has jurisdiction over cultural heritage, a total of 750 monuments were damaged, and 133 completely collapsed. 140 historic buildings were damaged, representing about 17% of the total number of listed monuments of KVWHP.[58]

---

[56] National Reconstruction Authority (2022) About Us. http://www.nra.gov.np/en/pages/view/fk2lRwucsHVwn9q-LAxpTW9mGJgIRz25rUWNDHdbkYk. Accessed 20 May 2022.

[57] National Planning Commission (2015) Nepal Earthquake 2015: Post-disaster needs assessment, executive summary. Government of Nepal, Kathmandu, p. 10.

[58] Based on a presentation by Besh Narayan Dahal, Director General of DoA. Tomoda T, Yamada H (eds) (2016) FY2015 International Contribution Project for the Protection of Cultural Heritage Commissioned by the Agency for Cultural Affairs: Survey Project on the Damage Situation of Cultural Heritage in Nepal, Summary Report National Research Institute for Cultural Properties, Tokyo, p. 102–105.

3.4.2 *Early Recovery Activities and Organizations for Reconstruction*

In the immediate aftermath of the earthquake, Nepalese soldiers and the local community quickly searched and rescued lives first, then rescued carved decorative pillars and statues from the rubble of the damaged buildings and moved them to a safe place. UNESCO held the first coordination meeting on saving cultural heritage in May 2015 to share information among the concerned parties. Then, UNESCO supported damage assessment, curing to prepare for the rainy season, repairing and storaging of components, and urgent reinforcement to prevent further collapse following the Post Disaster Needs Assessment (PDNA) prepared by the National Planning Commission with the participation of national and international experts.

To recover from the devastating damage, in December 2015, the National Reconstruction Authority (after this referred to as NRA) was established for five years (six years with a one-year extension) based on the Act Related to the Reconstruction of Earthquake Affected Structures (2015) [Article 3]. The NRA provided a framework[59] for reconstructing the disaster area in May 2016 as the initial plan to start the recovery process.

DoA still handles the procedures for restoration of cultural heritage, but the subsidies for restoration of damaged cultural heritage have been provided through the NRA. The "Central Level Project Implementation Unit (Building)"[60] was established within the NRA and plays a major role in the procedures.

3.4.3 *Restoration of the Buildings Damaged by the Gorkha Earthquake*

According to the NRA's document[61] in January 2022, the NRA signed agreements with about 830,000 beneficiaries, 95.8% of the total number of private houses to be rehabilitated. Among them, 99.9% started reconstruction, and 84.8% received the final subsidy, which means the completion of the reconstruction of their houses. In addition, 606 of 920 cultural heritage (65.9%) identified for restoration by the NRA have been restored completely, and 288 restoration projects (31.3%) are under construction.

[59] National Reconstruction Authority (2016) Post Disaster Recovery Framework.

[60] Website of Central Level Project Implementation Unit (Building) http://www.moudclpiu.gov.np/. Accessed 10 June 2022.

[61] National Reconstruction Authority (2021) Rebuilding Nepal. p. 28–29, http://www.nra.gov.np/en. Accessed 10 June 2021.

In December 2021, The National Reconstruction Authority (NRA) handed over the remaining works, liability, property, accounts, and other related documents to the National Disaster Risk Reduction and Management Authority (NDRRMA).

3.5 Legal Issues Exposed in the Recovery Process from the Gorkha Earthquake

This section summarizes the main legal issues exposed in restoring cultural heritage buildings from the Gorkha Earthquake focusing on the authenticity[62] and integrity in the Operational Guidelines to consider "whether the restoration of KVWHP has been achieved in full consideration of its OUV". The three reports of the Reactive Monitoring Mission submitted to the World Heritage Committee by experts dispatched to the site in October 2015, March 2017, and October 2019 explains in detail the problems encountered during the restoration process of damaged historic buildings. Therefore, the Committee has deliberated on whether to inscribe KVWHP on the LWHD for six times, from 2015 to 2021.[63]

These issues exposed the fact that fundamental issues related to the conservation and management of KVWHP remained unresolved during the restoration of earthquake-damaged monuments. Problems with the protection system for cultural heritage existed even before the Gorkha Earthquake, which led to KVWHP being inscribed on the LWHD in 2003. Following improvements in the flawed cultural heritage protection system, KVWHP was removed from the LWHD in 2007. However, in reality, the system had remained immature, as was seen in the restoration projects after the Gorkha disaster. There seemed to be a large gap between the ideal system and its operation on the sites.

Even though experts have pointed out numerous problems in restoring KVWHP through the reports of Reactive Monitoring Missions, the Convention seemed unable to take sufficient measures. This section summarizes the main issues in Nepal's cultural heritage protection system causing problems in the restoration of KVWHP in terms of the system and its operation through specific examples of restoration projects.

---

[62] Paragraph 82 of the Operational Guidelines lists attributes for understanding the conditions of authenticity, "*including form and design; materials and substance; use and function; traditions, techniques and management systems; location and setting; language, and other forms of intangible heritage; spirit and feeling; and other internal and external factors*".

[63] In 2020 and 2022, World Heritage Committee sessions were not held due to the outbreak of the covid-19 virus and the Russian invasion of Ukraine.

3.5.1 Issues in the World Heritage System

3.5.1.1 Issues in the System

Decision-Making Methods that Do not Directly Reflect Experts Monitoring

The report of the Reactive Monitoring Mission in 2019 shows in detail the problems in the restoration of KVWHP.[64] The World Heritage Committee requests the Reactive Monitoring Mission to ascertain, in consultation with the State Party concerned, the condition of the property, the dangers to the property, and the feasibility of adequately restoring the property or assessing progress made in implementing such corrective measures and report to the World Heritage Committee. Based on this report, the World Heritage Centre prepared a draft decision to inscribe KVWHP on the LWHD for the 44th session of the World Heritage Committee in 2021.[65] However, it was rejected by the Committee, not only in 2021 but also at every session after the Gorkha Earthquake. The final decision-making authority is not the ICOMOS or the World Heritage Centre but the Committee, represented mainly by ambassadors from the 21 committee members. The Committee is not obliged to pass the draft decision prepared by the World Heritage Centre based on the report through site monitoring. Some committee members may decide their own opinions considering the protection system in their own country and prioritizing the requests, so-called lobbying, from the concerned State Party rather than the State of Conservation of the discussed cultural heritage. The Committee members who have insufficient protection system for their cultural heritage and do not want a World Heritage property will be inscribed on the LWHD due to inadequate property management. Because it will be a precedent. Therefore, as a reason for opposing the draft decision, some committee members commented that the restoration of cultural heritage should be left to the self-efforts of the State Party.[66] Each committee member is in a position to make a decision on World Heritage properties owned by other countries, as well as to nominate its own cultural heritage to the WHL and provide protection for it. However, because the Committee is an intergovernmental committee, international political considerations influence its decisions. The reality is that decisions cannot be passed based on idealistic theories of the Convention, as stated in its articles. In the current situation, criticism of other countries' cultural heritage management will likely meet with

[64] UNESCO (2019) Report of the joint World Heritage Centre/ICOMOS/ICCROM Reactive Monitoring mission to the Kathmandu Valley (Nepal). UNESCO, https://whc.unesco.org/document/187827. Accessed 20 May 2022.

[65] World Heritage Committee Draft Decision (2021) 44 COM 7B.33 https://whc.unesco.org/en/soc/4087 Accessed 20 June 2022.

[66] The Committee members such as China, Uganda, and Zimbabwe commented that restoration works should be let Nepal, in the discussion on the State of Conservation of "Kathmandu Valley" in the 42nd World Heritage Committee https://www.youtube.com/watch?v=iyWab4ivMrU. Accessed 8 June 2022.

criticism of their own management in later discussions. It has led to a reluctance among the committee members to inscribe properties on the LWHD. The problems happening on the site are not disclosed to the Committee, and discussions on actual restoration are not deepened. Thus, it is a structural issue in the World Heritage Committee that the experts' (often ICOMOS') report based on monitoring the actual site is not given due weight enough, and decisions are sometimes made based on the political agenda of Committee members who are not directly related to the cultural heritage in the discussion.

Absence of Means to Stop the Implementation of Significant Changes in Restoration

The protection of World Heritage properties is entrusted to the State Parties that own the properties following the Convention. Paragraph 172 of the Operational Guidelines states that:

> The World Heritage Committee invites the States Parties to the Convention *to inform* the Committee, through the Secretariat, of *their intention to undertake or to authorize in an area protected under the Convention major restorations or new constructions* which may affect the Outstanding Universal Value of the property. *Notice should be given as soon as possible* (for instance, before drafting basic documents for specific projects) and *before making any decisions that would be difficult to reverse*, so that the Committee may assist in seeking appropriate solutions to ensure that the Outstanding Universal Value of the property is fully preserved.

Although there is a system of six-yearly Periodic Reporting[67] Cycle and the state of conservation reporting by State Parties to the Committee, the World Heritage Centre is usually not informed in advance of any restoration work that may affect the OUV of a World Heritage property if the State Party does not consider reporting is necessary. Thus, the World Heritage Centre has no way to stop it in advance. For example, major changes[68] during the restoration of the south wing of Sundari Chok in the Patan Durbar Square were not reported to the World Heritage Centre. The collapsed part of the south wing of Sundari Chok has been restored as a stairwell, and the internal structure has been modified. However, this restoration that may affect its OUV was treated as a minor change and completed in 2017 without notification to the World Heritage Centre, despite World Heritage Committee in 2016 made a decision requesting Nepal to submit detailed information about major

[67] Operational Guidelines (2021), Paragraph 199–210 and the World Heritage Convention (1972), Article 29.

[68] The collapsed part of the south wing of Sundari Chok has been reconstructed but modified as a double-height gallery.

restoration to the World Heritage Centre.[69] The problem is that even if there were major changes to a World Heritage property by restoration, the World Heritage Centre is not informed, and the Committee is forced to fall behind in its response (Figs. 3.2, 3.3 and 3.4).

Under these circumstances, in 2019, the Committee added to the Operational Guidelines a requirement that States Parties should ensure a Heritage Impact Assessment (after this referred to as HIA)[70] to be carried out as a pre-requisite for development projects and activities planned for implementation within or around a World Heritage property. KVWHP was also required in the decision of the Committee in 2021.[71] However, it is questionable whether it is possible to carry out an HIA by the State Parties under the condition of developing or reconstructing rapidly after the disaster.

Limitation of the Authority of the UNESCO Field Office

UNESCO has 53 UNESCO Field Offices (after this, referred to as Field Offices) around[72] the world at present (June 2022), including one in Kathmandu, established in 1998 (After this, referred to as the UNESCO Office in Kathmandu). Although the Field Offices take a role in collecting information on the World Heritage properties, they do not have direct authority over the properties held by the State Parties. Their intervention is limited, especially for cultural heritage not on the WHL. For example, after the earthquake, the U.S. Ambassadors Fund for Cultural Preservation supported the restoration of the Gaddi Baithak (New Royal Palace), and the Chinese government supported the restoration of the Basantapur Bhawan (Nine-story Pagoda) in the Hanuman Dhoka Durbar Square. The UNESCO Office in Kathmandu was not involved with these projects. In international cooperation projects funded by foreign countries in Nepal, historically, the donor countries and their experts selected their restoration methods, and DoA approved them.[73] In order to improve the quality of restoration of monuments of KVWHP, it would be desirable for every donor country to share the concept and method of restoration to

---

[69] The World Heritage Committee stated in Decision: 40 COM 7B.41 (2016), paragraph 15. "*Requests furthermore the State Party to submit to the World Heritage Centre, before any irreversible decision is made, detailed information about any major restoration, rehabilitation or reconstruction works foreseen within and in the vicinity of the property, for review by the Advisory Bodies in accordance with Paragraph 172 of the Operational Guidelines;*".

[70] Operational Guidelines (2021), Paragraph 118bis.

[71] WHC/21/44.COM/7B.Add. (2021), Paragraph 10.

[72] Fifty-three offices include UNESCO Liaison Offices as well. https://en.unesco.org/fieldoffice. Accessed May 2022.

[73] The history of the early restoration projects in Nepal is explained in the following book. Theophile E, Gutschow N (eds) (2003) *Sulima Pagoda: East Meets West in the Restoration of a Nepalese Temple*. Orchid Press, Bangkok.

Fig. 3.2 Before the reconstruction of the south wing of Sundari Chok in Patan Durbar square (© TNRICP)

be implemented at each restoration project with Nepal and other concerned countries. However, this has not been conducted.

After the Gorkha Earthquake, in recent years, there seems to be a movement to prevent donor countries from getting involved in the restoration of domestic cultural heritage, partly due to emotional reasons caused by growing nationalism. In this current situation, strong coordination by the UNESCO Office in Kathmandu was required, but its authority and activities were limited. The World Heritage Committee's recommendations do not link directly to the restoration projects in KVWHP. Under these circumstances, unlike usual, UNESCO Office in Kathmandu directly surveyed the damage to the Jagannath and Gopinath temples in the Hanuman Dhoka Durbar Square and prepared a restoration plan by themself. However, the plan had to be withdrawn due to opposition from some local people who wanted the restoration to be done solely with local funds and local experts and communities without international assistance.[74] This situation shows difficulties of international intervention in restoration projects, by the UNESCO World Heritage

[74] UNESCO (2019) UNESCO withdraws from restoring Jagannath and Gopinath Temples at Hanumandhoka Durbar Square World Heritage Site, https://en.unesco.org/news/. Accessed 10 November 2022.

Fig. 3.3 After the reconstruction of the south wing of Sundari Chok in Patan Durbar square (© TNRICP)

Centre and UNESCO Field Offices, especially when the property is not on the LWHD.

Ambiguity in the Definition of Authenticity

Restoration works in the Kathmandu Valley often mean demolition and reconstruction, even while it is assumed that the historic buildings could be restored. Paragraph 86 of the Operational Guidelines states that:

> In relation to authenticity, the reconstruction of archaeological remains or historic buildings or districts is justifiable only in exceptional circumstances. Reconstruction is acceptable only on the basis of complete and detailed documentation and to no extent on conjecture.

This guideline explicitly forbids reconstruction without complete and detailed survey documentation. It requires full consideration of authenticity. However, reconstructions that do not follow this requirement have often occurred in Nepal. In addition, damaged buildings are often not thoroughly surveyed before restoration, which may lead to an attitude that gives little consideration to authenticity. Furthermore, there are sometimes disagreements between responsible persons for the restoration (especially domestic carpenters or architectural firms) and experts

Fig. 3.4 The collapsed 2nd floor changed into a colonnade of a gallery atrium without reconstruction (© TNRICP)

(especially international experts) as to whether authenticity is maintained after a restoration. The formers might explain that they conduct minor repairs or reconstruction with full consideration of authenticity, while the latter denies it, as shown in the reports of Reactive Monitoring Missions. One of the factors that cause confusion and disagreement when considering authenticity in restoration is that the authenticity of each historic building cannot be defined uniformly. In the early 90's, an international discussion on authenticity was sparked initially by the restoration project conducted by Japanese experts in Nepal.[75] The total dismantling and conservation[76] was conducted when the building was restored. The decayed components were replaced, and the building was reassembled. This method was considered to be unsuitable for the "anastylosis" concept described in paragraph 15 of the Venice Charter. It states that:

> All reconstruction work should however be ruled out "apriori". Only anastylosis, that is to say, the reassembling of existing but dismembered parts can be permitted.

[75] Watanabe K (ed) (1998) The Buddhist monasteries of Nepal: a report on the I Baha Bahi restoration project.

[76] "*Konponshuuri*" in Japanese.

This restoration project led to a discussion that the idea of authenticity is not only the one described in the Venice Charter and that methods of restoration to preserve the authenticity of the OUV may vary from one State Party to another depending on their cultural context. With this background, the discussion was concluded in the Nara Document on Authenticity (after this, referred to as the Nara Document) in 1994. Paragraph 11 states.

> All judgements about values attributed to cultural properties as well as the credibility of related information sources may differ from culture to culture, and even within the same culture. It is thus not possible to base judgements of values and authenticity within fixed criteria. On the contrary, the respect due to all cultures requires that heritage properties must be considered and judged within the cultural contexts to which they belong.

In other words, there is no uniform standard of authenticity. The Nara document left an ambiguity that, in the worst case, could be conveniently interpreted to suit each State Party's position.

KVWHP was inscribed on the WHL in 1979 before the discussion on the authenticity was deepened. Moreover, KVWHP includes many reconstructed monuments after the Bihar Earthquake in 1934. Integrated Management Framework (IMF) in 2007 shows the idea of the authenticity of KVWHP that rebuilding after a disaster is a traditional method in the Kathmandu Valley, and these rebuilding activities do not diminish the OUV of KVWHP. IMF explains that:

> The authenticity of the Kathmandu Valley World Heritage property is retained through the unique form, design, material and substance of the monuments, displaying a highly developed traditional craftsmanship and situated within a traditional urban or natural setting, which have however throughout history gone through *the process of cyclical renewal.* (IMF p. 5)

and

> Cyclical renewal in the case of the Kathmandu Valley has clearly meant reconstruction. This is especially obvious after the reconstruction of monuments due to earthquakes. (IMF p. 5)

The Operational guidelines explain that conditions of authenticity depend on the type of cultural heritage and its cultural context. However, this Non-uniformity of authenticity affects demolishing and reconstruction of damaged historic buildings in Nepal, even if it is in a repairable state. The decision of the World Heritage Committee in 2016,[77] Paragraph 6. states that:

> Considers that a *renewal process [...] must be based on a review and analysis of precisely what has been damaged and could be recovered*, of what has been lost and will need to be replaced by new structures, as well as on a clear understanding of the attributes of OUV for each monument zone and how each has been impacted;

The ambiguity in the definition of authenticity and the renewal process in Nepal is a significant issue for restoring KVWHP.

---

[77] World Heritage Committee (2016) Decision: 40 COM 7B.41.

Insufficient Protection System for World Heritage Properties Inscribed During the Early Years

The development of the system related to the Convention can be seen in the development of the Operational Guidelines. For example, when the Convention was established, the Operational Guidelines at that stage did not require the establishment of buffer zones and comprehensive management plans for the properties. In order to inscribe an own property in the WHL, the State Party must prepare a nomination file following the Operational Guidelines. With the development of the Operational Guidelines, it is not uncommon today for a nomination file to exceed 1000 pages.

In the early days of the World Heritage system, when the "Kathmandu Valley" was inscribed on the WHL in 1979, there were fewer requirements for a nomination file. The management plan required by the current Operational Guidelines after 2005 had not yet been established. KVWHP was inscribed on the WHL without establishing the appropriate protection system required by the current Operational Guidelines.

Following the inscription on the LWHD in 2003, with the support of the World Heritage Centre, Nepal took steps to strengthen the protection system presented in IMF. However, it is still obscure because some documents, such as the management plan, are still not opened on the Website of the UNESCO World Heritage Centre.

An imbalance can be pointed out as an issue of the World Heritage system in that the protection system for the World Heritage properties prior to the mandatory preparation of a management plan tends to be insufficient compared to that after the mandate.[78]

3.5.1.2 Issues in the Operation

Continued Rejection towards Being Inscribed on the List of World Heritage in Danger

The inscription on the LWHD shall be an inherently beneficial opportunity for a State Party holding property, as it provides international support. However, the Nepalese government has strongly resisted the inscription of KVWHP on the LWHD even after the extensive damage caused by the Gorkha Earthquake, same as in the case of the first inscription on the LWHD in 2003. There had been many discussions in the World Heritage Committee since 1993 that KVWHP should be inscribed on the LWHD, and many problems related to the protection system for

[78] Badia F, Donato F (2011) The Management Plan for the UNESCO Heritage Sites: some Critical Reflections from a Managerial Point of View. Conference: 11th International Conference on Arts & Cultural Management.

cultural heritage were pointed out. However, KVWHP had not been inscribed on the List until 2003. These discussions had been perceived as a threat to the government of Nepal that KVWHP would be stripped of the title of World Heritage property because the protection system of Nepal was not sufficient.[79]

With the IMF established in 2007, the seven Monument Zones came under the jurisdiction of local authorities as defined by the Local Self Governance Act (1999), and Site managers from the local authorities were established in each Monument Zone. Historic ritual buildings that temples had previously managed (monks) and communities concerned were getting more substantial interference from DoA, the government authority. Delegating authority to local administrations was a desirable direction for the protection system of the World Heritage property. However, since the cultural heritage in the Kathmandu Valley historically belongs to the Newars, it was emotionally unacceptable for the Newars to have their cultural heritage managed by the central government, consisting mainly of non-Newars. Moreover, the complex historical background that preceded it is also related to the fact that they dislike the management system based on Western logic. The historical background includes the transition from the Malla period, when the Newars ruled the entire Kathmandu Valley, to the Shah dynasty (1768–1846) and the Rana dynasty (1846–1951), in which non-Newars were the prominent rulers. After 1951, Nepal shifted to a constitutional monarchy modeled after the British one, and Western-style management systems such as DoA and the Guthi Sansthan were established, and the cultural heritage of the Newars became controlled by the central government. The Newars, in particular, are thought to have had a long-standing grievance against these transitions.

The series of events surrounding the first inscription on the LWHD was seen as the imposition of external standards on their cultural heritage by the Newars. The Nepalese government, which was in a position to receive complaints from the local people, might also be frustrated by the opinions on the management from outside the country. These might lead to the present attitude that Nepal should avoid inscription on the LWHD, which has been under the discussion since the Gorkha Earthquake. This attitude would be a source of concern for establishing international cooperation to take remedial measures after the inscription on the LWHD. It would be problematic if it were perceived as a disgraceful imposition of foreign logic.

[79] Chapagain (2008) Heritage Conservation in Nepal: Policies, Stakeholders and Challenges. In: Third Annual Himalayan Policy Research Conference, Madison, 16 October 2008, p. 22.

3.5.2 Issues in the Domestic System

3.5.2.1 Issues on the Protection System for Individual Historic Monuments

The World Heritage Committee recommended that some restoration projects in KVWHP have not been realized as required by the Operational Guidelines.[80] This section focuses on the actual restoration implemented under the domestic cultural heritage protection system in Nepal and summarizes its institutional issues that are barriers to the required restoration.

Issues in the System

Laws that define reconstructed buildings as Ancient Monument almost unconditionally

The term "Ancient Monument" covered by the Ancient Monument Preservation Act (1956) is defined in Article 2(a) as *"temple, monument, house, abbey, cupola, monastery, stupa, Bihar* etc. *which have their importance above one hundred years"*. It does not mean more than 100 years after construction. A building after a full reconstruction was also covered as Ancient Monument if it has a history above 100 years from its foundation. Article 4.5 of Ancient Monuments Preservation Rules (1989) states.

> While performing the *maintenance and renovation* of an ancient monument, it has to be performed or caused to be performed in a research-oriented way and by preserving the originality, delicacy of the monuments and art and culture of the monument.

However, the reality is that "maintenance and renovation" include "reconstruction". If the same building remains unconditionally as an "Ancient Monument" in the Act even after the full reconstruction with other techniques and materials, there is no need to respect the attributes of authenticity in the Operational Guidelines, which emphasize the importance of the original materials.

Lack of acknowledgment of traditional management systems in Laws

The Ancient Monument Preservation Act, the primary law for protecting cultural heritage in Nepal, was established in 1956. This year was during the transition to a constitutional monarchy after the return of the monarchy in 1951 and the reform of the feudal system under the reign of King Mahendra beginning in 1955. Under this national regime, the Guthi Sansthan (Guthi Corporation) was established in 1964. Although the monarchy was abolished in 2008, the preamble of the Ancient Monument Preservation Act still states that it was enacted and promulgated by King Mahendra on the advice of the Cabinet of Ministers and the Guthi Sansthan.

---

[80] For example, World Heritage Committee (2019) Decision: 43 COM 7B, paragraph 10.

Guthi is a religious and customary management organization system, as mentioned above, and is a historical system that has been deeply connected with the social structure of the Newari people and continues until today. However, the Ancient Monument Preservation Act sets forth the principle of a top-down approach to the maintenance and management of traditional tangible and intangible cultural heritage, the treasure of the community, by Guthi Sansthan, an institution founded close to the central government under the monarchy.

The Role of Guthi Sansthan is also mentioned in the Integrated Management Framework (IMF) (2017), but there was little mention of traditional management systems[81] involving ordinary citizens in the IMF. Many traditional small-scale Guthis were dissolved after the earthquake, and it has also been highlighted that the almost cultural heritage owned by small-scale Guthis has been left without a national framework to guarantee their maintenance and reconstruction.[82] To continue using the many cultural heritage sites as living heritage for the communities, these are significant issues how to incorporate the Guthi system which was deeply rooted in the culture of the Newars, and how to reconstruct the relationship with the Guthi Sansthan into the modern protection system of cultural heritage at the present that the monarchy has been abolished.

Lack of Seismic performance standards for ancient monuments
The structure of traditional Newari buildings is a mixture of wooden and brick masonry (Fig. 3.5), but the National Building Code (NBC) does not have standards for it. While research and studies have shown that traditional materials and structures cannot hold sufficient seismic performance (strength against earthquakes),[83] the seismic performance standard for ancient monuments such as temples has not been established yet in Nepal. In order to restore ancient monuments in compliance with the attributes of the authenticity, construction methods should be selected following the level of desirable seismic performances. Setting the seismic performance standards is the crucial issue for the restoration and reconstruction.

Issues in the Operation

Traditional housing in historic settlements left uncatalogued
The Ancient Monument Preservation Act indicates that any structure above 100 years is eligible for protection as an ancient monument. Within the scope of the

[81] The Guthi established by individuals on the scale of "Raj Guthi" are called "Niji Guthi," and their guthi lands are subject to taxation. (Source: Shakya L (2013), p10).

[82] Shakya S (2019) The Guthi Act amendment bill may end the Guthi system altogether. Available at the Record. https://www.recordnepal.com/the-guthi-act-amendment-bill-may-end-the-guthi-system-altogether. Accessed 20 May 2022.

[83] Tomoda M, Yamada H (eds) (2016) *Project for Investigation of Damage Situation of Cultural Heritage in Nepal, Structural Survey of Historic Buildings*. National Research Institute for Cultural Properties, Tokyo,

Fig. 3.5 Exposed wooden column inside brick masonry, Changu Narayan (© TNRICP)

WHL, ancient monuments are classified (catalogued) by the IMF. On the other hand, privately owned traditional houses are a significant component of the streetscape of historic settlements, but the reality is that they are not fully catalogued, even if the properties are more than 100 years old. Outside of the component parts of KVWHP, ancient monuments that are supposed to be managed by local governments (municipalities) according to the Local Government Operation Act are not catalogued. In addition, traditional houses with a history of more than 100 years and general houses in traditional structures with a history of fewer than 100 years in the Kathmandu Valley and Kavre Valley[84] are treated almost in the same way. One of the reasons why the demolition of privately owned traditional houses is progressing is that the traditional houses with a history of more than 100 years which the law system should protect, are not adequately catalogued and protected by the Ancient Monument Preservation Act or the Local Government Operation Act.

[84] The Kavre Valley is located southeast of the Kathmandu Valley and has the same cultural background. Panauti, one of the historic cities listed on the Tentative List of World Heritage Property of Nepal as "The early medieval architectural complex of Panauti", is located in the Kavre valley.

Bidding system without technical guarantees

After the earthquake in 2015, in response to the public's desire for early restoration of temples, many projects for conserving and reconstructing ancient monuments were needed to order simultaneously. However, as seen in the failed case[85] of the Rani Pokhari Temple, some projects were conducted by companies with little experience conserving damaged historic buildings. Bidding for public works is conducted in accordance with the Public Procurement Act (2007).[86] It recommends that bids should be awarded at the lowest possible cost. On the other hand, it was a significant problem that contractors who did not have sufficient knowledge of historic buildings could conduct the restoration projects, although Sect. 4.5.2. of Ancient Monuments Preservation Rules (1989) states that the:

> Department (of Archaeology) may perform or cause to perform such works by quotation or in wages basis from the person or Firm, *who has the experience of ancient monuments*, 「...」 if there are possibilities of ruin down or may ruin-down the monuments.

There was another incident that DoA conducted a simultaneous price bidding in selecting contractors for the restoration of 49 historic buildings, even though there were only a limited number of contractors who could adequately restore cultural heritage.[87] The way of price bidding did not guarantee the contractors' skills and led to concerns about poor restoration. Strong criticism erupted from inside and outside of the country, including UNESCO. Although the bidding was canceled before the projects started, this incident highlighted the confusion of the restoration procedure at the time. Some restoration projects, such as the case of Rani Pokhari Temple, were halted after restoration works had begun due to widespread outcry or intervention by DoA because of the use of inappropriate building materials and techniques.[88,89] Restoration of historic buildings requires an appropriate organizational structure and skilled carpenters for the contractors who undertake the restoration work. However, it is impossible to hold the technical qualified and sufficient human resources enough to restore many damaged historic buildings in the immediate aftermath of a disaster. Without earthquakes, there would be fewer

[85] The contractor ordered to restore the Yamaleshwor temple in Lani Pokhali restored the lake wall and the temple with concrete. It became a major social issue and caused a significant community opposition movement. Bajracharya N (2020) Ranipokhari reconstruction in retrospection: 4 years of disputes followed by 1.5 years of deeds. Available at: https://english.onlinekhabar.com/ranipokhari-reconstruction-in-retrospection-4-years-of-disputes-followed-by-1-5-years-of-deeds.html. Accessed 20 May 2022.

[86] Financial Administration Rules (1999) and the Rules Relating to Financial Administration (1985) is also concerned.

[87] Bell T (2016) A second disaster awaits Nepal's heritage. https://www.aljazeera.com/opinions/2016/4/17/a-second-disaster-awaits-nepals-heritage. Accessed 30 May 2022.

[88] Ojha A (2017) Concrete Wall around Rani Pokhari Draws Flak. Capital-The Kathmandu Post. DIALOG. https://kathmandupost.com/valley/2017/12/20/concrete-wall-around-rani-pokhari-draws-flak. Accessed 20 May 2022.

[89] Mathema P (2017) Contractors Threaten Nepal's Heritage. Gulf-times, http://www.gulf-times.com/story/539799/Contractors-threaten-Nepal-s-heritage. Accessed 20 May 2022.

opportunities to restore damaged historical buildings compared to the period after the earthquake. For this reason, carpenters have limited to gain continuous experience, or the number of skilled carpenters is limited. It is an issue not only in the early stages of restoration but also at the time when the six-year restoration plan set by the NRA was approaching its final phase and when the restoration of many damaged buildings needed to proceed rapidly.

3.5.2.2 Issues on the Protection System for Historic Settlements

Issues in the System

The National Building Code prohibiting traditional three-stories brick masonry
The traditional style of Newari architectural housing that constitutes the historic townscape in the Kathmandu Valley is a three-storied mixed wood and brick masonry structure, which does not conform to the current NBC and exists in a state of existing non-conformity. It is impossible to build new houses or reconstruct them (even restore them) in the same way as before the earthquake due to the current NBC. It has become a fatal problem for the legal system to conserve historic townscapes. According to the Grant Distribution Guideline for Completely Destroyed Private Houses by Earthquakes (2015) by NRA, which stipulates the eligibility of subsidies for the reconstruction of damaged houses in order to ensure the structural safety of the damaged houses when they are reconstructed in brick masonry, they must be built with cement mortar instead of the fragile mud mortar used in traditional housing. That reconstructed houses should be no more than two stories high. This guideline is mainly intended for houses in the mountainous areas of the Gorkha region outside the Kathmandu Valley, where many houses have collapsed. While traditional houses on the side of the mountains are one or two-story structures, the typical form of traditional houses in the Kathmandu Valley is a three-story structure with an attic. Thus, there is no legal system for conserving traditional houses in the Kathmandu Valley. In addition, conserving traditional buildings was not eligible for subsidies by NRA. It is more beneficial for the owners to demolish and build new buildings than conservation. These circumstances have become a strong impetus to demolish the damaged traditional houses, replace them with reinforced concrete structures, and change the historic townscape in the Kathmandu Valley. Although structural safety is a prerequisite, creating a legal system for preserving traditional houses is required (Fig. 3.6).

Limitations of building by-laws
In response to uncontrolled urbanization, which was the most significant cause of KVWHP inscription on the LWHD in 2003, building by-laws have been formulated

Fig. 3.6 Rebuilding a traditional housing built by reinforced concrete structure (© TNRICP)

for the PMZs.[90] However, even the building by-laws, intended to conserve the historic townscapes, have limits. Even in the PMZ of Bhaktapur, which has the strictest building by-laws in Nepal, a new building that differs significantly in story height from traditional houses can comply with the building by-laws if bricks are attached to the surface of a new reinforced concrete building complied with the NBC. The building by-laws also permit the installation of terraces on the roof, although this is not a form of the traditional house. In other words, even if rebuilt according to the current building by-laws, new buildings will be constructed that differ from the traditional houses of the past (Fig. 3.7).

Lack of effective incentives and penalties in building by-laws

Effective incentives and penalties are necessary for owners to comply with the building by-laws formulated by each municipality. Bhaktapur municipality has a subsidy system for conservation and reconstruction following the building by-laws, such as providing bricks in kind before the Gorkha Earthquake. However, in Patan of Lalitpur Metropolitan City, many owners did not comply with the building by-laws, and the subsidy system itself was canceled (at least, it have been not

[90] Building by-laws basically hang on city planning classifications, so they do not necessarily match the scope of what the Antiquities Act says is required.

Fig. 3.7 A traditional building under reconstruction after the earthquake of which façade is different from the original in KVWHP (© TNRICP)

used).[91] Though there are penalties (fine, demolition, etc.), some municipalities were simply ineffective in enforcing the building by-laws. Moreover, the municipalities must rely on Chief District Officers to penalize defaulters. Implementing penalties and incentives that work effectively along with the building by-laws is necessary.

The building by-laws require that new buildings be inspected on-site by government officials for compliance with the NBC and the municipality's building by-laws at the time of building application (first inspection) and when the first floor is constructed (second inspection). However, some owners changed plans without permission after the inspection and incentive payment. It shows that the administrative guidance following building by-laws still seems insufficient. It is necessary to strengthen the legal system by checking the plans and strengthening penalties for alterations after the inspection (Fig. 3.8).

[91] Based on the interview with Ms. Chandra Shova Sakya, Chief, Heritage Conservation Section, Lalitpur Sub-Metropolitan City office (In the training program conducted by the National Research Institute for Cultural Properties, Tokyo, from 4 March to 12, 2017).

Fig. 3.8 Example of the building that altered the upper part after the second inspection (© TNRICP)

Issues in the Operation

Miscommunication between central and local governments
The "Basic Construction By-laws for Settlement Development Urban Planning and Building Construction (2015)" (basic building by-laws) was promulgated after the earthquake. It was led by the Department of Urban Development and Building Construction (DUDBC) of the central government and is of great significance in that it has uniformly applied the basic building by-laws to all historic settlements[92] in the Kathmandu Valley and the Kavre Valley. Each city can adjust it into own building by-laws. However, the historic settlements to which basic building by-laws apply were based on a survey[93] of historic settlements conducted from the 1960s to the 70s. It was impossible to apply this basic building by-laws to all historic settlements surveyed at that time because many had already lost their original townscape due to rapid urban development since the 70s. Furthermore, for the basic building by-laws to be applied, the municipalities needed to submit a master plan

[92] The number of historic settlements is not apparent, but it will be 53 historic settlements, according to the document of Carl Pruscha.

[93] Pruscha (1975) *Kathmandu Valley, the preservation of the physical environment and cultural heritage: a protective inventory*. Schroll.

within one year, but even after one year, none of the municipalities had responded to this requirement.[94,95] Thus, the basic building by-laws by the Ministry of Urban Development itself had not been communicated well to most of the administrative staff of the municipalities in the Kathmandu Valley and the Kavre Valley, and the system has not been put into practice (Fig. 3.9).

Insufficient staffing and capacity of administrative staff
Local government officials (Engineering officers) who implement building by-laws in the field are essential. The conservation of historic settlements, in particular, depends mainly on their abilities. Although building by-laws regulate the form of buildings, such as height and window forms, in reality, local government officials who carry out building inspections have not been able to control new construction fully. This situation probably depends partly on the ability and authority of the local government officials who check the application drawings and provide on-site guidance. In addition, although DoA approves the conservation and reconstruction of buildings in the PMZs,[96] the approval procedure is conducted with only the documents without actual drawings. There was confusion during the post-disaster, the lack of staff numbers, and the lack of experience, especially at the beginning of the recovery process. Strengthening the personnel and capacity of the administrative staff of DoA and local governments is an essential and ongoing issue for better operation of the protection system.

3.6 Conclusion

This chapter discussed issues related to the restoration of damaged historic buildings from two aspects: the effectiveness of the World Heritage system and the cultural heritage protection system in Nepal, using the case of KVWHP undergoing restoration after the 2015 Gorkha Earthquake as an example. In the World Heritage system based on the Convention, the properties of each world heritage are supposed to be protected under the sovereignty of their countries and their domestic cultural heritage protection system. Because of this premise, in countries where the domestic system and operation of cultural heritage protection still need development, the restoration considered inappropriate to the OUV still occurs. Many issues that emerged during the restoration of damaged cultural heritage have already been mentioned in the Reactive Monitoring Mission reports submitted in 2015, 2017, and 2019. Many of them can be improved by adhering to the Operational

[94] Shrestha (2020) Heritage Settlement Development and Basic Building By-laws for Historic Settlements. In: Shrestha BK, Tomoda M, Asada N (eds) Proceedings of The Third Mayors' Forum on Conservation of Historic Settlements in Kathmandu and Kavre Valleys, 5 January 2020 at Kirtipur, p.35–37.

[95] Ministry of Federal Affairs and Local Development (2015) Terms of Reference for the "Preparation of Building and Planning By-laws for Municipalities.

[96] Preservation Ancient Monument Act (1956), Paragraph 3(7).

Fig. 3.9 Some buildings were constructed without following the basic building by-laws during the chaos of the reconstruction period in the historic settlement of Khokana (Not in KVWHP, but on the Tentative List) (© TNRICP)

Guidelines as response measures. However, because the situation has not improved enough even more than seven years after the disaster, as seen in the decision of the World Heritage Committee, this may suggest that it is difficult to put all the responsibility on the State Party damaged by a large-scale disaster.

The World Heritage system has a role in supporting the State Parties with insufficient cultural heritage protection systems or in abnormal situations for protecting the properties. This chapter will conclude with the point of view on how international support should be provided to such State Parties to strengthen their domestic cultural protection system. It is considered adequate to inscribe the property on the LWHD as the first step to establish the basis and organization for actively promoting the cooperation between foreign and domestic experts. The inscription on the LWHD will make it easier for the UNESCO Field Office and foreign experts to become involved in the site project. However, the reality is that inscription of KVWHP on the LWHD has been rejected at every World Heritage

Committee deliberation, which is a fatal issue for the World Heritage system. It is partly due to the way of discussion in the World Heritage Committee that does not accurately and deeply reflect the actual situation on the site. Although the content of the Convention cannot be changed, it would be desirable to improve the operation of the World Heritage Committee by minimizing the time for discussion among the Committee members, limiting participation to resolutions only, and focusing on discussions with experts and the State parties related to the property.

From the perspective of realizing the appropriate restoration of damaged historic buildings in KVWHP in consideration of its OUV, it is necessary to clarify each property's characteristics and identify its authenticity. A detailed field survey is an essential step. The direct intervention in domestic cultural heritage from outside the State Party is not allowed, but it is necessary to research with international and domestic experts. The restoration methods for each historic building must be discussed in an open forum in which all parties concerned can participate, based on detailed documentation. Restoration methods should be selected through these discussions, the restoration process should be documented, and the results should be evaluated. Although it is a basic cycling process, it must be repeated. Through these continuous cycles, good examples and experiences of restoration can be accumulated in the State Party and in each administrative staff managing the property on the site. In order to achieve this goal, the World Heritage Centre and the Field Offices should take a decisive leadership role in holding international forums for discussion and create opportunities to use World Heritage Fund[97] and human resources to support strengthening the capacity of government officials and engineers in local government concerned with protecting cultural heritage in the State Party. This process is a slow but steady way to improve the cultural heritage protection system through international cooperation.

References

Amatya, S. (2007). *Monument conservation in Nepal: My experience with the world heritage sites of Kathmandu valley*. Vajra Publications.

Bonapace, C., & Sestini, V. (2003). *Traditional materials and construction technologies used in the Kathmandu valley*. UNESCO.

Chapagain, N. K. (2008). Heritage conservation in Nepal: Policies, stakeholders and challenges. In *Third annual Himalayan policy research conference*.

Department of Archaeology. (2007). *Integrated management framework, Kathmandu valley world heritage site*. UNESCO

Government of Nepal, National Planning Commission. (2015). *Nepal earthquake 2015, post disaster needs assessment, executive summary, Vol. A: Key findings, Vol. B: Sector reports*.

[97] The Fund for the Protection of the World Cultural and Natural Heritage of Outstanding Universal Value, called "the World Heritage Fund", was established in 1977 under Article 15 of the World Heritage Convention.

Government of Nepal. (2016). *Basic guidelines for the preservation and rebuilding of monuments damaged by the earthquake, 2072.*

Gutschow, N., & Roka, R. (Eds.). (2017). *Nepal patan palace—The restoration of Sundari Cok 2006–2016.* Kathmandu Valley Preservation Trust.

Gutschow, N., & Gellner, D. N. (1997). *The Nepalese Caitya: 1500 years of Buddhist votive architecture in the Kathmandu Valley.* Axel Menges.

Gutschow, N. (2011). *Architecture of the Newars: A history of building typologies and details in Nepal* (Vol. 3). Serindia Publications.

ICOMOS. (2011). *Guidance on heritage impact assessments for cultural world heritage properties.*

ICOMOS. (1964). *International charter for the conservation and restoration of monuments and sites.* The Venice Charter

ICOMOS. (1994). *The Nara document on authenticity*

Jing, F., Forbes, C., & Wijesuriya, G. (2016). *Report on the joint world heritage centre/ICOMOS/ ICCROM reactive monitoring mission to the Kathmandu valley (Nepal, C 121bis), world heritage Patrimoine Mondial 40 COM.* UNESCO.

Korn, W. (1977, Reprint 2016). *The traditional newar architecture of the Kathmandu valley.*

Korn, W. (2014). *The Traditional newar architecture of the Kathmandu valley: The Śikharas.*

Korn, W. (2015). *The Traditional newar architecture of the Kathmandu valley: The Stūpas and the Chaityas.*

Mishra. A. K. (2019). Development of building bye-laws in Nepal. *Journal of Advanced Research in Construction and Urban Architecture, 4*(3–4), 17–19.

National Reconstruction Authority. (2015). *Grant distribution guideline for completely destroyed private houses by earthquakes, 2072.*

Pruscha, C. (1975a). *Kathmandu valley: The preservation of physical environment and cultural heritage: Protective inventory.* Schroll.

Pruscha, C. (1975b, Reprint 2015). *Kathmandu valley, the preservation of physical environment and cultural heritage: A Protective Inventory* (Vol. 2).

Regmi, D. R. (1952, Reprint 2007). *Medieval Nepal* (Vol. 1). Rupa & Co.

Sanday, J. (1979). *Monuments of the Kathmandu valley.* UNESCO.

Sekler, E. F., et al. (1977). *Master plan for the conservation of the cultural heritage in the Kathmandu valley.* UNESCO, UNDP.

Sekler, E. F. (1979). Use of collective space in Patan and other historic towns of the Kathmandu valley Nepal. *Monumentum, XVIII–XIX*:97–108.

Shakya, L. (2013). *The management system of communal space of courtyard-style settlement in the historic city of Nepal: A case study of the old residential area of Patan.* The Doctoral Dissertation of Kyoto University.

Shrestha, S. S. (2016). *Swayambhu: A world heritage destination.* OCHSPA.

Shrestha, S. M. (2020). *Heritage settlement development and basic building by-laws for historic settlements, the third mayors' forum on conservation of historic settlements in Kathmandu and Kavre Valleys, Kirtipur* (pp. 35–37).

Theophile, E., & Gutschow, N. (Eds.). (2003). *Sulima pagoda: East meets west in the restoration of a Nepalese temple.* Orchid Press.

Tomoda, M., Kanai, K., Asada, N., Kansha, H., & Var, E. R. (2020). *Investigation report and proposal of rehabilitation plan for the Aganchen temple and associated buildings, Hanumandhoka Durbar Square.* Tokyo National Research Institute for Cultural Properties.

Tomoda, M., & Asada, N. (Eds.). (2020). *Interim report of the investigation of the Aganchen temple and associated buildings in the Hanumandhoka palace.* Tokyo National Research Institute for Cultural Properties.

Tomoda, M., Yamada, H., & Shrestha, BK. (Eds.). (2017). The conference on the preservation of historic settlements in the Kathmandu valley on 30 Nov 2016. In *Proceedings.* Tokyo National Research Institute for Cultural Properties.

Tomoda, M., Yamada, H., & Asada, N. (Eds.). (2020). *The first Mayors' forum on conservation of historic settlements in Kathmandu and Kavre valley on 26 Dec 2017 at Panauti municipality.*

Proceedings. Panauti Municipality and Tokyo National Research Institute for Cultural Properties.
UNESCO. (1972). *Convention concerning the protection of the world cultural and natural heritage*. UNESCO.
Watanabe, K. (Ed.). (1998). *The Buddhist monasteries of Nepal: A report on the I Baha Bahi restoration project*. Nippon Institute of Technology.
Weise, K. (Ed.). (2013). Revisiting Kathmandu: Safeguarding living urban heritage. In *Proceeding of an international symposium, Kathmandu valley*, 25–29 Nov 2013. UNESCO.
Wijesuriya, G., & Forbes, C. (2019). *Report on the joint world heritage centre/ICOMOS/ICCROM reactive monitoring mission to the world heritage property of the Kathmandu valley (Nepal, C 121bis)*. UNESCO.
World Heritage Committee. (2008). *Operational guidelines for the implementation of the World heritage Convention*. UNESCO World Heritage Centre.
Wright, D. (1877). *History of Nepal*. Cambridge.
Yamada, H., & Furukawa, N. (2016). The transformation of the traditional building units and lots of the historical town of Khokana in Kathmandu valley from 1934 until immediately after the 2015 Nepal Gorkha earthquake: Case study along Nyala Dan street. In *The international symposium on architectural interchanges in Asia (ISAIA2016)* (pp. 1883–1888).

Hiroki Yamada (Senior Assistant Professor, Research Institute of Cultural Properties, Teikyo University, Japan) is Registered Architect and Professional Engineer on Urban & Regional Planning in Japan. He has worked in various countries including Chile, Tajikistan, China, Iran, Vietnam and Nepal etc. After the Gorkha Earthquake in 2015, He has conducted technical assistance projects for conservation of historic monuments and settlements in the Kathmandu Valley as a core member of the Project "Technical Assistance for the Protection of the Damaged Cultural Heritage in Nepal" commissioned by the Agency for Cultural Affairs of Japan. He conducted more than 20 missions to the Kathmandu Valley and published various research reports as an author and editor. He continues to support engineers in Nepal as a coordinator of the Mayors' Forum on Conservation of Historic Settlements in the Kathmandu Valley and the Kavre Valley, as a visiting researcher of Tokyo National Research Institute for Cultural Properties.

Part II
Legal Governance Models for Cultural Heritage in Post-trauma Situations

Chapter 4
Introduction

Toshiyuki Kono

The World Heritage Committee endorsed the recommendations adopted by the experts in Warsaw in 2018, which encouraged the advisory bodies to conduct case studies on the reconstruction and recovery of the World Heritage sites. As a result, ICOMOS and ICCROM jointly organized a project of case studies. However, besides this project, fewer case studies were conducted from a comparative perspective applying the same thresholds. Moreover, almost none analyzed cases on recovery or reconstruction of cultural heritage through the lens of law. Part II of this book contributes to filling this lacuna.

Japan is a country where many types of disasters frequently occur, and cultural heritage sites have suffered because many of Japan's cultural properties are made of wood and paper. The ways Japan's law and practices handle post-traumatic situations may offer valuable perspectives to various stakeholders. Hence, Part II begins with a contribution that provides an overview of Japanese law and practices from the viewpoint of disaster prevention which has consistently been one of the significant issues in the protection of cultural properties in Japan. On the other hand, in terms of managing cultural heritage in post-traumatic situations, a case study of Kumamoto that the earthquake in 2016 heavily damaged identified many issues in Japanese law and practices. Before Kumamoto, Christchurch in New Zealand suffered massive damage to its cultural heritage in 2010 and 2011. At that time, there was no coordination between cultural heritage protection legislation and emergency response legislation and no collaborative relationship between the organizations involved. The fact that there was no collaboration between the cultural heritage organizations and the organization with emergency jurisdiction badly resulted in the post-earthquake response and recovery process. In 2014, according to the new law, an institutional collaboration between the two organizations was introduced. Japan should learn this

T. Kono (✉)
Kyushu University, Fukuoka, Japan
e-mail: konoto@law.kyushu-u.ac.jp

T. Kono and J. Okahashi (eds.), *Post-Trauma and the Recovery Governance of Cultural Heritage*, https://doi.org/10.1007/978-981-19-6041-3_4

lesson because there is no coordination between the authorities in cultural heritage protection and emergency response.

In France, Law No. 2019-803 on the conservation and restoration of Notre-Dame de Paris and the establishment of a system for receiving donations for this purpose passed in 2019, after the Notre-Dame de Paris was damaged by fire. It examines why such a Special Law was necessary for an emergency beyond France's regular cultural heritage protection system and what effects it could bring. Furthermore, to comprehensively consider whom within the public framework to entrust with what kind of response in the context of post-disaster reconstruction, one should see such Special Law and Public Establishment as an example of a suggested post-disaster governance response and institutional measure.

Toshiyuki Kono Distinguished professor, Kyushu University, Japan. Toshiyuki Kono was born in Osaka, Japan, in 1958. After graduating from the Faculty of Law, Kyoto University, he went on to obtain his LL.M. from the Graduate School of Law, Kyoto University. He is a specialist in private international law, international civil procedure law, and international cultural heritage law. He was a member of UNESCO's Expert Groups for the drafting of the Convention for the Safeguarding of the Intangible Cultural Heritage (2003) and the Convention on the Protection and Promotion of the Diversity of Cultural Expressions (2005). He was appointed as a member of the Executive Committee of the International Council on Monuments and Sites (ICOMOS) in 2011. After working as vice president, he was elected as the 8th president of ICOMOS in 2017. As the former president, he continues as an honorary president of ICOMOS. He is the series editor of Springer's book series Perspectives in Law, Business and Innovation.

Chapter 5
Japanese Approach and Practice for Cultural Heritage in Post-disaster Situations

Kazuhiko Nishi

Abstract This paper is an overview of the institutional positioning and history of implementation of disaster countermeasures for cultural properties in Japan, in order to provide basic information to understand the essays in this book. In reality, the system has undergone various changes, such as the expansion of its scope and changes in the way of thinking about the utilization of cultural properties, until now. However, disaster prevention has consistently been one of the major issues in the protection of cultural properties in Japan. This is mainly due to the fact that many of Japan's cultural properties are made of wood and paper, and that Japan is prone to many disasters.

Keywords Legal framework · Post-disaster restoration · Preventive measures

5.1 Introduction

5.1.1 Purpose of This Chapter

This paper is an overview of the institutional positioning and history of implementation of disaster countermeasures for cultural properties in Japan, in order to provide basic information to understand the essays in this book.

In reality, the system has undergone various changes, such as the expansion of its scope and changes in the way of thinking about the utilization of cultural properties, until now. However, disaster prevention has consistently been one of the major issues in the protection of cultural properties in Japan. This is mainly due to the fact that many of Japan's cultural properties are made of wood and paper, and that Japan is prone to many disasters.

K. Nishi (✉)
Agency for Cultural Affairs, Tokyo, Japan
e-mail: EZZ00603@nifty.com

T. Kono and J. Okahashi (eds.), *Post-Trauma and the Recovery Governance of Cultural Heritage*, https://doi.org/10.1007/978-981-19-6041-3_5

Although there are many different types of cultural heritage, this paper mainly discusses buildings and other structures that are often the most problematic in relation to disasters.[1] It should also be noted that the opinions expressed in this paper are those of the author and do not necessarily represent those of the organization to which he belongs.

5.1.2 About Previous Studies

There are many discussions on the technical aspects of disaster countermeasures for cultural properties. In particular, seismic and fire countermeasures have been developed through the accumulation of countless studies and experiences on architecture in general, and cultural properties are no exception. However, research on the system and operation of these measures concerning heritage is extremely limited compared to research on the technical aspects.

In this context, a recent summary of the institutional aspects of seismic countermeasures is "Development of Seismic Resistance in Conservation for Architectural Cultural Properties in Japan" by Satoshi Nishioka (Journal of the Society of Architectural Historians of Japan No. 74, 2020, p. 146). Regarding fire countermeasures, Tomoya Inagaki's "Progress in Fire Prevention Measures for Cultural Property Buildings in Japan, in Light of Notre Dame Cathedral Fire and the Shurijo-castle Site Fire" (Journal of the Society of Architectural Historians of Japan No. 75, 2020, p. 97) is a good example. In addition to these, there are other essays published in the "Gekkann bunkazai" (Gyosei).

However, since these are essays limited to their respective subjects, the purpose of this essay is to draw an outline of the overall disaster countermeasures for cultural property buildings that are not summarized beforehand, with referring to these essays.

[1] Although Groups of historical buildings, or conservation areas are another important area concerning risk preparedness, this section focuses on single buildings such as important cultural properties and registered tangible cultural properties. In addition, from a broader perspective, there is a need to take measures by integrating other types of cultural properties, such as statues, paintings or various type of intangible heritage. However, since these have only recently come to be emphasized, I only mention them as issues.

5.2 Japan's Cultural Property System

5.2.1 Until the Enactment of the Law for the Protection of Cultural Properties

First of all, I would like to briefly review the history of the cultural property protection system before the enactment of the Law for the Protection of Cultural Properties, which forms the basis of the current system in Japan.[2]

5.2.1.1 Grand Council of State Proclamation "How to Preserve Old and Antique Artifacts"

It is well known that the Law for the Protection of Cultural Properties, which governs most of the current cultural property protection measures, was enacted as a consolidation of the earlier Law for the Preservation of National Treasures (Law No. 17 of 1929), the Law for the Protection of Historic Sites and Natural Monuments (Law No. 43 of 1919), and the Law for the Protection of Important Art Objects (Law No. 43 of 1933).[3] Due to various social changes and turmoil after the Meiji Restoration, traditional Japanese culture and historical artifacts were in danger. In particular, there were fears that cultural assets would be scattered, destroyed, or lost to foreign countries due to the effects of the so-called "separation of Shintoism and Buddhism," which began in the first year of the Meiji era with a Shinto Office Circular No. 165, dated March 17, 1868, and was followed by the anti-Buddhist movement and the abolition of Buddhism. Under these circumstances, the earliest countermeasure was a proclamation by the Grand Council of State, "How to Preserve Old and Antique Objects," which was issued in response to a proposal from the *Daigaku*.[4] Although it did not intend to protect immovables, it is recognized as the first in a series of measures that led to the current cultural property system.[5]

5.2.1.2 Subsidies for Preservation of Ancient Shrines and Temples

The money for the preservation of old shrines and temples, which was provided by the Ministry of Home Affairs from the 1880 to the FY 1894, is the origin of the subsidies for cultural properties that continue to this day. However, unlike the current subsidies

[2] Mainly based on "Fifty-Year History of the Law for the Protection of Cultural Properties," supervised by the Agency for Cultural Affairs (2001).

[3] Ibid., p.3 etc.

[4] Ibid., p.5. *Daigaku* was established in 1872 as a governmental educational institution and educational administration organization, and was renamed *Daigakko* shortly after its establishment.

[5] For example, Study Group on the Law for the Protection of Cultural Properties (ed) (2006) The Latest Amendment to the Law for the Protection of Cultural Properties. Gyosei, Tokyo, Sect. 5.3.

that target specific projects, this was more of an aid for the operation of shrines and temples themselves.[6] However, the fact that such subsidies were provided in the very early days of the system is strongly related to the current system for the protection of cultural properties, which will be discussed later.[7]

5.2.1.3 Law for the Preservation of Ancient Shrines and Temples

In 1888, the Imperial Household Agency established the "Temporary bureau for the National Survey of Treasures" to conduct further surveys.[8] Based on these surveys, the Law for the Preservation of Ancient Shrines and Temples (Law No. 49 of 1897) was enacted in 1897. The basic approach of specifying the objects to be protected and establishing protection measures for them, such as specifying "specially protected buildings or objects qualified as national treasures," notifying these objects in the official gazette, obliging these objects to exhibit, and providing them with subsidies, forms the basis of the cultural property protection system that continues to this day.[9]

5.2.1.4 Law for the Preservation of Historic Sites, Places of Scenic Beauty and Natural Monuments

While legal frameworks mentioned above was intended to protect objects (movable or immovable), the Law for the Preservation of Historic Sites, Places of Scenic Beauty and Natural Monuments (Law No. 44 of 1919) was enacted in 1919 to establish a general protection system for monuments. Although the basic framework of the Act is the same as that of the Law for the Preservation of Ancient Shrines and Temples, there are some differences. For example, such as the provisional designation system and the allowance of not issuing a public notice where appropriate, due to the different targets and backgrounds.

5.2.1.5 National Treasures Preservation Law

Since the Meiji era (1868–1912), the Law for the Preservation of Ancient Shrines and Temples has provided for the protection of buildings and treasures owned mainly by shrines and temples, but it did not cover properties owned by other entities

[6] "Fifty-Year History of the Law for the Protection of Cultural Properties" p. 5.

[7] The nature of the money for the preservation of old shrines and temples, and its inner reality, was "a system in which religious administration and the will to preserve buildings overlapped, with the buildings themselves being the main object of preservation in actual operation, while showing the attitude of religious administration to maintain old shrines and temples". (Shimizu (2013) A Generative History of Architectural Conservation Concepts. Chuokoron Bijutsu Shuppan, Tokyo 2013, p. 125).

[8] "Fifty-Year History of the Law for the Protection of Cultural Properties" p. 6.

[9] Ibid., p. 7.

(public organizations including the national government, individuals, and corporations). National Treasures Preservation Law (Law No. 17 of 1929) was therefore enacted in 1929 to expand the scope of conservation measures to include castles, treasures of former feudal lords, and other items that require similar conservation measures. This law not only expanded the scope of conservation, which was the main impetus for the law's enactment, but also clarified the order in which conservation measures should be taken and the identification of the objects to be protected. Previously this had been handled in a chronologically mixed manner, were first designated as objects to be protected, and then various systems for the protection of the designated national treasures were established.[10] This is one of the ideas that forms the basis of today's system.

Furthermore, regulations on export or transfer,[11] and subsidies for the maintenance and repair of other types of building in addition to temples and shrines, are closer to the provisions of today's Law for the Protection of Cultural Properties.

5.2.1.6 Law concerning the Preservation of Important Objects of Art, etc.

The Law for the Preservation of National Treasures and the Law for the Protection of Natural Monuments and Historic Sites almost established the system for the protection of cultural properties in Japan before the Law for the Protection of Cultural Properties. However, in the economic situation of the early Showa period, it was needed to quickly respond to the increasing outflow of art works overseas. Therefore, the Law concerning the Preservation of Important Objects of Art, etc. (Law No. 43 of 1933) was established. In light of the purpose of this law, it mainly regulates only export controls by making recognized objects subject to the permission of Minister of Education. Recognition was granted not only at the time of its enactment, but also after World War II until 1949.[12]

---

[10] Ibid., p. 8. This fundamental principle has already been incorporated in the Act on the Protection of Historic Sites, Scenic Beauty and Natural Monuments.

[11] This refers to the removal of items to other countries or overseas territory at that time (ibid., p. 8).

[12] Ibid., p. 11. Although the Important Art Object system was abolished at the time of introduction of the Law for the Protection of Cultural Properties, the system remains in force for the time being as a transitional measure. Originally, it was assumed that the works would be designated and transferred to Important Cultural Properties, or that the recognition of Important Art Works would be cancelled, some part of them are still remains.

5.2.2 *Law for the Protection of Cultural Properties*

5.2.2.1 Establishment of the Law for the Protection of Cultural Properties

The Law for the Protection of Cultural Properties, which defines the current framework for the protection of cultural properties in Japan, was enacted in 1950 with the historical background described above. After the Pacific War and the confusion that followed, the recognition of important works of art and the designation of scenic spots and natural monuments, which had been suspended since February 1944, resumed in October 1945, followed by the restoration works of buildings.[13] At the same time, there were changes in the departments in charge within the administration,[14] and in the midst of the great confusion and economic exhaustion of the postwar period, consideration was given to a new system for the protection of cultural properties. A fire which caused damage of wall paintings of the main hall of Horyuji temple was also the trigger for the introduction of the new legal frameworks.

As a result, the Law for the Preservation of National Treasures, the Law for the Preservation of Important Art Objects, and the Law for the Preservation of Historic Sites, Scenic Beauty, and Natural Monuments, which had been the basis for the protection of cultural properties, were integrated. Because of this, the cultural property protection system was enhanced. Specifically, a new system for the protection of intangible cultural properties and buried cultural properties was established. In addition, the position of local governments and the public in the protection of cultural properties was clarified, the preservation and utilization of cultural properties was coordinated with the guarantee of property rights, and a committee for the protection of cultural properties was established to administer the protection of cultural properties.[15]

However, although there were references to the right to order fire prevention facilities for national treasures in the early stages of the study,[16] and the content of the bill was studied with fire incidents involving cultural properties in mind, it cannot be said that fire prevention and disaster prevention were major themes in the study of the new system as a whole. It was not explicitly stated, and was considered to be part of "management".[17]

---

[13] Ibid., p. 17.

[14] According to the "Fifty Year History of the Law for the Protection of Cultural Properties" p. 18. As the Imperial Household Museum of the Ministry of the Imperial Household became the National Museum in May 1947, the duties related to research and repair of national treasures and important art works were also transferred from the Ministry of Education to the National Museum.

[15] Study Group on the Law for the Protection of Cultural Properties (ed) (2006) The Latest Amendment to the Law for the Protection of Cultural Properties. Gyosei, Tokyo, p. 6.

[16] "Fifty-Year History of the Law for the Protection of Cultural Properties" p. 21.

[17] The process of the enactment of the Law for the Protection of Cultural Properties is detailed in the "Fifty-Year History of the Law for the Protection of Cultural Properties" as well as in the research by Ms. Asuka SAKAINO ("Research on the Process of the Enactment of the Law for the Protection of Cultural Properties: Background of Drafting and Changes in Drafts and Bills as

5.2.2.2 Major Revisions

The Law for the Protection of Cultural Properties has undergone various revisions since its enactment in 1950, including the expansion of the scope of the law. We will not go into the details of each amendment here, but the main changes are as follows.[18]

Amendment of 1954

Establishment of a new management system for important cultural properties and others.

Establishment of a new designation system for intangible important cultural properties.

Separation of folk materials from tangible cultural properties and establishment of a new designation system.

Development of the system for buried cultural properties.

Improvement of other regulations (clarification of the definition of monuments, establishment of a scheme of restitution in integrum, improvement of regulations concerning local governments, etc.)

Amendment of 1968

With the establishment of the Agency for Cultural Affairs, the authority of the Commission for Protection of Cultural Properties was transferred to the Minister of Education and the Commissioner for Cultural Affairs.

Establishment of the Council for the Protection of Cultural Properties.

Amendment of 1975

Improvement of regulations of Folk Cultural Properties (clarification of the status of folk performing arts, establishment of a new designation system for Important Intangible Folk Cultural Properties, etc.)

Establishment of a system for the protection of groups of historic buildings.

Seen in the GHQ/SCAP Documents", 2006). In this dissertation, as part of conclusions, SAKAINO states, "The major points of contention in the process of the enactment of the Law for the Protection of Cultural Properties can be said to be the provisions concerning the Commission for Protection of Cultural Properties, national museums, intangible cultural properties, historic sites/place of scenic beauty/natural monuments, and tax exemption".

[18] In addition to the above, other necessary amendments have been made, such as those accompanying the establishment of the Environment Agency, the establishment of the core city system, the so-called decentralization system reform, and the conclusion of the Convention on the Prevention of the Illicit Export of Cultural Properties.

Expansion of restrictions on the activities of important cultural properties, and establishment of a compensation system for losses associated with restrictions on changes to the current status of important cultural properties and monuments.

Expansion of the system of Important Intangible Cultural Properties (introduction of the system of recognition of holding organizations).

Improvement of the system for the protection of buried cultural properties.

Establishment of a new system for the protection of conservation techniques for cultural properties.

Improvement of regulations on the administrative system for the protection of cultural properties in local governments.

Amendment of 1996

Establishment of a new registration system for cultural properties.

Delegation of authority to designated cities and core cities.

Amendment of 2004

Establishment of a new selection system for important cultural landscapes.

Expansion of the scope of folk cultural properties (addition of folk techniques).

Expansion of the cultural property registration system (to include tangible cultural properties other than buildings, tangible folk cultural properties, and monuments).

Amendment of 2008

Establishment of a planning system for the conservation and utilization of cultural properties (prefectural general principles for the conservation and utilization of cultural properties, approval system for regional plans by municipalities, and approval system for conservation and utilization plans).

Establishment of a new designation system for organizations that support the conservation and utilization of cultural properties.

Relaxation of requirements for appointing a person in charge of management.

Changes to the system for the protection of cultural properties in local governments (enabling the transfer of the administration for the protection of cultural properties to the chief executive's department from the board of education.

Ordinance Revised in 2021

Expansion of the cultural property registration system (to include intangible cultural properties and intangible folk cultural properties).

Add provisions for registration system by local governments.

5.2.2.3 Classification of Cultural Properties based on the Law

As mentioned above, since the enactment of the Law for the Protection of Cultural Properties, the scope and methods of protection have been consistently expanded. The current system of cultural properties is as follows.[19]

5.3 How are Disaster Prevention and Disaster Response Measures for Cultural Properties and Buildings being Implemented?

5.3.1 Target Disasters

First of all, I will discuss the disasters that need to be addressed in relation to the protection of cultural property buildings. The Agency for Cultural Affairs' subsidy programs for cultural property buildings are defined in its Guidelines as follows.[20]

Projects to be Supported

Projects eligible for subsidies shall be those listed below (including research projects necessary for the accomplishment of these projects). With regard to projects in Important Cultural Landscape and Important Preservation Districts for Groups of Historic Buildings, the projects, in which the local government subsidizes the expenses for projects conducted by the owner, etc., and the projects conducted by itself are eligible.

---

[19] Fig. 5.1 is prepared by the author based upon the information on the website of the Agency for Cultural Affairs (https://www.bunka.go.jp/seisaku/bunkazai/shokai/gaiyo/pdf/taikeizu.pdf).

There are also mechanisms based on other laws and regulations related to cultural properties, such as the Landscape Law, and there are cultural properties designated or registered by local governments within the framework of the Law for Protection of Cultural Properties. In addition, subsidies based on frameworks other than cultural properties may be used for the conservation of cultural properties. In particular, when considering post-disaster responses, it is necessary to consider such cases thoroughly, but please refer to the separate article of this book for more details.

[20] "Guideline for National Subsidies for Repair of Important Cultural Properties (Buildings, Arts and Crafts) and Disaster Prevention Projects" (issued by the Commissioner for Cultural Affairs in May 1, 1979, and last revised on April 1, 2015). In addition, the rules and regulations regarding subsidies related to the Law for the Protection of Cultural Properties described below can be found on the Agency for Cultural Affairs website.

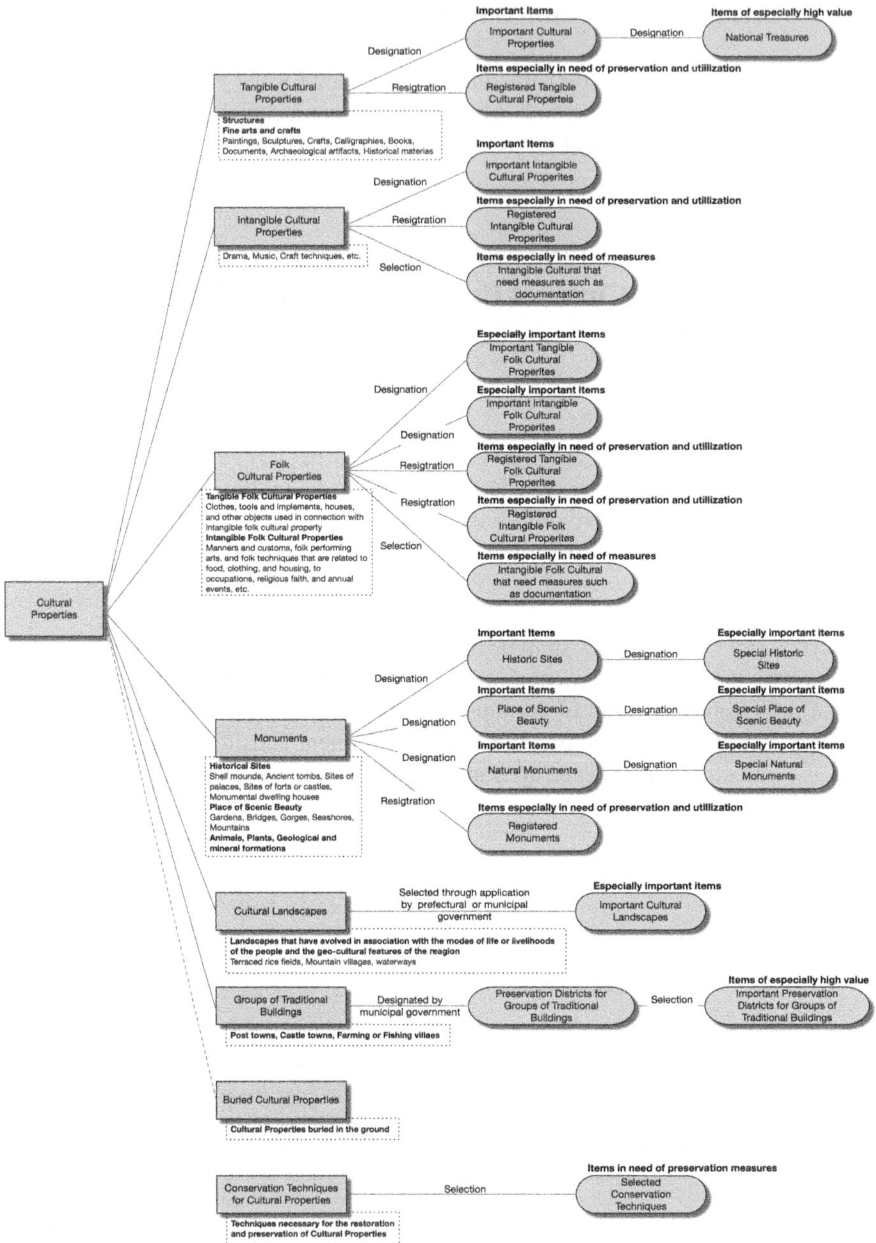

Fig. 5.1 Schematic diagram of cultural properties

If the Regional Resilience Plan specifically mentions cultural properties to be covered by the subsidy project, measures in the following priority order, for instance, will be taken:

(1) Disaster prevention facilities
(2) Installation of fire extinguishing facilities, lightning protection facilities, alarm facilities, and burglar/crime prevention facilities (limited to civil engineering and construction works that are integrated with the facilities)
(3) Establishment of firebreaks, roads for fire engines, disaster prevention warehouses, protective fences, and installation ((including expansion and renovation) of sheds (including storage sheds), Installation of fire walls, retaining walls, and drainage facilities
(4) Earthquake-proofing work
(5) Disaster recovery work

Another reference document concerning the scope of project related to disaster is the "Guidelines for National Subsidies for Projects to Repair and Prevent Disaster of Important Cultural Properties (Buildings, Arts and Craft)", which was the main reference document until the above-mentioned guidelines were established in 2019, and is still in effect today. It stipulates the contents of subsidized projects for disaster prevention of cultural properties, (a) Installation of alarm equipment, fire extinguishing equipment, lightning protection equipment, burglary prevention equipment, security equipment, and evacuation equipment; (b) Establishment of fire breaks, roads for fire engines, protective fences, and sheds (including storage sheds), installation (including expansion and renovation) of retaining walls and drainage facilities; (c) bird, animal, and insect control, diagnosis of dangerous trees and countermeasures against dangerous trees; (d) earthquake resistance diagnosis and countermeasures, and (e) disaster recovery.[21]

---

[21] The relationship between these two Guidelines is somewhat complicated. Before the new "National Government Subsidy for Disaster Prevention Facilities for Important Cultural Properties" was enacted, the "National Government Subsidy for Disaster Prevention Facilities for Important Cultural Properties (Buildings, Arts and Crafts)" was applied to the construction of disaster prevention facilities, but with the enactment of the former, most of the projects related to disaster prevention came to rely on the latter. The former was enacted because of the fires at Notre Dame Cathedral and the Shuri Castle, as described below. The purpose of introduction of the new guidelines was to treat them as expenses subject to public debt issuance (public works-related expenses). It is necessary to juxtapose the two when considering the scope of current disaster prevention-related subsidy projects.

Mr. Tomoya Inagaki provided advice on the background and rationale for this process.

While these are regulations for subsidized projects and do not necessarily list all the disasters that need to be addressed, they do give us an idea of the types of disasters that are expected to be addressed in the system. These include human-caused damage, fires (including arson), earthquakes, dangerous tree measures,[22] bird and animal damage, and landslides.[23] These are interrelated, for example, the issue of fire prevention after earthquakes and the fact[24] that arson is one of the major causes of fires in general. In the following, I will focus on fire and earthquakes, which are considered to be the most important factors affecting cultural properties in terms of the necessity and scale of countermeasures.

5.3.2 Position in the Law for the Protection of Cultural Properties

The following is an overview of how disaster response for cultural property buildings is carried out under the current system, its institutional positioning and actual operation.

5.3.2.1 Important Cultural Properties (Buildings)

Under the Law for the Protection of Cultural Properties the "management" of Important Cultural Properties is, in principle, to be carried out by the owner or a "person in charge of management" appointed by the owner (Article 31). However, the Commissioner for Cultural Affairs may designate a "person in charge of management" to carry out the necessary management "in cases where the owner is not known, or where it is clearly recognized that management by the owner or the person in charge of management is extremely difficult or inappropriate" (Article 32–2). This term

[22] "Hazardous tree control" refers to measures to prevent damage to buildings caused by falling trees. The actual measures include felling of dangerous trees, wiring to prevent them from falling onto buildings, and clearing branches to ensure sunlight to keep buildings dry. As for damage to cultural properties caused by fallen trees, the damage to the five-story pagoda of Murouji Temple caused by a typhoon No. 7 in 1998 is well known.

[23] Among the disasters that are generally assumed, those not included here are heavy snowfall, typhoons, and flooding/inundation damage. Heavy snowfall can have a significant impact on social infrastructure, while cultural properties can be affected in many ways such as rain leaks, which are dealt with on a case-by-case basis as necessary. Typhoons affect cultural properties in the form of wind damage and flooding, and wind damage is dealt with through measures against dangerous trees and disaster restoration work (e.g., roof repair). Floods and inundation damage are not considered to be the main target of prior countermeasures, since shrines and temples are historically located in relatively safe areas. It is clearly stated in the guidelines that restoration work after a disaster has occurred is included in the scope of the project.

[24] According to the "Fire and Disaster Management Agency's White Paper on Firefighting for FY 2020" (the Fire and Disaster Management Agency, 2021), arson and suspected arson accounted for 12.1% of the total number of fires that broke out during 2020, making it the most common cause.

"management" includes not only the installation of disaster prevention facilities, but also the maintenance of the surrounding environment, daily measures such as weeding, cleaning and patrolling, and minor repairs as emergency measures, and is understood as legal basis of projects of disaster countermeasures. It is stipulated that "repair" of important cultural properties is also, in principle, to be carried out by the owner or the aforementioned management organization (Article 34–2).[25]

For the management and repair of these important cultural properties, "in cases where a large amount of money is required and the owner or the management organization of the important cultural property is unable to bear the burden, or in other special circumstances, the government may provide a subsidy to the owner or the management organization of the important cultural property to cover part of the cost" (Article 35). This provision is understood as the basis for granting subsidies for repairs, disaster restoration, and construction of disaster prevention facilities. The only reference to "disaster" in the text of the Law for the Protection of Cultural Properties is about an exception to the regulations on alteration of the status quo in case of disaster, and there are no explicit provisions on disaster preparedness or post-disaster response.[26]

5.3.2.2 Registered Tangible Cultural Properties (Buildings)

The same institutional framework is applied to registered tangible cultural properties as to the aforementioned important cultural properties. It is assumed that the owner is responsible for the management of the property, and if necessary, a person in charge of management or a management organization is appointed or designated (Article 60). Repairs are also to be carried out by the owner or management organization (Article 63). However, there is no provision for a subsidy system as seen in the provisions for Important Cultural Properties, and this difference is the reason why the subsidy

[25] In addition, there are other related orders and recommendations stipulated in the articles. However, almost none of these orders and recommendations are actually implemented. Katsuhiko WADA, commenting on the actual situation, said, "At the time of the Law for the Protection of Cultural Properties, there was a strong reflection that the system of responsibility for the management and repair of national treasures under the Law for the Preservation of National Treasures and the nature of the involvement of the State were unclear, and a detailed system of orders and recommendations for management and repair was established as described below. However, there are few cases where these systems have actually been put into practice as planned, and the management and repair of important cultural properties are mostly carried out through voluntary plans by the owners and relevant local governments based on actual guidance from the Agency for Cultural Affairs and other factors, and government subsidies for such plans. (Kawamura et al., (2002) Introduction to Cultural Heritage Policy: Toward New Developments in the Protection of Cultural Heritage. Tokai University Press, Tokyo p. 89).

[26] For example, Article 43 (Restriction on Alteration of Existing State) says that "Any person who intends to alter the existing state of an Important Cultural Property or to perform an act affecting its preservation shall obtain the permission of the Commissioner of the Agency for Cultural Affairs; however, this shall not apply to cases where the act of altering the existing state is merely a maintenance measure or emergency measure taken in the event of disaster, or to cases where the effects of the act on preservation are negligible".

system for registered tangible cultural properties (buildings) is more limited than that for Important Cultural Properties (buildings).

5.3.3 Subsidies (Requirements, etc.)

Based on the aforementioned legal provisions on subsidies, a subsidy system has been established for the management of cultural property buildings, focusing on repair and improvement of disaster prevention facilities.

Cultural properties, especially buildings, were originally created for a specific purpose, and then the value of cultural properties was added later. In other words, they have their own purposes and uses before they become cultural properties, and they were not built for the purpose of being cultural properties. In addition, repairing them as cultural properties and building disaster prevention facilities require a large amount of money, so the position of subsidized projects in the protection of cultural properties is extremely important. Therefore, it can be said that the system or operational rules (including those that are not explicitly stated) for subsidized projects have an extremely large role in defining the way cultural properties are protected. This is also true for disaster response, whether pre- or post-disaster. Therefore, in order to understand the operation of cultural property protection, it is also important to understand the subsidy system.

As for the subsidies, besides the provisions in the Law for the Protection of Cultural Properties itself, as mentioned above, there is no law other than the Act on general rules concerning subsidies (Act on the Appropriate Execution of Budgets pertaining to Subsidies). Basic rules concerning implementation are "Regulations for the Grant of Cultural Property Subsidies by the Agency for Cultural Affairs" (Commissioner for Cultural Affairs notification on December 26, 1966, and last revised on March 12, 2009), and the "Guidelines for Implementation of National Subsidies for Conservation of Cultural Properties" (Decided by the Commissioner for Cultural Affairs on May 1, 1979, and last revised on April 20, 2021). These guidelines stipulate applications, reports, a list of persons who will implement the subsidized projects for each type of project, conditions for grant, and other procedures. However, since these are general regulations on subsidies for cultural properties, it is necessary to check the individual regulations for each project type or the regulations on subsidy rates under these regulations in order to discuss the contents of disaster prevention projects.

With regard to the repair of important cultural properties and disaster prevention projects, there are "Guidelines for National Treasury Subsidies for Repair of Important Cultural Properties (Buildings, Arts and Crafts) and Disaster Prevention Projects" (approved by the Commissioner for Cultural Affairs on May 1, 1979, and last revised on April 1, 2015) and "Guidelines for National Treasury Subsidies for Disaster Prevention Facilities Improvement Projects for Important Cultural Properties" (approved by the Commissioner for Cultural Affairs on December 13, 2019, and last revised on April 1, 2021). The former is used for repair projects including post-disaster restoration, while the latter is mainly used for the construction of disaster prevention facilities. In these guidelines, in addition to the aforementioned eligible projects, the eligible expenses and subsidy rates are presented. The basic rate of subsidy is 50%, but for parties other than local governments or profit-making corporations, the subsidy rate can be increased in 5% steps according to the "project scale index". This index is calculated by dividing the project cost for a single year (the total project cost to be subsidized divided by the number of years of the subsidized project) by the financial scale of the subsidized entity. In practice, 50 to 85% of the costs are paid out as subsidies in increments of 5%. In addition, depending on the municipality in which the cultural properties are located, there are many cases in which the prefectural and municipal governments independently provide subsidies, and in many cases the actual burden on the owner is even lower.

Furthermore, the subsidy rate is increased by 20% in the case of disaster recovery projects,[27] and may be further increased in the case of severe disasters[28] or when certain conditions are met for World Heritage sites and national treasures.[29]

On the other hand, regarding registered tangible cultural properties (buildings), the "Guidelines for Government Subsidies for Repair of Buildings of Registered Tangible Cultural Properties" (approved by the Commissioner for Cultural Affairs on July 11, 1997, and last revised on July 2, 2020) are applicable. As mentioned above, this is a subsidy for the cost of design and supervision for conservation and repair, or for the cost of projects related to public use (including planning, equipment, maintenance of disaster prevention facilities, and seismic measures). As mentioned above, there is a large difference in both the eligibility for subsidy and the subsidy rate for registered tangible cultural properties compared to important cultural properties, and the subsidy rate is set at 50% with some exceptions.[30] In the case of disaster restoration, the subsidy rate is increased by 20%.[31]

---

[27] In the "Subsidy Rate for Cultural Properties Related to Disaster Restoration" (issued by the Commissioner for Cultural Affairs on November 20, 1998, last revised on April 1, 2020), it is stated that "The subsidy rate for a project carried out as a disaster restoration project shall be the rate calculated in accordance with the above guidelines plus 20%. However, the upper limit shall be 85% of the subsidized cost".

[28] In the "Subsidy Rate for Cultural Properties in Relation to Disaster Restoration of Cultural Properties Damaged by Severe Disasters" (decided by the Commissioner for Cultural Affairs on November 1, 2016, revised on April 1, 2020), it is stated that "If all of the following conditions are met, an additional 5% will be added to the subsidy rate. However, the upper limit shall be 90% of the subsidized cost".

[29] Based on "The subsidy rate for the installation of fire prevention facilities and equipment at World Heritage Sites, National Treasures (buildings), or museums which store Important Cultural Properties (arts and crafts), which were found to be in need of maintenance, etc., based on an on-site survey, etc., based on a request from the Agency for Cultural Affairs on April 1, 2019.", issued by the Commissioner for Cultural Affairs on December 13, 2019".

[30] Depopulated areas, special exceptions for Okinawa Prefecture, etc.

[31] In addition to these, there are also subsidized projects for the purpose of regional revitalization and tourism promotion, but since there are not many examples of such projects being applied to disaster response, either pre- or post-disaster, they are outside the scope of this discussion.

5.3.4 *Actual Operation*

So far, we have summarized the legal frameworks and subsidy-related provisions. However, since it is difficult to understand the actual operation of these systems, I would like to give an overview of what is actually being done based on these systems, dividing it into pre-disaster measures and post-disaster measures.

5.3.4.1 Pre-disaster Measures

The measures that are currently being taken in advance can be broadly categorized as (1) seismic reinforcement, (2) construction of disaster prevention facilities, (3) planning, and (4) public awareness and training.

Seismic Reinforcement

Although seismic reinforcement is one of the most important themes in Japanese architecture, it has been almost neglected for cultural properties. But then, since the Great Hanshin-Awaji Earthquake, the damage to cultural properties has attracted a great deal of attention, and with the expansion of the scope of cultural properties and the increase in the percentage of buildings that are used daily, it has become almost universally recognized that a certain level of earthquake resistance is necessary even for cultural properties. However, seismic reinforcement of cultural properties is not an easy task. Seismic reinforcement has a large impact on the cultural properties and on their heritage value, hence its implementation is very difficult from the perspective of "minimum intervention," which is one of the fundamental principles of cultural property protection.

The study of building structures in Japan has evolved along with the countermeasures against earthquakes. However, unlike the construction of new buildings, it is difficult to grasp the current status of cultural properties because they are already there and their detailed specifications differ greatly from modern construction methods. For this reason, seismic countermeasures for cultural properties have been studied starting with seismic diagnosis. In addition, because of the fundamental principle that cultural properties should not be unnecessarily altered, and because of the practical difficulties involved, the prevailing view has been that seismic measures should be taken only during large-scale conservation and repair projects. In recent years, however, this view has changed, and seismic reinforcement is no longer subordinate to repair work. In other words, subsidized projects that focus on seismic reinforcement have become viable, and the concept of "transitional reinforcement" is becoming more widespread. As a result, as of November 2019, among 4080 buildings as national treasures and important cultural properties that require seismic reinforcement, countermeasures have been completed for 2536 buildings (62.2%), and of these, 651 have been reinforced.[32]

With a few exceptions,[33] most of these projects were carried out in the framework of the repair and disaster prevention projects on a large scale.

The basic principles and implementation details for cultural properties as a whole, which are not limited to the framework of subsidized projects, are summarized in the "Guide for Seismic Evaluation and Seismic Reinforcement of Important Cultural Properties (Buildings) (Revised)" (2017), edited and published by the Counselor of the Cultural Properties Department of the Agency for Cultural Affairs.

Development of Disaster Prevention Facilities

Disaster prevention facilities, mainly for fire prevention, was promoted earlier than that of seismic reinforcement. This is because, although there are special factors of heritage buildings, it is basically possible to apply the concept of fire prevention for general buildings, and because there are fewer technical problems. Another reason is that while designated important cultural properties are exempted from applying the Building Standards Act,[34] installing some disaster prevention equipments is obligatory under the Fire Service Act.

Automatic fire alarms, fire extinguishing equipment (fire hydrants, water guns, etc.), and lightning protection equipment are the main equipments that have been installed in this way. The details are mainly based on the "Guidelines for the Project concerning Disaster Prevention Facilities for Important Cultural Properties".[35]

According to a survey[36] conducted by the Agency for Cultural Affairs in response to the fire at Notre Dame Cathedral in April 2019, of the total number of important cultural properties (including national treasures), 3983 historic buildings (87.7%), were equipped with automatic fire alarms, while 358 historic buildings (7.9%) were

[32] Nishioka (2020) Seismic Countermeasures for National Treasures and Important Cultural Property Buildings. Architectural History 74; p. 150.

[33] For example, for the Marunouchi Main Building of Tokyo Station (an important cultural property), funds were raised through the use of the specific floor area ratio application zone system (as it was called at the time) by transferring and selling the unused floor area ratio on top of the building to the surrounding area, and conservation and repair work was carried out without using the framework of subsidized projects for cultural properties.

[34] The provisions of Article 3 of the Building Standards Law.

[35] This is an internal regulation for the subsidized projects of the Agency for Cultural Affairs. However, it is widely used as a guideline for the projects. The guidelines are revised in 2022.

[36] "Results of a Urgent Questionnaire Survey on Fire Prevention Equipment for National Treasures and Important Cultural Properties (Buildings)" (https://www.bunka.go.jp/koho_hodo_oshirase/hodohappyo/1420029.html).

not.[37] As for the installation of fire extinguishing systems other than fire extinguishers indoors or outdoors, 3529 buildings (77.7%) have already installed such systems, indicating that countermeasures to cope with the fire have been taken for many historic buildings compared to seismic reinforcement.

Planning

Installing such facilities or taking physical counter measures should be integrated in a comprehensive management plan for each building. However, because of the emphasis on individual specificity of each heritage building and decisions taken based on expert knowledge, the protection of cultural properties has mainly been implement on a case-by-case basis, with decisions made based on regulations. There are many problems with this working method, hence today the focus has been gradually shifted from restriction for each case to control based on relevant plans.

In the amendment of the Law for the Protection of Cultural Properties in 2018, the "general plan" for the protection of cultural properties in each prefecture and the "district plan" for each municipality as hierarchical master plans for the protection of cultural properties, as well as the "conservation and utilization plan" for individual cultural properties were established. If a "conservation and utilization plan" meets certain conditions and is approved by the Commissioner for Cultural Affairs, the procedural and other requirements will be relaxed.[38] According to the "Guidelines for the Formulation, etc. of the General Plan of the Preservation and Utilization of Cultural Properties, the Regional Plan for the Preservation of Cultural Properties, and the Plan for the Preservation and Utilization of Cultural Properties based on the Law for the Protection of Cultural Properties" (March 4, 2019, Agency for Cultural Affairs),[39] formulated in response to the amendment, "matters related to disaster prevention and crime prevention" is listed as one of the "contents of specific measures to be taken for the preservation and utilization of the important cultural properties concerned".

In these Guidelines, it is stated that the plan should include "plans for fire prevention, crime prevention, earthquake resistance, wind resistance, and other measures to be taken during the planning period, based on the current status and issues of preservation." It is expected that various projects will be carried out based on the respective plan for each cultural property.

---

[37] The remaining 4.4% are either not obligated to be installed or have been removed during repair work.

[38] Article 53, 4 etc. of the Law for the Protection of Cultural Properties. Although the preparation of this type of plan has been recommended in the past, and standard examples have been provided in the form of guidelines for the preparation of such plans, this amendment clarified the legal position of the plan and made it possible to relax the regulations. This means that planning can now play a clear and central role in the protection of cultural properties, whereas before it was only subordinate to controls by permission systems.

[39] (https://www.bunka.go.jp/seisaku/bunkazai/1402097.html).

Public Awareness, Training, etc.

When dealing with disasters involving cultural properties, it is undisputed that it is important not only to maintain and reinforce facilities, but also to conduct drills and raise awareness of the importance of disaster prevention. According to the results of the aforementioned survey questionnaire, in many cases the number of people who can respond to emergencies such as fires is very limited.[40] 21% of the respondents said that fire drills are not conducted throughout the year. In general, it is understood that "more than half of disaster preventive facilities are deteriorated and not suitable for the reality of use and maintenance in an aging society with a declining birthrate".[41]

The Agency for Cultural Affairs and the Fire and Disaster Management Agency have designated January 26 of each year as Fire Prevention Day for Cultural Properties, and drills are conducted at individual cultural properties during the period around January 26. In addition, notices are issued whenever there is a fire that has had a major impact on a cultural property building. However, it is questionable to what extent the owners of cultural properties are aware of these administrative notices, and it is necessary to continue to implement concrete disaster prevention measures for each cultural property. These measures include the formulation of disaster prevention plans in the conservation and utilization plans.

5.3.4.2 Post-disaster Response

Immediately after a Disaster, Issues of Removal of the Designation or Registration

To restore damaged buildings after a disaster using the framework of the cultural property system, it is first assumed that the value of the property as a cultural property survives and that its designation or registration will not be cancelled. In fact, except in the case of loss of properties by fire, restoration work may be carried out even in the case of severe damage that is generally considered to be challenging to restore, provided that, as a result of detailed examination, it is evaluated as possible to maintain the value of the property.[42] However, in some cases, especially with regard to registered tangible cultural properties, it is difficult for the owner to restore the

---

[40] Even during the daytime, 18.9% of the respondents answered that they had less than two people, and 35.4% answered that they had less than two people at night.

[41] Inagaki (2020) Progress in Fire Prevention Measures for Cultural Property Buildings: Based on the experience from Notre Dame Cathedral Fire and the Shurijo Site Fire. Architectural History 75: p. 97, p. 101.

[42] In particular, when a wooden structure collapses, it is almost always possible to restore it because at least all of its components remain in place. Typical examples of this are the former Kobe residence hall No.15 after the Great Hanshin-Awaji Earthquake and the Aso Shrine after the Kumamoto Earthquake.

property, and there are cases where restoration work is technically possible but is not carried out for economic reasons, leading to cancellation of the registration.[43]

In addition, post-disaster cultural heritage buildings are often in a vulnerable situation in terms of public perception. In particular, the lessons learned from previous large-scale disasters have led to a more rapid response to buildings in general. The smoother the social flow of recovery is, the more difficult it will be to decide to restore and continue using cultural properties rather than dismantling them. Although the Agency for Cultural Affairs and the Ministry of Land, Infrastructure, Transport and Tourism jointly confirmed that "the emergency assessment of danger level of damaged buildings is to determine the risk of collapse and the risk of falling exterior walls and windows in order to prevent secondary disasters caused by aftershocks, etc., and does not require uniform and immediate demolition,"[44] it is clear that there is a strong need to present a clear and economically feasible path to restoration as cultural properties.

On the other hand, for important cultural properties and other cultural properties that are easily noticed by the public, the damage is reported in the media, and as a symbol of recovery and reconstruction, it is easier to take budgetary measures.[45] In the future, it is necessary to expand the social recognition of the recovery of cultural properties in the event of a disaster to a wider range of objects, including undesignated cultural properties.

Restoration Work

As we have already seen, the guidelines clearly state that the repair of cultural property buildings after a disaster is eligible for subsidies and that the subsidy rate will be raised for a disaster recovery work. However, there are many problems caused by the fact that this is defined within the same framework as ordinary repair projects. There is indeed a consideration for the exceptional and urgent nature of disaster response, such as allowing some projects to begin before the grant decision, but for registered tangible cultural properties, for which the portion eligible for subsidies is originally tiny in relation to the overall construction cost, the subsidy rate is still insufficient even with a slight increase. It must be said that this is a limited response to the situation that could lead to immediate removal or cancellation of registration if repairs are not realized.[46]

---

[43] For more information on this point, please refer to the other article in this book.

[44] "Handling of cultural properties that have been assessed as being in danger of being damaged by the earthquake", (Notice issued by the director of Architecture and other structure division of Agency for Cultural Affairs dated April 7, 2011, https://www.bunka.go.jp/earthquake/tsuchi_bunkazai/pdf/toriatsukai_01.pdf).

[45] Kumamoto Castle after the Kumamoto Earthquake is a clear example of this.

[46] Of course, there are various factors involved in the realization of restoration, such as public awareness in the region of cultural properties or the securing of engineers and technicians, in addition to the economic aspect, but as this is beyond the scope of this paper's consideration, I will only point out the issue of subsidies here.

For this reason, especially for registered tangible cultural properties or other undesignated cultural properties, restoration projects are often carried out by combining various subsidy programs. For more information on this point, please refer to the articles by Yatsunami and Tanaka in this book.

5.4 Recent Progress of Disaster Prevention and Response for Cultural Heritage Buildings

So far, we have reviewed the current institutional framework and its operation for dealing with disasters involving nationally designated cultural properties. Such a framework was established based on the historical background as described above, but since the Great Hanshin-Awaji Earthquake disaster countermeasures for cultural properties have made significant progress, I would like to summarize the changes.

5.4.1 Great Hanshin-Awaji Earthquake

The Great Hanshin-Awaji Earthquake, which occurred on January 17, 1995, is often said to have been an opportunity to take full-fledged measures for cultural properties against earthquakes and organized disaster response. This evaluation is now well established. For a long time, there was a vague understanding that cultural properties should have few seismic problems because of their long survival history.[47] Although many academic studies had been accumulated from technical points of view, it was not until the Great Hanshin-Awaji Earthquake that the need for earthquake-resistant measures for cultural property buildings was strongly recognized as an administrative response.[48]

After the earthquake, which caused serious damage to various types of cultural properties, including 116 important cultural properties,[49] the Agency for Cultural Affairs established the "Research Collaborators' Meeting on Improving the Seismic

[47] For example, the Agency for Cultural Affairs' pamphlet "Protecting Cultural Properties from Earthquakes: Questions and Answers" (https://www.bunka.go.jp/seisaku/bunkazai/hogofukyu/pdf/pamphlet.pdf) states in its introduction, "We tend to think that old buildings that are cultural properties are safe because they have survived earthquakes and windstorms for a long time".

[48] This does not mean that seismic reinforcement had not been carried out before then. Especially for castles and brick buildings, various studies and measures have been taken. For example, the former Yamagata Prefectural Assembly Building, an important cultural property that was undergoing conservation and repair work between 1986 and 1990, is known for its innovative method of exposing the steel reinforcement to the outside.

[49] Nishioka (2020) Seismic Countermeasures for National Treasures and Important Cultural Property Buildings. Architectural History 74; p. 148.

Also, according to a survey conducted by the Architectural Institute of Japan, among 1260 buildings surveyed including undesignated buildings, 75% is damaged. (The Architectural Institute of Japan (ed) (1999) Report on the Hanshin-Awaji Earthquake Disaster, Building Series Volume 8,

Performance of Cultural Property Buildings" and, after discussions at the meeting, formulated the "Guidelines for Ensuring the Safety of Cultural Property Buildings in the Event of Earthquakes" in 1996. In 1999, "Guidelines for Seismic Diagnosis of Important Cultural Properties (Buildings)" and "Guidelines for the Implementation of Diagnosis by Owners of Important Cultural Properties (Buildings)" were formulated, and two years later in 2001, "Guidelines for the Implementation of Basic Diagnosis of Important Cultural Properties (Buildings)" were adopted.

As a result, there have been several cases where seismic reinforcement has been implemented in regular conservation works of important cultural properties other than disaster restoration. Since 2005, it is possible to carry out seismic diagnosis as an independent subsidized project, which was possible only as part of conservation and repair work.[50] Furthermore, in 2007, the Earthquake Resistance Section was established in the division in charge of heritage buildings of the Agency for Cultural Affairs, and a senior specialist who is devoted to anti-earthquake initiatives was assigned.[51] From FY2009, in addition to the seismic diagnosis, the seismic reinforcement work can be subsidized independently from the conservation work.[52] These measures were discussed by the "Study Group on Measures to Promote Seismic Evaluation of Important Cultural Properties (Buildings)"[53] from 2007 to 2012. In parallel with these studies, the "Study Group on Comprehensive Disaster Prevention Measures for Important Cultural Property Buildings" was established in 2008 jointly by the Cabinet Office, the Ministry of Land, Infrastructure, Transport and Tourism, the Fire and Disaster Management Agency, and the Agency for Cultural Affairs, based on the discussions of the Central Disaster Management Council. In April 2009, this was summarized as "Comprehensive Disaster Prevention Measures for Important Cultural Properties and Surrounding Areas".[54] This can be evaluated as a positive sign that cultural properties, especially disaster prevention measures for them, have changed their significance, i.e. from "being recognized as a special field of expertise" to "being widely discussed as a social issue".

The Great Hanshin-Awaji Earthquake was a major turning point not only in terms of how cultural properties perceive a large-scale disaster, but also in terms of how society perceives cultural properties in the event of a large-scale disaster. However, at that time, the importance of cultural properties in times of disaster was not yet widely recognized, and those in charge at local governments had a great deal of difficulty.[55] On March 22, about two months after the earthquake, the Hyogo Prefecture

Architectural Planning and Design, History and Theory of Architecture. The Architectural Institute of Japan, Tokyo, p. 249).

[50] Nishioka, ibid., p. 149.

[51] Ibid., p. 149.

[52] Ibid.

[53] From 2008 onwards, the name has been changed to "Conference of Collaborators on Seismic Countermeasures for Important Cultural Properties (Buildings)".

[54] (https://www.bunka.go.jp/seisaku/bunkashingikai/kondankaito/kenzobutsu_bosai/sogo_bosai.html).

[55] Michio Yamada, who was then Director of the Social Education and Cultural Properties Division of the Hyogo Prefectural Board of Education, wrote about the situation at the time in "The Great

Council for the Protection of Cultural Properties made an emergency proposal entitled "Towards the Succession and Revival of Culture." In it, the Council expressed its awareness of basic issues that have continued to this day, such as the necessity of giving consideration to the recovery of undesignated cultural properties and the importance of positioning cultural properties in the general recovery plan.[56] In particular, the framework regarding undesignated cultural properties will be realized in the post-disaster rehabilitation phase of the Kumamoto Earthquake.

5.4.2 Great East Japan Earthquake

In the Great East Japan Earthquake that occurred on March 11, 2011, a large number of cultural properties were damaged over an extremely wide area in Japan. In response, the aforementioned guidelines for seismic diagnosis, preliminary seismic diagnosis, and basic seismic diagnosis were revised in June 2012.[57] The revised guidelines incorporate new academic findings on the seismic performance of cultural property buildings, as well as the concept of "transitional reinforcement" as a transitional measure before full-scale reinforcement is undertaken. This is a way of incorporating the concept of "disaster mitigation," which has been discussed in various ways in general buildings, into the concept of reinforcing cultural heritage buildings. In addition, a liaison document was issued to request that seismic countermeasures for non-structural parts,[58] which have been identified as one of the causes of earthquake damage in buildings, be included in large-scale repair projects, as well as in more partial restoration works such as roof replacement. As a result, the seismic retrofitting of cultural property buildings progressed rapidly.[59]

In addition, the "Great East Japan Earthquake Restoration Support Project for Cultural Properties" was launched as the first attempt concerning heritage buildings. This project, also known as the "Cultural Property Doctor Project," is a real estate version of the so-called "Cultural Property Rescue Project", which was launched for movable cultural properties after the Great Hanshin-Awaji Earthquake. In this context, the fact that separate organizations carried out the response to buildings and

Hanshin-Awaji Earthquake and the Restoration of Cultural Properties: Current Situation and Issues" (Monthly Cultural Properties, No. 389, 1996, p. 4),

Hiromichi Murakami, a specialist in cultural properties in Hyogo Prefecture, also described the situation at the time. (The Architectural Institute of Japan (ed) (1999) Report on the Hanshin-Awaji Earthquake Disaster, Building Series Volume 8, Architectural Planning and Design, History and Theory of Architecture. The Architectural Institute of Japan, Tokyo, p. 249).

[56] Yamada, ibid., p. 7.

[57] (https://www.bunka.go.jp/seisaku/bunkazai/hogofukyu/taishin_shishin.html).

[58] For example, it refers to countermeasures for ceiling components, which are not part of the main structure of a building but can pose a serious hazard if they fall.

[59] "Seismic Countermeasures for Buildings of Cultural Properties" (issued by the director of Architecture and other structure division of Agency for Cultural Affairs dated June 22, 2012 (https://www.bunka.go.jp/seisaku/bunkazai/hogofukyu/pdf/r1411329_02.pdf)).

movable property and the establishment of a cooperative system among specialists in each field were raised as issues. It is expected that the Disaster Prevention Center[60] for Cultural Properties, established in the National Institutes for Cultural Heritage in 2020, will be responsible for the integrated management of this issue.

5.4.3 Kumamoto Earthquake

As mentioned above, after the Great Hanshin-Awaji Earthquake and the Great East Japan Earthquake, awareness of the need for earthquake-resistant measures for cultural property buildings has increased dramatically. In response to this, the Agency for Cultural Affairs has continued to study various issues. In FY2013, a pamphlet[61] on earthquake-resistant measures was prepared for a wide range of owners, and a guide for experts on earthquake-resistant diagnosis and reinforcement of important cultural properties (buildings, etc.) was prepared. In addition, the aforementioned guidelines to earthquake resistance was revised based on the results of studies conducted between 2014 and 2016.[62] This revision includes measures for brick and reinforced concrete structures, as well as measures for non-structural parts, which were previously announced in the form of a liaison document.[63]

The Kumamoto Earthquake that occurred on April 14–15, 2016 caused damage to 39 important cultural properties (buildings) and 74 registered tangible cultural properties (buildings).[64] Notable post-earthquake developments related to cultural properties include: (1) the damage to Kumamoto Castle and other cultural properties attracted a great deal of attention, and its position as a symbol of reconstruction was strongly recognized: (2) not only municipalities officials but also architects and researchers collaborated and responded in a timely manner, and (3) a new subsidiary scheme was established for undesignated cultural properties. As for (1), due to the symbolic nature of the castle, the ease of understanding the damage, such as the

---

60 This center was established to further strengthen "the Network for Disaster Mitigation of Cultural Heritage", which succeeded the Cultural Property Rescue Project. The National Institutes for Cultural Heritage had been in charge of this network as a project to be renewed every year, but the new center would be operated as a permanent organization.

61 See note 71.

62 Architecture and other structure division of Agency for Cultural Affairs, "Guide for Seismic Evaluation and Seismic Reinforcement of Important Cultural Properties (Buildings, etc.) (Revised Edition)" (March, 2017), (https://www.bunka.go.jp/seisaku/bunkazai/hogofukyu/pdf/kokko_hojyo_taisin16.pdf).

63 In general, guidance on cultural properties emphasizes the individuality of each case, thus often reference cases are provided rather than just uniform guidelines.

64 Nishioka (2020) Seismic Countermeasures for National Treasures and Important Cultural Property Buildings. Architectural History 74; p. 150.

collapse of the stone walls, and the clear connection with tourism and other reconstruction measures, it can be evaluated that the trend started at the Great Hanshin-Awaji Earthquake is accelerated. As for (2) and (3), I will leave the details to the articles by Yatsunami and Tanaka in this book, but I would like to say that the efforts to improve the post-earthquake system for cultural heritage buildings, which have been sought since the Great East Japan Earthquake, have been accelerated by the efforts of various parties involved and by the efforts of the pre-disaster preparations. Furthermore, point (3) is a concrete answer to an unresolved issue that was already raised at the time of the Great Hanshin-Awaji Earthquake, and can be considered groundbreaking. It has been repeatedly pointed out that whether or not a list of historical buildings to be surveyed in the event of a disaster exists in advance makes a big difference in the response, and concrete efforts have been made, such as the ongoing creation of a nationwide database by the Architectural Institute of Japan.[65] However, while these measures play a major role in the response of the experts who conduct the survey, it is clear that for the owners who carry out the subsequent restoration, the presence or absence of some kind of financial support will be the major difference. The significance of the subsidies for undesignated cultural properties introduced here is extremely significant in considering the cultural property protection system in Japan in a broader sense.[66]

5.4.4 Fire at Notre-Dame de Paris and Shuri-jô Main Hall

As mentioned above, fire prevention has been the main disaster prevention measure for cultural properties in Japan, but after experiencing major earthquake damage in the Hanshin-Awaji and East Japan earthquakes, technical and institutional progress in earthquake resistance measures has been remarkable. Two years after the Kumamoto earthquake, the Agency for Cultural Affairs issued a liaison document to ensure that earthquake-resistant measures are taken more thoroughly, calling for the formulation of "policies" for each cultural property building as necessary. In this way, there is a growing need to promote earthquake-resistant measures. As described above, there has been a great deal of progress in the area of earthquake-resistant measures, while fire prevention measures have been relatively stable in terms of both system

[65] The Historical Architecture Database Subcommittee was established as a standing research body of the Architectural Institute of Japan (AIJ), and has been building a database of historical architecture located throughout Japan for many years.

[66] The Law for the Protection of Cultural Properties stipulates that the definition of "cultural properties" does not depend on designation, etc. (Article 2), and says that "The owner of any tangible cultural property other than Important Cultural Properties and Registered Tangible Cultural Properties may, … ask the Commissioner of the Agency for Cultural Affairs for technical guidance in regard to the custody or repair of such tangible cultural property." (Article 70). However, it cannot be said that this is a concrete protection measure for undesignated cultural properties, because it is almost impossible to imagine a case in which only "technical guidance" is requested for post-disaster measures, and there is no common recognition that undesignated cultural properties can also be recognized as cultural properties.

and operation, as there was almost no damage caused by fires in cultural property buildings even after several earthquakes.

However, the fire at the Notre Dame de Paris Cathedral in April 1991 attracted a great deal of attention, which led to a reconsideration of fire prevention measures for cultural property buildings in Japan. In response to the fire, the Agency for Cultural Affairs and the Fire and Disaster Management Agency immediately issued a message from the Commissioner for Cultural Affairs as well as notifications focusing on bringing attention.[67] In addition, as mentioned above, a survey was conducted to ascertain the current situation. Based on the results of this survey, the "Guidelines for Fire Prevention of National Treasures and Important Cultural Properties (Buildings)" were formulated in September 2019.[68] The guidelines aim to break away from the fixed image of fire prevention measures for cultural properties, which has been built up over many years and tends to focus on installation of facilities, and encourages each owner to consider the maintenance of facilities, training, and other measures, and to create a specific fire prevention plan, based on an understanding of the individual situation. The report also encourages owners to prepare specific fire prevention plans.

In October of the same year, several buildings, including the Main Hall of Shuri Castle, located within the designated historic site, were destroyed by fire. This building was originally designated as a national treasure under the National Treasure Preservation Act, but was destroyed by fire during World War II and restored after the war. In addition to this fact, since the building was a symbol of the Okinawa and the site was inscribed as a World Heritage site, it was considered a major event. In this case, due to the management problems pointed out in the questionnaire and in the examination of the guidelines, various fire prevention equipment and systems did not work, although the legal requirements for fire prevention were met. For this reason, the aforementioned guidelines were immediately revised,[69] and in December 2019, the "Five-Year Plan for Fire Prevention in World Heritage Sites and National Treasures" was decided. This was exceptional, as an action plan of this kind had only been prepared after World War II.[70]

Based upon this plan, the subsidy rate for disaster prevention projects for World Heritage Sites and National Treasures has been raised[71] and the total budget for disaster prevention measures has been increased. In addition, the "Guidelines for

[67] Also in the past, when a large-scale fire broke out in a cultural property building, notices were issued in many cases to alert the public.

[68] (https://www.bunka.go.jp/koho_hodo_oshirase/hodohappyo/1420851.html, last accessed on September 29, 2021). The fact that such a comprehensive guideline was formulated less than half a year after the Notre Dame Cathedral fire shows the strong interest in fire prevention measures for cultural properties.

[69] (https://www.bunka.go.jp/koho_hodo_oshirase/hodohappyo/pdf/91957201_03.pdf).

[70] Inagaki (2020) Progress in Fire Prevention Measures for Cultural Property Buildings: Based on the experience from Notre Dame Cathedral Fire and the Shurijo Site Fire. Architectural History 75: p. 104.

[71] The subsidy rate is based on the "Subsidy Rate for Cultural Properties for Installation of Fire Prevention Facilities and Equipment at Museums and Other Institutions that Store World Heritage Sites, National Treasures (Buildings), or Important Cultural Properties (Arts and Crafts), which were found to be in need of maintenance, etc., based on an on-site survey, etc., based on a request

Subsidized Projects for Disaster Prevention Facilities for Important Cultural Properties", which has a significant impact on the development of disaster prevention facilities through subsidized projects, was revised in 2022.

5.4.5 Summary of Recent Changes

The above is an overview of the institutional framework and operation of pre- and post-disaster response for cultural properties in Japan, as well as the changes since the Great Hanshin-Awaji Earthquake. In summary:

(1) Disaster prevention measures for cultural heritage buildings in Japan are not directly mentioned in the law, but are mainly promoted as subsidized projects.
(2) In the past, disaster prevention measures for cultural properties in Japan focused on fire prevention, but since the Great Hanshin-Awaji Earthquake, earthquake-resistant measures have been developed. On the other hand, fire prevention measures have been mainly focused on installation of facilities until recently, but after the fires at Notre Dame Cathedral and the Main Hall of Shuri-Jô Castle, the contents of these measures have been greatly reviewed.
(3) In Japan's system for the protection of cultural properties, subsidized projects have a large significance, but anti-seismic measures, which used to be treated as an incidental part of conservation projects, have gradually become independent and more important. On the other hand, for post-disaster restoration, etc., the same framework is applied as that for ordinary conservation projects as far as subsidy projects are concerned.
(4) Regarding the recovery system after a large-scale disaster, past experience has been accumulated, but the situation regarding the integrated operation of movable and immovable properties is expected to be studied in the future.

5.5 Conclusion

Finally, based on the current situation described so far, I would like to express my personal views on possible issues to be addressed in the future.

Issues related to the protection of cultural properties in general are piling up in various ways due to changes in social conditions. In particular, the situation of custodians (owners, local communities, restoration technicians, etc.) has changed drastically due to changes in the social structure, and there is an urgent need to respond to these changes. The aforementioned amendment to the Law for the Protection of Cultural Properties in 2018 can be evaluated as facilitating the participation of not only owners but also local communities against the background of these problems.

---

from the Agency for Cultural Affairs dated September 2, 2019″ (decided by the commissioner for Cultural Affairs dated December 13, 2019).

However, it is expected that problems will become apparent from various perspectives, such as the fact that temples and shrines, which account for a large percentage of cultural property, are rapidly losing the basis of their existence in local communities, especially for small-scale corporations. Therefore, further consideration on the systems for protection should be discussed.[72]

While I do not doubt the necessity of financial support such as subsidies, it is necessary to shift the focus to the formulation of plans for individual cultural properties, with greater emphasis on so-called "soft" measures, including daily management of cultural properties and disaster prevention facilities, training, and public awareness. In doing so, it will be important to integrate measures for buildings, Buddhist statues, and other treasures located in temples, for example, rather than for each type of cultural property.

More specifically, I believe that a clearer and more independent framework should be given not only to disaster prevention measures in advance but also to restoration projects after the fact.[73] As already mentioned, the subsidies for restoration projects for cultural property buildings are basically provided under the same framework as that for ordinary restoration projects, although there are certain specific considerations such as a higher subsidy rate and quicker operational response. In the future, it will become more important to examine this point, including who should take primary responsibility for disaster recovery under the system.

References

Inagaki, T. (2020). Progress in fire prevention measures for cultural property buildings: Based on the experience from Notre Dame Cathedral fire and the Shurijo Site Fire. *Archit Hist, 75*, 97–111.

Kawamura, T., Nemoto, A., & Wada, K. (Eds.). (2002). *Introduction to cultural heritage policy: Toward new developments in the protection of cultural heritage*. Tokai University Press.

Nishioka, S. (2020). Seismic countermeasures for national treasures and important cultural property buildings. *Architectural History, 74*, 146–162.

Sakaino, A. (2009). A study on the process of the establishment of the law for the protection of cultural properties: Background of drafting and changes of drafts and bills in the GHQ/SCAP documents. Dissertation, University of Tsukuba.

Study Group on the Law for the Protection of Cultural Properties (Ed.). (2006). *The latest amendment to the law for the protection of cultural properties*. Gyosei

Supervised by the Agency for Cultural Affairs. (2001). *A fifty-year history of the law for the protection of cultural properties*. Agency for cultural affairs

[72] For example, with regard to securing materials for repairing cultural properties in order to preserve them permanently, various initiatives and surveys have been conducted by the Agency for Cultural Affairs. However, except for a few cases such as those related to conservation techniques, this has not been adopted as a legal framework at present, and is a major issue for the future.

[73] For example, in the case of registered tangible cultural properties (buildings), where, with some exceptions, subsidies are provided mainly for design and management costs and not for construction costs, this framework could be changed in the event of disaster recovery. Currently, in order to avoid such difficulties, it is necessary to carefully consider to use various systems, but it can be said that the system itself should be able to guarantee these things.

The Architectural Institute of Japan (Ed.). (1999). Report on the Hanshin-Awaji earthquake disaster, building series volume 8, architectural planning and design, history and theory of architecture. The architectural institute of Japan

Kazuhiko Nishi (Chief Senior Specialist for Cultural Properties at the Agency for Cultural Properties, Government of Japan) He holds a Master of Engineering in History of Architecture from the University of Tokyo. He has more than 25 years experiences in architectural conservation, disaster preparedness as well as international cooperation in conservation in the Agency and Tokyo National Research Institute for Cultural Properties. He worked for ICCROM (International Centre for the Study of the Preservation and Restoration of Cultural Property) as a staff member from 2004 to 2006 and currently serves as a council member. His selected publications include: NISHI Kazuhiko (2003), "Japanese Style Architecture in Modern Age." Arts of Japan, Vol. 450. Shibundo Publishing; NISHIMURA Yukio, MOTONAKA Makoto, NISHI Kazuhiko et al. (2017), "Introduction to the World Cultural Heritage," University of Tokyo Press; NISHI Kazuhiko et al. (2021), "Attributes, a way of understanding OUV" Tokyo National Research Institute for Cultural Properties.

Chapter 6
Cultural Heritage Protection Challenges Seen from the Kumamoto Earthquake

Ren Yatsunami

Abstract This paper examines the legal issues related to preserving historical townscapes in times of disaster, reviewing the case of the Kumamoto Earthquake of 2016 in Japan. Since May 2020, the author participated in a research team conducting interviews with local experts, government officials, and owners of damaged cultural properties in Kumamoto Prefecture to examine legal needs and challenges in the cultural heritage protection they faced after the occurrence of the earthquake. In considering the results of the interview survey conducted in 2020 and the follow-up survey conducted under this project, this paper discusses the recent trends of legal institutions for preserving historical townscapes in post-traumatic situations. Efforts to systematize the knowledge on disaster mitigation of cultural heritages and those to build up a sustainable network of industry-academia-government-private sector cooperation are observed. Especially the establishment of the Cultural Heritage Disaster Risk Management Center in 2020 deserves particular attention as a milestone in Japan's recent development of cultural heritage protection in post-trauma situations.

Keywords Kumamoto earthquake · Legal resilience · Cultural heritage protection

6.1 Introduction

The Great East Japan Earthquake in 2011 exerted a considerable impact on society, and since then, there have been many efforts to re-examine desirable disaster recovery legislation. In particular, attempts have been made to systematize the institutions for disaster response, recovery, and revitalization as a legal field called "Disaster Recovery and Revitalization Law."[1] Also, it is noteworthy that efforts are being made to compile the legal needs and know-how for reconstruction using the concept

[1] Okamoto (2014, 2018a, b).

R. Yatsunami (✉)
Kyushu University, Fukuoka, Japan
e-mail: yatsunami@law.kyushu-u.ac.jp

T. Kono and J. Okahashi (eds.), *Post-Trauma and the Recovery Governance of Cultural Heritage*, https://doi.org/10.1007/978-981-19-6041-3_6

of "legal resilience."[2] However, while these studies have been conducted from the perspective of victims' relief and livelihood protection, research focusing on legal issues of disaster recovery based on the consideration of cultural heritage preservation should be required.[3]

Specifically, the issue of disaster mitigation for cultural properties has recently received renewed attention due to the frequent occurrence of disasters. As recent major examples in Japan, the Kumamoto Earthquake in 2016, the East Japan Typhoon in 2019, the fire at Shuri Castle in 2019, and the torrential rains in Kyushu and Central Japan in July 2020 have caused damage to cultural properties. While some of the damaged cultural buildings have been successfully restored, a considerable number of historical buildings have been dismantled. On the other hand, critical recent developments in this field can be observed, including the establishment of the "Cultural Heritage Disaster Risk Management Center" in 2020. Thus, it can be said that the demand for re-examining disaster recovery legislation from the perspective of cultural heritage preservation has increased. This paper examines the legal issues related to preserving historical townscapes in times of disaster, reviewing the case of the Kumamoto Earthquake of 2016.

This paper is a part of the results of the research project "International Joint Research to Develop an Integrated Governance Methodology for Cultural Heritage Protection" (Principal Investigator: Toshiyuki Kono), which was adopted by the Japan Society for the Promotion of Science (JSPS) as a project in the "Topic-Setting Program to Advance Cutting-Edge Humanities and Social Science Research." In this project, Notre Dame Cathedral, Kathmandu, Christchurch, and Kumamoto have been taken up as subjects of case studies on cultural heritage conservation efforts in post-traumatic situations. The case studies have been conducted by project members from several different jurisdictions, including Japan. For the Kumamoto case study, the Kumamoto research team conducted interviews with local experts such as heritage managers and owners of damaged cultural properties, visiting damaged buildings.[4] At the same time, through local study meetings and online meetings to exchange opinions with local experts, the Kumamoto research team summarized the actual situation of the efforts from the post-earthquake period to the present and examined the legal needs and challenges. Based on these research activities, this paper will first summarize the information and suggestions obtained from the interviews and follow-up surveys conducted in 2020, and it will then examine the current status and issues of disaster recovery legislation from the perspective of preserving cultural heritage and historical townscapes (6.2). Then, this paper will focus on the trend toward developing a more systematic and permanent system for disaster response in the future, based on the disaster recovery efforts revealed by these surveys (6.3).

---

[2] Masuda et al. (2020), pp. 2–21.

[3] See, for example, Okahashi (2020), pp. 67–88, Hisasue (2020).

[4] The interviews and other research activities in Kumamoto Prefecture conducted under this project were conducted jointly by Toshiyuki Kono (Kyushu University; Principal Investigator of this project), Eisuke Tanaka (Hokkaido University), and Ren Yatsunami (Kyushu University).

6.2 The 2020 Survey

6.2.1 The 2020 Interview Survey

6.2.1.1 Objective and Method

Since May of 2020, the Kumamoto research team of this project has conducted interviews with experts, government officials, and owners of damaged cultural properties who have been working on cultural heritage conservation in the post-traumatic state in order to identify legal needs that were recognized in the local areas immediately after the occurrence of the 2016 Kumamoto Earthquake and during the reconstruction period (hereinafter referred to as "2020 interview survey"). During the period of the survey, we also conducted on-site inspections of damaged buildings.

This section will firstly summarize the results of the 2020 interview survey, focusing on the four systems that were the focus of attention during the Kumamoto Earthquake in 2016 (6.2.1.2). Then, the follow-up survey, which was conducted in the latter half of the same year in order to supplement the results of the 2020 interview survey, will be explained (6.2.1.3).

6.2.1.2 Results of the 2020 Interview Survey

Emergency Risk Judgments

In the 2020 interview survey, critical opinions were raised regarding the method of implementing the emergency risk judgments. The emergency risk judgment is an urgent and temporary measure to prevent secondary damage from occurring.[5] It is carried out by government officials and private architects registered as emergency risk assessors. In order for the capacity buildings for large-scale disasters, prefectural governments train and register private architects and other professionals who have taken a course and meet other requirements as emergency risk judges.

Under the emergency risk judgment system, the results of the judgments will be displayed on the "emergency risk judgment sticker" at an easily visible location on the building. The attachment of the sticker is essential for clearly indicating the risk of secondary damages, including damage from collapsing, falling exterior walls, and falling accessories that may occur due to aftershocks.[6] Since the emergency risk judgment is an urgent measure to determine only a limited number of items in a short period, there is no continuity or consistency between the judgment and the damage survey conducted after the fact. However, since it is easily misunderstood that the assessment is not related to the survey for disaster certification, it was pointed out

[5] Sasaki (2017), p. 64.

[6] See, for example, Japan Building Disaster Prevention Association (JBDPA) (2021).

in the 2020 interview survey that it would be desirable to make the meanings of the judgments more widely known during normal times.

In the case of the 2016 Kumamoto earthquake, a total of 6,819 emergence risk judges participated in the survey from April 15, 2016, to June 4, 2016, and 57,570 judgments were conducted. One of the problems that came up repeatedly in the course of the 2020 interview survey was that, although there is no doubt that the emergency risk judgment is an important first-aid measure to prevent secondary disasters, there were cases where the psychological impact of having a "danger" sticker ("red judgment") on the property prevented the restoration of damaged cultural properties. In the immediate aftermath of the earthquake, when information was complicated, there were many cases where the assessment result was mistakenly perceived as if the restoration of the building in question was impossible.[7]

Dismantling Using Public Funds

Publicly fund dismantling refers to a system in which the government or local government bears the cost of dismantling damaged houses on behalf of the owners from the perspective of preserving the living environment and preventing secondary disasters. In the case of the 2016 Kumamoto earthquake, buildings certified as half-destroyed or buildings that suffered more damage were subject to public expenditure for demolition.[8] Once the decision was made to target buildings that were half-destroyed or more, municipalities began accepting applications. On June 27, 2016, Kosa Town became the first municipality in Kumamoto Prefecture to start publicly funded demolition, and other municipalities also started demolition work.

In the 2020 interview survey, some critical comments on public fund dismantling pointed out that the way the application deadline was set encouraged the demolition of cultural properties. As for the application deadlines set by local governments in Kumamoto Prefecture within the fiscal year 2017, measures such as the extension of application deadlines were taken as appropriate. However, as an actual result, in several cases, the information on the deadlines of public fund dismantling encouraged owners' decisions to demolish their cultural buildings at the stage when they were unsure about whether there will be any other subsidies for restoring the damaged historical buildings.[9] In addition, as will be discussed later, the subsidy system by the Fund for Restoration and Rehabilitation of Cultural Properties Damaged by the Kumamoto Earthquake (discussed later in "Subsidies by the Funds for the Restoration of Damaged Cultural Properties") was decided in April 2017, and its full-scale operation did not start until November of the same year. Therefore, for owners of

[7] It is reported that there was a misunderstanding that buildings with "danger stickers" (so-called "*akagami*" or "red judgment") at the site had lost their property value. See Japan ICOMOS (International Council on Monuments and Sites) National Committee (2019), p. 72 [Tsuji].

[8] Kobayashi et al. (2017), pp. 161–162.

[9] Japan ICOMOS National Committee (2019), p. 102 [Sasaki]. For more information on extension of the deadline for applying for the dismantling of public funds in this period, see Owaki et al. (2017), p. 65.

historical buildings who were struggling to choose between restoration and demolition in their post-traumatic situation, it was apparent that they had to be aware of the impending deadline for applying for dismantling at public expense, before the necessary assistance was sufficiently prepared and made known to them.[10] This was an unavoidable situation at the time, considering that the public expenditure for dismantling was a subsidy for disaster waste disposal projects administered by the Ministry of the Environment, which was used by the affected municipalities. In the future, it would be desirable to develop this system to coordinate with other institutions that can be used for cultural heritage conservation.

Furthermore, as a related institutional issue, it was pointed out that, even if the building itself must be dismantled, it may be possible to preserve and utilize components with historical value. However, such utilization of components would be difficult to achieve with public fund dismantling. Therefore, voluntary dismantling was chosen in cases where owners wanted to convert specific components, such as pillars and beams, which they were attached, into houses that could be built later.[11]

In addition, there are reports of cases where contractors from both parties applied for public fund dismantling and self-financed dismantling simultaneously, resulting in a collision of contractors at the site.[12] In addition to the issue of coordination between the institutions, it will also be necessary to devise ways to make the public aware of the system (e.g., providing information on restoration support in addition to easy-to-understand explanations).

There is no doubt that public fund dismantling is an important measure in general. Still, from the perspective of historical townscape preservation, its coordination with other institutions is an issue that cannot be overlooked. Careful consideration must continue to be given to whether there were aspects that encouraged the demolition of cultural buildings that could have been fully restored. The follow-up survey (6.2.2) described below is meaningful as a data collection tool for this study.

Group Subsidies

The "Small and Medium Enterprise Group Facility Reconstruction and Improvement Subsidy" (hereinafter referred to as the "Group Subsidy") is a system whereby the prefecture approves, through examination and evaluation, the "Reconstruction Project Plan" formulated by a "Small and Medium Enterprise Group" that is expected to play an important role in reconstruction, and provides subsidies for the expenses required for the reconstruction and improvement project of facilities, etc., implemented by the Small and Medium Enterprise Group or its members. Once a "reconstruction business plan" formulated by "small and medium-sized business groups" are adopted, subsidies are provided for the expenses required for restoration and

[10] Japan ICOMOS National Committee (2019), p. 78 [Fujikawa]. See also Japan ICOMOS National Committee (2019), p. 109 [Kariya]; Japan ICOMOS National Committee (2019), p. 69 [Kotani].

[11] Japan ICOMOS National Committee (2019), p. 67 [Kotani].

[12] Japan ICOMOS National Committee (2019), p. 75 [Tsuji].

improvement projects of facilities, conducted by small and medium-sized business groups or their members.[13] This system was established after the Great East Japan Earthquake and was also implemented after the Kumamoto Earthquake in 2016 to support affected Small and Medium-sized Enterprises. A "small and medium-sized enterprise group" is defined as "a group consisting of multiple small and medium-sized enterprises" (Article 2, Paragraph 3 of the Kumamoto Prefecture Small and Medium-sized Enterprise Group Facility Restoration and Improvement Subsidy Guidelines). Also, "small and medium-sized enterprises" here refers to those stipulated in Article 2, Paragraph 1 of the Small and Medium-sized Enterprise Support Act (Act No. 147 of 1963) (Article 2, Paragraph 2 of the Kumamoto Prefecture Small and Medium-sized Enterprise Group Facility Restoration and Improvement Subsidy Outline). Since the buildings damaged by the 2016 Kumamoto earthquake include Machiya (townhouses) as merchant houses, there are many cases where group subsidies were used to restore the business portions of these buildings.

In the Shinmachi and Furumachi areas of Kumamoto City, Kumamoto Prefecture, a human network of castle town research and historical building preservation that can be traced back to 1986, has been fostered before the 2016 Kumamoto Earthquake. Since 1997, it has developed into a private organization, the Kumamoto Machinami Trust (see 6.3.1.1). Thanks to the personal connections built up through these activities, the Kumamoto Machinami Trust was requested by local merchants to provide various support activities during the 2016 Kumamoto Earthquake. In relation to group subsidies, from August to September of the same year, the Kumamoto Machinami Trust hosted a series of meetings regarding subsidy applications.[14] As a result, the reconstruction project plan for the "Castle Town Stopping Place" was approved.

In addition, in Ogawa-machi, Uki City, Kumamoto Prefecture, the teachers and alumni of Kumamoto College of Technology played a central role in forming a network for the preservation of Machiya houses during normal times (see 6.3.1.1).[15] As part of the results of these efforts, the reconstruction project plan applied for as the "Association for the Creation of a Town of Traditional Townhouses and Experiences in Ogawa-machi Shopping Street" was approved in the framework of the group subsidy in September 2016.

In the 2020 interview survey, the positive evaluation of the group's subsidy was that the application was started early after the earthquake and that there were many cases where the prefectural government acted as a contact point and handled the related procedures and inquiries relatively smoothly. In particular, with regard to the timing of the call for applications, it was suggested that the Group's subsidy played a

---

[13] The "Kumamoto Prefecture Small and Medium Enterprise Group Facility Reconstruction and Improvement Subsidy Project Reconstruction Project Approval Outline" and "Kumamoto Prefecture Small and Medium Enterprise Group Facility Reconstruction and Improvement Subsidy Outline," which were formulated as part of the reconstruction policy after the 2008 Kumamoto Earthquake, can be found on the following webpage of Kumamoto Prefecture. See Kumamoto Prefecture—Commerce, Industry and Industry Promotion Finance Division—Corporate Reconstruction Support Office (2016).

[14] Japan ICOMOS National Committee (2019), p. 77 [Fujikawa].

[15] Japan ICOMOS National Committee (2019), p. 57 [Isoda].

significant role in the period when the subsidy system under the Fund for Restoration and Rehabilitation of Cultural Properties Damaged by the 2016 Kumamoto Earthquake, which will be discussed in the next section, was not yet available. During that period, there were no specific subsidies that were applicable for the conservation of undesignated cultural properties. In particular, the significance of the group subsidies was that they were effective in motivating owners of historical buildings to stay away from "demolition," which was confirmed again in the 2020 interview survey.[16]

On the other hand, since the group subsidies are not primarily focused on the preservation of cultural heritage, it was unavoidable that the restrictions on the eligibility of the subsidies have caused some difficulties in the field of cultural heritage restoration. In other words, under this framework, the subsidy must be for "facilities or equipment of a small or medium-sized business group or its members," "essential for a small or medium-sized business group to carry out a project based on a reconstruction business plan," and "expenses required for a project to restore and improve facilities and equipment and promote the restoration of commercial functions in the prefecture in principle. (Article 4, Section 2 of the Kumamoto Prefecture Small and Medium Enterprise Group Facility Restoration and Improvement Subsidy Outline). Therefore, if a townhouse that has been damaged includes a business part and a home part, only the cost of restoring the business part will be covered by the group subsidy, and the cost of restoring the home part will have to be funded in another way.[17]

Subsidies by the Funds for the Restoration of Damaged Cultural Properties

Even among the undesignated cultural properties, there are a considerable number of properties with high historical value that should become designated as cultural properties in the future. Article 3 of the Law for the Protection of Cultural Properties stipulates that "the government and local governments shall endeavor to thoroughly implement the purpose of this Law with due care, so that cultural properties […] may be properly preserved," and the obligation of the government and local governments set forth here extends to undesignated cultural properties as well.[18] However, at the time of the Kumamoto Earthquake in 2016, under the existing framework, national, prefectural, and municipal designated cultural properties were eligible for assistance from the national government and local governments, but there was no supporting framework for undesignated cultural properties.

On the other hand, after the Kumamoto Earthquake of 2016, there were donations and fundraising activities from the private sector for the restoration of damaged cultural assets. Such fundraising activities became more serious when the private sector organization "Kumamoto Castle, Aso Shrine and Other Damaged Cultural

[16] Japan ICOMOS National Committee (2019), p. 78 [Fujikawa].

[17] As an example of the need to deal with such problems, the example of "Kiyonaga Honten" is reported. See Japan ICOMOS National Committee (2019), p. 29 [Fujikawa].

[18] Hidaka (2015), pp. 186–187.

Properties Restoration Support Committee" was formed in July 2016.[19] In October 2016, Kumamoto Prefecture enacted the "Fund for Restoration and Recovery of Cultural Properties Damaged by the 2016 Kumamoto Earthquake" Ordinance (Ordinance No. 44, October 11, 2016) and established the "Fund for Restoration and Recovery of Cultural Properties Damaged by the 2016 Kumamoto Earthquake" using donations from the private sector as its financial source (Article 1 of the same ordinance). In addition to the Fund for the Restoration and Recovery of Cultural Properties Damaged by the 2016 Kumamoto Earthquake, Kumamoto Prefecture has established a new subsidy system to support the restoration of designated and undesignated cultural properties by utilizing the reconstruction funds granted by the government. Under this new subsidy, the private owners will be subsidized for 1/2 of the cost of restoration of designated cultural properties and design and management of registered tangible cultural properties, which the public could subsidize even before this new system is established.[20] In addition, for construction costs of registered tangible cultural properties and undesignated cultural properties, which were not subject to the public subsidy system in the past, subsidies of up to 2/3 of the private owner's share become possible with this new subsidy.[21]

In the 2020 interview survey, we heard a positive evaluation that the realization of the subsidy system for undesignated cultural properties was a breakthrough. On the other hand, because it took time to establish and start the operation of the new subsidy, there were cases where the decision to dismantle damaged cultural properties was made before the support menu was fully known to the public.

6.2.1.3 Implementation of the Follow-Up Survey Based on the 2020 Interview Survey

As mentioned above, the 2020 interview survey was meaningful because it allowed us to listen to opinions from various local actors about the roles that each system played in the preservation of historical buildings during the Kumamoto Earthquake of 2016 and the challenges which each system faces. In addition, the Kumamoto research team thought it necessary to compare the results of the 2020 interview survey with the other local cases of different jurisdictions taken up in this project. In addition, while examining the results of the 2020 interview survey, we became aware of the need to conduct a survey to track the current status of how many historical buildings have actually been demolished due to various problems with the multiple institutions. Based on these considerations, the two follow-up surveys were conducted in the latter half of 2020 under this project.

Firstly, a survey was conducted to apply the "case study matrix" developed in the ICOMOS Global Case Study Project on Reconstruction to the case of the

[19] For more details on the fundraising campaign to support the restoration of damaged cultural properties such as Kumamoto Castle and Aso Shrine, see Kumamoto Prefecture (2016).

[20] Japan ICOMOS National Committee (2019), p. 79 [Fujikawa].

[21] Ibid.

Kumamoto Earthquake. The "Case Study Matrix" was developed in response to the 2017 ICOMOS Guidance on Recovery and Reconstruction of World Cultural Heritage from Traumatic Events document.[22] It is significant as an effort to organize and accumulate the results of surveys on cultural heritage damaged by the disaster in a comparable form, rather than just individual case studies.

From August to September 2020, the Kumamoto research team had a series of discussions with the Kumamoto Machinami Trust on preparing matrix reports for case studies. As a result, by January 2021, two matrix reports were prepared for the Kumamoto case studies. One matrix report is written by Juko Itoh (Faculty of Advanced Science and Technology, Kumamoto University, and Kumamoto Machinami Trust), describing the conservation and restoration of cultural heritage in Kumamoto City in relation to the 2016 Kumamoto Earthquake. Also, Kazuhiro Fujikawa (Institute for Humanity and Urban Research, Kumamoto Machinami Trust) wrote a matrix report describing the current situation of Nishi-Tojin-machi and Naka-Tojin-machi in the Shinmachi-Furmachi district of Kumamoto City.

Secondly, another follow-up survey was conducted by the Architects and Building Engineers Association of the Kumamoto Prefecture under the leadership of Mitsukiyo Yamakawa.[23] This follow-up survey was designed to ascertain the status of buildings that the Society has identified as having historical value, regardless of whether or not they have been designated as such, from the time of the Kumamoto Earthquake of 2016 to the present. The committee is a graduate school of Kyushu University. The committee compiled the results of this survey, which was commissioned by Toshiyuki Kono's Office at the Kyushu University, as the "Report on the Current Status of Historical Buildings Damaged by the Kumamoto Earthquake" (2021) of the Historical Buildings Committee of the Kumamoto Prefecture Association of Architects and Building Engineers. It is expected that the data will be widely used beyond the framework of this project for the activities of local governments, architect associations, NPOs, and so on.

The results of these follow-up surveys were discussed at the project's research meetings in January 2021 and April 2021. At the workshop held on April 10, 2021, we were able to exchange opinions not only with the project members and the members of the Kumamoto Machinami Trust but also with the staff of the Cultural Properties Division and the Urban Design Division of Kumamoto City Hall. Based on the discussions at the research meetings and workshop in 2021, the following section will discuss the results of the historical building survey conducted by the Architects and Building Engineers Association of the Kumamoto Prefecture on the historic buildings damaged by the Kumamoto Earthquake.

---

[22] International Council on Monuments and Sites (ICOMOS) (2017).

[23] Yamakawa (2021).

6.2.2 Results and Analysis of the Current Status Survey of Historic Buildings Damaged by the Kumamoto Earthquake

6.2.2.1 Objective and Method

In order to connect the lessons learned from the 2016 Kumamoto Earthquake to future policy discussions, it became clear through the study groups of this project that the historical buildings committee of the Kumamoto Prefecture Society of Architects and Building Engineers shared the problem of the lack of post-event surveys that include undesignated cultural properties. Therefore, we decided to focus on the data of the project to support the restoration of cultural properties damaged by the Kumamoto earthquake (hereinafter referred to as the "cultural property doctors"), which targeted damaged cultural properties, including undesignated cultural properties, and to plan a follow-up survey for this project based on the results of the 2020 interview survey.

The program to dispatch cultural property doctors is an initiative to conduct damage surveys and provide technical advice for the restoration of historic buildings, including undesignated cultural properties, through collaboration between the public and private sectors. The program was established at the time of the Great East Japan Earthquake and played an important role in the 2016 Kumamoto Earthquake. In the Kumamoto Earthquake of 2016, the Committee for Supporting the Restoration of Damaged Cultural Properties was established on April 20, 2016, six days after the earthquake, and it was decided at an early stage that the project to dispatch cultural property doctors would be implemented with the Japan Federation of Architects & Building Engineers Associations as the secretariat.[24] In May of the same year, the Agency for Cultural Affairs formulated the "Guidelines for the Implementation of the Project to Support the Restoration of Cultural Properties Damaged by the Kumamoto Earthquake," and the project was implemented in June.[25] During the period from then until March 2017, as the first survey of the dispatch of cultural property doctors, the current status of 1,687 buildings that had been identified as necessary for the preservation of historical townscapes, including undesignated cultural properties, was surveyed (hereinafter referred to as the "primary survey").[26] Of the buildings that were the subject of the primary survey, a detailed survey of the damage was conducted for 435 buildings for which a high degree of urgency for restoration assistance was recognized and the owners requested (hereinafter referred to as the "secondary survey").[27] The secondary survey included internal surveys, drawings, and interviews. The second survey included internal surveys, drawings, and interviews, and involved emergency measures, recovery planning, and technical advice for these measures. In the tertiary survey, advice on the selection of design and

[24] Japan ICOMOS National Committee (2019), pp. 81–82 [Tanaka].

[25] Ibid.

[26] Japan ICOMOS National Committee (2019), p. 83 [Yamanaka].

[27] Ibid.

supervision firms and contractors, advice on design, supervision, and construction details, and completion inspections were provided.[28]

For the follow-up survey of this project, the subjects were narrowed down to 443 buildings in Kumamoto Prefecture. In addition to the 435 buildings that were identified as needing restoration support in the dispatch of the cultural property doctor program, targeted for the secondary survey of the cultural property doctor, eight additional buildings were added to the list for this survey. It is important to note that buildings with recognized historical value are included regardless of whether they are designated or registered.

As for the structure of the follow-up survey, a working group was organized within the Historical Buildings Committee to conduct the survey, with the Heritage Manager of the Kumamoto Prefecture Association of Architects and Building Engineers as the surveyor, and the Architectural History and Design Committee of the Kyushu Branch of the Architectural Institute of Japan, the Prefectural Culture Division, and Toshiyuki Kono's Office at Kyushu University as observers.

6.2.2.2 Results and Analysis

Overall

The current status of the 443 cases surveyed was classified into six categories: "Dismantled," "Reconstructed," "Renovated," "Restored," "Emergency Measures," and "No measures" (see Fig. 6.1).

As a general trend, the first thing to note is that only about 64% of the buildings have been restored or are in the process of being restored, and about 1/3 of the historic buildings have been transformed by the 2016 Kumamoto Earthquake. Looking at the breakdown of non-restored buildings, besides those whose condition has been changed (approximately 11%, including reconstructed and renovated buildings), approximately 9% of the surveyed buildings have been dismantled or are in the process of being dismantled. It was also confirmed that 15.8% of the damaged buildings are left to be as they are with no measures or only with emergency measures.

From the perspective of preserving historic townscapes, this data shows again that the earthquake's impact cannot be overlooked. In addition to the overall results, the survey on the status of historic buildings damaged by the Kumamoto earthquake presents two comparative summaries: one is a comparison between privately owned buildings and the other buildings, and the other is a comparison between buildings located in concentration districts (the terminology will be explained later) and the buildings in the other districts. In the following, these reports will also be discussed in light of the suggestions made through the 2020 interview survey and matrix reports ("Comparison: Privately Owned Buildings and the Other Buildings" and "Comparison: Concentration Districts and the Other Districts"). In addition,

[28] Japan Federation of Architects and Building Engineers Associations (2020), p. 4 [Remarks by Yamakawa].

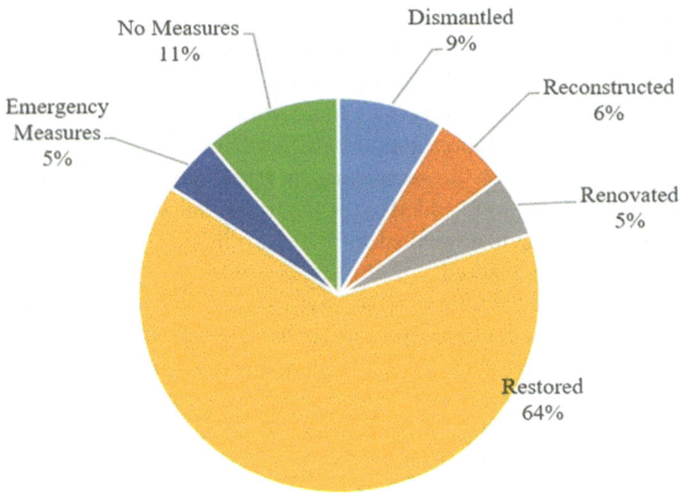

Fig. 6.1 Overall observation

using the data obtained from the current status survey of historic buildings damaged by the Kumamoto earthquake, the results of an additional comparative study between designated or registered cultural properties and the other properties will also be presented and discussed ("Comparison: Designated or Registered Buildings and the Other Buildings").

Comparison: Privately Owned Buildings and the Other Buildings

The report on the current status of historic buildings damaged by the Kumamoto earthquake examines whether there is any difference in the rate of restoration between privately owned buildings (houses, stores, workshops, warehouses, storehouses, etc.) and the other buildings (religious facilities, public facilities, etc.). Of the total surveyed, 181 were specified as privately owned, and 262 were seen as the other buildings. Figure 6.2 shows the survey result summarized from this comparative viewpoint.

In terms of the percentage of "restored" in each graph, the number in the chart of "Privately Owned Buildings" is slightly smaller than that in the graph for "The Other Buildings."

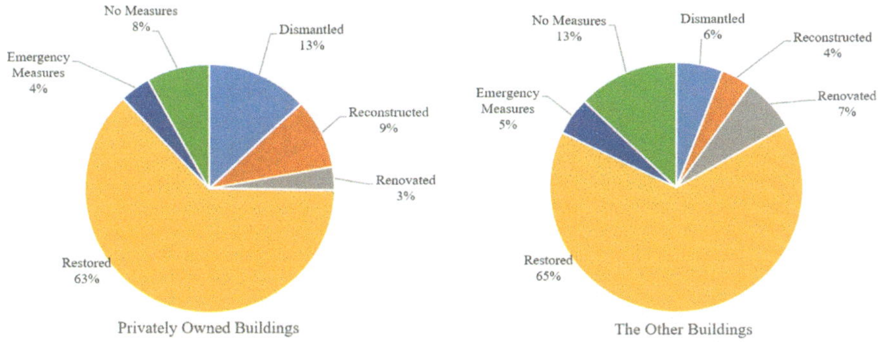

Fig. 6.2 Privately owned buildings and the other buildings

However, the difference between the two companies is more conspicuous in the item "dismantled" in Fig. 6.2, where there seems to be a tendency that the privately owned buildings were more likely to be dismantled. In light of the information obtained in the 2020 interview survey, the experts recognized that moving toward restoring privately owned cultural properties was pretty challenging. Because of the considerable financial and emotional burdens placed on the owners, it was difficult for them to receive advice and support unless they were connected to a network of experts, including heritage managers, researchers, NPOs, and government officials, on a regular basis.[29]

On the other hand, if we focus on the "no measures" item in Fig. 6.2, we can observe that the percentage is smaller in the case of private ownership. The first reason may be that the privately owned buildings contain more items that need to be used on a daily basis, such as houses. Secondly, in Kumamoto Prefecture, historic buildings include many religious facilities such as temples. The aforementioned matrix report by Juko Ito suggests that the delay in the restoration of temples may have something to do with the decrease in the number of Buddhist monks and "danka" (financial supporters of temples).

Comparison: Concentration Districts and the Other Districts

The report on the current status of historic buildings damaged by the Kumamoto earthquake identifies the four districts of (1) Shinmachi-Furumachi, (2) Kawashiri, (3) Ogawa, and (4) Otsu as "concentration districts" and compares buildings in the concentrate districts with those in the other districts. The term "concentration area" is used for convenience in the survey report to mean "an area where historical buildings

[29] For example, since the experts and the owner of the cultural properties had been involved in the survey for the application for the registration of cultural properties in 2014 before the earthquake, they were able to be involved in the confirmation of the damage situation of the owner's cultural properties immediately after the earthquake. This example will be further described later in (6.3.1.1) of this paper. See Isoda et al. (2019), pp. 189–198.

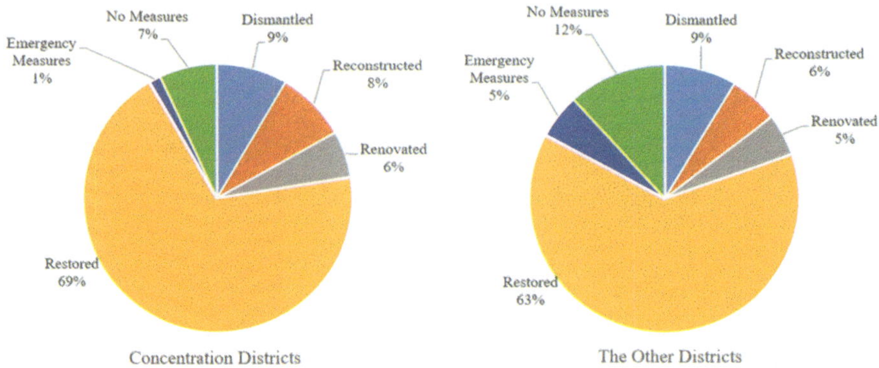

Fig. 6.3 Concentration districts and the other districts

are grouped together to form a townscape unique to that area" (in the following, it is understood to refer to the above four areas). Looking at the breakdown of the total number of cases, 71 buildings are located in the concentration districts, and 372 buildings are located in the other districts. Figure 6.3 shows the result of the survey summarized from this comparative viewpoint.

First, a comparison of the item "restored" shows that the restoration rate is slightly higher for the buildings located in the concentration districts. Furthermore, the total percentage of buildings in the "emergency measures" and "no measures" categories is about 8 percent in the concentration districts, while it is about 17% in the other districts. Considering the results of the 2020 interview survey, the reason for this difference in trend may be that the human network of experts who share the awareness of heritage conservation is well developed, especially in the concentrated areas.[30]

On the other hand, looking at the item "dismantled" in Fig. 6.3, there was almost no difference at about 9% in both cases (8.5% in the concentration districts and 8.6% in the other districts). This result may remind us of the criticism that various systems, such as the emergency risk judgment and public fund dismantling, may have affected the abandonment of the restoration of historic buildings, as we heard in the above-mentioned interview survey in 2020. Therefore, if additional surveys can be conducted in the future, we would like to supplement the information necessary for verification by asking about the reasons for choosing to dismantle and whether it was done with public funds or with self-funded measures.

[30] See, for example, Moriyama and Isoda (2018), pp. 799–800.

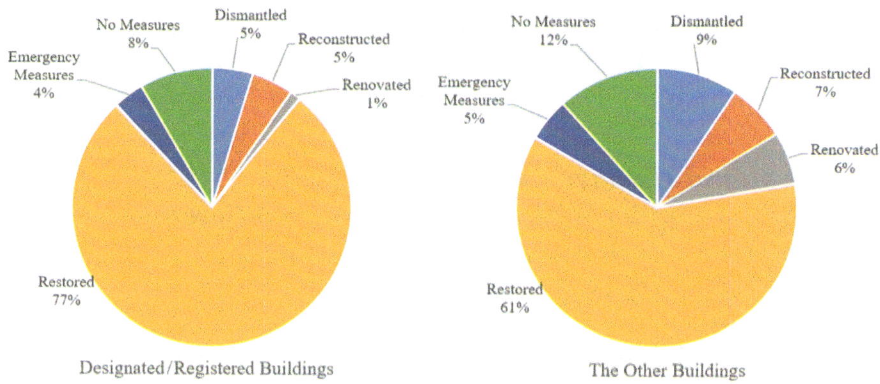

Fig. 6.4 Designated/registered buildings and the other buildings

Comparison: Designated or Registered Buildings and the Other Buildings

Utilizing the data obtained from the survey on the current status of historic buildings damaged by the Kumamoto Earthquake, the Kumamoto research team of this project also confirmed the differences in trends between designated or registered buildings and the other buildings. Of the total surveyed, 83 are the designated or registered buildings, and 360 are not. Figure 6.4 shows the result of the survey summarized from this comparative viewpoint.

As a natural result, in Fig. 6.4, it was confirmed that the restoration rate of the undesignated buildings is lower than that of buildings that have been designated or registered. Also, focusing on the item of "dismantled," it is clear that buildings that have been designated or registered as cultural properties tend to be more easily preserved.

This result reminds us that it is effective for designating or registering cultural properties with high historical value for the purpose of ensuring their conservation. It also reaffirms the importance of preserving for future generations those cultural properties that have not yet been designated, even though they have the value to become designated cultural properties in the future. In this regard, it is hoped that the system of "tentative registration," which will be discussed later, will be further expanded to provide information on undesignated cultural properties and to support their restoration.

6.3 Development and Challenges of Legislation for Cultural Heritage Disaster Mitigation After the Kumamoto Earthquake in 2016

6.3.1 Cultural Heritage Conservation Network in Cooperation with Industry, Academia, Government, and the Private Sector in Times of Disaster or Reconstruction

6.3.1.1 Efforts up to the 2016 Kumamoto Earthquake: Collaborative System Relying on Existing Human Networks

Based on the suggestions from the 2020 interviews and the follow-up survey summarized in the previous sections, the following sections will examine institutional issues for preserving historical townscapes in post-traumatic situations.

This section will firstly look at initiatives implemented up to the Kumamoto Earthquake in 2016, in which existing networks of industry-academia-government-private sector collaboration were utilized for cultural heritage conservation at the time of the disaster and during reconstruction (6.3.1.1). Then this section will secondly discuss the establishment of the Disaster Mitigation Center for Cultural Properties as an initiative to foster and make permanent a network of collaboration between industry, academia, government, and the private sector during normal times in order to enhance the resilience of cultural heritage, for examining the expected future role of the center (6.3.1.2).

As the first example where the availability of an existing network of industry-academia-government-private sector collaboration came into play, it can be observed that the activities related to archiving undesignated cultural properties, that had been promoted mainly in Miyagi Prefecture before the earthquake, positively influenced the preservation of cultural properties at the time of the Great East Japan Earthquake. Following the 2003 earthquake in northern Miyagi Prefecture, the Miyagi Network for the Preservation of Historical Materials (hereinafter referred to as "Miyagi Shiryo Net") was established. This occurred through the collaboration of researchers in universities, administrative staff of municipalities, and citizens, including cultural property owners. Through their collaborations, the rescue and preservation activities of historical materials such as ancient documents were implemented.[31] Through locating and compiling a database of historical materials, mainly undesignated cultural properties, the members of Miyagi Shiryo Net deepened their relationships with government officials and owners of cultural objects and built a system for constant cooperation.[32] As a result, when the Great East Japan Earthquake struck in 2011, the existence of this human network connecting cultural

[31] Sato (2019), p. 56.

[32] Hirakawa (2005), pp. 33–45.

property owners, government officials, researchers, and other experts was put to good use, and private-sector-led cultural heritage preservation activities were swiftly carried out in Miyagi Prefecture. On the day after the earthquake, Miyagi Shiryo Net members, including Arata Hirakawa (Tohoku University), began touring the Sendai City Museum of History and Folklore and other facilities, contacting administrative officials and owners of collections with whom they had been in contact before the earthquake, for organizing information.[33] Furthermore, on March 15, 2011, just four days after the earthquake, they resumed updating the online materials called "Miyagi Shiryo Net News," which played an essential role in disseminating information and recruiting volunteers.[34] Subsequently, the "Rescue Project for Cultural Properties Damaged by the Tohoku Earthquake" (the "Rescue Project for Cultural Properties" at the time of the Great East Japan Earthquake) was launched under the leadership of the Agency for Cultural Affairs. Then, Miyagi Prefecture was the first prefecture to send a request for rescue to the Agency for Cultural Affairs in March 2011 and start the project in April of the same year.

The second example is the response taken by the Ogawa-machi shopping street in Uki City, Kumamoto Prefecture, during the 2016 Kumamoto Earthquake. In 2014, Setsuko Isoda (National Institute of Technology of Kumamoto College) and Junichi Sakata (Japan Cultural Heritage Consultancy) conducted a survey on Shin-Kojiya in the shopping street.[35] In addition, surveys of Machiya houses in Ogawa-machi, such as the former Iwasaki-ke residence (Shioya) and Hasegawa-tei, were conducted.[36] In these researches, the buildings in the Ogawa-machi shopping street have often been the subjects of graduation research conducted by students of the National Institute of Technology of Kumamoto College.[37] It is clear that a human network centered on the people involved in the National Institute of Technology of Kumamoto College has been fostered as social capital for the preservation of Ogawa's historical townscape. As a result, immediately after the earthquake in April 2016, support for the owners of cultural properties and surveys of the damage were started. For example, on April 17, 2016, the day after the earthquake, Sakata inspected the damages to Machiya houses in the area. One week after the earthquake, Isoda received a consultation from the owner of Shin-Kojiya about the damage to Machiya houses, and on April 26, 2016, they made a visual inspection of each Machiya house.[38] As mentioned above, this

[33] Sasaki et al. (2013), p. 137.

[34] Hirakawa (2011).

[35] See Sakata et al. (2014), pp. 505–508. As a result, the following items were registered in 2016: Shin-Kojiya Kashiwabara Family Residence Main Building (Registered Tangible Cultural Property No. 43-0153), Shin-Kojiya Kashiwabara Family Residence Detached Area (Registered Tangible Cultural Property No. 43-0154), and Shin-Kojiya Kashiwabara Family Residence Gate and Fence (Registered Tangible Cultural Property No. 43-0155). In 2021, the courtyard wall of the Shin-Kojiya Kashiwabara Residence (Registered Tangible Cultural Property No. 43-0183) was also registered.

[36] See Narukawa and Isoda (2015), pp. 65–72. "Shioya" was registered as "Former Iwasaki Family Residence (Shioya) Store and Main Building (Registered Tangible Cultural Property No. 43-0180)" in 2020.

[37] Isoda et al. (2019), pp. 189–198.

[38] Ibid.

human network supported the owners of cultural properties in their efforts during the reconstruction period, such as applying for group subsidies ("Group Subsidies").

As the third example, during the reconstruction period of the 2016 Kumamoto Earthquake, the activities of the Kumamoto Machinami Trust strengthened the cooperation between cultural property owners, government officials, and experts. Since 1986, researchers in the Shinmachi and Furumachi areas of Kumamoto City, Kumamoto Prefecture, have been working together as the "Furumachi Study Group" to study the castle town and preserve its buildings. Still, the efforts to protect the company building of the former Kumamoto branch of the Dai-ichi Bank led to the establishment of the Kumamoto Machinami Trust in 1997, initially as a voluntary organization.[39] As mentioned above, the fact that the local merchants, who are the owners of cultural assets, were able to directly consult with the Kumamoto Machinami Trust, especially regarding group subsidy applications, was an essential factor that encouraged the reconstruction ("Group Subsidies"). In addition, in November 2016, the Kumamoto Machinami Trust served as the secretariat of the "Council for Cooperation of Affected Cultural Heritage Owners," a group of 25 owners of cultural heritage in the Shinmachi and Furumachi areas. In addition, the Kumamoto Machinami Trust has been established as an organization to promote cooperation among cultural property owners.[40] The Kumamoto Machinami Trust was registered as an NPO in 2009. As a result of the central role played by the Kumamoto Machinami Trust, it was seen in the 2020 interview survey how the industry, academia, government, and private sectors had developed channels to respond to consultations from cultural property owners in Kumamoto Prefecture.

6.3.1.2 Cultural Heritage Disaster Risk Management Center

As mentioned above, in cases where experts and government officials are acquainted with the owners of cultural properties before the disaster, post-disaster support can efficiently reach the owners. As a result, the preservation of cultural heritage and historic townscapes can be promoted. On the other hand, the 2020 interview survey reveals that when there was no acquaintance before the disaster, even if the experts offered support in the post-traumatic state, the owners could not afford to accept the advice and sometimes refused it. As a direction for developing a system to prepare for future disaster response, a system that relies on accidentally fostered human networks is insufficient. It is desirable to seek a more systematic and permanent approach to industry-academia-government-private sector cooperation by consolidating lessons learned from past efforts. In this regard, the establishment of the "Cultural Heritage Disaster Risk Management Center" in 2020 should be noted as a noteworthy milestone.

The Cultural Heritage Disaster Risk Management Center was established on October 1, 2020, as an organization of the Independent Administrative Institution

---

[39] Fujikawa (2013), p. 33.

[40] Japan ICOMOS National Committee (2019), pp. 86–87 [Fujikawa].

National Institutes for Cultural Heritage. The basis for its establishment was the results of the "Project for Promotion of the Network for Disaster Mitigation of Cultural Properties," which the National Institutes for Cultural Heritage has been implementing for six years since 2014 with a subsidy from the Agency for Cultural Affairs.[41] The framework of the "Network for the Promotion of Disaster Mitigation of Cultural Properties," which was established through the rescue project for cultural properties in the Great East Japan Earthquake, could be continuously utilized even after the dissolution of the Rescue Project for Cultural Properties. It has contributed to establishing a system for disaster mitigation of cultural properties. In response to the frequent occurrence of natural disasters in recent years, it is crucial to improve the legal system further to preserve cultural heritages.

As for the structure of the Cultural Heritage Disaster Risk Management Center, the headquarters of the Cultural Heritage Disaster Risk Management Center has been established in the Nara National Research Institute for Cultural Properties.[42] Tokyo National Research Institute for Cultural Properties and Nara National Research Institute for Cultural Properties will serve as the core centers for eastern and western Japan respectively. In addition, the Tokyo National Museum, Kyoto National Museum, Nara National Museum, and Kyushu National Museum join as member institutes.[43] In carrying out its project activities, the Cultural Heritage Disaster Risk Management Center cooperates and collaborates with the Agency for Cultural Affairs (especially the Disaster Countermeasures Committee for Cultural Properties), the Network Conference on Disaster Mitigation of Cultural Heritage, the expert committees on Disaster Mitigation of Cultural Heritage, local governments, research institutes, and international organizations.[44]

Based on the results of the 2020 interview survey and follow-up survey, it seems that the effectiveness of the subsidy system would be further enhanced if the application deadline and the method of dissemination were coordinated between the publicly funded dismantling system administered by the Ministry of the Environment and the various subsidy systems that can be used for cultural heritage conservation. In addition, it was suggested that the subsidies that can be used for cultural heritage conservation include group subsidies administered by the Small and Medium Enterprise Agency, regardless of the original purpose of the institutions. From this perspective, in the future operation of the Cultural Heritage Disaster Risk Management Center, it would be desirable to periodically confirm opportunities for exchanging information and maintaining channels for cooperation, not only with the Agency for Cultural Affairs but also with the competent authorities of these peripheral systems.

---

[41] Okada (2021), pp. 16–18.

[42] Cultural Heritage Disaster Risk Management Center (2021), p. 2.

[43] Ibid.

[44] Ibid.

6.3.2 Information Management on Cultural Properties, Including Non-designated Cultural Properties

6.3.2.1 Efforts up to the 2016 Kumamoto Earthquake: Utilization of the List of Cultural Properties Created Voluntarily or on a Project Basis for Emergency Measures After the Earthquakes

In the event of a large-scale disaster, whether or not an exhaustive survey of cultural heritage was conducted before the occurrence of the disaster and whether or not there is a list of cultural properties available for initial investigations will affect the path to cultural heritage conservation. In this section, examples of past efforts to understand information on cultural heritage damaged by earthquakes will be discussed (6.3.2.1). Then, as a systematic development to ensure the understanding of a wide range of information, including undesignated cultural properties during normal times, the role of the "Tentative Registration of Cultural Properties" system, an initiative of Kyoto Prefecture, will be reviewed (6.3.2.2). Also, the "Outline for the Preservation and Utilization of Cultural Properties" institutionalized by the amendment of the Law for the Protection of Cultural Properties in 2018 will be discussed (6.3.2.3).

Looking back at the past situation, at the time of the Great Hanshin-Awaji Earthquake, the national government did not have information on historical buildings other than designated cultural properties.[45] Therefore, as a trend after the earthquake, in addition to the survey of designated cultural properties conducted by the national government and local government officials, a damage survey covering even undesignated cultural properties was conducted by the Architectural Institute of Japan.

On the one hand, it was difficult to conduct surveys by national and local government officials immediately after the earthquake. For example, for about a week after the earthquake in southern Hyogo Prefecture occurred on January 17, 1995, local government officials were quite busy with life-threatening surveys and protection measures. During that time, there was naturally no time to devote personnel to the survey of cultural properties, and even the request from the prefecture to the municipalities for the survey of cultural properties was canceled under the direction of the Hyogo Prefecture Reconstruction Headquarters.[46] Later, on January 25, 1995, the Buildings Division of the Agency for Cultural Affairs, the Association for the Conservation of Cultural Properties and Buildings, and those in charge of buildings in the Kinki region decided that the Agency for Cultural Affairs becomes responsible for surveys of nationally designated cultural properties, while the Kinki region becomes responsible for surveys of Hyogo Prefecture-designated cultural properties and important traditional building preservation areas.[47]

[45] Futagami and Kumamoto (2011), pp. 42–56.

[46] Tani (1998), pp. 3–4.

[47] Ibid.

On the other hand, the survey of damage to historical buildings by members of the Architectural Institute of Japan was conducted by volunteers immediately after the earthquake. The survey by the Architectural Institute of Japan has unique inclusive features, providing an extensive list of buildings that the Institute considers important, including undesignated cultural properties. For each of the survey targets, valuable records were compiled, including the characteristics of the damage, the status of measures taken at the time of the survey, interviews with the owners about their intentions, and photographic records.[48]

Compared to the situation after the Great Hanshin-Awaji Earthquake, in the case of the Kumamoto Earthquake of 2016 there were several lists that could be utilized immediately after the earthquake, including those related to undesignated cultural properties. In 1970, an emergency survey of Minka (traditional Japanese houses) was conducted, mainly focusing on houses built in the Edo period (1603–1868), and it was recorded as the "Kumamoto Prefecture Minka Survey Emergency Survey Summary Report."[49] However, there are some criticisms of this survey in 1970, such as the fact that some of the upper layer houses that were not thatched were excluded from the survey.[50] In Kumamoto Prefecture, this survey started in September 2015 and was still ongoing at the time of the Kumamoto Earthquake in April 2016.[51] As a result, a list of Machiya houses in Kumamoto Prefecture, including undesignated cultural assets, was compiled to some extent, which was helpful for the private sector volunteers to visit the damaged cultural assets immediately after the earthquake.[52] However, some issues were pointed out, such as the fact that some Machiya houses had not yet been surveyed, which resulted in insufficient information on the architecture of shrines and temples in the early modern period.[53]

Such issues related to listing undesignated cultural properties have been frequently pointed out in recent disasters. For example, in the case of Asakura City, Fukuoka Prefecture, in response to the torrential rains in northern Kyushu in July 2017, any list of undesignated cultural properties did not exist in advance. Hence, a list had to be prepared after the occurrence of the torrential rains. In order to respond to the damage caused by the torrential rains in northern Kyushu in July 2017, Fukuoka Prefecture, in consultation with municipalities, confirmed the damage to cultural properties and took emergency measures to protect them. When Fukuoka Prefecture provided assistance, it consulted with the Cultural Properties Section, Culture and Lifelong Learning Division of the Asakura City Board of Education and provided support in line with the city's intentions.[54] After the dispatch of the prefectural

---

[48] Ibid.

[49] Kumamoto Prefectural Board of Education, Miyazaki Prefectural Board of Education, Okinawa Prefectural Board of Education, Kagoshima Prefectural Board of Education (1999), pp. 3–4.

[50] Japan ICOMOS National Committee (2019), p. 65 [Kimoto].

[51] Eriguchi and Moriyama (2019), p. 17.

[52] Japan ICOMOS National Committee (2019), p. 109 [Kariya].

[53] Ibid.

[54] Cultural Heritage Disaster Risk Management Center (2021), pp. 46–47 [Kyushu National Museum].

staff, the staff of the Amagi Museum of History and Archives, who had a good understanding of the area, accompanied the prefectural staff on a tour of designated cultural properties, and about a week after the dispatch began, an investigation of undesignated cultural properties was conducted.[55] However, since neither the prefecture nor the city had an organized list of undesignated cultural properties before the disaster, the prefectural staff collected information from surveys by universities and other organizations and from the compilation of the city's history at the same time as the inspection of designated cultural properties, and made a list and carried out mapping.[56]

6.3.2.2 "Tentative Registration of Cultural Properties" System: Kyoto Prefecture's Approach

Looking at the examples of previous efforts described above, it is clear that an exhaustive survey of cultural properties, including undesignated cultural properties, and the existence of a list are essential for protecting cultural heritage from large-scale natural disasters. From this perspective, Kyoto Prefecture's "Tentative Registration of Cultural Properties" system deserves close attention as a pioneering effort for local governments to obtain information on the locations of undesignated cultural properties and to clarify their values to the public officially.

In 2017, Kyoto Prefecture partially amended its Ordinance for the Protection of Cultural Properties to establish a system under which undesignated cultural properties with significant historical value can be registered as "tentatively registered" cultural properties.[57] In the same year, it also enacted the Kyoto Prefecture Regulations on Tentatively Registered Cultural Properties (Kyoto Prefecture Board of Education Regulation No. 5). This system is noteworthy as a way to collect information on undesignated cultural properties that should be designated as cultural properties in the near future and to motivate the preservation of such properties for future designation by publicly valuing them. Traditionally, Kyoto Prefecture has been supporting the conservation activities of undesignated cultural properties through its own "Kyoto Prefectural Subsidy Program for the Preservation of Cultural Materials of Shrines and Temples," funded by the prefecture's budget.[58] The Tentative Registration of Cultural Properties system is intended to develop this effort into a more comprehensive approach and build a more reliable cultural heritage conservation system by regularly listing cultural properties on the tentative list. It also provides a mechanism to subsidize the management of cultural properties through the Kyoto Prefectural tentative registration (Article 23 of the Regulations Concerning Kyoto Prefecture's Tentative Registration of Cultural Properties).

---

[55] Ibid.

[56] Ibid.

[57] Kyoto Prefectural Government—Cultural Properties Protection Division (2017).

[58] For the further details on Kyoto Prefecture's subsidized projects for the preservation of cultural materials of shrines and temples, see Kyoto Prefectural Board of Education (2020a), p. 2ff.

However, remembering the aforementioned analysis of the current status of historic buildings damaged by the Kumamoto Earthquake, it is even more desirable for such "tentative registers" of cultural properties to work as an effective motivation for realizing suitable designations or registrations in the next step ("Comparison: Designated or Registered Buildings and the Other Buildings"). From this point of view, in Kyoto Prefecture, there are many examples of cultural properties that were provisionally registered as cultural properties that have become designated cultural properties, and this initiative is steadily producing results.[59]

6.3.2.3 Reference to Undesignated Cultural Properties in the "Outline for the Utilization of Cultural Properties"

As another system that can work together with the efforts to understand information on undesignated cultural properties at normal times, the system for planning the conservation and utilization of cultural properties (the "Outline for the Conservation and Utilization of Cultural Properties" of prefectures, the certification system of "Regional Plans for the Conservation and Utilization of Cultural Properties" of municipalities, and the approval system of "Plans for the Conservation and Utilization of Cultural Properties" of owners, etc.) was established by the 2008 amendment of the Law for the Protection of Cultural Properties.

The "Outline for the Conservation and Utilization of Cultural Properties" was institutionalized by the amendment of the Law for the Protection of Cultural Properties in 2008, and it is to be formulated by prefectural boards of education based on Article 183-2 of the Law for the Protection of Cultural Properties. The boards of education of municipalities may prepare their own "Regional Plan for the Conservation and Utilization of Cultural Properties" and apply for approval from the Commissioner of the Agency for Cultural Affairs, taking into consideration the general guidelines for the conservation and utilization of cultural properties if such guidelines have been established (Article 183-3 of the Law for the Protection of Cultural Properties). In addition, the owners of cultural properties may prepare a "Conservation and Utilization Plan."

In the Law for Protection of Cultural Properties, there is no reference to undesignated cultural properties. In contrast, the Guidelines for the Formulation of the Outline of the Preservation and Utilization of Cultural Properties, the Regional Plan for the Preservation and Utilization of Cultural Properties, and the Plan for the Preservation and Utilization of Cultural Properties based on the Law for the Protection of Cultural Properties formulated by the Agency for Cultural Affairs indicates the necessity of making use of tangible and intangible cultural properties, including undesignated cultural properties, for community development, while securing bearers of

[59] For example, in 2019, two buildings, four arts and crafts, and one historic site that had been provisionally registered as Tangible Cultural Properties in Kyoto Prefecture were designated as Kyoto Prefecture-designated Cultural Properties. With the designation of these cultural properties as Kyoto Prefecture-designated cultural properties, their registration as Kyoto Prefecture provisionally registered cultural properties was cancelled. Kyoto Prefectural Board of Education (2020b), p. 2.

the inheritance of cultural properties and creating a system that enables the whole community to work on it. In the same guideline, it is stated that it is necessary to make use of tangible and intangible cultural properties, including those that have not yet been designated, for community development, while securing those who will be responsible for the inheritance of cultural properties, and creating a system that enables the entire local community to work on this issue.[60] In addition, the guideline explains that the regional plans for the conservation and utilization of cultural properties formulated by municipalities should be a framework for promoting the conservation and utilization of cultural properties by comprehensively surveying and grasping various cultural properties, including undesignated cultural properties. In fact, as shown in the following example, looking at the trend of the formulation of the Outline for the Preservation and Utilization of Cultural Properties in each prefecture, when the Outline for the Preservation and Utilization of Cultural Properties is formulated, it is examined in a way paying attention to undesignated cultural properties.[61] It seems that the practice of including a broader scope of conservation and utilization of cultural properties in the general guidelines is spreading.

For example, in March 2021, Kumamoto Prefecture formulated the Kumamoto Prefecture Outline for the Preservation and Utilization of Cultural Properties.[62] Looking at the Kumamoto Prefectural Outline for the Preservation and Utilization of Cultural Properties, Kumamoto Prefecture has considered the requests from municipalities to the prefecture for financial support and policies to deal with undesignated cultural properties.[63] To preserve cultural properties and pass them on to the next generation, it is necessary to steadily promote measures needed for their preservation, such as protection measures through designation and the creation of records of cultural property information, and at the same time to carry out comprehensive surveys and other primary research as appropriate, including those on undesignated cultural properties, to gain an understanding of cultural properties in the prefecture.[64] Considering that the results of the comprehensive survey, including undesignated cultural properties, were used as basic materials in the dispatch of cultural property doctors and the cultural property rescue project at the time of the Kumamoto Earthquake in 2016 and the torrential rains in July 2020, we will continue to collect more information and create a database.[65]

In the Fukuoka Prefectural Outline for the Protection of Cultural Properties formulated by Fukuoka Prefecture, it is noteworthy that the prefecture's role in the event of a disaster is described, including its response to undesignated cultural properties.[66] With regard to the preservation and restoration of undesignated cultural properties, it states that together with municipalities, the prefecture will consult with owners of

---

[60] Agency for Cultural Affairs (2009), p. 1.

[61] Agency for Cultural Affairs (2009), p. 4.

[62] Kumamoto Prefectural Board of Education (2021), p. 1ff.

[63] Kumamoto Prefectural Board of Education (2021), p. 29.

[64] Kumamoto Prefectural Board of Education (2021), p. 37.

[65] Kumamoto Prefectural Board of Education (2021), pp. 43–44.

[66] Fukuoka Prefecture Board of Education (2021), p. 55ff.

cultural properties and seek cooperation from related organizations and groups as necessary and that concerning movable cultural properties, the prefecture will take measures to preserve and restore them so that they can be returned to their owners in an appropriate condition, mainly at the Kyushu Archives of History. This can be evaluated as a meaningful policy that reflects the results of the cultural property rescue activities in various regions.[67]

For example, Saga Prefecture has been working since October 2020 to formulate a general plan for the conservation and utilization of cultural properties. As a part of this plan, it has decided to create a hazard map of cultural properties.[68] The hazard map is planned to include undesignated cultural properties and natural monuments and to make efforts to grasp information on cultural properties from normal times.[69] To identify undesignated buildings, it is essential to collaborate with the Association of Architects and Building Engineers and Heritage Managers, and the data accumulated by the Association of Architects and Building Engineers will be used for the hazard map.[70] As for the future plans to formulate the outline for the conservation and utilization of cultural properties in Saga Prefecture, discussions will continue in an ad-hoc committee of the Saga Prefecture Council for the Protection of Cultural Properties, and the content will be finalized while seeking advice from outside. After public comments from September to December 2021, Saga Prefecture aims to complete the plan by the end of the same year.[71]

As described above, it is significant that both the national and prefectural guidelines for the conservation and utilization of cultural properties now clearly state that conservation and utilization should be promoted, including for undesignated cultural properties. Hopefully, this awareness will be reflected in the regional disaster reduction plans of local governments throughout Japan.[72]

---

[67] Fukuoka Prefecture Board of Education (2021), p. 61.

[68] Cultural Heritage Disaster Risk Management Center (2021), pp. 15–16 [Kyushu National Museum].

[69] Ibid.

[70] Saga Prefecture has been implementing the "Historical Roads Research Project" under a nine-year plan starting in 2009, and the results of the project are expected to be used for disaster prevention. For more information on this project, see, for example, Hattori et al. (2021), p. 1ff.

[71] Ibid. See also Saga Prefecture (2021).

[72] Some local prefectural or city governments, including Ishikawa prefecture, Akita prefecture, Niigata prefecture, Sendai city, and Kyoto city, already have descriptions of undesignated cultural properties in their local disaster prevention plans. Nakajima et al. (2018), p. 149ff.

6.3.3 *Temporary Evacuation of Cultural Properties*

6.3.3.1 Efforts up to the 2016 Kumamoto Earthquake: A Case Study of the Rescue Project for Cultural Properties

In this section, we first examine examples of past large-scale disasters that addressed the issue of securing places and bearers for temporary evacuation of cultural properties in the event of a disaster (6.3.3.1). Then, we will examine recent efforts to stabilize the operation of facilities for the temporary storage and restoration of damaged cultural properties and to make the commissioning system permanent (6.3.3.2).

As mentioned above, the project for the rescue of cultural properties at the time of the Great East Japan Earthquake was launched in March 2011, and the first meeting of the Committee for the Rescue of Affected Cultural Properties was held in April of the same year. It is a project that covers even undesignated cultural properties. As an example of the project's activities, an effort was made to restore water-damaged materials damaged by the tsunami and sludge, such as the Oshima Fishing Cooperative in Kesennuma City, Miyagi Prefecture, which were rescued from the Kanagawa University Research Institute for Japanese Everyday Culture, using the vacuum freeze dryer at the Nara National Research Institute for Cultural Properties.[73] If left unattended, water-damaged ancient documents will decompose and become moldy in a short period of time, so it is necessary to freeze them before vacuum freeze-drying to prevent them from decomposition. However, since Nara National Research Institute for Cultural Properties could not store these large volumes of ancient documents alone, Nara Ichiba Refrigeration Corporation provided its facilities for securing temporary preservation.[74]

In contrast to the rescue activities for cultural properties in Miyagi Prefecture, in Fukushima Prefecture, due to the impact of the accident at the TEPCO's Fukushima Daiichi Nuclear Power Station, it has been impossible to develop rescue activities for cultural properties. As a result, full-scale rescue activities for cultural properties did not start until the beginning of 2012.[75] In particular, in the towns of Futaba, Okuma, and Tomioka, which were designated as restricted areas, not only were damaged cultural properties left unattended for a year and a half after the disaster, but even after the rescue work began, it was necessary for the workers to wear Taibek suits and to measure the environmental radiation and the radiation dose of the materials.[76]

In the case of the 2016 Kumamoto earthquake, in the week immediately after the disaster, the prefectural executive and local government officials were busy facing emergencies that were completely different from normal times.[77] In such a situation, voluntary cultural property rescue activities by private organizations were carried

[73] Takatsuma (2013), p. 75ff.

[74] Sato (2011).

[75] Tanno (2013), p. 65ff.

[76] Ibid.

[77] Murata (2017), p. 22.

out ahead of others. For example, in April 2008, the "Kumamoto Affected Historical Materials Rescue Network" (hereinafter referred to as "Kumamoto Historical Materials Network") was launched with Tsuguharu Inaba (Kumamoto University Eiseibunko Research Center) as the representative, and Jun Misawa (Kumamoto University) and other university faculty members and museum curators in Kumamoto Prefecture as participants. In the immediate aftermath of the earthquake, the Kumamoto Archives Network worked hard to rescue and temporarily store damaged houses and restore damaged cultural assets to the minimum level.[78] It also reports on the Kumamoto Prefectural Museum of Art's voluntary efforts, such as the rescue of Buddhist statues designated as national important cultural properties at a temple in the city on April 18, 2016, and the rescue of Tsuguharu Fujita's works owned by the elementary school attached to the Faculty of Education of Kumamoto University on April 27, 2016.[79]

After that, a cultural property rescue project led by the Agency for Cultural Affairs was launched in Kumamoto Prefecture in July 2016. Then, the groups that had already been implementing the project voluntarily joined the project. The rescue project led by the Agency for Cultural Affairs continued until the end of 2016. Even after the rescue project led by the Agency for Cultural Affairs ended, activities protecting the unrescued movable cultural properties were still necessary. From 2017 onward, the Cultural Affairs Division of the Kumamoto Prefectural Government's Education Agency took the lead in the "Kumamoto Prefecture Support Project for Affected Cultural Properties (Kumamoto Prefecture Rescue Project for Cultural Properties)" and continued the activities with the same purpose.[80] The cultural properties rescued in this project were given first aid and are being returned in order as soon as the owners are ready to accept them.[81]

6.3.3.2 Preparations for the Temporary Storage of Damaged Cultural Properties During Normal Times

For the temporary storage of damaged cultural properties and emergency measures, it is desirable to consolidate the accumulated know-how on cultural property rescue activities and to establish a permanent place and persons for temporary storage. In terms of know-how accumulation, research is underway to clarify universal activity patterns related to cultural property rescue from individual data of past earthquakes through quantitative analysis of daily reports of cultural property rescue activities.[82]

Concerning the issues of places for the temporary storage of damaged cultural properties and who is in charge of such storage, in recent years, efforts have been made

78 Inaba (2020), p. 145.

79 Japan ICOMOS National Committee (2019), p. 8 [Kurihara].

80 Cultural Heritage Disaster Risk Management Center (2021), pp. 44–46 [Kyushu National Museum].

81 Ibid.

82 Murai et al. (2016), p. 4ff, Murai et al. (2019), p. 301ff, Murai et al. (2020), p. 1ff.

to verify past examples and improve the environment for the future, including the establishment of permanent facilities. For example, the National Research Institute for Cultural Properties, Tokyo, has been verifying the conservation environment of facilities that were used as temporary storage facilities for damaged materials at the time of a large-scale disaster.[83] At present, at the initiative of the National Research Institute for Cultural Properties, Tokyo, concerning the rescue activities for cultural properties in Fukushima Prefecture conducted by the Committee for the Rescue of Cultural Properties Affected by the Tohoku Earthquake, efforts are being made to improve the environment for the continued stable operation of the temporary storage facility built on the grounds of the Fukushima Prefectural Cultural Properties Center Shirakawa Building "Mahoron."[84] These efforts are ongoing.

In addition, another attempt can be observed as an example of regularly securing temporary storage facilities for damaged cultural properties. The Kyoto National Museum is conducting a study to secure a shelter for cultural properties from normal times, to examine the commissioning system regarding the acceptance of damaged cultural properties, and to verify the improvement of the storeroom environment. The Kyoto National Museum has leased two storerooms (storerooms 113 and 217) in the Keihanna Open Innovation Center (KICK) from the Kyoto Prefectural Government and continues to develop and maintain the storerooms. Research and studies are underway to identify issues in the system for entrusting cultural properties in the event of a disaster.[85]

As shown in the examples discussed above, efforts to develop temporary storage sites and acceptance procedures from normal times are meaningful for securing a place for quick evacuation of movable cultural properties in the event of a disaster. Compared to these trends, establishing a system for temporary consignment of real estate has not made much progress due to barriers such as the large scale of the place required for the temporary storage of damaged materials. Another issue is the verification of cultural property rescue activities from securing the sites and tools necessary to preserve intangible cultural heritage.[86] In the future, it should be required to increase the available institutions to support temporary storage immediately after the earthquake, including for historic buildings and intangible cultural heritage.

---

[83] See, for example, Sano et al. (2016), p. 89ff.

[84] Cultural Heritage Disaster Risk Management Center (2021), p. 19 [Tokyo National Research Institute for Cultural Properties]. See also Sano and Yamamoto (2015), p. 59.

[85] Cultural Heritage Disaster Risk Management Center (2021), p. 28; Kyoto Sangyo 21 Keihanna Branch Office (2020), p. 21.

[86] Kubota (2016), pp. 41–42.

6.4 Conclusion

Based on the results of the 2020 interview survey and the follow-up survey conducted under this project, this paper discusses the recent trends of institutions for the preservation of historical townscapes in post-traumatic situations. From the recent trends of institutional development, such as the establishment of the Cultural Heritage Disaster Risk Management Center and the Kyoto "Tentative Registration of Cultural Properties", it can be seen as significant that there are efforts to systematize the knowledge on disaster prevention and disaster mitigation of cultural properties, which has been built up through various efforts until the Kumamoto Earthquake in 2016, for the future preservation of historical townscapes.

On the other hand, it has been pointed out that future disaster prevention and recovery legislation should include a discussion of resilience in the context of combined natural, social, and biological disasters.[87] Indeed, in the case of the cultural property rescue activities in Fukushima Prefecture mentioned in this paper, the post-traumatic situation caused by the combined effects of natural disasters and the nuclear power plant accident created more severe difficulties for cultural property conservation activities. This is one of the issues that should be addressed in future research activities based on the results of this project.

References

Agency for Cultural Affairs. (2009). Bunkazai-hogo-ho Ni Motozuku Bunkazai Hozon Katsuyo Chiiki Keikaku, Hozon Katsuyo Keikaku No Sakutei To Ni Kansuru Shishin (guidelines for the formulation, etc. of the outline of the preservation and utilization of cultural properties, regional plans for the preservation and utilization of cultural properties, and preservation and utilization plans based on the law for the protection of cultural properties) (March 4, 2019). Accessed November 13, 2021, https://www.bunka.go.jp/seisaku/bunkazai/pdf/r1402097_10.pdf

Cultural Heritage Disaster Risk Management Center. (2021). Reiwa 2 Nendo Bunkazai Bosai Center Nenji Hokoku Sho (2020 annual report of cultural heritage disaster risk management center). Accessed May 20, 2022, https://sitereports.nabunken.go.jp/94676

Eriguchi, H., & Moriyama, M. (2019). Kumamoto-ken Yatsushiro-shi No Kindai Wafu Minka Kiyomatsu-ke Jutaku Ni Kansuru Kenkyu (a study on the Kiyomatsu residence, a modern Japanese-style house in Yatsushiro-City, Kumamoto prefecture). *Kumamoto Kosen Senmongakko Kenkyu Kiyo, 11*, 17–26.

Fujikawa, K. (2013). Dai-ichi Ginko Kumamoto Shiten (PS Orangerie) (Dai-ichi Bank Kumamoto Branch (PS Orangerie). In: Kumamoto Industrial Heritage Study Group and Kumamoto Machinami Trust (Ed.), *Kumamoto o Kindai-ka Isan (jo): Kumamoto-shi Ken-o (Modernization Heritage of Kumamoto (1): Kumamoto City and Central Prefecture)*. Genshobo, Fukuoka.

Fukuoka Prefecture Board of Education. (2021). Fukuoka-ken Bunkazai Hogo Taiko (Fukuoka prefecture outline for the protection of cultural properties). Accessed 13 November 2021, https://www.pref.fukuoka.lg.jp/uploaded/attachment/135371.pdf

Futagami, Y., & Kumamoto, T. (2011). Kokuho Bunkazai Kenzobutsu No Jishin Taisaku No Genjo To Kadai: Jishindo Yoso Chizu Tono Renkei No Kanosei (current status and issues of earthquake

[87] Yamazaki (2021), p. 16.

countermeasures for national treasures and cultural property buildings: possibility of linking with earthquake motion prediction maps). *Jishin Journal, 52*, 42–56.

Hattori, H., Kaneko, S., Ito, R., Shigeto, T., Tsuru, S., Nagasaki, H., Kusaba, S., Ono, M. (2021). Karatsu Kaido No Kenzo-butsu (Buildings on the Karatsu Road). In: Saga Prefecture (Ed.), *Karatsu Kaido: Rekishi No Michi Chosa Hokokusho (Karatsu Road: report on the survey of the historic roads)* (Vol. 3). Saga Prefecture, Saga.

Hidaka, S. (2015). Seikatsu Bunka No Kioku Wo Torimodosu: Bunkazai Rescue No Genba Kara (Reclaiming the Memory of Living Culture: From the Field of Cultural Asset Rescue). In: N. Kibe (Ed.), *Saigai Ni Manabu: Bunka Shigen No Hozen To Saisei (learning from disasters: conservation and revitalization of cultural resources)* (pp. 186–187). Bensei Shuppan, Tokyo.

Hisasue, Y. (2020). *Toshi-saigai To Bunkazai-hogo-hosei (Les Catastrophes Urbaines et le Droit du Parimoine Culturel)*. Seibundo, Tokyo.

Hirakawa, A. (2005). Saigai "Go" No Shiryo-hozen kara Saigai "Mae" No Bosai-taisaku e (from 'post-disaster' material conservation to 'pre-disaster' disaster prevention measures). *Rekishi Hyoron, 666*, 33–45.

Hirakawa, A. (2011). 3gatsu 11nichi: Tohoku Kanto Daishinsai Kakuchi De Mizo No Higai (March 11: Tohoku-Kanto earthquake: unprecedented damage in various areas). *Miyagi Shiryo Net News*, 94 (March 15, 2011). Accessed November 13, 2021, http://miyagi-shiryounet.org/news94/

Inaba, T. (2020). *Rekishi Ni Ima Wo Yomu: Kumamoto, Eiseibunko Kara No Hasshin (Reading the Present in History: Transmissions from Kumamoto, Eiseibunko)*. Kumanichi Service Kaihatsu—Kumanichi Publishing, Kumamoto.

International Council on Monuments and Sites (ICOMOS). (2017). ICOMOS Guidance on post trauma recovery and reconstruction for world heritage cultural properties. Accessed November 13, 2021, http://www.openarchive.icomos.org/id/eprint/1763/19/ICOMOS%20Guidance%20on%20Post%20Trauma%20Recovery%20.pdf

Isoda, S., Sakata, J., Kashiwabara, T., Fujita, S., Hirakawa, A., Takagi, J., Ito, R., & Matsushita, R. (2019). Kumamoto-jishin Ni Yoru Dentoteki-machiya No Hisai-jittai Fukko-katei No Kiroku To Machizukuri: Kumamoto-ken Uki-shi Ogawa-machi-shotengai No Rekishiteki-machinami No Keisho Wo Mezashite (record of the actual condition of damaged old historical houses "Machiya" by Kumamoto earthquake, the restoration process and community development intend to inherit historical townscape of Ogawa machi Shopping Street, Uki City, Kumamoto prefecture). *Jyuso Kenku Ronbunshu Jissen Kenkyu Hokoku Shu, 45*, 189–198.

Japan Building Disaster Prevention Association (JBDPA). (2021). Post-earthquake quick inspection of damaged buildings. Accessed January 13, 2022, http://www.kenchiku-bosai.or.jp/nwcon017/wp-content/uploads/2021/09/panf2.pdf

Japan Federation of Architects & Building Engineers Associations. (2020). Kumamoto-jishin Bunkazai Doctor Dai-san-ji Chosa-hokoku-kai Kiroku (record of the third investigation report meeting of the Kumamoto earthquake cultural properties doctor). Accessed November 13, 2021, https://kenchikushikai.or.jp/data/machizukuri/machizukuri_doc_202005.pdf

Japan International Council on Monuments and Sites (ICOMOS) National Committee. (2019). The 2016 Kumamoto earthquake report on damages to the cultural properties and recommendation for their restoration and rehabilitation. Accessed May 20, 2022, https://icomosjapan.org/news/news190425

Japan Building Disaster Prevention Association, National Council for the Assessment of the Emergency Risk of Damaged Buildings. Accessed January 13, 2021, http://www.kenchiku-bosai.or.jp/assoc/oq-index/

Kobayashi, Y., Konishi, H., Hirohata, M., Baba, K. (2017). Kumamoto-jishin Ni Okeru Saigai-haikibutsu-shori No Genjo Ni Tsuite (current status of disaster waste disposal in Kumamoto earthquake). *Haikibutsu Shigen Junkan Gakkai Kenkyu-happyo-kai Koen-shu, 28*(2), 161–162. https://doi.org/10.14912/jsmcwm.28.0_161

Kumamoto Prefecture. (2016). Kumamoto-jo Aso-jinja To Hisai-bunkazai Fukko-shien Iinkai No Hakkai Ni Tsuite (launch of the committee for supporting the recovery of cultural properties damaged by Kumamoto Castle and Aso Shrine). Accessed November 13, 2021, https://www.pref.kumamoto.jp/soshiki/125/65117.html

Kubota, H. (2016). Mukei Bunka Isan No Rescue To Bosai (rescue and disaster mitigation of intangible cultural heritage). *Tobunken News, 61*, 41–42.

Kumamoto Prefectural Board of Education, Miyazaki Prefectural Board of Education, Okinawa Prefectural Board of Education, Kagoshima Prefectural Board of Education. (1999). *Kyushu Chiho No Minka (2) Miyazaki, Kagoshima, Okinawa, Kumamoto ((Minka in the Kyushu Region (2) Miyazaki, Kagoshima, Okinawa, Kumamoto) Survey Reports on Minka in Japan, 16*. Toyo Shorin, Tokyo

Kumamoto Prefecture—Commerce, Industry and Industry Promotion Finance Division—Corporate Reconstruction Support Office. (2016). Chushokigyo-to Group Shisetsu-to Fukkyu-seibi Hojokin (Group Hojokin) (small and medium enterprise group facility reconstruction and improvement subsidy (group subsidy)). Accessed November 13, 2021, https://www.pref.kumamoto.jp/soshiki/61/2288.html

Kumamoto Prefectural Board of Education. (2021). Kumamoto-ken Bunkazai Hozon Katusuyo Taiko (Kumamoto prefecture outline for the conservation and use of cultural properties). Accessed November 13, 2021, https://www.pref.kumamoto.jp/uploaded/life/91060_128978_misc.pdf

Kyoto Prefectural Board of Education. (2020a). Kyoto-fu Bunkazai Hozon Katsuyo Taiko (Kyoto prefecture outline for the conservation and use of cultural properties). Accessed November 13, 2021, http://www.kyoto-be.ne.jp/soumu/bunkazai/bunkazai38.pdf

Kyoto Prefectural Board of Education. (2020b). Bunkazai Hogo: Mamori Sodateyo Min-na No Bunkazai (protection of cultural properties: let's protect and nurture everyone's cultural properties) (38). Accessed November 13, 2021, http://www.kyoto-be.ne.jp/bunkazai/cms/?action=common_download_main&upload_id=3143

Kyoto Prefectural Government—Cultural Properties Protection Division. (2017). Kyoto-fu Bunkazai Hogo Jorei No Ichibu Wo Kaisei Suru Jourei (ordinance partially amending the ordinance for the protection of cultural properties in Kyoto prefecture (Kyoto prefecture ordinance No. 20)), Kyoto prefecture public relations, No. 7 (March 28, 2017). Accessed November 13, 2021, http://www.kyoto-be.ne.jp/bunkazai/cms/?action=common_download_main&upload_id=2180

Kyoto Sangyo 21 Keihanna Branch Office. (2020). Keihanna open innovation center (KICK) Nyukyo Kigyo No Go-shokai (introduction of Keihanna open innovation center (KICK) residents). Accessed November 13, 2021, http://kick.kyoto/uploads/12250e8dd7e92f3980622da927299214.pdf

Masuda, Y., Okamoto, T., Asakawa, T., Maki, N., & Takaguchi, H. (2020). Legal resilience: legal systems to support livelihood reconstruction and recovery. *Kenchiku Zasshi, 2020–9*, 1–21.

Moriyama, M., & Isoda, S. (2018). Kumamoto-jishin Ni Yori Kohi-kaitai Sareta Hinagu Aka-renga-soko No Jumin-sanka-gata Ni Yoru Atochi-seibi Ni Tsuite (on the development of the site of the Hinaku Red Brick Warehouse, which was demolished at public expense due to the Kumamoto earthquake, by the participation of local residents). *Kenchiku-Rekishi Isho, 2018*, 799–800.

Murai, G., Naito, Y., Kubota, H., Yamanashi, E., Tarashima, S., Okada, K., Morii, J., Futagami, Y., Emura, T., Kikuchi, R., Sarai, M., Imaishi, M., Sano, M., & Yoshihara, D. (2016). Higashi-nihon Daishinsai Go No Bunkazai Rescue Katsudo Nippo No Inshi Bunseki (analysis on records of activities conducted to rescue cultural property after the Great East Japan earthquake). *Archives Gaku Kenkyu, 25*, 4–23.

Murai, G., Futagami, Y., Naito, Y., Hayashi, M., Yamanashi, E., & Okada, K. (2019). Keiryo Bunseki Ni Yoru Kumamoto Jishin To Higashi-nihon Daishinsai Deno Bunkazai Rescue Katsudo No Hikaku (comparison of the rescue activities for cultural property between the Kumamoto earthquake and the Great East Japan earthquake based on quantitative analysis). *Jinmonkon Ronbunshu, 2019*, 301–308.

Murai, G., Hayashi, M., Futagami, Y., Naito, Y., & Yamanashi, E. (2020). Hanshin-Awaji Daishinsai No Nippo Bunseki To Mittsu No Shinsai Ni Okeru Bunkazai Rescue Katsudo No Hikaku (an analysis of daily reports of the Great Hanshin-Awaji earthquake and a comparison of cultural heritage rescue activities at three disasters based on daily reports). *Hozon Kagaku, 60*, 1–18.

Murata, S. (2017). Shinsai eno Taio Kara Mietekita-mono (what we have seen from the response to the earthquake). *Hogaku Seminar, 62*(6), 21–24.

Nakajima, S., Hamada, T., & Takatsuma, Y. (2018). Todofuken Chiiki Bosai Keiaku Chu Ni Okeru Bunkazai To No Hozen Ni Kansuru Kisai No Genjo To Korekara (descriptions on cultural property preservation in prefectural disaster management plans: a review and future recommendations). *Hozon Kagaku, 58*, 149–168.

Narukawa, N., & Isoda, S. (2015). Kumamoto-ken Uki-shi Ogawa-machi Ni Okeru Machiya "Hasegawa-tei" No Kenchiku-teki Tokucho To Hozon Ni Mukete No Hosaku Ni Kansuru Kenkyu (a study on the architectural characteristics of Machiya at Ogawa-machi, Uki, Kumamoto and Machiya conservation circumstances in the future: a case study on the HASEGAWA silk reeling mill and the residence). *Kumamoto Koto Senmon Gakko Kenkyu Kiyo, 7*, 65–72.

Okada, K. (2021). Bunkazai Rescue Kara Bosai Network e: Bunkazai Bosai Center Secchi No Igi (from cultural property rescue to disaster prevention network: significance of the establishment of the disaster prevention center for cultural properties). *Gekkan Bunkazai, 691*, 16–18.

Okahashi, J. (2020). Notre-Dame de Paris Wo Meguru Giron (discussing the special law for the restoration of Notre Dame Cathedral of Paris). *Seishin Joshi Daigaku Ronso, 135*, 67–88.

Okamoto, T. (2014). *Saigai Fukko Hogaku (an encouragement of disaster recovery and revitalization law)*. Keio University Press.

Okamoto, T. (2018a). *Saigai Fukko Hogaku (an encouragement of disaster recovery and revitalization law II)*. Keio University Press.

Okamoto, T. (2018b). *Saigai Fukko Hogaku No Taike: Legal Needs To Fukko Seisaku No Kiseki (system of disaster recovery and revitalization law: legal needs and reconstruction policy trajectories)*. Keiso Shobo, Tokyo.

Owaki, S., Okada, Y., Ohikata, N., Kurata, K., Suzuki, K., & Hamada, E. (2017). Kumamoto-jishin To Horitsugaku No Yakuwari (Dai-5-kai) Zadankai: Seikatsu-saiken Ni Chokumen Shita Hisaisha Ni Donoyona Te Wo Sashinoberunoka (Jo) (the Kumamoto earthquake and the role of Jurisprudence (5) roundtable: what help can we give to disaster victims faced with rebuilding their lives (1)). *Hogaku Seminar, 62*(11), 64–75.

Saga Prefecture. (2021). Reiwa-san-nendo Public Comment Jisshi Anken (public comment items for 2021). Accessed November 13, 2021, https://www.pref.saga.lg.jp/kiji00380150/index.html

Sakata, J., Kimura, K., Isoda, S., & Harada, T. (2014). Shin-koji-ya No Heimen To Kenchiku Nendai Ni Tsuite: Kumamoto-ken Uki-shi Ogawa-machi Shotengai No Kindai-ka Isan Ni Kansuru Kenkyu (Sono 1) (the plan and the date of construction of Shin Koujiya: a study on the modernization heritage at Ogawa-machi, Uki city, Japan (No. 1)). *Nihon Kenchiku Gakkai Kyushu Shibu Kenkyu-Hoku-Sho, 53*, 505–508.

Sano, C., & Yamamoto, T. (2015). Fukushima-ken Bunkazai Center Shirakawa-kan Mahoron Ni Secchi Sareta Hisai Bunkazai Kari-hokan Shisetsu Nai No Hozon Kankyo (environmental study on temporary storehouses for rescued historical objects from the restricted area in Fukushima prefecture). *Hozon Kagaku, 54*, 59–73.

Sano, C., Kitano, N., & Sugisaki, S. (2016). Fukushima-ken Bunkazai Rescue Jigyo De Ichiji Hokan Basyo To Natta Kyu Soma Joshi Koko No Hozon Kankyo Ni Tsuite (environment of temporary storage rooms in a closed school at Soma city in Fukushima prefecture). *Hozon Kagaku, 55*, 89–101.

Sasaki, K., Mizumoto, Y., & Ogawa, C. (2013). Hanshin-awaji Daishinsai Kara Higashi-nihon Daishinsai e: Daishinsai Sono-go Ni Kansuru Chosa (from the Great Hanshin-Awaji earthquake to the Great East Japan earthquake: a survey on the aftermath of the great earthquake). *Records Management, 65*, 120–129.

Sasaki, S. (2017). *Disaster prevention and recovery legislation: commentary on the disaster prevention, emergency, recovery, and reconstruction system based on the Great East Japan Earthquake* (Dai-ichi Hoki, 2017) (p. 64).

Sato, D. (2011). Nara eno Tabi: Tsunami Hisai Shiryo No Toketsu Kanso Syori (journey to Nara: freeze-drying treatment of tsunami-affected materials). *Miyagi Shiryo Net News, 147*. Accessed November 13, 2021, http://miyagi-shiryounet.org/news147/

Sato, D. (2019). NPO Hojin Miyagi Rekishi Shiryo Hozen Network No Hisai Shiryo Rescue (the rescue activity of Miyagi Shiryo net for the damaged historical materials 2011–2018). *Rekishi, 132*, 56–59.

Takatsuma, H. (2013). Nara Bunkazai Kenkyujo No Bunkazai Rescue Katsudo (rescue activities for cultural properties at the Nara National Research Institute for Cultural Properties). In Committee for Salvaging Cultural Properties Affected by the 2011 Earthquake off the Pacific Coast of Tohoku and Related Disasters (Ed.), *Heisei-24-nendo Katsudo Hokokokusho (activity report for 2012). Committee for Salvaging Cultural Properties Affected by the 2011 Earthquake off the Pacific Coast of Tohoku and Related Disasters*. Tokyo. Accessed November 13, 2021, https://www.tobunken.go.jp/japanese/rescue/report/index.html

Tani, N. (1998). Hanshin-Awaji Daishinsai Ni Yoru Higai No Jittai (the actual state of damage caused by the great Hanshin-Awaji earthquake). In: K. Kato (Ed.), *Hanshin-Aswaji Daishinsai To Rekishiteki Kenzobutsu (The Great Hanshin-Awaji Earthquake and Historic Buildings)*. Shibunkaku, Kyoto.

Tanno, T. (2013). Fukushima-ken Ni Okeru Bunkazai Rescue Jigyo No Torikumi (efforts of the rescue project for cultural properties in Fukushima prefecture). In *Committee for salvaging cultural properties affected by the 2011 Earthquake off the Pacific Coast of Tohoku and Related Disasters*, Heisei-24-nendo Katsudo Hokokokusho (Activity Report for 2012). Committee for Salvaging Cultural Properties Affected by the 2011 Earthquake off the Pacific Coast of Tohoku and Related Disasters, Tokyo. Accessed November 13, 2021, https://www.tobunken.go.jp/japanese/rescue/report/index.html

Yamakawa, M. (2021). Kumamoto-jishin Hisai-rekishiteki-kenzobutsu Genkyo Chosa Hokoku (report on the current status of damaged historical buildings after the Kumamoto earthquake). Accessed June 13, 2022, http://ch.policy.integration.kyushu-u.ac.jp/activity/img/survey07.pdf

Yamazaki, E. (2021). Saigaitaisaku Ni Kansuru Kihonteki Hoseido No Kadai (challenges in basic legal systems for disaster countermeasures). *Horitsu Jiho, 93*(2), 13–20.

Ren Yatsunami (Associate Professor in the Faculty of Law at Kyushu University, Japan) Since November 2019, he serves as a member of the ICOMOS International Committee on Legislative, Administrative and Financial Issues (ICLAFI). Before joining Kyushu University in 2017, he was Associate Professor at Kagawa University. Prior to becoming Associate Professor, he was a post-doctoral fellow at the University of Tokyo and recipient of a fellowship from the Japan Society for the Promotion of Science (JSPS). While being a post-doctoral fellow, he co-edited a book titled "Regulatory Hybridization in the Transnational Sphere" (Martinus Nijhoff, 2013). He obtained a doctoral degree in law from Kyushu University in 2012. He earned his master's degree from Kyushu University in 2009. In 2012, he was awarded the JSPS Ikushi Prize, as well as the Kyushu University Award for Academic Research Activities.

Chapter 7
Lessons from the Earthquakes in Christchurch and Legislative Responses

Toshiyuki Kono

Abstract Christchurch was severely damaged by earthquakes in 2010 and 2011. At that time, there was no coordination between cultural heritage protection legislation and emergency response legislation and no collaborative relationship between the organizations involved. As a result, the decision to dismantle damaged buildings was made only based on the scheme planned in the emergency response legislation. Under the Heritage New Zealand Pouhere Taonga Act, enacted in 2014 after the earthquake, a linkage between the two is created, and collaboration between the organizations involved is required. The fact that there was no collaboration between the cultural heritage organizations and the organization with emergency jurisdiction was reflected in the post-earthquake response and recovery process. The fact cannot be ascertained when information on unlisted cultural properties is unavailable, even if they are damaged and dismantled. Christchurch was not the case since the list of heritage buildings in Christchurch is extensive and comprehensive. In Japan, however, the protection of unlisted buildings remains a big issue.

Keywords Christchurch · Earthquake · Emergency response · Legislation · Listing · Funding

7.1 Introduction

Christchurch, the largest city on the South Island of New Zealand, does not have any cultural heritage on the World Heritage List. However, it is one of the most representative cities in New Zealand, with its grid layout of streets from the 1850s and many buildings from the British colonial period. Although New Zealand has experienced many earthquakes in the past, it has been thought that an earthquake of a potentially life-threatening scale occurs only once every fifty-five years. The magnitude 7.1 earthquake that occurred in September 2010 and the magnitude 6.3 earthquake that occurred five months later in February 2011 are considered to be

T. Kono (✉)
Kyushu University, Fukuoka, Japan
e-mail: konoto@law.kyushu-u.ac.jp

T. Kono and J. Okahashi (eds.), *Post-Trauma and the Recovery Governance of Cultural Heritage*, https://doi.org/10.1007/978-981-19-6041-3_7

Fig. 7.1 Christchurch Cathedral after the earthquake. © Win Clark copyright credit

once every three hundred years. The September 2010 earthquake had heightened the vulnerability of many historic buildings, and the following February's quake was a devastating blow. One hundred eighty-five people lost their lives, and the city's iconic Christchurch Cathedral and other historic buildings, large and small, were severely damaged (Figs. 7.1 and 7.2).

This paper aims to examine the legal system in New Zealand in order to cope with traumatic situations through an analysis of the damage and recovery of cultural heritage caused by this earthquake and to draw some lessons.[1]

[1] Due to the COVID-19 pandemic, on-site interviews became impossible. Hence a joint work of the International Council on Monuments and Sites (ICOMOS) and the International Centre for Conservation and Restoration Research (ICCROM) under the author's initiative, ICOMOS/ICCROM (2021), Analysis of Case Studies in Recovery and Reconstruction, Case Studies, Vol. 1, pp. 273. http://openarchive.icomos.org/id/eprint/2447/ was used as the basis of this paper. In addition, an online interview with Catherine Forbs and Amanda Ohs, the report's authors in Case Studies, was conducted on May 25, 2022.

Fig. 7.2 Cashel St, between High St and Oxford St after the earthquake. This area has been completely rebuilt. © Win Clark copyright credit

7.2 New Zealand's Cultural Heritage Protection Legislation and Emergency Response Legislation[2]

7.2.1 National Level

Under current New Zealand law, the Heritage New Zealand Pouhere Taonga Act[3] (hereafter HNZPT Act), enacted in 2014 after the earthquake, is the basic law for cultural heritage protection at the national level. However, for the purposes of this paper, in order to compare two legal systems before and after the earthquake, it is necessary to look at the system in place at the time of the earthquake, so the Historic Places Act (hereafter HP Act) 1993, the predecessor of the HNZPT Act, will be examined first.[4]

The HP Act establishes and maintains the Registry, which consists of four parts: (1) Historic Places (divided into those of particular importance and value (Category 1) and those of particular value (Category 2)), (2) Historic Areas, (3) Wahi Tapu (Maori traditional, religious, ceremonial or legendary sacred places), and (4) Wahi Tapu Areas (Section 22). The listing of the Registry is done following the evaluation

---

[2] Also see Osamu Goto (2018), p. 2 et seq. (in Japanese).

[3] https://www.legislation.govt.nz/act/public/2014/0026/latest/DLM4005414.html.

[4] https://www.legislation.govt.nz/act/public/1993/0038/latest/whole.html#DLM300597.

criteria set forth in Section 23 of the HP Act.[5] Once listed, the Registry will have the following effects: (1) general public notice, (2) notification to owners, and (3) support for conservation under the Resource Management Act (hereafter RM Act) (para 2 of Section 22 of the HP Act[6]). In other words, the HP Act, as the primary law for the protection of cultural heritage, identifies and advocates the protection of cultural heritage, but it leaves the legal tools for protection to the RM Act.[7] Section 6 of the HP Act stipulates the Heritage Covenant. Once the New Zealand Historic Places Trust (hereafter NZHT), responsible for implementing the HP Act makes this agreement with the owner or lessee of a property, the agreement is entered into the land register. It is enforceable even if the ownership is transferred (Section 8 of the HP Act and Section 62 of the Land Transfer Act, 1952).[8] Except pursuant to an

---

[5] Section 23 Criteria for registration of historic places and historic areas.

(1) The Trust may enter any historic place or historic area in the register if the place or area possesses aesthetic, archaeological, architectural, cultural, historical, scientific, social, spiritual, technological, or traditional significance or value.

(2) The Trust may assign Category 1 status or Category 2 status to any historic place, having regard to any of the following criteria:

(a) the extent to which the place reflects important or representative aspects of New Zealand history:

(b) the association of the place with events, persons, or ideas of importance in New Zealand history:

(c) the potential of the place to provide knowledge of New Zealand history:

(d) the importance of the place to the tangata whenua:

(e) the community association with, or public esteem for, the place:

(f) the potential of the place for public education:

(g) the technical accomplishment or value, or design of the place:

(h) the symbolic or commemorative value of the place:

(i) the importance of identifying historic places known to date from early periods of New Zealand settlement:

(j) the importance of identifying rare types of historic places:

(k) the extent to which the place forms part of a wider historical and cultural complex or historical and cultural landscape:

(l) such additional criteria for registration of wahi tapu, wahi tapu areas, historic places, and historic areas of Maori interest as may be prescribed in regulations made under this Act:

(m) such additional criteria not inconsistent with those in paragraphs (a) to (k) for the purpose of assigning Category 1 or Category 2 status to any historic place, and for the purpose of registration of any historic area, as may be prescribed in regulations made under this Act.

[6] Section 22 (2) The purposes of the register shall be as follows:

(a) to inform members of the public about historic places, historic areas, wahi tapu, and wahi tapu areas:

(b) to notify owners of historic places, historic areas, wahi tapu, and wahi tapu areas where necessary for the purposes of this Act:

(c) to assist historic places, historic areas, wahi tapu, and wahi tapu areas to be protected under the Resource Management Act (1991).

[7] https://www.legislation.govt.nz/act/public/1991/0069/latest/whole.html?search=qs_act%40bill%40regulation%40deemedreg_resource+management+act_resel_25_h&p=1#DLM230265.

[8] Also, the Council may treat and agree with the owner or lessee for a covenant to provide for the management of that land in a manner that will achieve the particular purpose or purposes of conservation of historical values in accordance with Section 77 of the Reserves Act (1977). https://www.legislation.govt.nz/act/public/1977/0066/latest/DLM444305.html.

authority granted under Section 14, it shall not be lawful for any person to destroy, damage, or modify, or cause to be destroyed, damaged, or modified, the whole or any part of any archaeological site, knowing or having reasonable cause to suspect that it is an archaeological site (para 1 of Section 10 of the HP Act).

There are some critical changes in the amendment from the HP Act to the HNZPT Act of 2014. The NZHT was replaced by the Heritage New Zealand Pouhere Taonga (hereafter HNZTP), which the HNZTP Act established. As a public corporation, the HNZTP is supported by the government and receives financial assistance from the Ministry of Culture and Heritage. The scope of work, powers, and functions of the HNZPT are set out in the HNZPT Act. The Registry under the HP Act has been renamed the New Zealand Heritage List (hereafter NZH List) and taken over (Section 65 of the HNZTP Act). Under the HP Act, the Registry consisted of four parts, as described above. However, the NZH List now consists of five parts with the addition of Wahi Tupuna (a place of importance to Maori, their ancestors, and associated with their cultural values).

On the other hand, there are no changes to the assessment criteria for inclusion (Section 65(4) and 66 of the HNZTP Act). The effect of the listing on the NZH List is the same as the effect of the listing on the Registry under the HP Act, which includes a general public notice and notification to owners, and a supporting function when applying the RM Act (para 3 of Section 65 of the HNZTP Act). Restrictions or regulations on land and buildings are not derived from the listing, and the regulatory structure remains unchanged in that the legal tools for regulation are the RM Act, Heritage Covenant,[9] and restrictions on archaeological sites (Section 39 et seq. of the HNZTP Act).

The most significant amendment to the HNZTP Act from its predecessor, the HP Act, from the perspective of this paper, is the inclusion of provisions referring to the Civil Defence Emergency Management Act 2002[10] (hereafter CDEM 2002), the basic and comprehensive law for emergency response. In New Zealand, a policy shift was made in 1964 to prioritize natural disasters rather than nuclear attacks. Since then, it has become customary to use the term "civil defence" to refer to all efforts to ensure the general public's safety from various types of emergencies. The CDEM 2002 adopted a four-step approach, i.e., the four Rs (Reduction, Readiness, Response, and Recovery) to deal with a wide range of hazards, including natural disasters, epidemics, infrastructure damage, food safety, and terrorism.[11] At the national level, at the time of the earthquake, the National CDEM Plan (2005) systematized the principles and implementation system for emergencies under the National CDEM Strategy (2007). In addition, the New Zealand Coordinated Incident Management System (hereafter CIMS) was introduced to ensure functional coordination among multiple agencies in dealing with emergencies. However, the HP Act did not make any reference to the CDEM 2002. This non-reference means a lack of coordination

---

[9] https://www.heritage.org.nz/protecting-heritage/heritage-covenants.

[10] https://www.legislation.govt.nz/act/public/2002/0033/51.0/DLM149789.html. See Michitaka Umemoto (2017), p. 37 et seq. (in Japanese).

[11] Umemoto, ibid., 38–39.

between cultural heritage protection legislation and emergency legislation, which is said to have led to the loss of many historic buildings. In contrast, the HNZPT Act provides that the HNZPT should provide advice on cultural heritage in the event of a national or regional emergency (as defined in Section 4 of the CDEM 2002) or during a transition period (Sections 94A and 94B of the CDEM 2002) as defined in the CDEM 2002 (para 1(d) of Section 13 of the HNZTP Act. In addition, provisions on Emergency Authorities are newly added under Subpart 3 Emergency Authorities of the HNZTP Act. It intends to regulate the process for obtaining emergency powers to destroy or alter archaeological or historical sites in areas or districts where a state of emergency has been declared or a transitional period notified under the CDEM 2002. Any person may apply for such emergency powers (Section 61 of the HNZTP Act), and the HNZTP must take into account the requirements of para 2 of Section 45[12] of the HNZTP Act and the items set out in Section 62[13] of the HNZTP Act in deciding whether to grant such powers (para 3 of Section 61 of the HNZTP Act). The HNZTP may also conduct a field survey if necessary (Section 63 of the HNZTP Act).

However, under the HP Act at the time of the earthquake, which lacked such a linkage provision, Section 85 of the CDEM 2002, which allows for the removal and disposal of damaged buildings for security purposes, and Section 92 of the CDEM 2002, which allows for the "destruction of any property for the purpose of investigation," were applicable without any connection to cultural heritage legislation.

---

[12] A person must not be approved to carry out an activity under subsection (1) unless Heritage New Zealand Pouhere Taonga is satisfied that the person—

(a) has sufficient skill and competency, is fully capable of ensuring that the proposed activity is carried out to the satisfaction of Heritage New Zealand Pouhere Taonga, and has access to appropriate institutional and professional support and resources; and

(b) in the case of a site of interest to Māori—

(i) has the requisite competencies for recognising and respecting Māori values; and

(ii) has access to appropriate cultural support.

[13] 62 Determination of applications.

(1) Heritage New Zealand Pouhere Taonga may—

(a) grant an emergency authority in whole or in part, with or without conditions; or

(b) refuse to grant an emergency authority, giving reasons for doing so.

(2) In determining an application for an emergency authority, Heritage New Zealand Pouhere Taonga must have regard to—

(a) the purpose of this subpart; and

(b) the need to protect public health and safety; and

(c) to the extent that they are relevant, the matters referred to in Section 47(1)-(a); and

(d) all of the matters set out in Section 59(1)-(a) (the matters to which the Environment Court must have regard when determining an appeal); and

(e) the views of the owner of the land, to the extent that they can reasonably be ascertained.

7.2.2 Local Level

Cultural heritage protection at the local level is done through designations made by each municipality within the framework of a District Plan. In Christchurch, this is currently through the Christchurch District Plan of 2016, which has been operative since December 2017. But for this paper, it is essential to look at the Christchurch City District Plan of 1995 and the Banks Peninsula District Plan[14] of 1997.

There were five hundred eighty-eight listed buildings in the whole of Christchurch City and three hundred and nine listed buildings in the central part of Christchurch before the earthquake.[15] According to Statement 1.1 in Part 10, Heritage and Amenities of the 1995 Christchurch City District Plan,[16] updated in 2005, historic buildings, places, and objects were listed in four groups according to the following classification criteria: (1) those with international or national significance, whose protection is essential; (2) those with national or regional significance, whose protection is extremely important and feasible; and (3) those with regional or city-level significance, whose protection is extremely important and feasible, and (4) those that have city-level significance or are related to the city's cultural heritage and whose protection is desirable. To be listed as a cultural heritage site, an object must represent a variety of factors, including the following ones: (1) historic and social significance, (2) cultural and spiritual significance, (3) architectural and artistic significance, (4) group significance and setting, (5) landmark significance, (6) archaeological significance, and (7) technological significance and craftsmanship.[17] Of these, factors (1) through (3) were considered with double the weight of the other factors.[18] That resulted in certain types of buildings, such as churches, being favored. The report that forms the basis of the assessment includes information on the critical elements of the building facade and interior.[19] The currently valid assessment criteria are set out in the Christchurch District Plan of 2016, Chap. 9, Historic Heritage, Appendix 9.3.7.1. They are slightly revised from the old criteria.[20] In the Banks Peninsula District Plan, there were two categories, i.e., (1) structures, buildings, places, sites,

---

[14] It is the district plan for the area of Banks Peninsula prior to its amalgamation with Christchurch City.

[15] Amanda Ohs/Catherine Forbes (2021), p. 112–149, p128.

[16] Christchurch City Plan (1995), Vol. 3, The Statement of Rules, Part 10, Heritage and Amenities. https://ccc.govt.nz/the-council/plans-strategies-policies-and-bylaws/plans/christchurch-district-plan/districtplans/operative-christchurch-city-plan/.

[17] Statement 1.1, ibid.

[18] Ohs/ Forbs, ibid., p. 120.

[19] Ibid.

[20] https://districtplan.ccc.govt.nz/pages/plan/Book.aspx?exhibit=DistrictPlan&hid=314085.

(a) historical and social value; (b) cultural and religious value; (c) architectural and aesthetic value; (d) technical and artisanal value; (e) contextual value (e.g., relationship to the natural environment); and (f) archaeological and scientific value.

and areas with significant cultural heritage value, and (2) "silent file areas" as the area that are important to Maori and should not be identified in regional plans.[21]

As mentioned earlier, using the RM Act, which includes Heritage Orders,[22] or Covenant with the owner, in the case of Christchurch, the City Council[23] and the Canterbury Regional Council[24] are tasked with scrutinizing historical heritage and incorporating and protecting it in the formulation of the district and regional plans.[25]

In terms of emergency response at the local level, the CDEM 2002 introduced the CDEM Group system as a local core, a joint organization for emergency response established by several local governments and related organizations in each Regional Council.[26] The CDEM 2002 required that the CDEM Groups be established by June 1, 2003, and that CDEM Group Plans be developed in consultation with communities within two years of their establishment.[27] As a result, 16 CDEM Groups have been established across the country. In the case of Christchurch, there is Canterbury CDEM[28] at the regional level and Christchurch CDEM at the city level.[29] At the scene of the disaster, Fire and Emergency New Zealand (hereafter FENZ) is the agency responsible for search and rescue. Safety and law enforcement is the responsibility of the New Zealand Police. From a technical point of view, the Building Act of 2004, which sets safety standards, is essential. Before the 2010 earthquake, the City of Christchurch was aware that many of its historic buildings had seismic problems, but only a few had been surveyed and retrofitted.[30]

Prior to the earthquake, the City of Christchurch's Department of Cultural Heritage and the HNZPT had established a working relationship, including at an informal level, and reportedly had good communication with the property owners. However, neither of these organizations had any relationship with CDEM-related organizations or the

---

[21] https://ccc.govt.nz/assets/Documents/The-Council/Plans-Strategies-Policies-Bylaws/Plans/district-plan/banks-peninsula/Chapter14-bpdplistofpdfs.pdf.

[22] https://www.environmentguide.org.nz/issues/heritage/managing-historic-heritage/heritage-orders/.

[23] In New Zealand, there are two basic units of local government, City and District, each of which has its own council, and a directly elected mayor who is also the chairman of the council. The administrative divisions of each municipality are positioned under the council in terms of organizational structure, and these divisions are called City Council or District Council, which is the Territorial Authority. See Umemoto, above, p. 38.

[24] There are 17 Regional Authorities in the country. Six of these consist only of a single City or District and are integrated with the Regional Authority. This system combines the functions and authority of both regional and local governments. Regional governments also have their councils and administrative divisions. Therefore, regarding administrative structure, regional and local governments have a parallel and equal relationship. Umemoto, above, p. 38.

[25] Ohs/Forbes, ibid., p. 125.

In addition, the City of Christchurch adopted the ICOMOS New Zealand Charter (adopted in 1987, the current version in 2010) as its cultural heritage preservation policy in the 1990s.

[26] Umemoto, ibid., p. 44.

[27] Umemoto, ibid.

[28] https://www.cdemcanterbury.govt.nz/canterbury-cdem/about-us/.

[29] Ohs/Forbes, ibid., p. 125.

[30] Ohs/Forbes, ibid., p. 126.

FENZ.[31] Although the HNZPT is required to work with various government agencies as an independent organization, the fact that there was no collaboration between the cultural heritage organizations and the organization with emergency jurisdiction was unfortunately reflected in the post-earthquake response and recovery process. Furthermore, the RM Act broadly defines historic heritage in Section 2 as "those natural and physical resources that contribute to an understanding and appreciation of New Zealand's history and cultures". There were many cultural heritage sites in Christchurch, including representative settings and historical buildings from the colonial period. However, it is said that there were some critical voices because they could not see the Maori value. In this way, the understanding of Christchurch's unique cultural heritage values among national and local policymakers, and cultural heritage stakeholders was not always consistent. It was during these circumstances that a series of earthquakes occurred.[32]

In summary, there are three fields of laws and regulations: (1) the RM Act, the Regional Plan and District Plan to implement the RM Act at the local level, (2) the HP Act and its successor, the HNZTP Act to establish and manage the cultural heritage list using this scheme, and (3) the CDEM 2002 as an emergency response law. However, the relationship between cultural heritage-related laws and the CDEM 2002 was fragmented at the time of the earthquake. There was no communication between the departments in charge.

7.3 The 2011 Earthquake and the Subsequent Response

The cultural heritage sites, which had been made vulnerable by the September 4, 2010 earthquake (M.7.1), were devastated by the February 22, 2011 earthquake (M.6.4). There were two more disasters; one on June 13, 2011 (M.6.4) and the other on December 23, 2011 (M.6.2). These have been rated as once in every five hundred years.[33]

The damage from the February 22, 2011 earthquake was so severe that some city center areas were closed for two years.[34] About a quarter of the listed cultural heritage sites, including those on the Banks Peninsula, were destroyed. In Christchurch, two hundred and four buildings, or thirty-five percent of the city's five hundred eighty-eight registered historic buildings, were lost. In the city center, one hundred thirty-five buildings, or forty-four percent of three hundred and nine buildings, were lost.[35] According to a recent survey by the Council, some buildings still have received only temporary emergency measures. Some have been announced to be reinforced and

[31] Ohs/Forbes, ibid.

[32] Ibid.

[33] Ibid.

[34] Ibid.

[35] Ibid., p. 128.

restored, while others will be demolished. In addition, about thirty heritage places in the city center included in the district plan remain vacant, damaged, and unrepaired.[36]

Following the earthquake, the central government declared a state of emergency in accordance with the CDEM 2002. The Civil Defence Controller assumed primary responsibility for the immediate aftermath of the disaster. In April 2011, the Canterbury Earthquake Recovery Act (CER Act) was enacted[37] after the Canterbury Earthquake Recovery Authority (CERA) was established as a central government agency to lead the recovery process in March, 2011. As mentioned above, the CDEM 2002 allows for the removal and disposal of damaged buildings for safety purposes (Section 85). However, this authority was transferred to the CERA under Section 38 of the CER Act. This transfer makes the CERA the supreme authority to decide on demolishing the affected buildings.

As mentioned above, the HP Act was not relevant to the exercise of this authority.[38] As suggested by the fact that the then Minister of Earthquake Reconstruction referred to historic buildings as "dangerous and unnecessary," the CERA made decisions that led to the demolition of historic buildings.[39] First, it revised the District Plan, overriding the existing agreement between the owner and the cultural heritage protection authority for buildings approved for demolition by the CERA, thus eliminating the need for consent for demolition. With the rapid creation and implementation of this emergency response system, the process of cultural heritage protection, which is based on consent and involves the community at large, has been dramatically reduced.[40] The Central City District Plan has also been amended to bring damaged historic buildings into compliance with building code standards.[41] The ICOMOS/ICCROM report points out that the damage to the city center, which lost forty-four percent of its area, was not only caused directly by the 2011 earthquake but also by a combination of aftershocks and post-quake decisions by the CERA, insurance companies, and property owners.[42] As mentioned above, before the earthquake, cultural heritage organizations, both at the national and local levels, had no relationship with CDEM-related organizations or the FENZ. In addition, there was a lack of understanding between national and local reconstruction policy makers and cultural heritage stakeholders regarding the unique value of Christchurch's cultural heritage. The lack of understanding of the unique value of Christchurch's cultural heritage

---

[36] Ibid., p. 129.

[37] The Greater Christchurch Regeneration Act replaced the CER Act in 2016. https://dpmc.govt.nz/our-programmes/greater-christchurch-recovery-and-regeneration/greater-christchurch-regeneration-act.

[38] When the HNZTP Act was enacted in 2014 as the successor legislation to the HP Act, the CER Act was also amended to relate it to the HNZTP Act (para 3 of Section 71 of the CER Act).

[39] Ohs/ Forbes, ibid., p. 133.

[40] Ibid., p. 140.

[41] Ohs/Forbes, ibid., p. 133. In 2016, the Greater Christchurch Regeneration Act (GCR Act) replaced the CER Act. It made Regenerate Christchurch (a joint agency of the city and state) charged with taking control of the recovery and regeneration process.

[42] Ohs/Forbes, ibid., p. 133.

between national and local decision-makers and cultural heritage stakeholders has also contributed to this trend.[43]

7.4 Cultural Heritage Conservation and Economic Support in the Reconstruction Process

Almost half of Christchurch's historic buildings were lost, but there were still owners and community groups who wanted to restore them to their former glory. The most important thing for them is financial support for repair or restoration.

One program available before the earthquake was the Christchurch Council Heritage Incentive Grants. These grants provide up to fifty percent of the cost. For large buildings, Christchurch Council Central City Landmark Grants are more generous. After the earthquake in September 2010, the Canterbury Earthquake Heritage Building Fund was established to provide support for repairs and seismic retrofitting and incentivize owners to preserve their buildings. In addition, the HNZTP's National Heritage Preservation Fund provides grants for buildings of national significance.[44]

Since most of the insurance policies[45] taken out by owners of historic buildings did not cover the cost of repairing, restoring, and reinforcing them against earthquakes, the fund established after the earthquake aims to make up the difference between the amount covered by the insurance and the actual cost, and existing subsidy policies have been operated in the same direction.[46] Making up the difference between the insurance payment and the insurance premium may be a helpful tool to protect historic buildings that are not landmarks that are ranked low in the value hierarchy.[47]

One of the most significant grants available was the Christchurch Council Central City Landmark Grants for the former McLean Mansion, one of the largest Victorian wooden buildings in New Zealand and internationally. The 53-room building, constructed in 1899, was listed on the NZH Registry as a Category 1 Historic Place in 1983. In addition, the Christchurch District Plan listed the building and its setting as "highly significant" in 1995.[48] Christchurch Academy purchased the building in 1987, which was still the owner at the time of the earthquake. The building escaped destruction due to the flexible structure of its wooden construction, but the interior and decorative elements were severely damaged and declared unsafe and unusable (Fig. 7.3).[49]

---

[43] Ibid., p. 140.

[44] https://www.scoop.co.nz/stories/AK2108/S00175/loss-of-heritage-equip-funding-a-blow.htm.

[45] https://www.eqc.govt.nz/what-we-do/insurance-overview/.

[46] Ohs/Forbes, ibid., p. 139.

[47] Ohs/Forbes, ibid., p. 143.

[48] Forbes/ Clark (2021), pp.150–179, p.160.

[49] Ibid., p. 165.

Fig. 7.3 The interior ground floor of McLean's Mansion, front north room after the earthquake. © Win Clark copyright credit

It was estimated that a complete restoration of the building would cost over 9.1 million NZ dollars, so the owner put it up for sale in its damaged state.[50] After failing to find a buyer for the property, even though it was clear that assistance was possible, a group of local self-employed people established the McLean's Mansion Charitable Trust in 2016 to purchase and restore the building.[51] An enthusiastic fundraising campaign raised 2.5 million NZ dollars, and a grant with 1.9 million NZ dollars from the Christchurch Council Central City Landmark Grant was awarded, making the purchase possible on August 7, 2018.[52] A six-stage plan was drawn up to complete the restoration in March 2022.[53]

To be mentioned from a funding perspective are the McKenzie and Wills Building[54] and New Regent Street.[55] Christchurch's most famous shopping street was built in the early twentieth century for commercial use on Christchurch's main street.

The McKenzie and Wills Building, built in the early twentieth century for commercial use on the main street of Christchurch, was listed as a Category 2 Historic Place by the NZH Registry in 1981 as a good example of late Victorian and Edwardian

---

[50] Ibid., p. 172.

[51] Ibid.

[52] Ibid. p. 174.

[53] Ibid., p. 176.

[54] Catherine Forbes (2021), pp. 224–247.

[55] Wykes/ Forbes (2021), pp.248–273.

Fig. 7.4 The McKenzie and Wills Building after the earthquake (the building on the left side). © Win Clark copyright credit

style commercial buildings.[56] At the time of the earthquake, the building was still used as a showroom for the furniture company McKenzie and Wills.[57] However, the unreinforced masonry building was listed as a seismically unsound building in 2009.[58] After the earthquake, the back half of the building was reduced to rubble, and the owner, not wanting to bear the cost, applied for demolition of the remaining part of the building (Fig. 7.4).

The CERA recommended demolition on June 13, 2011.[59] On the other hand, Christchurch Council proposed the option of demolishing everything and incorporating the original stone into the new building and another option of leaving the facade on site and repairing and reinforcing it. The Council recommended the latter. The latter option was less expensive and preserved some of the cultural heritage significance.[60] Nevertheless, the initial cost was estimated at 540,000 NZ dollars. The owner followed Christchurch Council's recommendation and applied for the Canterbury Earthquake Heritage Building Fund but sold the property in 2014 to a property developer who promised to incorporate the facade into a new building. In the end, Christchurch Council provided a Heritage Incentive Fund to cover 40 percent of the cost (240,000 NZ dollars), while the remainder and increased costs (which grew

[56] Forbes, ibid. (McKenzie and Wills Building), p. 230.

[57] Ibid., p. 229.

[58] Ibid., p. 231.

[59] Ibid., p. 233.

[60] Ibid., p. 234.

at ca. one million NZ dollars) were covered by private donations and the Canterbury Earthquake Heritage Building Fund.[61]

New Regent Street is a group of more than 40 two-story buildings built as stores in the 1930s and constitutes one of Christchurch's most famous urban landscapes.[62] In 1990 it was listed as a Category 1 Historic Place and in 1994 as a Historic Area in the NZH Registry.[63] Unlike the above examples, in the case of New Regent Street, on the one hand, more than 40 buildings belonged to 24 owners. In assessing the value of a building as cultural heritage, it is not only the interior of the building but, more importantly, the exterior of the building, especially the facade, which forms a beautiful landscape with buildings of the same architectural style (Fig. 7.5).[64]

Although traffic was restricted, the stores of each building were open during the day. Therefore, restoration work had to be done early in the morning and later in the evening. In order to maintain a uniform landscape and carry out the work efficiently, the same contractor should be in charge, and the owners had to agree to this. In the end, most of the owners agreed, and the restoration was completed in 2012. Traffic restrictions were lifted in 2013. The street is said to have once again earned the reputation as the most beautiful street in New Zealand (Fig. 7.6).[65]

The cost of the restoration and seismic reinforcement was covered by the Canterbury Earthquake Heritage Building Fund (about $76,000 NZ dollars), Christchurch Council Heritage Incentive Grant (about $100,000 NZ dollars), and the insurance of each owner (amount unknown). Grant (about $100,000 NZ dollars), Christchurch Council Central City Landmark Heritage Grant ($900,000 NZ dollars), and also a grant from the HNZTP (about $300,000 NZ dollars).[66] Without these grants, the owners would have been forced to sell or demolish the buildings, and many of them would have been lost.[67]

From the above examples, it is clear that a combination of multiple funding schemes has been used to obtain financial support for the conservation of damaged historic buildings. The HNZTP and the Christchurch Council Cultural Heritage Section were responsible for communicating this information to the owners and other stakeholders and coordinating the whole process. After the earthquake, under the HNZTP Act, which linked cultural heritage legislation and emergency response legislation, the HNZTP started institutional dialogues with CDEM-related bodies.[68]

---

61 Ibid., p. 240.

62 Wykes/Forbes, ibid. (New Regent Street), p. 252.

63 Ibid., p. 254.

64 Ibid., p. 255.

65 Ibid., pp. 269–270.

66 Ibid., p. 269.

67 One of the owners of the five buildings did not agree to the project for insurance policy reasons and commissioned another contractor to restore the buildings. Wyles/Forbes, ibid.

68 The explanation was provided in the online interview with Catherine Forbs and Amanda Ohs, conducted on May 25, 2022.

Fig. 7.5 New Regent street after the earthquake. © Christchurch City Council Heritage Files copyright credit

7.5 Dismantling and the Value of Cultural Heritage

The Isaac Theater Royal Theatre,[69] which was one of the most important centers of exchange for the people of Christchurch, and the Knox Presbyterian Church,[70] which was built in 1904 as a Presbyterian church, were severely damaged in the main part of the building, and they concluded that they had no choice but to demolish them technically. As both buildings are facilities where many people enter and stay simultaneously, ensuring safety is a top priority. So the buildings were dismantled, and the structures were rebuilt to meet earthquake resistance standards (Fig. 7.7).

[69] Fiona Wykes/Catherine Forbes (2021), pp.180–199.

[70] Catherine Forbs (2021), pp. 200–223.

Fig. 7.6 New Regent street in 2022. © Christchurch City Council Heritage Files copyright credit

Fig. 7.7 The Knox Church after the earthquake. © Win Clark copyright credit

On the other hand, in both cases, the interior of the building was restored to its pre-earthquake condition as much as possible by using the original components. In the case of the Isaac Theatre, the original facade was preserved and combined with the new building. In the case of the Knox Church, it was decided that the original building site would be maintained and a new building would be constructed there, rejecting the theory of relocation. The ICOMOS/ICCROM report states that although the Isaac Theatre "lost authenticity and integrity through the disaster and recovery process, it has retained historic, aesthetic, architectural and social values."[71] Knox Church retains its "social and spiritual significance" and continues to contribute to "the social fabric of the community."[72] Interestingly, the Isaac Theatre is still listed as a Category 1 Historic Place in the HNZPT list today. The District Plan states that it meets the criteria for a significant place.[73] The Knox Church has not lost its status as a Category 2 Historic Place, which was listed in 1984. Nevertheless, the assessment has been revised to focus on the value of the interior of the building.[74]

It cannot be said that the demolished and newly constructed buildings still retain the same value assigned to them before the disaster. However, it is not impossible for people who have a relationship with the building to find some significance in it, even if it is a new building. It was seen when the State Hall of Shuri-jô Castle in Naha, Japan, was destroyed by fire in 2019. The building was reconstructed in 1992 and was not listed as cultural property. However, many people were moved to tears and donated money for reconstruction. Also, large donations were made when the Kumamoto Castle tower, also not a designated cultural property, was heavily damaged by the earthquake in 2016. New Zealand's cultural heritage practice seems to be taking this head-on by adding new value even after demolition or new construction.

7.6 Conclusion from a Comparative Perspective with Japan

This paper has examined the governance of cultural heritage in post-traumatic situations through a case study of Christchurch, severely damaged by earthquakes in 2010 and 2011, and an analysis of New Zealand's cultural heritage protection legislation and emergency response legislation. In New Zealand, it is necessary to keep an eye on legal systems at the national and local levels. However, in both cases, before the earthquake, there was no coordination between cultural heritage protection legislation and emergency response legislation and no collaborative relationship between the organizations involved. As a result, it became clear that the decision to dismantle was made only based on the scheme planned in the emergency response legislation. However, under the HNZTP Act enacted in 2014 after the earthquake, there is a

71 Wykes/Forbes, ibid. (Isaac Theatre Royal), p. 194.
72 Forbes, ibid. (Knox Presbyterian Church), p. 216.
73 Wykes/Forbes, ibid. (Isaac Theatre Royal), p. 197.
74 Forbes, ibid. (Knox Presbyterian Church), p. 221.

linkage between the two. At least in terms of the law, there is now a requirement for collaboration between the organizations involved.

In the context of cultural property protection legislation alone, some examples can be referred to, such as the use of economic support schemes and how to add value after the event. On the other hand, under Japanese law, damage to cultural heritage has been dealt with using the framework of ordinary "repair."[75] In addition, there is no linkage between the Law for the Protection of Cultural Properties and the emergency response legislation. Should the legal system in Japan, a country with frequent disasters, remain in such a state? It seems that further discussion is needed. On the other hand, the New Zealand cases were all about treating listed cultural heritage sites after they were damaged, so there is no issue of how to treat damage to undesignated cultural heritage sites. The earthquake in Kumamoto raised this issue. As of December 2021, there were five national, eleven prefectural, and thirty municipal designated cultural properties in Kumamoto City with 740,000 residents, for a total of forty-six buildings. In Christchurch, with 380,000 residents, five hundred and eighty-eight heritage buildings, places, and objects were listed before the earthquake. Even after the earthquake, three hundred and seventy-four items are listed.[76] This overwhelming difference may be explained by the very selective nature of Japan's operation. Nevertheless, it may be problematic from the viewpoint of how much information on cultural heritage the city government would receive, keeping track of information on historic buildings and places. Because information on undesignated cultural properties is unavailable, even if they are damaged and dismantled, the fact cannot be ascertained. In addition, there are no funds for damaged undesignated cultural properties at the national or local level, except for the restoration of famous reconstructed monuments like Kumamoto Castle and Shuri-jô Castle. The cases in Christchurch suggest that there is much work to be done in japan.

References

[Reports in ICOMOS/ICCROM Case Studies]

Amanda Ohs/ Catherine Forbes. (2021). Christchurch: heritage recovery from the Canterbury earthquakes. *ICOMOS/ICCROM, Analysis of Case Studies in Recovery and Reconstruction, Case Studies, 1*, 112–149.

Catherine Forbes/ Winston Clark. (2021). McLean's Mansion (Holly Lea). *Christchurch, ICOMOS/ICCROM, Analysis of Case Studies in Recovery and Reconstruction, Case Studies, 1*, 150–179.

Fiona Wykes/ Catherine Forbes. (2021). Isaac theatre royal. *Christchurch, ICOMOS/ICCROM, Analysis of Case Studies in Recovery and Reconstruction, Case Studies, 1*, 180–199.

Forbs, C. (2021). Knox Presbyterian Church. *Christchurch, ICOMOS/ICCROM, Analysis of Case Studies in Recovery and Reconstruction, Case Studies, 1*, 200–223.

[75] See Nishi's report in this volume.

[76] Appendix 1, List of Protected Buildings, Places, and Objects (updated on 26, August 2016), Part 10, Heritage and Amenities, the Christchurch City District Plan (1995).

Forbes, C. (2021). McKenzie and Wills Building (former A. J. Whites). *Christchurch Commercial Building Façade and Setting, ICOMOS/ICCROM, Analysis of Case Studies in Recovery and Reconstruction, Case Studies, 1*, 224–247.
Fiona Wykes and Catherine Forbes. (2021). New Regent Street. *Christchurch, ICOMOS/ICCROM, Analysis of Case Studies in Recovery and Reconstruction, Case Studies, 1*, 248–273.
http://openarchive.icomos.org/id/eprint/2447/

[Articles]

Goto, O. (2018). Disaster prevention measures for cultural property buildings in New Zealand. *Fire and Disaster Management, 68*(5, 356), 2 et seq. (in Japanese)
Umemoto, M. (2017). The system of disaster response in New Zealand and its characteristics. *Essays of the Association on Regional Safety* (31), 37 et seq. (in Japanese)

[National Legislation]

Canterbury Earthquake Recovery Act. (2011). https://www.legislation.govt.nz/act/public/2011/0012/latest/DLM3653522.html
Civil Defence Emergency Management Act. (2002). https://www.legislation.govt.nz/act/public/2002/0033/51.0/DLM149789.html
Greater Christchurch Regeneration Act. (2016). https://dpmc.govt.nz/our-programmes/greater-christchurch-recovery-and-regeneration/greater-christchurch-regeneration-act
Heritage New Zealand Pouhere Taonga Act. (2014). https://www.legislation.govt.nz/act/public/2014/0026/latest/DLM4005414.html
Historic Places Act. (1993). https://www.legislation.govt.nz/act/public/1993/0038/latest/whole.html#DLM300597
Reserves Act. (1977). https://www.legislation.govt.nz/act/public/1977/0066/latest/DLM444305.html
Resource Management Act. (1991). https://www.legislation.govt.nz/act/public/1991/0069/latest/whole.html?search=qs_act%40bill%40regulation%40deemedreg_resource+management+act_resel_25_h&p=1#DLM230265

[District Plans]

Banks Peninsula District Plan. (1997). https://ccc.govt.nz/assets/Documents/The-Council/Plans-Strategies-Policies-Bylaws/Plans/district-plan/banks-peninsula/Chapter14-bpdplistofpdfs.pdf
Christchurch City District Plan. (1995). https://ccc.govt.nz/the-council/plans-strategies-policies-and-bylaws/plans/christchurch-district-plan/districtplans/operative-christchurch-city-plan/
Christchurch District Plan. (2016). https://districtplan.ccc.govt.nz/pages/plan/Book.aspx?exhibit=DistrictPlan&hid=314085

Toshiyuki Kono Distinguished professor, Kyushu University, Japan. Toshiyuki Kono was born in Osaka, Japan, in 1958. After graduating from the Faculty of Law, Kyoto University, he went on to obtain his LL.M. from the Graduate School of Law, Kyoto University. He is a specialist in private international law, international civil procedure law, and international cultural heritage law. He was a member of UNESCO's Expert Groups for the drafting of the Convention for the Safeguarding of the Intangible Cultural Heritage (2003) and the Convention on the Protection and Promotion of the Diversity of Cultural Expressions (2005). He was appointed as a member of the Executive Committee of the International Council on Monuments and Sites (ICOMOS) in 2011. After working as vice president, he was elected as the 8th president of ICOMOS in 2017. As the former president, he continues as an honorary president of ICOMOS. He is the series editor of Springer's book series Perspectives in Law, Business and Innovation.

Chapter 8
The Significance of Special Laws in Post-disaster Restoration and Recovery of Cultural Heritage: The Case of the Special Law for the Conservation and Restoration of Notre-Dame de Paris

Junko Okahashi

Abstract This paper discusses the process and significance of the "Law No. 2019-803 on the conservation and restoration of Notre-Dame de Paris and the establishment of a system for receiving donations for this purpose", which was passed in 2019, during the same year as the Notre-Dame de Paris having been damaged by fire. It examines why such a Special Law was necessary in an emergency, beyond the normal cultural heritage protection system in France, and what effects could be seen. Furthermore, to comprehensively consider who within the public framework should be entrusted with what kind of response in the context of post-disaster reconstruction, such Special Law and Public Establishment shall be positioned as an example of a suggested post-disaster governance response and institutional measure.

Keywords Special law · Public establishment · Post-disaster restoration · Leadership · Emergency operations · Notre-Dame de Paris

8.1 Introduction

This paper discusses the process and significance of the "Law No. 2019-803 on the Conservation and Restoration of Notre-Dame de Paris and the Establishment of a Donation System for the Conservation and Restoration of Notre-Dame de Paris",[1] which was passed in 2019, during the same year as the Notre-Dame de Paris having

[1] Loi n° 2019-803 pour la conservation et la restauration de la cathédrale Notre-Dame de Paris et instituant une souscription nationale à cet effet. https://www.legifrance.gouv.fr/affichTexte.do?cidTexte=JORFTEXT000038843049&categorieLien=id (2021.9.14 accessed). This law, developed in the aftermath of a disaster, will be referred to in this paper as the "Special Law in Charge of the Conservation and Restoration of Notre-Dame de Paris" or "Special Law".

J. Okahashi (✉)
University of the Sacred Heart, Tokyo, Japan
e-mail: okahashi@u-sacred-heart.ac.jp

T. Kono and J. Okahashi (eds.), *Post-Trauma and the Recovery Governance of Cultural Heritage*, https://doi.org/10.1007/978-981-19-6041-3_8

been damaged by fire. It examines why such a Special Law was necessary for an emergency, beyond the normal cultural heritage protection system in France, and what effects could be seen. Furthermore, to comprehensively consider who within the public framework should be entrusted with what kind of response in the context of post-disaster reconstruction, such Special Law and Public Establishment shall be positioned as an example of a suggested post-disaster governance response and institutional measure.

8.2 The Legal Framework for the Protection of Cultural Property in France

As a background to the establishment of the Special Law on the Conservation and Restoration of Notre-Dame de Paris, we shall examine the legal features of the normal French cultural heritage protection system to understand why this Special Law was necessary.

State-designated historic monuments such as Notre-Dame de Paris, i.e., buildings that are important cultural properties, have been protected for many years under the "Law on Historic Monuments"[2] promulgated on 31 December 1913. The Code has been replaced by the "Code of Cultural Heritage" (Code du Patrimoine), promulgated by Ordinance[3] 2004-178. The "Code of Cultural Heritage" became a definitive legal document with no time limit by Article 78 of the "Law for the Simplification of the Law"[4] issued on 9 December 2004. As for the detailed regulations, they were made official by a decree[5,6] of 24 May 2011.

The "Code of Cultural Heritage" covers the totality of immovable or movable property that exhibits historical, artistic, archaeological, aesthetic, scientific, or technical value, belonging to public or private ownership. It also integrates a detailed system that covers city blocks, settlements, and scenic spots that are considered to have scenic value, and does not only deal with the historic monuments (buildings) directly concerning this paper and the landscape management area of a radius of 500 m around them. It provides income tax deductions for the management costs of buildings designated as historic monuments, deductions for private enterprises that donate cultural properties to the state within 10 years of purchase, deductions for real estate income from the restoration of buildings in historic monuments, and

[2] Loi de 31 décembre 1913 sur les monuments historiques.

[3] Ordinances are enacted by the government based on the legislative power on specific matters delegated by the parliament for a limited period of time, and have the same effect as laws.

[4] Loi n° 2004-1343 du 9 décembre 2004 de simplification du droit.

[5] A decree is an executive decision with general or specific effect, signed by the President or Prime Minister of the Republic.

[6] Décret n° 2011-573 du 24 mai 2011 relatif à la partie réglementaire du code du patrimoine (Décrets en Conseil d'État et en conseil des ministres) and Décret n° 2011-574 du 24 mai 2011 relatif à la partie réglementaire du code du patrimoine (livres Ier à VI) Les dispositions réglementaires du code du patrimoine font l'objet d'une publication spéciale annexée au Journal officiel de ce jour).

landscape protection areas, and deductions for corporate and individual donations for the protection of cultural properties. Tax incentives for corporate and individual donations related to the protection of cultural properties, and exemption of gift taxes on buildings designated as historic monuments, provided that they are open to the public, are some of the incentives for general cooperation in the protection of cultural properties.

It should be noted, however, that the French Ministry of Culture is solely responsible for the implementation of this Code as an administrative organization. In an emergency after a disaster, if a single ministry is responsible for mid-to-long-term operations that will continue until it is possible to determine that the desired recovery status has been reached, it may be feared that in reality, it will not be able to maintain the driving force to overcome the complex situation. From this perspective, it is understandable how a Special Law was deemed necessary for post-disaster emergencies that require responses that transcend the scope of the "Code of Cultural Heritage" and the jurisdiction of the Ministry of Culture.

8.3 Question of Authenticity Under the "Convention for the Protection of the World Cultural and Natural Heritage"

Notre-Dame de Paris was inscribed on the World Heritage List under the "Convention for the Protection of the World Cultural and Natural Heritage" (hereinafter referred to as the "World Heritage Convention") by the World Heritage Committee[7] in 1991 as one of the components of the World Cultural Heritage, which is comprised of 365 hectares as the "Banks of the Seine in Paris".[8] The scope of the inscription is limited to the center of Paris, from the Sully Bridge at the eastern end of Saint-Louis Island in the east to the Iena Bridge in front of the Eiffel Tower in the west and the architectural complex surrounding the Champ de Mars Park, which housed the five World Expositions during the nineteenth and twentieth centuries. While modern buildings such as the Eiffel Tower and wide avenues created by Baron Haussmann under the Second Empire in the Nineteenth Century exemplified the transformation of Paris and influenced later urban planning, Notre-Dame de Paris, located on Cité Island, a sandbar in the middle of the Seine River and the cradle or origin of the city of Paris, remained for centuries as representative of medieval Gothic architecture. As Notre-Dame de Paris is thus part of the World Cultural Heritage of Outstanding Universal Value under the World Heritage Convention, it must meet the definition of authenticity, as described in paragraphs 79 to 86 of the "Operational Guidelines

[7] A regular annual intergovernmental meeting of the United Nations Educational, Scientific and Cultural Organization (UNESCO), which serves as the secretariat. The World Heritage Committee is composed of 21 countries elected by the General Conference of the States Parties to the World Heritage Convention, which meets once a year.

[8] Paris, Banks of the Seine. https://whc.unesco.org/en/list/600/.

for the Implementation of the World Heritage Convention". Paragraph 86 of the Guidelines reads the following:

> In relation to authenticity, the reconstruction of archaeological remains or historic buildings or districts is justifiable only in exceptional circumstances. Reconstruction is acceptable only on the basis of complete and detailed documentation and to no extent on conjecture.

The recovery of cultural properties that have been destroyed or damaged is not limited to restoration, but may also include work that can be called reconstruction, even if only in part. It is necessary to take into account the fact that Notre-Dame de Paris is required to ensure its authenticity, during its recovery, under the World Heritage Convention.

8.3.1 The Universal Symbolism of Notre-Dame de Paris and Its Current State Through Historical Changes

Regarding the aforementioned guarantees of authenticity, it is crucial to be ascertained of the phases of various restoration works that Notre-Dame de Paris has undergone until now, taking into account the requirements under the guidelines of today's international conventions (Fig. 8.1).

Notre-Dame de Paris is the cathedral of the Archdiocese of Paris in the Catholic Church and is widely known in France and abroad as one of the masterpieces of

Fig. 8.1 Cathedral Notre-Dame de Paris before the 2019 fire. © Benjamin Mouton

French Gothic architecture, which gradually developed and blossomed from the first half of the twelfth century. In the history of France, the coronation and burial of kings took place mainly in the Cathedral Notre-Dame de Reims in the Champagne region and the church of Saint-Denis in the northern suburbs of Paris. Also, as masterpieces of Gothic architecture, the Cathedral Saint-Etienne in Bourges and the Cathedral Notre-Dame in Chartres are known to be the most representative. However, among them, Notre-Dame de Paris is the most famous. Perhaps due to its location, it has a universality which is not too much to say that its symbolic value is shared by all people in France and abroad. This universal symbolism is evidenced by the fact that the fire that broke out on 15 April 2019 affected the emotions of people all over the world, and by the fact that the reconstruction of the site has continued to attract attention.

Notre-Dame de Paris has undergone many additions and restorations over the years, and it has not been the same since its original construction in the Middle Ages. The initial construction started in 1163 under the reign of King Louis VII of France under Bishop Maurice de Sully and was completed around 1250 with four design revisions during the work. In the centuries that followed, the building underwent numerous changes. During the French Revolution, it was subjected to vandalism, including the destruction of statues, and temporarily lost its function as a church and was used for secular purposes. In 1802 it was restored as a Catholic Church, and in 1844, King Louis-Philippe ordered the restoration of the cathedral during the restoration of the monarchy. The mid-nineteenth century restoration, which brought the cathedral much closer to the existing Notre-Dame de Paris, involved major alterations designed by the two architects Eugène Viollet-le-Duc and Jean-Baptiste Lassus, including the rebuilding of the spire, which had previously been lost.

8.3.2 Past Restoration Works at Notre-Dame de Paris

In the middle of the nineteenth century, when the architectural culture and Gothic art of the Middle Ages were not yet widely recognized as valuable and were in a state of disrepair, Victor Hugo, a popular writer of the time, aroused public interest in the historical memory of Paris through his writings. Hugo's novel, *Notre-Dame de Paris*, became a bestseller in France as soon as it was published in 1831, sparking the public's interest in the medieval period and its architecture. Hugo combined the historical site of Notre-Dame de Paris with a dramatic narrative, focusing on the cathedral as a centre to describe the chaotic aspects of Paris in the fifteenth century. A big bulk of the novel takes place in the Notre-Dame tower, where the bellman, Quasimodo, is the central character. Noting the cathedral's terrible state of disrepair at the beginning of the nineteenth century, and believing that great architecture takes centuries to build, like a great mountain, Hugo joins the great campaign to restore Notre-Dame de Paris. The fact that the restoration work began in 1845 following the king's order was the result of the campaign by Hugo and others to mobilize public opinion, which aroused widespread interest in cultural properties in France and led to a full-scale movement of policies for the restoration of buildings into action.

Notre-Dame de Paris embodies the Gothic architectural style of pointed arches, ribbed vaulted ceilings, flying buttresses, high ceilings, and large interior spaces. The structural parts of this architectural style were shaped according to the structural needs of each phase during the construction. External flying buttresses and piers were introduced to support the lateral dynamics of the vaulted roof and masonry side walls. These structural supports also made it possible to create large openings to light up the interior spaces. The doors on the main western façade and transepts of the cathedral were decorated with many statues, but they were destroyed during the French Revolution. The subsequent restoration projects of the nineteenth century brought back those stone statues of the thirteenth century. As for the spire that rises above the nave in the centre of the cathedral, Viollet-le-Duc decided to rebuild it after it had been struck by lightning several times and had been removed by the end of the eighteenth century. He developed drawings for the spire and designed it more than 10 m higher than it had been in the past, using wood and lead. The spire was completed in 1859 as a decorative element, without any function such as a bell tower. Bronze statues of the four evangelists and twelve apostles of Jesus Christ were also added around the base of the spire on the roof. In addition to the drastic changes, the fact that the models for the statues were Viollet-le-Duc himself and the staff involved in the construction was later criticized. Moreover, the gutters on the lower part of the roof of the side walls were decorated with stone statues of gargouille. The restoration of Notre-Dame de Paris in the nineteenth century shows the thinking of the architect who tried to emphasize the development and function of the building as an architecture, rather than adhering to the restoration that faithfully rewinds the building to its past form according to historical documents.

In the twentieth century and after World War II, Notre-Dame de Paris was restored in stages. In 1965, the windows of the nave were covered with coloured glass replicating stained glasses from the twelfth and thirteenth centuries. The interior of the cathedral was extensively cleaned in 1982, and the north facade was restored and cleaned in the 1990s. The restoration of the pipe organ was carried out over two years from 1990.

Nevertheless, the state of preservation of this cathedral in the early 2000s was not good. Many of the decorative stone statues, including the gargouille and handrails, had deteriorated, the masonry of the flying buttresses had become structurally unstable, and the spire was held to the roof by a metal belt to prevent it from collapsing. Therefore, a restoration project was approved in 2013 based on the report of the Chief Architect of Historic Monuments (architecte en chef des monuments historiques),[9]

---

[9] An architect who specializes in historic monument restoration and who is nationally certified. All buildings designated as historic monuments in France have a responsible expert assigned to them for restoration. It is the French national mission to train professionals in the restoration of cultural properties. Training is given to young people already with architectural qualifications, at a specialized national institution, to become qualified architects of historic monuments (Architecte en Chef des Monuments Historiques) or professional civil servants who are involved in the preservation of streetscapes (Architectes des Bâtiments de France).

and the restoration of one of the flying buttresses on the south side and the spire on the roof began in 2018. Since the first task of this latest restoration project was to restore the spire, a large steel scaffolding was erected on the roof at the beginning of 2019. The 16 bronze statues that stood around the spire were lifted by crane on 12 April and were moved to southwestern France for restoration.[10] A few days later, the fire destroyed the spire and the roof.

8.4 Background of the Legislative Process of the Special Law

8.4.1 Immediate Response to Fire in April 2019

On 15 April 2019, smoke was seen rising from the roof of the cathedral, and the alarm went off at 18:20. When the alarm sounded again at 18:43, the source of the fire was identified, but the fire had already engulfed the entire roof structure.

The roof structure of Notre-Dame de Paris was made of wood and had covered the thin stone vaults 24 cm thick that served as the ceiling of the nave of the cathedral and the central intersection with the transept in cruciform when viewed from above, like a complex forest. The wood, which had been dry for centuries, was fast disappearing. It is also believed that the flames were further activated when the lead that covered the roof melted. More than 600 firefighters arrived on the scene by 19:00 and proceeded[11] with rescue work, but an hour later, the spire standing at the cross-roof intersection of the nave and transept collapsed, and the fire consumed the roof and spire. Amid the fire, the roof frameworks began to burn at 19:37 from the eastern part of the nave and collapsed completely by 20:00. As an emergency measure, the relics inside the cathedral, including the Crown of Thorns, were evacuated one by one while water was pumped from the Seine and sprayed on the fire. The destruction of the wooden roof structure, which was built in the thirteenth century, was an enormous loss from the perspective of cultural assets.

The steel scaffolding that had been used to repair the spire remained on the roof, deformed and welded by the high temperatures. At this point, the wood of the roofing structure had fallen through many parts of the stone vault and into the interior of the cathedral. The firefighters, using drones and water-dropping robots, were able to finish extinguishing the fire by 2:00 AM the next morning (Fig. 8.2).

From the day after the fire, robots were used for the initial debris disposal and site inspection. Fortunately, the three rose windows (stained glasses), the artifacts in the side aisles, the north and south towers, and the bell tower escaped the fire.

[10] These restorations were completed in September 2021, and they are displayed at the Cité de l'architecture in the Palais de Chaillot in Paris until the restoration of the roof of the cathedral will have been completed.

[11] Weise, Kai. and Joshi, Anie. Notre-Dame de Paris 2019 Fire: Notes on the response and early discussions on rehabilitation. September 2019. p. 1.

Fig. 8.2 Damage to the cathedral's roof after the disaster. © Philippe Villeneuve

Cultural heritage conservators were also involved in the evacuation of 1300 objects of religious and artistic importance. Among the wreckage that fell from the roof to the floor, a bronze weather vane attached to the top of the spire, which was 96 m above the ground, was found, which was considered miraculous.

8.4.2 Donation Premised on Cathedral Restoration and the Statement Made by the President of the Republic

As the fire department worked to prevent further disasters, the city of Paris and other French and foreign donors began to show up one after another with large-scale donations for the restoration of Notre-Dame de Paris, including the Pinault family of the Kering Group, which owns Gucci and Yves Saint-Laurent, the Arnault family of the LVMH Group, which owns Louis Vuitton and other luxury brands, French oil company Total, cosmetics company L' Oréal, and Disney in the United States.

French President Emmanuel Macron visited the disaster site on the evening of 16 April and announced to the media that the rebuilding of Notre-Dame de Paris would be a priority and that international experts would be brought in if necessary. The next day, he was more specific, stating that the cathedral would be rebuilt more beautifully than ever before and that he hoped to achieve this within 5 years, by the time of the 2024 Paris Olympics. The next day, Prime Minister Philippe announced that an international design competition would be held to determine whether the Nineteenth Century spire of Viollet-le-Duc would be restored or whether a new design that challenged the technology of the day would be selected. The series of statements made by the president and his ministers in the immediate aftermath of the fire baffled experts in the field of cultural heritage.

8.4.3 Discussions Leading to the Enactment and Promulgation of the Special Law

In the immediate aftermath of the fire, preparations were underway to create the conditions for the future preservation of the cathedral building and to protect the people involved from further damage. How, then, were the norms and policy frameworks developed to ensure that the future restoration of Notre-Dame de Paris would be carried out on a national basis?

On 29 July 2019, a new law was enacted consisting of 11 Articles.[12] It is the aforementioned "Law No. 2019-803 on the conservation and restoration of Notre-Dame de Paris and the establishment of a system for receiving donations for this purpose". This was published in the official bulletin of the French government the next day.[13]

This section observes the debates in the French parliament that led to the enactment and promulgation of the above-mentioned Special Law. This law, which consisted of

[12] Loi n° 2019-803 pour la conservation et la restauration de la cathédrale Notre-Dame de Paris et instituant une souscription nationale à cet effet.

[13] Journal Officiel n°0175 du 30 juillet 2019 texte n° 1. https://www.legifrance.gouv.fr/affichJO.do?idJO=JORFCONT000038843046 (accessed 2021.8.13).

9 Articles in the original draft, was intended to establish a National Fund to finance the restoration of Notre-Dame de Paris, which was made known by the President of the French Republic on the day after the fire. First, it was the Minister of Culture, Franck Reister, who submitted the draft of the law to the National Assembly on 24 April 2019, 9 days after the fire. On the same day, the French government pledged to expedite the process of passing the bill. However, the bill was not immediately passed by the two houses of parliament, and it was reviewed several times over three months, going back and forth between the two houses each time.

The French National Assembly held its first reading on 10 May and requested a clause that would create a special public corporation that would be fully commissioned to carry out conservation and restoration work at the Cathedral. This is what was eventually defined in Article 9 of the Special Law.

In the Senate, two committees considered this bill in parallel. On 30 April, the Finance Committee of the Senate took up the bill, and on 15 May, they appointed Albéric de Montgolfier as the rapporteur of the bill, and on 22 May of the following week, they presented and discussed the Montgolfier Report over the bill that had passed the National Assembly. On the other hand, the Committee on Culture, Education, and Communication Committee of the Senate appointed Senator Alain Schmitz as the rapporteur of the bill on 7 May. This committee also presented and discussed the Schmitz Report on 22 May and made amendments to the bill. The amendment demanded that the donations received to be used only for the limited purpose of preserving and restoring Notre-Dame de Paris and that the newly proposed Public Establishment should be placed under the supervision of the Ministry of Culture. On 27 May, the first reading of the bill was held in the Senate plenary session, and further amendments were proposed. The proposed amendments included the following: if building materials were to be used differently from those used before the fire, the person in charge of the work would make available to the public a study plan for restoration with changes; the National Council for Architectural and Cultural Heritage (Commission national du Patrimoine et de l'architecture, CNPA) should be regularly informed and consulted.

On 2 July, the National Assembly held another reading and passed the bill. In response to the bill, the Senate's Committee on Culture, Education, and Communication prepared a new Schmitz Report, based on which further amendments were proposed on 8 July. The proposed amendments included: the use of the donation would not include the normal maintenance and personnel costs of the cathedral; the work would be guaranteed to respect the authenticity and integrity of its outstanding universal value as a World Heritage site[14]; the work would be charged with restoring the cathedral to its last visible appearance before the fire[15]; and to ensure that the work is carried out for this nationally designated historic monument under the authority of the Chief Architect of Historic Monuments of Notre-Dame de Paris[16]; to ensure that the Scientific Committee of the Public Establishment is composed of qualified

[14] Repeated requests for amendments by the committee on 22 May 2019.

[15] Idem.

[16] Idem.

experts in architecture, medieval history and archaeology, and that its members are appointed among the cultural heritage conservators, the official architects of Buildings of France (ABF),[17] the Chief Architects of Historic Monuments and researchers from the National Centre for Scientific Research (CNRS), and that the Public Establishment would be dissolved once the intended work had been accomplished. In the further reading at the Senate plenary session on 10 July, these conditions were approved, and further amendments were made to specify, concerning the phrase "around the cathedral" in the proposal being too vague, the extent of the periphery, whether it includes the parvis, the public space surrounding the building, and the sidewalk on the south side of the Cité Island.

Then, on 16 July, the National Assembly held the last reading of the bill. Here, the bill was amended to read, "The restoration work will preserve the historical, artistic and architectural assets of the building". The Senate's frequent proposal that "the work shall restore the cathedral to its last visible appearance before the fire" was not accepted, and the Senate's insistence on this point was dropped from the final bill.

In this context, a law governing the restoration of the cathedral of Paris was passed three months after the fire that destroyed its spire and roof. The new law, promulgated on 29 July, suggested that the restoration work of Notre-Dame de Paris intended to preserve the historical, artistic, and architectural assets of the building i.e., to rebuild it in its harmonic context. The law also specifies special measures that exempt the contents of existing codes for the protection of cultural heritage, urban planning, the environment, and construction, although it was deliberated that those special measures should be kept to the minimum necessary to respect the existing laws.

8.5 Content and Characteristics of the Special Law

8.5.1 Inter-Sectoral Inclusiveness

Reading the text of the Special Law, we can see that out of all the 11 articles, Articles 1–7 are related to donations, and that the law emphasizes how to guarantee the budget and provide tax benefits to the donating organizations. Article 11 establishes a system for accepting donations from 16 April 2019 onward, and then Article 2 indicates that the use of the donations will be limited to funding the work for the conservation and restoration of Notre-Dame de Paris. It defines such work to be above all the preservation of the historical, artistic, and architectural assets of the building in question. Article 4 calls for donations to be made not only by individuals and companies but also by local governments. Article 5 clearly states that tax deductions are available to the donating organizations.

[17] It is the French national mission to train young people already with architectural qualifications, at a specialized national institution, to become qualified architects of historic monuments (Architecte en Chef des Monuments Historiques) or professional civil servants who are involved in the preservation of streetscapes (Architectes des Bâtiments de France, ABF).

In addition to the part about securing and consolidating the budget, the purpose of this law was to specify the institutions and responsibilities that could coordinate the various measures to achieve the goal of preserving and restoring the cathedral of Paris. Article 8 describes the obligation of a Public Establishment to manage funds and report, and Article 9 is an important clause that announces the setting up of such a Public Establishment. In other words, under this Special Law, a special national Public Establishment is established by decree, and it is publicly stated that the Public Establishment will be under the supervision of the Minister of Culture and will carry out its duties in cooperation with the Ministry of Culture. Following this, it is stated that a designated responsible authority would take up the work on the building, wavering Article 621-26-2 of the "Cultural Heritage Code" which states that "the owner of a registered or designated building shall be responsible for the work on the building, and the assignee of the land is also responsible, depending on the terms of the donation". In addition, Article 10 indicates that the National Council for Architectural and Cultural Heritage (CNPA) will be periodically informed and consulted on the progress of the construction work and related surveys, so it is a clear assumption that the Public Establishment should respect the scientific knowledge on cultural heritage and professional judgment on conservation and restoration.

The last Article 11 states that, as this is a Special Law, the above-mentioned Public Establishment can carry out archaeological surveys as an exception to the Cultural Heritage Code, that it is exempt from consulting the Regional Council of Architectural and Cultural Heritage of Île-de-France in the event of a disagreement with the ABF over a temporary structure. It also states in detail that public relations activities using historic monuments are prohibited according to the "Environmental Code," but that educational publicity and postings that do not have a commercial purpose but are intended to draw attention to the restoration work are permitted, and that exception can be made to road traffic, environmental and urban planning regulations according to the needs of the work. Article 11 can be fully considered a multidisciplinary legal text in that it provides exemptions to various provisions of the Cultural Heritage Code and on the other hand follows other codes which do not involve cultural property. The details are as the following.[18]

About archaeological investigations, "by the exemption in Article L.523-9 of the Cultural Heritage Code, the Public Establishment referred to in Article L.523-1 of the same Code is the entity in charge of carrying out preventive archaeological excavations required in connection with the restoration work."

About important cultural heritage urban landscapes, "by the exemption provided for in the second paragraph of Article L.632-2 of the Cultural Heritage Code, the administrative body that adjudicates appeals in cases of disagreement with the ABF concerning temporary buildings shall be exempt from consultation with the Regional Commission on Heritage and Architecture.

As for outdoor advertising at the site, "At the site of the restoration of the cathedral, the prohibition of all advertising falling under Article L.581-3-1° applies to buildings

---

[18] The following quotations, indicated by " ", are the author's translation from the original legal text.

designated or registered as historic monuments, as provided for in Article L.581-4-1° of the Environmental Code. However, advertisements that are not commercial and whose sole purpose is to arouse public interest in the work, to inform the public of the importance of the initial and ongoing training of the professionals who will carry out the work, and to list the donors, may be permitted under the conditions outlined in the first paragraph of Article L. 621-29-8 of the Cultural Heritage Code. This is a provision that allows for the construction of scaffolding necessary for the restoration of historic monuments and the provision of a space for posting on part of the scaffolding. Furthermore, "as an exemption from the 1° and 4° of Section I of Article L.581-8 of the Environmental Code and the local advertising regulations, advertising within the meaning of the second paragraph of 3° of Section I of the same may also be permitted on the fence of the work site. The first paragraph of the current 4° applies concerning all temporary or permanent installations located within the worksite site (Fig. 8.3)."

About the occupation and use of the site of the restoration work, "without prejudice to the application of the rules of access and use of the buildings assigned to religious activities, as provided in Article L.2124-31 of the General Code on the Property of Public Persons, with a view to the cultural, artistic and educational valorization of the work site, and without prejudice to the application of the building for the implementation of religious activities resulting from the Article 13 of the Law of 9 December 1905 on the Separation of Church and State as well as Article 5 of the

Fig. 8.3 The site team in front of the safety fences with an exhibition on the works of artisans. © C2RMF/Alexis Komenda

Law of 2 January 1907 on the Implementation of Public Religious Activities," "by the exemption in Article L.2122-1-1 of the General Code on the Property of Public Persons, the competent authorities may permit the occupation or use of public land for economic activities. To do so, they shall inform the applicant in advance that they will accept appropriate declarations of intent and shall decide on the authorization after presenting general conditions to the applicant." "By the exemption in the first paragraph of Article L.2125-1 of the aforementioned Code, the competent authority may grant a permit for the occupation of public land free of charge."

Furthermore, the last part of Article 11, section III, suggests the acceptance of additional matters, stating that bylaws may be established by Ordinance to specifically facilitate the implementation of this special national law. "Subject to the conditions outlined in Article 38 of the Constitution, the Government may, within a period of one year from the promulgation of this law, determine by Ordinance any matter relating to all the categories outlined in the provisions of this law which may facilitate the completion of the conservation and restoration of the Cathedral Notre-Dame de Paris as soon as possible and in a satisfactory and safe condition, and the improvement of its surroundings. This may be determined by Ordinance. This includes, among other things, projects that serve to accommodate the public during the restoration work itself and the work period, the installation of equipment, and transportation methods that allow for the supply of goods to the work site." "To the extent strictly necessary to achieve this objective, these Ordinances may provide for adaptations or exemptions to the rules on roads, environment, and urban planning, in particular about the consistency of planning documents, the issuance of the necessary authorizations, and the procedures and deadlines to be applied." "The Regulations by the Ordinance promulgated under this section shall respect the principles laid down in the 2004 Environmental Charter, and shall be without prejudice to France's compliance with its commitments in Europe and the international community, in particular in terms of the protection of health, safety, public health, nature, the environment, and the landscape, by intentions stated in Articles L.181-3, L.211-1 and L.511-1 of the Environmental Code. The government bill, if any, to be pursued must be submitted to the parliament within 3 months after the delivery of the Ordinance."

By Article 11 section III of this Special Law, an Ordinance was issued within one year of the law's entry into force. Ordinance No. 2020-1395 of 18 November 2020,[19] "exempting quarrying decisions justified by the need to restore Notre-Dame de Paris from the obligation to comply with local quarrying plans," was issued jointly by the Ministry of Ecological Transition and the Ministry of Culture, both of which are responsible for environmental policy and sustainable development.

Overall, it can be said that this Special Law is characterized by the following: first, it ensures that contributions from various sources are collected and secured in a single national implementing agency that transcends ministries and agencies;

---

[19] Ordonnance n° 2020-1395 du 18 novembre 2020 dispensant d'obligation de compatibilité avec les schémas régionaux des carrières les décisions d'exploitation de carrières justifiées par les besoins de la restauration de la cathédrale Notre-Dame de Paris.

second, it ensures budget execution with clear responsibilities and inter-sectoral comprehensiveness to oversee complex concurrent tasks.

8.5.2 Public Establishment Under the Special Law, in Charge of the Conservation and Restoration of Notre-Dame de Paris

In French law, a Public Establishment (établissement public) is a public law entity, distinct from a local government, that is granted legal personality and is tasked with managing public service activities within the scope of its limited purpose. Although it is said that the uniqueness of this legal category of administrative law, which used to be very strong and unique, is fading,[20] the "Public Establishment for the Conservation and Restoration of Notre-Dame de Paris" was established by the relevant decree by the "Special Law for the Conservation and Restoration of Notre-Dame de Paris" is, so to speak, an administrative Public Establishment. Its mission is to manage traditional public service activities, and its existence is governed by administrative legal norms.

The Public Establishment referred to herein was established by Decree No. 2019-1250 of 28 November 2019[21] on the Organization and Role of the Public Establishment for the Conservation and Restoration of Notre-Dame de Paris. It was published in the official bulletin the following day.[22] This Decree was based on the aforementioned Article 9 of the Law of 29 July and consists of 25 Articles. The Public Establishment was established on 1 December as an organization with independent authority. It is stated in the Decree that the President of the Public Establishment is appointed by a Presidential Decree and that the dissolution of the organization will also be ordered by a Decree. The purpose of this special public institution is limited to the conservation and restoration of the Gothic Notre-Dame de Paris, which was damaged by fire in April 2019. The scope of its authority is broad and inter-sectoral, and it has the task of coordinating and managing the entire work process.

General Jean-Louis Georgelin, former Chief of the French Defence Staff, was appointed by President Macron as the president of the Public Establishment. Even before his official appointment in December, General Georgelin had his office in the Elysée Palace as the future president of the Public Establishment. He was thus near the President of the Republic and could report directly to him. It is highly unusual for a military officer to lead a conservation organization for cultural properties. As

[20] Koichi Nakamura, Osamu Niikura and Gensei Imazeki (2012), *Dictionary of French Legal Terms*, 3rd edition, Sanseido, pp. 187–188 [in Japanese].

[21] Décret n° 2019-1250 du 28 novembre 2019 relatif à l'organisation et au fonctionnement de l'établissement public chargé de la conservation et de la restauration de la cathédrale Notre-Dame de Paris. Available at: https://www.legifrance.gouv.fr/affichTexte.do?cidTexte=JORFTEXT000039429294&categorieLien=id (accessed 2021.9.13).

[22] Journal officiel "Lois et Décrets" n°0277 du 29 novembre 2019. https://www.legifrance.gouv.fr/affichJO.do?idJO=JORFCONT000039428894 (accessed 2021.9.13).

for why the Presidential Decree appointed a retired general, it can be judged that the situation required a strong organization with firm leadership like the military, to carry out a big-scale national project in a state of emergency. President Macron's five-year restoration schedule seemed quite unrealistic, nevertheless, or perhaps because of this, the General was appointed to lead a complex and large-scale operation that would involve many parties from different sectors and contractors from different industries, confronting all the factors that could delay the work, even if it could not be entirely completed in five years. A general was appointed to the role, having experienced key positions in the French military, with leadership skills, and would follow orders of the head of state.

Philippe Jost, a technical officer from the Ecole Polytechnique who had served for many years as the financial officer of the French Armed Forces, was appointed as the right-hand man of President Georgelin as the special secretary-general of the Public Establishment. 40 people have been hired to work for the Public Establishment. The Public Establishment is responsible for all of these staff operations, as well as for the receipt and commercialization of all national funds received from domestic and foreign sources, the signing of contracts, the execution of budgets, the implementation of plans, and the sharing of information with local shopkeepers and residents.

By the Decree, various advisory committees have been established to advise the Public Establishment. The Steering Committee includes the Governor of the Ile-de-France region, the Mayor of Paris, the Archbishop of Paris, as well as former ministers of culture, foreign affairs, and other important public officials. The Scientific Committee is composed of 14 experts in the fields of historical buildings, archaeology, history, art history, engineering, and material science. In addition, there is a Donor Committee consisting of major donors. The organization has a staff member from the Ministry of Culture in charge of communication, public relations, and Mecenat, and an engineer from the Direction of Arts and Culture of the Ile-de-France Region in charge of field operations.

Although the Public Establishment is positioned under the supervision of the Ministry of Culture, it can enter into contracts with all public and private persons at the same time and is required to work closely with the City of Paris and the Archdiocese of Paris in particular. The necessary scientific and technical insights into the works, to be accomplished, are to be found within the framework of the "Cultural Heritage Code", but its characteristic is that it operates under special national law and as an independent body distinct from the Ministry of Culture.

In the past, Notre-Dame de Paris has never needed such extensive repairs as this current one. In the Nineteenth Century, the spire was rebuilt, and in recent years, the spire on the roof had been half restored to improve its stability and design condition. In addition, the cleaning of the gargouille, which serves as a flume, the removal of soot from the walls throughout the building, and various other design repairs are carried out regularly. The most recent restoration of the spire was studied and planned by the Chief Architect and was being executed, including the construction of scaffolding over the roof. Then, in the aftermath of the 2019 fire, an unprecedented need arose for complex operations, including structural safety measures for the entire monument, not just for the missing upper part, and the need to implement a budget that far exceeded the existing framework under the Ministry of Culture. It can be said that a strong driving force beyond the existing organization became necessary to lead these activities in an emergency.

8.5.3 Duties and Challenges of the Public Establishment in Charge of the Conservation and Restoration of Notre-Dame de Paris

On 22 January 2020, shortly after the founding of the Public Establishment for the Conservation and Restoration of Notre-Dame de Paris, the Committee for Culture, Education and Communication of the French Senate held a public hearing with General Georgelin, its president. He stated that a detailed post-fire assessment would be carried out on the entire building, not just the missing part above the cathedral and that the restoration plan would be completed on that basis.[23] The restoration plan for Notre-Dame de Paris would be submitted to the National Council for Architecture and Cultural Heritage (CNPA) for deliberation, and after its approval, the operation was expected to start in 2021.[24]

The first major practical task of this Public Establishment was to remove the steel scaffolding that had been welded by flames and smoke from the roof. The scaffolding, which had been in place before the fire for the restoration of the spire, was not structurally dependent on the medieval wooden roofing system, so it did not fall off when the entire roof went up in flames. If it had fallen, it would have caused even more damage. In addition to the removal of the welded scaffolding, the reinforcement of the entire building, which was structurally unstable due to the loss of equilibrium normally supported by the gravity of the roof tiles, was a priority safety issue. In addition, structural, architectural, and archaeological investigations were to be conducted to develop and implement a restoration plan, and to work with the city of Paris on the improvement of the environment around the cathedral. Another important task was to organize training for the restoration workers and to hold Scientific Committee meetings to check the progress of the work and to stimulate discussion and advice that would be key to the future direction of the work. All activities are documented in an annual report, submitted to the Steering Committee, and made available to the public through the Ministry of Culture.

---

[23] Audition du général Jean-Louis Georgelin, président de l'Établissement public chargé de la conservation et de la restauration de la cathédrale Notre-Dame de Paris, 22 janvier 2020. http://videos.senat.fr/Datas/senat/portail/video.1492984_5e2637517a077.patrimoine---audition-du-general-jean-louis-georgelin-president-de-letablissement-public-charge-de (accessed 2021.9.12).

[24] Despite some lockdown periods due to COVID-19, restoration phase was ready to begin in the latter half of 2021, after completion of cleaning, consolidation and safety clearance of the entire damaged site.

Immediately after the fire, the vaulted ceiling was covered to protect it from rainwater, using cordists'[25] techniques, but the roof intersection around the former spire had to remain uncovered until the dissolving steel scaffolding was safely removed. Once the roof area was stabilized and secured, the entire area could be covered with white sheets. The metal tip of the burnt-down spire, which had been buried in the stone vault since the fire, was also rescued and a damage assessment started.

Urgent structural reinforcement of the building started immediately after the fire. It is visually clear that the fire destroyed the wooden roof structure and the spire, and it is also true that wood and molten lead fell through the stone vault at the bottom of the roof, but the stone vault kept the fire from entering the cathedral. Therefore, investigations have been made on the impact of the fire on the stone vault of the ceiling, which served as a firewall, and on the damage to the stone pillars and masonry structure of the interior. The condition of the mortar that bonded the vault and the stones together was also vulnerable due to the direct exposure to rain, wind, heat, and cold waves since the fire. Besides recovery of the design, it was also and foremost a matter of ensuring the structural strength of the building. Even now that the structural strengthening work has been completed, a detailed architectural analysis of the vulnerability of the stone vault and a diagnosis of its state of preservation is underway. The stone vault is covered with fiberglass bundles to prevent collapse. Restoration work in Notre-Dame de Paris over the past few decades has been mostly architectural in design. The damage caused by the fire is much larger and more complex than that, and it is an opportunity to analyze and review the entire masonry structure from the twelfth and thirteenth centuries. The damaged interior columns were temporarily reinforced with steel cables tied together with thick wood panels. In the long run, the challenge will be how to ensure adequate maintenance to counteract the vulnerability of the monument and strengthen its resilience.

The loss of the roof structure and the possibility of damage to the vault covering the nave threatened to seriously undermine the structural stability of the entire building. Flying buttresses protruding from the outside of the building support the high stone pillars of the side walls from the side, but with the absence of the part that connected them as the weight from the top, there is a risk that the side walls will open outward structurally due to the pressure exerted on the stone pillars of the side walls, which have been deteriorated by the fire. It should be mentioned here that in the Middle Ages when Notre-Dame de Paris was built, the roof was built before the vaulted ceiling to ensure the overall structural rationality of the roof due to the vertical load is exerted on the side walls from above. Therefore, a characteristic and important part of Gothic church architecture is the flying buttresses that support the side walls from the outside. As a precautionary measure to hold the side walls firmly in place, wooden frames were installed on the inside of the arches of all the buttresses at an early stage to balance the forces acting laterally. This work of structural function

[25] A technician uses a rope to move to an area that is normally difficult to reach. They take pictures of damaged areas that are normally inaccessible and check the durability of the stones. They are stationed almost everywhere on the Notre-Dame de Paris site, and researchers and architects work with them to determine the most appropriate architectural measures.

Fig. 8.4 Ensuring security upon adjustment of the centrings supporting the buttresses. © C2RMF/Alexis Komenda

has been easily visible to Parisians from the outside even after the area around the cathedral was fenced off as a restoration site. The gable at the bottom of the roof, which remained unsupported as long as the roof was absent, was also reinforced with wood to prevent further damage. The work of fixing the fragile parts of the masonry with wooden frames can be seen in many places, which was carried out in coordination with a survey on the state of conservation of stones, crane operation, and carpentry work (Figs. 8.4 and 8.5).

The apse, side aisles, and stained-glass windows were unscathed by the roof fire. Also, the great pipe organ, which has been the voice of Notre-Dame de Paris since 1733, miraculously escaped the fire and destruction. However, as the vault collapsed into the interior in places, the interior of the cathedral was filled with dust and lead, and the pipe organ was exposed to so much water and dust. It was therefore dismantled in August 2020 and is in the process of being restored to its original state by removing the dust from its 8000 pipes of various sizes. The stained glass in the upper windows was temporarily removed to protect it from the risk of vibration at the work site, and the openings were sealed (Fig. 8.6).

In September 2021, less than two years and a half after the fire, halfway through the targeted five-year recovery period, the entire process of securing and structurally reinforcing Notre-Dame de Paris after the disaster was completed. At this point, it became possible to proceed to the stage of the so-called restoration and reconstruction work. There is no longer any danger of the side walls opening up or of hazardous

Fig. 8.5 Chevet of the cathedral undergoing work. © C2RMF/Alexis Komenda

Fig. 8.6 The great organ of Notre-Dame de Paris has been taken down for cleaning and restoration, to preserve the acoustics and soundscapes of the cathedral. © Benjamin Mouton

materials falling from the burnt roof. Currently, a forest of new metal scaffolding is being erected not only on the exterior of the cathedral but also on the interior walls and along the pillars, all the way from the floor to the height of 27 m of the vaulted ceiling.[26] The installation of the scaffolding inside the cathedral was a major work that took the whole summer of 2021 to complete. This new scaffolding serves as the foundation and pathway for future restoration work and will be dismantled after all the restoration work is completed.

In the work of surveying, reinforcing, and restoring cultural assets, each engineer and craftsman who is familiar with historical buildings constructed with traditional methods is an indispensable resource.

In addition, educational and public relations activities, such as talks and work demonstrations by engineers and craftsmen for the general public, are also actively carried out as a mission of the Public Establishment. Public activities are not only carried out through the Internet i.e. homepages and social networking sites, and publications, but also on occasions such as the annual "Journées européennes du Patrimoine" (Days of Cultural Heritage) in September, which provide opportunities for direct interaction between the operators and craftsmen and the general public. In fact, during the "Heritage Days" weekend of 2021, which began on 18 September, more than 20,000 visitors had the opportunity to meet carpenters, scaffolders, pre-roofing cover sheeting contractors, caulkers, coppersmiths, mural, statue, and metal restorers, architects, and archaeologists in the hands-on ateliers set up in the Cathedral Square, and learn about their roles and work (Fig. 8.7).

In October 2021, following the completion of the safety and structural reinforcement of Notre-Dame de Paris, the cleaning of the dust and dirt covering the entire interior of the cathedral began, which took seven months, from top to bottom, as it was intended to improve the environment for the next stage of restoration work and reduce lead damage. The Public Establishment now called for bids for the contracted projects from specialized companies and skilled craftsmen who would be responsible for the next phase of restoration, which is finally the restoration of the spire and roof, and the detailed parts inside the cathedral. It has already been decided that the roof structure will be made of wood and lead, and new scaffolding will be required. The project leaders were identified in early 2022,[27] to be able to initiate the operations.

In France, professional contractors, including artisans, who can handle the hands-on work of restoring historical monuments are involved in many restoration projects every year, but rarely have they experienced repairs on a scale exceeding 100,000 euros.[28] The situation in France, where major companies are rarely involved in the

[26] TF1. Notre-Dame presque hors de danger. 2021.9.16. Available at: https://www.tf1.fr/tf1/jt-20h/videos/notre-dame-presque-hors-de-danger-nos-images-exclusives-55992061.html?fbclid=IwAR20eu412YMtG9TIkialxuxeRm2L59Fd4bKsrL22LCPFf1Ke48TjGetbzhA (accessed 2021.9.23).

[27] Ouest France. 2021.11.5. Notre-Dame de Paris. L'appel à la mobilisation des entreprises pour la restauration. Available at: https://www.ouest-france.fr/faits-divers/incendie/incendie-de-notre-dame-de-paris/notre-dame-de-paris-l-appel-a-la-mobilisation-des-entreprises-pour-la-restauration-08f5e1aa-3ccd-11ec-8bc6-eb6b26766f3c (accessed 2021.11.13).

[28] Bandarin, Francesco. New law regarding Notre-Dame says restoration must preserve its 'historic, artistic and architectural interest'. *The Art Newspaper*. 2019.8.2.

Fig. 8.7 A carpenter on-site. © Benjamin Mouton

repair of cultural properties, is different from the situation in Japan, where the Association for the Conservation of Cultural Properties provides design supervision and general contractors carry out the construction. On the other hand, it seems that at Notre-Dame de Paris many major companies are hired for the current operations, such as scaffolding management and crane operation, which are not directly involved in the design. In this way, it is certain that a great variety of work of various qualities would be conducted in parallel, including both delicate surveys toward cultural property conservation measures and comprehensive large-scale works, and that skilled management is required to encompass this diversity. In light of the above, it becomes clear why it was necessary to establish a Public Establishment under a Special Law, an organization of an unusual scale and position regarding cultural properties, as part of the national post-disaster response.

8.5.4 Decision-Making and Leadership in the Conservation and Restoration of Notre-Dame de Paris

Looking back at President Emmanuel Macron's declaration to the French people and the world in the aftermath of the fire in April 2019, it is possible to focus on two important points. The first is about the future of Notre-Dame de Paris. Immediately after the fire, President Macron hinted that he would consider accepting new contemporary architectural expressions to rebuild the spire more beautifully than ever before. The second is the time frame for recovery, which would be accomplished within five years, until the spring of 2024. How these initial visions for reconstruction are being followed will be discussed here.

First, in the future vision and restoration plan for Notre-Dame de Paris, the French Ministry of Culture maintains a role in the approval and execution of the restoration plan by the Code of Cultural Heritage. Philippe Villeneuve, the Chief Architect of the Historic Monuments for Notre-Dame de Paris, was present for the restoration of the spire, which had begun before the fire, and after the fire, he directed all architectural emergency responses and reinforcement measures until the creation of the Public Establishment. The Ministry of Culture's position on the future of the cathedral of Paris will be maintained specifically through this Chief Architect and the Regional Direction for Arts and Culture. On the other hand, General Georgelin required Villeneuve to reserve his plans for the cathedral,[29] until the final decision is made by President Macron on the issue of the rebuilding of the spire, which has attracted the most attention from the domestic and international media. In this scene, it could be observed that the public institution entrusted with the restoration of the cathedral was willing to strictly follow the views of the head of state, even if it meant disagreeing with the Ministry of Culture on this point. Although the Public Establishment is under the supervision of the Ministry of Culture, the president of the organization himself has taken a position that could be described as directly subordinate to the President of the Republic, suggesting that the head of state is in a position to directly or indirectly control the entire process.

Although no formal architectural competition had been called for since the announcement by the President and the Prime Minister immediately after the fire, all sorts of innovative ideas, such as rooftop pools, deck roofs with plants, glass spires, etc., had been received from all over the world, and these ideas had been circulated through the media. According to an online poll conducted by Odoxa-Dentu Consulting between 7 and 9 May, a few weeks after the fire, 55 percent of a French public of 1003 individuals over the age of 18 wanted the spire design to remain the

[29] Audition du général Jean-Louis Georgelin, président de l'Établissement public chargé de la conservation et de la restauration de la cathédrale Notre-Dame de Paris, 22 janvier 2020. He urged the agreement of Senator Leroux, Chairman of the CNPA, who was present at the time of his reply.

same as it was before the fire.[30] From the viewpoint of those for cultural heritage preservation, this was only a little more than half of the population. In this context, Jean Nouvel, one of the most renowned contemporary architects representing France and leading the world of architecture on an international level, said in an interview, "Notre-Dame de Paris must be Gothic to the fullest extent".[31] It is possible that the prominent architect Nouvel's view had an impact on public opinion ever since.

The future of Notre-Dame de Paris, which had been left vague and unspecified in the Special Law for the Conservation and Restoration of Notre-Dame de Paris, was put into definite perspective when President Macron announced on 9 July 2020, a year and three months after the fire, that, unlike the policy announced immediately after the fire, he would restore Notre-Dame de Paris to its "last visible appearance before the fire," that is, to its appearance in the latter half of the nineteenth century. Here, it was the end of the debate on the design of the spire, as the government expressed its intention to restore the lost spire faithfully to the design of Viollet-le-Duc in 1859. It was also decided that oak would be used for the roofing of the cathedral and that lead would be used for the roofing material as before. In the end, it was decided to follow the aforementioned working guidelines for the implementation of the World Heritage Convention, as well as international principles for the conservation of cultural properties, such as the Venice Charter and the Nara Document, which were endorsed by UNESCO and ICOMOS (International Council on Monuments and Sites). It was decided to follow a technique that respects the authenticity of cultural properties.

Why was the initial presidential vision on design overturned? It may be pointed out that this had to do with another important point: the time frame for reconstruction. The National Council on the Architectural and Cultural Heritage (CNPA) was convened on 9 July 2020. The most conservative among three proposals presented, which was to restore the building to its "last visible appearance before the fire," i.e., to its appearance in the second half of the nineteenth century which burned, was unanimously approved by the Council.[32] Then Villeneuve submitted a 3000 page-long report to the President of the Republic. The presidential palace announced that President Macron trusted the experts' opinion and approved the restoration plan presented by the Chief Architect of Historical Monuments in charge of Notre-Dame de Paris. It was reported[33] that the President chose to clarify the direction of the project quickly,

---

[30] Franceinfo. Notre-Dame de Paris: les Français majoritairement opposés à une loi d'exception pour accélérer la reconstruction, selon un sondage. 2019.5.19. https://www.francetvinfo.fr/culture/arts-expos/architecture/notre-dame-de-paris-les-francais-majoritairement-opposes-a-une-loi-d-exception-pour-accelerer-la-reconstruction-selon-un-sondage_3435847.html (accessed 2021.9.14).

[31] Europe 1. Reconstruction de Notre-Dame: pour Jean Nouvel, "il faut être plus gothique que jamais". May 26, 2019. https://www.youtube.com/watch?v=fmP3k8edkX8 (accessed 2021.9.14).

[32] French Ministry of Culture website "Notre-Dame de Paris: Les travaux de sécurisation et de consolidation". https://notre-dame-de-paris.culture.gouv.fr/fr/travaux-securisation-et-consolidation (accessed 2021.9.14), and according to Benjamin Mouton, former Chief Architect of Notre-Dame de Paris and member of the Academic Committee of the Public Establishment (2021.7.28 interview by the author).

[33] Euronews. Notre-Dame cathedral: Spire to be rebuilt exactly as it was, Macron decides. 2020.7.10. https://www.euronews.com/2020/07/10/notre-dame-cathedral-spire-to-be-rebuilt-exactly-as-it-was-macron-decides (accessed 2021.8.24).

not wanting to delay or halt the ongoing work on-site, and not wanting to delay the entire project. In other words, it can be inferred that the President's top priority was to ensure that the recovery of the cathedral would be completed in 2024 and that he would have to cycle through the work to get it done in time.

It can be seen here that President Macron's time priorities coincided with the experts' opinions and detailed plans on how to restore the monument and its future. In addition to prioritizing the political goal of adhering to the schedule, the President may have understood the power of restoration that is based on historical documents, which is faithful and sincere to cultural heritage values, and that the resilient appearance of a prominent monument that transcends time and space exerts a universal impression and impact on people. The leadership for the recovery of Notre-Dame de Paris rests with the President of the Republic, but the institutional framework which respects scientific and technical perspectives supports a governance system that allows experts to mobilize and influence strong leadership.

The envisaged time frame is to open the cathedral to the public in April 2024 with a mass of thanksgiving singing *Te Deum*, before the Paris Olympics, five years after the fire, and to return the church to its function as a living place of prayer.[34] This work plan has not been changed even after the temporary suspension of work due to the COVID-19 pandemic in 2020. The removal of the scaffolding on the roof, which was an urgent issue at the beginning, was completed on schedule even after the COVID-19 calamities. Operations are now moving forward at a rapid pace, to symbolically return the cathedral of Paris from the site of its restoration to a place of prayer for the people. To prevent the spread of the new coronavirus infection, an Ordinance stipulates measures regarding delayed construction to prioritize the health of the people in the event of the pandemic, namely the Ordinance on the Extension of Deadlines during the Health Crisis Period and the Adaptation of Procedures during the Same Period,[35] which was issued a week after the first lockdown from 17 March 2020, which lasted for two months. At the Notre-Dame de Paris site, the removal of metal scaffolding, including 40,000 pieces that had been burnt and welded on the roof, was interrupted from 16 March. Then, the work resumed on 4 May after safety measures were taken for the workers. The progress of the work has been reported to the public through the website, images, and videos.

On the other hand, the development of the squares, parks, streets, and banks of the Seine around the cathedral, apart from the restoration work, is expected to undergo a different renewal in a way that is appropriate for Parisians and visitors of today. A plan for the development of the area would be drawn up within two years, and the actual development work would begin after the Paris Olympics in 2024.

---

[34] Franceinfo: Notre-Dame de Paris: en 2024, la cathédrale sera "plus lumineuse", assure le recteur, qui s'attend à devoir "réguler" les visiteurs. 2021.4.15. https://www.francetvinfo.fr/culture/patrimoine/incendie-de-notre-dame-de-paris/notre-dame-de-paris-en-2024-la-cathedrale-sera-plus-lumineuse-assure-le-recteur-qui-s-attend-a-devoir-reguler-les-visiteurs_4373105.amp (accessed 2021.9.13).

[35] Ordonnance n° 2020-306 du 25 mars 2020 relative à la prorogation des délais échus pendant la période d'urgence sanitaire et à l'adaptation des procédures pendant cette même période.

Strong leadership and accountable responsibility are effective in complying with time constraints in implementing plans through on-site operations. Clarification of the location of leadership is also important for budget execution. As of April 2021, the total amount of contributions pledged to the National Fund to finance the restoration of Notre-Dame de Paris under the Special Law amounted to 833 million euros, including contributions pledged by 338 thousand individuals. Of this amount, 165 billion euros were already used by the Public Establishment for various work contracts and operating expenses.[36] Donors who have pledged large sums of money need to be explained and understand what is a scientifically and technically necessary process. Also, the responsible organization for the works must balance the three directions of structural reinforcement of the damaged cathedral, detailed on-site investigation, and implementation of plans. It can be said that the concentration of duties and responsibilities in a special Public Establishment, entrusted with a national administration, allows the eyes of the French people, who hope for the revival of Notre-Dame de Paris in their hearts, to monitor the actual execution of the budget. It is important to note that leadership here is based on a firm emphasis on scientific research and serious respect for the views of experts. In addition to organizational clarity, such accountable leadership is enabled by the emergency response of high quality and professionalism assured based on scientific evidence.

8.6 Conclusion

This paper examined the process of policy measures that have been taken in the post-disaster situation since the fire incident that affected Notre-Dame de Paris in April 2019. The entire process has been and will continue to be, extremely complex with many parties involved. There is a high degree of political pressure and commitment on the part of the French government to show both nationally and internationally that the cathedral in Paris is on the road to recovery, and that progress is being made on various fronts.

The restoration of Notre-Dame de Paris has three major challenges: accurate analysis of the site, implementation of the restoration plan, and the duration of the process. Decisions on these issues require multi-sectoral cooperation and speed beyond the framework of the existing Cultural Heritage Code, which is why a Special Law was established. It is no exaggeration to say that the whole world is watching how the Public Establishment, which is based on a Special Law, will continue to be responsible for decision-making and enforcement. It should also be reiterated that the ongoing restoration work will have to meet the requirements of authenticity under the international norm, the World Heritage Convention and that the respected expertise supports such orientation.

[36] La Chaîne Info. Notre-Dame de Paris: faut-il vraiment 833 millions d'euros pour restaurer la cathédrale? 2021.4.15. https://www.lci.fr/societe/notre-dame-de-paris-restauration-faut-il-vraiment-833-millions-d-euros-pour-restaurer-la-cathedrale-2183502.html (accessed 2021.9.14).

In any case, the Special Law for the Conservation and Restoration of Notre-Dame de Paris, formulated as a policy instrument, and the Public Establishment specially created under it; such an entity is expected to meet the norms and requirements to be able to orchestrate the complex process. The operational strength lies in the fact that a public institution with a specially given mandate puts policy decisions into practice and steadily uses the budget to implement projects. In the context of disaster and recovery, this Special Law may be positioned as an instructive example of post-disaster governance and institutional measures that can be used to comprehensively consider who should be entrusted with what tasks and how to respond effectively. The significance of Special Laws and the setting up of a Public Establishment in post-disaster emergencies may include speed, decision-making power, clarification of the consensus-building process, and accountability. Since some exemptions from the cultural property protection system secured by the existing "Cultural Heritage Code" may be necessary for emergencies, the legitimization of specific measures into a legal text also ensured accountability for exemptions.

In the post-disaster recovery process, this type of Special Law may have a vital implementation power that goes far beyond the vertical division of labor among ministries and agencies, in that it clarifies where responsibility lies for the rapid leadership of complex operations. Doesn't it embody the legal responsibility to improve collaboration among all sectors, not allow for ambiguity in organizational roles and responsibilities, and publicly share a clear chain of command? Furthermore, the prompt legislative function of the parliament demonstrated an example of how post-disaster policy leadership can be achieved promptly. It was the Minister of Culture, Franck Reister, who submitted the bill to the National Assembly on 24 April 2019, 9 days after the fire. However, it was not at the discretion of the Minister of Culture alone to compile the bill, including specific details related to the budget, so quickly. This was swift legislation that would not have been possible without the President of the Republic himself exercising direct and strong leadership over his entire cabinet.

More than half of the Special Law emphasizes the issue of how to provide tax incentives to donor organizations and how to ensure that donations are not only announced but paid. The legislative significance of a Special Law in times of emergency that makes it possible to secure and execute budgets beyond the scope of individual ministries and agencies is not limited to cultural heritage issues. A strong organization to solve the problems of fund sharing, budget execution, and the ability to carry out large-scale operations can embody responsible leadership by being established on a legal basis, rather than on an ad hoc basis. To move large-scale public activities under clear leadership in times of emergency, it would be no exaggeration to say that strengthening the legislative functions that make this possible is the most pressing issue for consideration, even at normal times.

References

Audition du général Jean-Louis Georgelin, président de l'Établissement public chargé de la conservation et de la restauration de la cathédrale Notre-Dame de Paris, 22 janvier 2020. Accessed September 12, 2014, http://videos.senat.fr/Datas/senat/portail/video.1492984_5e2637517a077.patrimoine---audition-du-general-jean-louis-georgelin-president-de-letablissement-public-charge-de

Bandarin, F. (2019, August 2). New law regarding Notre Dame says restoration must preserve its 'historic, artistic and architectural interest. *The Art Newspaper.*

Décret n° 2019-1250 du 28 novembre 2019 relatif à l'organisation et au fonctionnement de l'établissement public chargé de la conservation et de la restauration de la cathédrale Notre-Dame de Paris. Accessed September 13, 2021, https://www.legifrance.gouv.fr/affichTexte.do?cidTexte=JORFTEXT000039429294&categorieLien=id

Euronews. (2020, July 10). Notre Dame cathedral: Spire to be rebuilt exactly as it was, Macron decides. Accessed August 24, 2021, https://www.euronews.com/2020/07/10/notre-dame-cathedral-spire-to-be-rebuilt-exactly-as-it-was-macron-decides

Europe 1. (2019, May 26). Reconstruction de Notre-Dame: pour Jean Nouvel, "il faut être plus gothique que jamais". Accessed September 14, 2021, https://www.youtube.com/watch?v=fmP3k8edkX8

Franceinfo. (2019, May 19). Notre-Dame de Paris: les Français majoritairement opposés à une loi d'exception pour accélérer la reconstruction, selon un sondage. Accessed September 14, 2021, https://www.francetvinfo.fr/culture/arts-expos/architecture/notre-dame-de-paris-les-francais-majoritairement-opposes-a-une-loi-d-exception-pour-accelerer-la-reconstruction-selon-un-sondage_3435847.html

Franceinfo. (2021, April 15) Notre-Dame de Paris: en 2024, la cathédrale sera "plus lumineuse", assure le recteur, qui s'attend à devoir "réguler" les visiteurs. Accessed September 13, 2021, https://www.francetvinfo.fr/culture/patrimoine/incendie-de-notre-dame-de-paris/notre-dame-de-paris-en-2024-la-cathedrale-sera-plus-lumineuse-assure-le-recteur-qui-s-attend-a-devoir-reguler-les-visiteurs_4373105.amp

French Senate. Restauration et conservation de la cathédrale Notre-Dame de Paris. Accessed August 25, 2021, https://www.senat.fr/espace_presse/actualites/201905/restauration_et_conservation_de_la_cathedrale_notre_dame_de_paris.html

Journal Officiel n°0175 du 30 juillet 2019 texte n° 1. Accessed August 13, 2021, https://www.legifrance.gouv.fr/affichJO.do?idJO=JORFCONT000038843046

Journal officiel "Lois et Décrets" n°0277 du 26 novembre 2019. Accessed August 13, 2021, https://www.legifrance.gouv.fr/affichJO.do?idJO=JORFCONT000039428894

La Chaîne Info. (2021, April 15). Notre-Dame de Paris: faut-il vraiment 833 millions d'euros pour restaurer la cathédrale? Accessed September 14, 2021, https://www.lci.fr/societe/notre-dame-de-paris-restauration-faut-il-vraiment-833-millions-d-euros-pour-restaurer-la-cathedrale-2183502.html

Loi n° 2019-803 pour la conservation et la restauration de la cathédrale Notre-Dame de Paris et instituant une souscription nationale à cet effet. Accessed September 14, 2021, https://www.legifrance.gouv.fr/affichTexte.do?cidTexte=JORFTEXT000038843049&categorieLien=id

Ministère de la Culture. Notre-Dame de Paris: les travaux de sécurisation et de consolidation. Accessed September 14, 2021, https://notre-dame-de-paris.culture.gouv.fr/fr/travaux-securisation-et-consolidation

Nakamura, K., Niikura, O., Imazeki, G. (Eds.). (2012). *Dictionary of French Legal Terms*, 3rd edn. Sanseido, pp. 187–188. [in Japanese]

TF1. (2021, September 16). Notre-Dame Presque hors de danger. Accessed September 23, 2021, https://www.tf1.fr/tf1/jt-20h/videos/notre-dame-presque-hors-de-danger-nos-images-exclusives-55992061.html?fbclid=IwAR20eu412YMtG9TIkialxuxeRm2L59Fd4bKsrL22LCPFf1Ke48TjGetbzhA

Web exhibition supervised by Toshiyuki Kono (University of Kyushu) and ICOMOS France. Notre-Dame de Paris Cathedral and Shuri-jo Castle: Reconstruct and Restore their Cultural Value Beyond the Fire 2019. Accessed April 29, 2022, https://www.notredame-shurijo.com

Weise, K., Joshi, A. (2019, September). *Notre Dame de Paris 2019 fire: notes on the response and early discussions on rehabilitation.*

Junko Okahashi is currently an associate professor in international cultural cooperation at the University of the Sacred Heart, Tokyo, Japan. She holds a Ph.D. in Arts and Sciences (Area Studies) from the University of Tokyo. As a staff member and program specialist of UNESCO from 2002 to 2011, she assisted states parties to the Convention concerning the Protection of the World Cultural and Natural Heritage. She continued to advocate for the implementation of their cultural heritage policies, in particular through formulating World Heritage site management plans in Asia and activating the process of World Heritage periodic reporting in Africa. Her research quest in cultural heritage policies and the theory/philosophy of conservation is sought through a combination of document-based work and fieldwork. She investigates the correlation and compatibility between multilateral governance of international norms related to cultural heritage (World Heritage, import and export of cultural properties, intangible cultural heritage, cultural diversity, historic urban landscapes) and case-specific on-site conditions, in an attempt to harmonize local needs and international orientations.

Part III
Governance through the Building of Local Systems in Post-trauma Situations

Chapter 9
Introduction

Toshiyuki Kono

The existing international legal framework is insufficient to govern the cultural heritage in the post-traumatic context, and more case studies are needed. However, case studies would not provide valuable lessons unless there is no coordination among the studies. Independent and uncoordinated case studies would not be more than fragmented pieces of information. There was no case study from a comparative legal perspective regarding the governance of cultural heritage in post-traumatic situations. National legal systems and practices for recovering cultural heritage are still developing. What is necessary under such current circumstances is firstly to create a local system to cope with post-traumatic situations. ICOMOS joined forces with ICCROM to establish a joint project that could harness both bodies' experience and expertise to clarify recovery and reconstruction issues and provide insights that could improve guidance. In Kumamoto, despite the lack of adequate legal mechanisms, some owners recovered their historic buildings with the support of experts in their networks. Human networks before traumatic events seem to play a decisive role in recovery. In the cases of the State Hall of Shuri-jô Castle in Okinawa, Japan, and Wangduephodrang dzong in Bhutan, destroyed by fire in 2019 and 2012, respectively, the authorities decided to reconstruct them as they were before the fire due to their cultural significance. However, the lost buildings were not legally protected heritage buildings. After the fire of Notre-Dame Cathedral in Paris and Shuri-jô Castle in Okinawa, social reactions have been pretty similar despite differences between the two buildings. This phenomenon suggests we reconsider the role of communities in recovering cultural heritage and societies.

Toshiyuki Kono Distinguished professor, Kyushu University, Japan. Toshiyuki Kono was born in Osaka, Japan, in 1958. After graduating from the Faculty of Law, Kyoto University, he went on to obtain his LL.M. from the Graduate School of Law, Kyoto University. He is a specialist

T. Kono (✉)
Kyushu University, Fukuoka, Japan
e-mail: konoto@law.kyushu-u.ac.jp

T. Kono and J. Okahashi (eds.), *Post-Trauma and the Recovery Governance of Cultural Heritage*, https://doi.org/10.1007/978-981-19-6041-3_9

in private international law, international civil procedure law, and international cultural heritage law. He was a member of UNESCO's Expert Groups for the drafting of the Convention for the Safeguarding of the Intangible Cultural Heritage (2003) and the Convention on the Protection and Promotion of the Diversity of Cultural Expressions (2005). He was appointed as a member of the Executive Committee of the International Council on Monuments and Sites (ICOMOS) in 2011. After working as vice president, he was elected as the 8th president of ICOMOS in 2017. As the former president, he continues as an honorary president of ICOMOS. He is the series editor of Springer's book series Perspectives in Law, Business and Innovation.

Chapter 10
The ICOMOS-ICCROM Studies Project on Post-disaster Recovery and Reconstruction Situations

Loughlin Kealy and Trevor H. J. Marchand

Abstract The instinct to rebuild and to recover what was lost is arguably a universal human reaction to the destruction of home and habitat. In recent decades, the rapid dissemination of information about the destruction of culturally significant environments and artefacts, both through human action and natural events, has brought renewed focus to the work of international bodies devoted to the protection of heritage. The scale and intensity of destruction has prompted serious rethinking about recovery, reconstruction and the meanings of authenticity in different contexts. ICOMOS recognised that the complexities attending ideas of reconstruction had to be set against the urgent need to introduce guidance for dealing with post-trauma recovery and reconstruction. In 2018, the World Heritage Committee formally directed the attention of its advisory bodies towards examining case studies. In response, ICOMOS joined forces with ICCROM to establish a joint project that could harness the experience and expertise of both bodies in order to clarify issues of recovery and reconstruction and provide insights that could improve guidance.

Keywords ICOMOS-ICCROM project · Case-study analysis · Post-trauma reconstruction

10.1 Introduction

The instinct to rebuild and to recover what was lost is arguably a universal human reaction to the destruction of home and habitat. That reaction is especially strong when what was destroyed had deep significance for the group affected.

From the nineteenth century onward, debates in Western nations about reconstruction were framed mainly by concern for the maintenance of physical traces as

L. Kealy (✉)
School of Architecture, University College Dublin, Dublin, Ireland
e-mail: loughlin.kealy@ucd.ie

T. H. J. Marchand
Social Anthropology, School of Oriental and African Studies, London, UK
e-mail: tm6@soas.ac.uk

T. Kono and J. Okahashi (eds.), *Post-Trauma and the Recovery Governance of Cultural Heritage*, https://doi.org/10.1007/978-981-19-6041-3_10

essential markers of authenticity and as a defence against falsification of evidence. The movement towards internationalism in built heritage protection was articulated in documents such as the Athens Charter of 1931 and the Venice Charter of 1964, and was consolidated in the World Heritage Convention of 1972. Nevertheless, the seeds for a more complex understanding of reconstruction were present from the very start. It took some time for them to blossom.

The post-war reconstructions of historic environments that were deliberately destroyed during World War Two were, for a time, seen as anomalies and they were reluctantly accepted as 'justifiable' in exceptional circumstances only. However, the rationale for acceptance in the international context lay in the recognition that cultural significance is not confined to material inheritances. Of necessity, it also encompasses spiritual and immaterial factors. The understanding and acceptance of significance within societies depends on that recognition.

In recent decades, the rapid dissemination of information about the destruction of culturally significant environments and artefacts, both through human action and natural events, has brought renewed focus to the work of international bodies devoted to the protection of heritage. The scale and intensity of destruction has prompted serious rethinking about recovery, reconstruction and the meanings of authenticity in different contexts.

ICOMOS (International Council on Monuments and Sites) recognised that the complexities attending ideas of reconstruction had to be set against the urgent need to introduce guidance for dealing with post-trauma recovery and reconstruction. It therefore organized an international colloquium in March 2016. The colloquium underscored the importance of case studies while also identifying some of their shortcomings. For example, a large number of individual case studies already existed at the time, but their very specificity meant that it was difficult to extrapolate lessons and learning that could be applied more broadly. The colloquium therefore concluded that a 'one-size-fits-all' approach to guidelines could not work across all social, cultural, geographical and economic contexts.

The colloquium was followed later that year by a workshop, which led to the publication in 2017 of the *ICOMOS Guidance on Post Trauma Recovery and Reconstruction for World Heritage Cultural Properties*. This was a working document to be amended following experience and reflection, and for which case studies could supply valuable learning.

10.2 Developing a Framework for Analysis: The Matrix for the Compilation of Case Studies in Recovery and Reconstruction

ICOMOS launched a project to assess the importance of case studies in formulating policies where problems were ill-defined. A small task force was assembled to generate a matrix, through which experts working on the recovery of post-trauma sites could systematically supply and share information, critically reflect on procedures and decision-making processes, and record experiences and outcomes. The project had several phases. As a starting point, case studies were analysed and a scoping text was developed as the basis for further discussion. This led to inviting six authors to write pilot case studies with the understanding that they were assisting the task force to draft a framework for writing case studies – a complex commission accepted by the authors. These studies were discussed in workshops, revised and later published as drafts on the ICOMOS website.

The six studies were carried out on heritage sites in Uganda, Bosnia, Italy, Japan, Chile, and West Jerusalem. The Uganda study concerned the Kasubi Tombs in Kampala, destroyed by fire in 2010, and undergoing reconstruction.[1] In Bosnia, the city of Sarajevo was examined from the perspective of the targeting of symbolic elements during conflict.[2] The Italian study focussed on the reconstruction of the Duomo di Venzone (Sant'Andrea Apostolo) in Udine, destroyed by the Friuli earthquake in 1976.[3] The Japanese study was of the reconstruction of Sensho-Ji Temple, involving characteristic replacement of materials.[4] The Chilean study was of the reconstruction of a section of the city of Valparaiso, in the aftermath of the 2007 fire.[5] And, the study of the Damascus Gate in West Jerusalem was not of reconstruction as such, but grappled with issues of displacement and appropriation of meaning.[6] The case studies were presented during an international seminar, and subsequently revised and published as draft documents on the ICOMOS website.

An illustration of the complexities encountered can be gained from a summary of the Uganda study.

10.2.1 The Kasubi Tombs, Kampala, Uganda[7]

The former palace of the kabakas (kings) of Buganda is located on a 30-hectare hilltop site in Kampala. It was built in 1882 and converted into a royal burial ground two years later. It is known as the Kasubi Tombs. At the heart of the complex is the Muzibu-Azaala-Mpanga, measuring approximately 30 m in diameter and 15 m high. Four 'sleeping' kabakas are interred within. Because the place transmits spiritual essence (*mwooyo*) from the past to the present and beyond, it continues to be an important spiritual and political site for the Baganda, who are Uganda's largest ethnic

[1] Nsubuga (2019).

[2] Badescu (2018).

[3] Doglioni (2018).

[4] Martinez de Arbulo (2018).

[5] Kaplan Depolo (2018).

[6] Pullan (2018).

[7] The summary description below is grounded in Nsubuga's case study and in communications between Nsubuga and Marchand.

group. The present kabaka and his representatives carry out important rituals there, and it is a place where communication is had with the spiritual world.

The site was inscribed on the UNESCO World Heritage List in 2001 (it is the only cultural WH site in Uganda), fulfilling four of the six cultural criteria for inscription:

> It is a major example of an architectural achievement in organic materials, principally wood, thatch, reed, wattle and daub. The site's main significance, however, lies in its intangible values of belief, spirituality, continuity and identity.'[8] It bears 'witness to the creative genius of the Baganda and as a masterpiece of form and craftsmanship' and is a strong representation of the 'continuity of a living tradition'.[9]

In March 2010, a suspicious fire engulfed the Muzibu-Azaala-Mpanga. Relations between the Baganda and Ugandan President Museveni had soured when the kabaka began demanding more local power over his traditional Baganda kingdom. His supporters accused the government of arson. Riots erupted at the site and three protesters were reportedly killed by police. UNESCO determined that loss of the main tomb structure compromised the site's authenticity, but it was nevertheless recognised that the building's traditional architectural craftsmanship and the required skills are still available to allow it to be recreated.[10] The site was added to the UNESCO List of World Heritage in Danger.

In 2013, the Japanese government pledged an emergency assistance fund for the rehabilitation of the property. Numerous cultural properties in Japan contain wooden buildings with thatched roofs, and the country's conservationists are renowned for preservation techniques that involve replacement of materials. In addition to conducting interviews with key stakeholders, Japanese technical experts visited cogon grass fields, surveyed thatching work, and interviewed thatched-roof workers to understand local techniques and maintenance skills (Fig. 10.1). The local population of the Buganda Kingdom commenced rebuilding the Muzibu-Azaala-Mpanga with support from the Uganda Ministry of Tourism, Wildlife and Antiquities and with technical assistance from Japanese experts, ICOMOS, UNESCO and CRATerre (International Centre on Earthen Architecture). Japanese funding was used to provide scientific support, to contribute to the costs of qualified supervision for the reconstruction, and to set up an efficient risk prevention scheme. The training of young apprentices by Baganda elders was at the core of the process, to learn traditional building techniques as well as intangible cultural practices and belief systems.

Decisions regarding approaches to reconstruction were not straightforward. The building destroyed in 2011 was itself a departure from earlier versions. In 1938, the British had reconstructed the original wood structures using concrete poles and steel-framed roof trusses. It was first intended that the twenty-first-century reconstruction would restore the tomb to its pre-fire state (Fig. 10.2). However, the Japanese funders soon identified a number of challenges. In addition to concerns about the capability of local construction companies, the most difficult issue was procuring sufficient supplies of high quality cogon grass and qualified workers for the project.

---

[8] UNESCO (2022).

[9] UNESCO World Heritage Convention (2001).

[10] Ibid.

Fig. 10.1 The Main House (Muzibu-Azaala-Mpanga) in the Kasubi Tombs complex, Kampala, Uganda. Rebuilt several times, the latest reconstruction followed its destruction by fire in 2010. The photograph shows the reconstruction in progress. The trimming of the thatch around the entrance has an important ritual function (photo courtesy of Jonathan Nsubuga)

Fig. 10.2 Detail of the restored royal house showing composite construction (photo courtesy of Jonathan Nsubuga)

Resolution of these challenges revealed that the reconstruction process would need to be accompanied throughout by Baganda religious and spiritual events, thereby introducing delays to the schedule of works.

Ugandan architect Jonathan Nsubuga was appointed as project manager. He observed that the UNESCO inscription criteria were essential for directing the recovery process, but their use was limited. To understand the past history of the site and the correct ways of reconstructing the main building, Nsubuga had to collaborate closely with Baganda oral historians and spiritual consultants. In his words, 'their knowledge involves time-travel experiences, and so the information they provide does not necessarily adhere to a linear sense of time.'[11] Spiritual consultants engaged in so-called '*Masengere*' meetings with past kabakas and the tomb's original builders in order to receive guidance. The social structure within the heritage resource is clearly defined. Titles, duties and control over ritualistic processes are divided along gender lines and between numerous clans. The array of traditional titleholders of the royal court played significant roles—some positively and some antagonistically—in the reconstruction. Knowledge that project funding existed encouraged some individuals to concoct cultural customs and rituals. These had to be continually verified through consultation with elders, clan leaders and mediums, which in turn strained social relations within the community.

Before work could begin, the Protector of the Palace, a member of the monkey clan, had to cleanse the foundations. Next, rituals were performed to identify a tree that would serve as the central pole of the new structure and pierce the thatch roof, 'creating a foundation in the air'.[12] Rituals were carried out through the night. The ground around the tree was soaked with traditional beer to loosen the roots so that *Abatabazi* (warriors) could uproot it with their bare hands. The tree was carried for nearly 45 kms to the Kasubi Tombs without once touching the ground. Further rituals were carried out before erecting the pole, and the most important ritual was cutting and trimming the lower *wankaki* (thatch) at the front prior to 'opening the house'.

When doubts arose about any procedures, *Bataka* (clan leaders) called for mediums to host a *Masengere* to seek solutions and truths from the sleeping kabakas and original builders. In this way, the architect was able to gather missing information about the heritage property and to complete the documentation process that he had been assigned.[13] In his own words, Jonathan concluded that 'the recovery programme yielded solid, viable, authentic records; cultural and spiritual consultation records, and a deeper understanding of risk management.'[14]

This study underscored key factors to be addressed in devising a framework to facilitate learning across case studies: more specifically, it highlighted the interconnection between intangible factors and decisions about reconstruction choices and practices.

---

[11] Nsubuga (2019).

[12] Ibid.

[13] Subsequently, CyArk produced X-Ray photos of the Muzibu-Azaala-Mpanga to produce a technical scientific record of the structure. The record provides a baseline for monitoring site conditions over time.

[14] Nsubuga (2019).

The Evolution of the Matrix Structure

Intensive workshop sessions examined how the six aforementioned case studies tested the draft Matrix from differing perspectives. For example, the Ugandan project shed light on the interdependence of the concrete steps taken to reinstate the architectural entity and the living beliefs and traditional practices of the community; the Italian study demonstrated how the established practice of anastylosis could be explored with the community, utilising local skills to identify, rescue and re-assemble surviving elements while maintaining the marks of destruction; the Chilean study drew attention to the organisational frameworks that impinged on responses to disaster; and the Damascus Gate study underlined issues of appropriation that are often present when historic sites are at the forefront of conflict, and also highlighted the facts that the causes of trauma may be repeated over time and their impacts can include the creation of a 'new normal' for those affected.

The issues encountered by the six authors led to the refinement of the Matrix. The process was by no means straightforward. The concept of a matrix as an underlying structure is challenging even though the issues that prompted the effort may be acknowledged and, indeed, its potential embraced. Transforming the concept into a tool required a shift in focus from the particularities of the cases to the meta-project of finding what categories of information might improve learning across a range of studies and, as a result, lead to improved guidance. The revised matrix was published online in April 2018 under the title *ICOMOS Global Project on Reconstruction: Matrix for the Compilation of Case Studies.*[15]

Simply put, the purpose of the tool is to capture the significance of the heritage resource in question, the nature of the destructive event and its impact on the resource, and what has happened in the aftermath—and to capture this information as objectively as possible. There are seven categories of information, supported by 'prompts' aimed at helping authors to provide appropriate descriptions and relevant supporting documentation. The seven categories are:

Description of the Resource
Nature of the Impacting Event(s)
Post-Event Appraisals
Response Actions, Timeframes, Resources and Costs
The Outcomes and Effects
Additional Comments
Details of the Expert(s) Completing the Study.

The matrix structure was designed for authors to document the nature of the their engagement with the resource, and to record any reflections on the case study itself and the experience of writing it.

[15] ICOMOS (2018).

10.3 The ICOMOS-ICCROM Project: Analysis of Case Studies in Recovery and Reconstruction

In 2018, the same year that the Matrix was published, the World Heritage Committee formally directed the attention of its advisory bodies towards examining case studies. In response, ICOMOS joined forces with ICCROM to establish a joint project that could harness the experience and expertise of both bodies in order to clarify issues of recovery and reconstruction and provide insights that could improve guidance. The project, *Analysis of Case Studies in Recovery and Reconstruction*, was developed and managed through a joint Working Group comprising members of both organisations and administered through the ICOMOS Secretariat and the office of ICCROM Sharjah.[16] It had two inter-connected aims: to analyse the studies and draw conclusions about the issues of recovery and reconstruction that they highlighted; and to use the studies for testing the utility of the Matrix as a structuring tool.

The project was launched in 2019 with an international call for proposals. From those received, 11 case studies were analysed, covering 16 significant sites and buildings, and representing a comprehensive set of factors, namely geographical, cultural and causational. The commissioned authors used the Matrix to structure their investigations and their final reports.[17] The selected case studies are described in the table below:

Country/region/place	Resource	Type of trauma	Event/time
Austria/Wachau WHS	Cultural landscape: terracing walls, buildings	Flooding	Flood of 2002; noting later flooding event
Bosnia-Herzogovina/Mostar	Sevri Hadzi Hasan Mosque with reference to the Nezir-agina and Tabačka mosques	Conflict	Successive events 1992–1995; destruction of mosque in 1950s
Chile/O'Higgins Region	Historic city/San Pedro de Alcántara	Earthquake and tsumani	Events of 2010
China/Taishun	Group of structures: three covered bridges	Flooding	Flooding arising from typhoon 2016
Italy/L'Aquila	Historic building: Palazzo Carli Benedetti	Earthquake	L'Aquila earthquake 2009
Mexico/San Luis Potosí	Temple of Nuestra Señora de la Asunción of Santa María Acapulco	Lightning strike	2007 strike and fire

(continued)

[16] The members of the Working Group were Loughlin Kealy (Coordinator), Zaki Aslan, Luisa de Marco, Amra Hadzimuhamedovic, Toshiyuki Kono, Marie-Laure Lavenir and Trevor Marchand.

[17] ICOMOS and ICCROM Sharjah (2021). The 11 case studies are published in two volumes.

(continued)

Country/region/place	Resource	Type of trauma	Event/time
Nepal/Kathmandu	Urban area: Patan Durbar Square/monument zone, civic and religious elements	Earthquakes	Principal seismic event 2015
New Zealand/Christchurch (6)	Historic city and specific sites (5 historic buildings)	Earthquakes	Seismic events in 2010 and 2011
Rwanda/Nyanza	Cultural landscape	Conflict	1994 genocide
Syria/Aleppo	Historic city: historic *suq*	Conflict	Successive events, 2012–2016
West Bank/Nablus	Historic city: and multiple sites	Conflict, also effects of earthquake	Incursion 2002–2004; events post 1967; 1927 earthquake

The case studies covered individual buildings, complexes, urban areas and landscapes of cultural significance. Their focus ranged from detailed exposition of repair methods to questions of cultural traditions and social organisation as these impacted on the processes of reconstruction.

The richness of data and the complexity of issues can be illustrated with reference to the case studies from Mexico and Syria.

10.3.1 Mexico: Reconstruction of the Symbolic and Physical Space of the Temple of Nuestra Señora de la Asunción of Santa María Acapulco[18]

Franciscan friars founded the Temple of Nuestra Señora de la Asunción in the village of Santa Maria Acapulco circa 1750. It was constructed of soil and stone, plastered with lime and clay, and covered with a palm-frond roof. Its interior was elaborately decorated in a baroque style, featuring four wooden altarpieces with sculptures and canvases and covered in silver leaf, and a wooden coffered ceiling that was plastered and richly decorated with iconography (Fig. 10.3).

The inhabitants of Santa María Acapulco are indigenous Pame (Xi'ói), who, until recently, lived a relatively isolated existence from the rest of Mexico. The temple is the seat of the community's civil and religious authorities. The governor, the treasurer and the sacristan are responsible for organising all religious celebrations and for maintaining the temple, and they are assisted by a council of elders.

During 2006, representatives from Mexico's National Institute of Anthropology and History (INAH) had been working together with members of the National

[18] See Schneider (2021). The summary description in this chapter is grounded in Schneider's text.

Fig. 10.3 The Temple of Nuestra Señora de la Asunción in the village of San Luis Potosí, Mexico was destroyed by lightening strike and fire in 2007. The photograph shows the interior of the church in 2006 before its destruction (photo courtesy of SMA project, by kind permission of Renata Schneider)

Cultural Heritage Conservation Coordination (CNCPC) in Santa María Acapulco. They were creating a photo documentation of the temple and had initiated the conservation of the building's façade and some of the polychrome sculptures. There are no colonial references to the building of the temple and little is known about the history of the settlement or about renovations carried out on its temple. Nevertheless, it remained little changed since the late eighteenth century.

Two workshops were also organised: one for creating an inventory of movable and immovable property and another to introduce the notion of 'local heritage' to the Pame population. Author of the report, Renata Schneider, explains that executing the inventory workshop was challenging due to the low literacy rate, and because contemporary everyday plastic objects also had to be registered since they were invested with sacredness.

The heritage workshop was yet more challenging. Terms such as 'heritage', 'valuation' and 'culture', which were easily translated and recognized as concepts in mestizo communities, meant absolutely nothing to Pame residents. For them, 'cultural heritage' as a concept was inseparable from everyday life as an activity. The idea of taking care of 'things' (i.e. material culture) made little sense because, like people and activities, objects are continually transforming. The things that need looking after are the seasonal cycles and the harvest.

Discussing the concept of 'national cultural heritage' and the existence of laws that protect it prompted questions among local residents: 'Are things yours or are they ours?'; 'Do you make decisions concerning things to be conserved and restored or do we make them freely?'; 'Why does the government say they belong to us but allocates money to take care of them?'; or conversely, 'Why do you say they are yours, but you want us to do it without directly giving us money?'.

On 1 July 2007, lightning struck the temple's roof and within five hours all immovable cultural heritage contained within the building was irretrievably lost, including altarpieces, the pulpit, benches, beams and the coffered ceiling (Fig. 10.4). Most movable heritage, however, was evacuated in time.

Members of the INAH and CNCPC who had worked there accompanied the villagers in their month-long mourning while initiating the necessary processes for collecting disaster insurance compensation on behalf of the residents. They also formulated a schedule of interventions to be carried out over an eight-year period that would result in the reconstruction, conservation and rehabilitation of the temple and, most importantly, of the religious, civil and daily life of its users. All stages would be implemented with the community and in accordance with the local system of decision-making. Schneider played a key role throughout.

Initially, the residents of Santa María Acapulco were in a state of shock and paralysis, which was broken only by rituals of forgiveness to God and the agricultural deities, especially that of thunder. Removal of ashes from the temple allowed the villagers to move forward with the recovery of their property. The following year, the community decided to integrate the ashes into the new rammed-earth floor.

A delegation of anthropologists from the INAH explored the community's expectations for the future of their temple. The results largely defined the proposal for the subsequent technical interventions on the building and its objects.

For the Pame, the temple is not only the material property, but rather includes all ceremonial activities that constitute it as a sacred space, including dressing and parading the statues, performing music and dances for rain and fertility, and placing offerings. On some occasions, the temple becomes a representation of the human body, with sections of the building taking the form of a vital organ or bodily appendage.

Fig. 10.4 The devasted interior of the church after the events of 2007 (photo courtesy of SMA project, by kind permission of Renata Schneider)

Schneider and her team thereby determined that it was essential to reproduce all that enabled the community to reconstitute its sacred space, despite the fact that reproduction of objects or spaces is generally disparaged in the field of conservation and restoration and sparks impassioned debate over material authenticity. They reasoned, for example, that a straightforward stabilization of a Virgin Mary statue with a missing arm would be pointless: not restoring the arm with which the Virgin grants her blessing during a celebration means simply that there would be no celebration. Similarly, in the case of the sacred books, which are constantly manipulated during processions and rituals, restoration included the addition of thick and resistant bindings to better protect them.

Mexico has an established legal framework for conservation and restoration practices that aligns strongly with the conservative Athens and Venice Charters, which prioritise tangible heritage and material authenticity. The CNCPC therefore had to elaborate a detailed proposal to justify the reconstruction of altarpieces and other immovable property. They successfully grounded their arguments in Pame convictions that material heritage cannot be separated from the intangible, and in the more recent Nara Document (1994) and Riga Charter (2000) on authenticity and historical reconstruction in relation to cultural heritage.

The temple remained a functioning site of worship throughout the conservation process, and parishioners continued to place medicinal offerings (e.g. eggs and corn) in different parts of the building, leaving them to naturally decompose.

Educational programmes were organized for schoolchildren that connected them to the recovery work. Most of the architectural interventions were carried out by community members who had greater knowledge of techniques used in building wooden structures, and apprentices were also introduced to the processes. In the case of the masonry walls, however, these were consolidated by a team of masons specialized in conservation work.

The restoration (and reproduction) of objects and immovable property was overseen by a team of professional conservators. In the case of the reconstructed coffered ceiling, the original painted scenes were not reproduced because photographs of sufficient quality were non-existent. It was agreed with the traditional authorities that if the Pame residents wished to repaint the coffered ceiling with the old or brand new motifs, the decision would be entirely their own.

The temple was officially reconsecrated on 29 January 2014. Schneider conveys that,

> After the fire, the patron Virgin of the village flew away and took shelter at the church of Tancoyol, a mestizo community (but of Pame origin) in the neighbouring state of Querétaro. When the restoration was finished, she returned to her place inside the temple and found herself at home. The people of Santa María Acapulco saw her "in the form of a beautiful bird" when she left, and also when she returned.[19]

This project illustrated the importance of supporting a community to reconstitute its cultural heritage from its own vantage point and grounded in the realities of its daily life, while providing them with basic management elements. Schneider calls for recovery and reconstruction efforts to take the time necessary to describe the social realities on the ground, so as to avoid adopting methodologies aimed mainly at satisfying professional and institutional requirements. Rather than standardise concepts and methods, the focus should be on the activities of regularly meeting and cooperating with local stakeholders and critically analysing decisions and processes (Figs. 10.5 and 10.6). She maintains that we must continually examine the vertical relationship that always exists when one party provides work for another, or manages

[19] Schneider (2021: 209).

Fig. 10.5 Consultation meeting held as part of the process of reconstruction (photo courtesy of SMA project, by kind permission of Renata Schneider)

the money, and to carefully consider the consequences and repercussions in order to minimise them.

10.3.2 Syria: Reconstruction of Suq al-Saqatiyya, Aleppo[20]

The study of the reconstruction of the Suq al-Saqatiyya in the historic city of Aleppo provided a detailed account of the technical decisions taken, and it placed these in the context of complex interactions between authorities, institutions, international agencies and donors, and those whose lives had been disrupted in the Syrian Civil War between 2011 and 2016. Suq al-Saqatiyya is one of many markets (*suqs*) located in the commercial quarter of the historic city centre. This area has been the core of public life for centuries, accommodating shops, workshops, warehouses, baths and religious buildings, and hosting the interactions of traders, European communities, consulates and religious missionaries.

[20] See Kasmo and Kutiefan (2021). The summary description in this chapter is grounded in their text.

Fig. 10.6 The restored entrance front of the church (photo courtesy of SMA project, by kind permission of Renata Schneider)

The Old City suffered from planning policies and inappropriate developments during the twentieth century, a situation that only ended in 1976 when the centre was declared a national historic area and the authorities discontinued the planning scheme that was in force at the time.[21] In 1986, the Old City was declared a UNESCO World Heritage Site (under criteria III and IV) on account of the exceptional importance of its cultural traditions and the outstanding quality of its architecture, representing the different periods of its history. The description of the historic city refers to Aleppo's role 'located at the crossroads of several trade routes since the second millennium B.C.'[22] The *suqs* are referred to as 'a part of the city's cohesive and unique urban fabric that contribute to the Outstanding Universal Value' representing 'an exceptional reflection of the social, cultural and economic aspects of what was once one of

[21] The Gutton Plan of 1954 proposed to separate the historic centre from the surrounding urban fabric with a ring road to facilitate direct vehicular access. The plan was only partially realised. The first phase of Gutton's proposal led to the destruction of some important monuments and brought development pressures to bear. Newly opened streets cut the traditional thoroughfares leading from the centre to the gates. New commercial activities along the sides of the new streets encouraged the replacement of old buildings with high-rise blocks. Gyoji Banshoya's plan of 1974 tried to respond to the shortcomings of the Gutton Plan, but did not change its basic concepts.

[22] UNESCO Silk Roads Programme.

the richest cities of all humanity'.[23] Following the inscription, several international initiatives were launched to promote awareness of the precarious condition of much of the physical fabric and to support training activities.

The Rehabilitation Project for the Old City of Aleppo was launched in 1992 by the municipal authorities with promised funding support from the German Development Agency and the Arab Fund for Social and Economic Development. The Directorate of the Old City was formed the following year to advance the rehabilitation works. Despite constraints, which were partly legal and financial, the Directorate achieved some important results. A major inhibitory factor lay in the social constraints that arose mainly from the fragmentation of ownership, whereby few owners occupied their premises and instead rented them to the shopkeepers. This led to difficulties in securing agreements that affected individual interests. Generally, the project was most successful in improving public spaces and what might be termed 'beautification' works, but it left many deficiencies in infrastructure and services provision.

As the Syrian Civil War unfolded from 15 March 2011 onwards, Aleppo became the locus of intensive fighting and the central area of the city became the frontline between government forces and opposing groups. The narrow streets of the Old City became a battleground, with the Great Mosque at the centre of the struggle. The Old City suffered major damage and the loss of significant structures including the minaret of the Great Mosque. From the beginning of the conflict, the Directorate General of Antiquities and Museums (DGAM) in collaboration with UNESCO was heavily involved in trying to safeguard and rescue the city's treasures, but the accumulating damage to the city fabric led to it being placed on UNESCO's Heritage in Danger list. While the conflict lasted, access to the area was difficult and information on damage was partial, some of which was recorded by concerned citizens on their personal devices.

Post-conflict assessment was initially made through a joint operation between UNITAR (United Nations Institute for Training and Research) and UNESCO, with the latter also supporting expert evaluation of the extent of loss of historic fabric. About ten per cent of the city's historic buildings had been destroyed. But the survey also established that over half of the buildings that had suffered damage were repairable. The Aga Khan Foundation became active in the established rehabilitation programmes, together with the Directorate for the Ancient City of Aleppo, and the Syria Trust for Development. From 2014, UNESCO (in collaboration with ICOMOS and ICCROM, and with support from Belgium and Austria) implemented an EU-funded programme to conduct technical meetings focussed on conditions in the Old City.

In this context, the reconstruction of the Suq al-Saqatiyya became one of the pilot projects to underpin wider regeneration efforts (Fig. 10.7). Built in 1574 as a revenue-generating structure belonging to the foundation of Sokullu Muhammed Pasha, the Suq al-Saqatiyya is an architectural complex whose shops sold nuts, pistachios, fruit, vegetables and meat. About half the shops were occupied by butchers (its name is derived from *saqatat*, meaning organ meats or offal). The shops were

[23] UNESCO World Heritage Convention (1986).

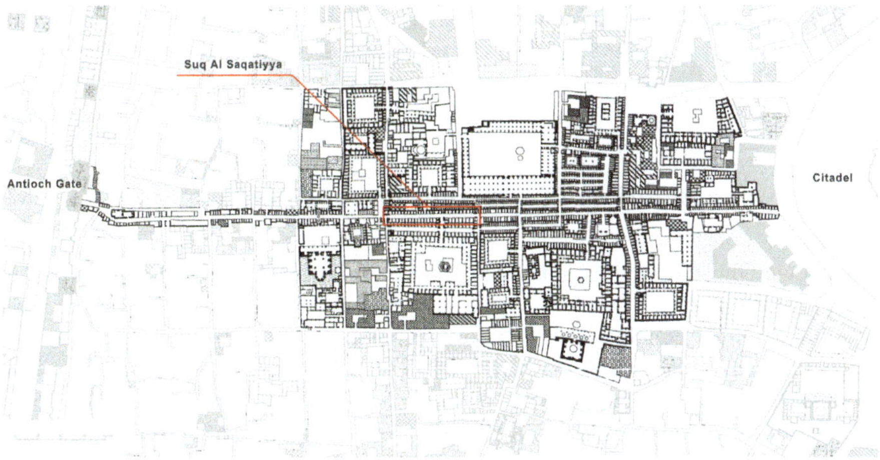

Fig. 10.7 Map of the central commercial area of Aleppo, showing the location of Suq al-Saqatiyya (image prepared from a map by Gaube and Wirth 1984, courtesy of Ruba Kasmo)

roofed with barrel vaults. The structure was two storeys high and its passages were covered by vaults and punctuated by four domes. Damage to the *suq* was considerable, including partial destruction of three domes and severe damage to the western entrance. The reconstruction work had to address not only damage directly attributed to the conflict, but also deterioration that had occurred due to lack of maintenance and the accumulation of inappropriate interventions over the years.

The case study provided considerable detail of the interventions to reconstruct the *suq*, the rationale behind them, and the difficulties encountered in sourcing materials. In this regard, authors Ruba Kasmo and Lina Kutiefa made an observation that resonates beyond the case of the Aleppo *suq*. Reconstructions during recovery from disasters frequently encounter problems of sourcing adequate supplies of essential materials and of finding skilled operatives to carry out the work. Where there has been major displacement of population, the shortage of necessary skills may be difficult to overcome, at least in the short term. In such situations, pilot projects are inevitably advantaged—they can take advantage of connections not always available to the generality of the reconstruction efforts across the wider environment, and they can attract such skill and expertise as still remains available. Thus the particular project under study is a well-documented snapshot of what can be achieved in difficult circumstances, rather than representing wider regeneration activities, or perhaps in the short term at least, as offering a model of how new projects, inevitably less-well resourced, may be conducted. At the same time, the importance given to education and training within the initiatives in Aleppo offers grounds for optimism. The observation serves to underline the need for the reader to understand the context in which the case study project has been executed.

The authors also note that the resumption of commercial activity in the *suq* has been slower than might have been hoped, encountering hesitation among sectors of the population on account of continuing shortages and uncertainties. Those components of recovery that are rooted in confidence and belief in the future may take longer than what is envisaged by official initiatives.

10.3.3 Some Additional Comments on the Studies

When reviewing the studies generated by the Analysis Project, it is important to reflect that its purpose was not to define reconstruction or to prescribe practice, but rather to draw conclusions from how reconstruction has been approached in a variety of circumstances, and to learn from those experiences. Reconstruction meant different things in different contexts, as illustrated by the following examples.

In the study of Austria's Wachau Valley following the major floods of 2002,[24] the discussion of reconstruction centred on how the flood defences were improved by being integrated within a territory that encompasses many settlements with multiple local authorities working within regional and national administrations. Challenges of recovery involved developing consensus across communities about the typology of physical interventions (while allowing local variations) and devising financial instruments that supported remedial works to private property as well as to the public realm.

In radical contrast, the authors of the report on the Royal Capital at Nyanza in Rwanda, Maya Ishizawa and Jerome Karangwa, asked: 'What is the role of "authenticity" in a context where the recovery of social life, relations and security are paramount, and where the driving objectives of reconstruction are not historical accuracy but rather to heal and to rebuild national identity?'[25] It is also important to note that, in accordance with Rwanda's National Policy of Unity and Reconciliation, it is forbidden to raise the issue of ethnicity. Thus, questions about the decision to reconstruct the residence of royal Tutsi elite as a symbol of 'Rwandanness' have been muted, as too are those about how this structure is perceived by different communities and different stakeholders. Ishizawa and Karangwa promote the neutral position that the reconstructed capital represents on a more general level a Rwandan inhabitation strategy that evolved over time and in response to a specific geography and set of environmental factors.[26]

[24] See Schimek (2021).

[25] See Ishizawa and Karangwa (2021).

[26] There are currently plans to develop Rukari hill as a cultural village, which would include reconstructing the 13 or so remaining huts of the Nyanza capital and populating the site with royal cattle to roam as they would have done on the original site. It is anticipated that the strategy will expand Rwanda's touristic attractions beyond its present focus on national parks, and that it will provide a place for Rwandan visitors to experience pre-colonial society and the traditional knowledge of their ancestors that was tied to the land. Aside from the display of a traditional hut in the country's ethnographic museum, there are no surviving remnants of Rwanda's vernacular architecture.

Finally, the studies of reconstruction in Christchurch, New Zealand, which comprise an overview and studies of five individual reconstruction projects, detailed the responses to catastrophe on the part of NGOs, institutions and authorities.[27] They provide insight into how reconstruction was addressed over time, demonstrating the shifts in focus as recovery matured, the inconsistencies of understanding that emerged, the influence of regulatory frameworks and professional orientations. Taken as a whole, the corpus of studies provides an in-depth review of response that will have wide resonance.

10.3.4 Summary Conclusions of the Analysis Project

The project report provides an analysis of the case studies, using the components of the Matrix as headings. It lists ten general conclusions, some relating to the understanding of reconstruction, others to issues of governance or social organisation.

On the understanding of post-trauma reconstruction:

- The case studies demonstrate the interrelationship between reconstruction of the damaged physical environment or resource and the processes of generating a new, post-trauma social reality. The relationship persists even though it differs in each case;
- The studies show that the relationship between physical/environmental reconstruction and the retention of cultural value can be made a priority in the aftermath of catastrophe, but is not a given;
- The word 'reconstruction' carries multiple meanings in post-trauma remedial action. It is widely accepted that reconstruction can be understood as describing a process rather than be understood as a singular event. The processes of recovery may involve physical reconstruction that is also supporting the intention or desire to re-establish pre-existing social or cultural conditions. Alternatively, they may also embrace the desire for change. Both considerations may apply in particular cases. Future case studies need to be conscious of the need to avoid conflating 'reconstruction' with 'recovery';
- Where the importance of retaining cultural value is recognised, restitution of physical, spatial and visual characteristics frequently takes priority over adherence to conservation principles as they relate to authenticity of materials and techniques. As well as creating challenges for resilience, uncertainties of supply and availability of material and skills result in changes to practice. Commensurate outcomes arise from how new regulatory requirements are implemented;
- The studies raise questions about interpretations and understandings of authenticity at a popular level and within cultural organisations, official bodies or professional bodies even where the immaterial attributes of a resource are taken to be significant components of its pre-event significance.

[27] The full six-part case study was produced by Amanda Ohs, Catherine Forbes, Winston Clark and Fiona Wykes. See Ohs et al. (2021).

On implications for governance:

- The case studies provide evidence of the critical importance of local population engagement for effective and socially responsible recovery actions and of the key role that governance structures and available policy instruments play in enabling such engagement. They also demonstrate that documenting such engagement is not always a priority in how remedial actions are described;
- Certain studies demonstrate the influence of donors in the prioritisation of and the preferential resourcing for projects. Special projects attract resources beyond what is available in the wider context of recovery;
- Certain studies highlight questions about the sustainability of recovery processes, where these processes involve relationships created in the pursuit of remedial actions;
- Where repeated destructive events are experienced, preparation for future events is a deep challenge for authorities. Even if it can be said that systems continue to learn, preparation for fresh events is sometimes not prioritised;
- The case studies suggest that capacity building was rarely an explicit priority in the recovery of social life and local economies.

10.4 Conclusion

The project identified six cross-cutting issues and drew conclusions about the Matrix and its usefulness. The cross-cutting issues were:

- Social justice: in a number of studies, the accounts shed light on existing social relationships, as well as on wide variations in the engagement of the local population in the recovery process and in the realisation of capacity-building;
- A number of studies dealt with inconclusive situations, even in circumstances where the impacting event(s) had ceased, demonstrating that in certain cases responses were ongoing and continuous, and thus becoming a feature of 'normal' life;
- The covert nature of where the learning from post-trauma recovery and reconstruction resides became apparent. The dynamic nature of knowledge-generation and the uncertainties of knowledge-sharing were implicit in several studies and evident in others. The role of donors (especially international ones) was significant in committing financial resources, knowledge and expertise and in influencing priorities;
- The economic perspective on recovery tended to be underrepresented in reportage. The exploration of how the reconstruction efforts of local populations are supported by the infusion of resources needs to be mainstreamed in case studies of recovery and reconstruction;
- Measures introduced in recovery processes can generate new relationships between sectors in society. Studies raised questions about sustainability of measures, relationships and lasting impacts;

- The question of where authenticity lies in the reconstructed resource, or how 'authenticity' is defined in the given context, was not comprehensively addressed across the various studies. In this context, the issue of establishing resilience is inseparable from discussion of recovery actions. New post-trauma regulations and standards that are introduced to improve resilience frequently challenge existing or traditional constructions. Further examination of the issue is required in relation to factors such as continuous response, sustainability, resources and authenticity.

The project drew conclusions about the experience of using the *Matrix for the Compilation of Case Studies*, drawn from the perspectives of analysing the case studies produced and the challenges experienced by the commissioned authors. The project report concluded that the Matrix was a valuable tool and made a significant positive contribution to the learning outcomes. In particular, the Matrix proved its value:

- In helping to structure complex information;
- In identifying aspects within studies that merited deeper exploration;
- In identifying cross-cutting issues common to many and diverse situations;
- In providing a solid basis for comparison and contrast;
- In providing ideas and information for further reflection and productive debate.

The Analysis Project provided a valuable resource for shared learning and improving practice. The experience suggests that the Matrix be developed further and amended to reflect the experiences of the case study authors and the project team. For bodies like ICOMOS and ICCROM, building up a resource of structured case studies should remain a priority. The project concluded that the Matrix, having established its usefulness in general terms, should be used and tested further with regard to more complex sites, and where authority structures are ill-defined or contested.

References

Badescu, G. (2018). Post-war Sarajevo: Heritage reconstruction in the Baščaršija quarter, including the Sarajevo City Hall, National Library and the Gazi Husrev Mosque *ICOMOS Global Case Study Project on Reconstruction.* https://issuu.com/icomos/docs/badescu-icomos_reconstruction_globa/25

Doglioni, F. (2018). The reconstruction of the Cathedral of Venzone. *ICOMOS Global Case Study Project on Reconstruction.* https://issuu.com/icomos/docs/doglioni_francesco_venzone_final_20

ICOMOS. (2017). *ICOMOS guidance on Post trauma recovery and reconstruction for world heritage cultural properties.* https://www.icomos.org/en/focus/reconstruction/40988-icomos-guidance-on-post-trauma-recovery-and-reconstruction-for-world-heritage-cultural-properties-document-2

ICOMOS. (2018). *ICOMOS global project on reconstruction: Matrix for the compilation of case studies.* https://www.icomos.org/images/DOCUMENTS/Secretariat/2018/Reconstruction_CaseStudies/ICOMOS_GlobalCaseStudyReconstr_Matrix_20180426.pdf

ICOMOS and ICCROM Sharjah. (2021). *Analysis of case studies in recovery and reconstruction*, 2 volumes. Available online at https://www.icomos.org/en/focus/reconstruction/91268-publication-of-icomos-iccrom-joint-project-analysis-of-case-studies-in-recovery-and-reconstruction

Ishizawa, M., & Karangwa, J. (2021). The interpretative reconstruction of the Royal Capital in Nyanz, Rwanda. *ICOMOS and ICCROM Sharjah, Analysis of Case Studies in Recovery and Reconstruction, 2*, 60–89.

Kaplan Depolo, P. (2018). Valparaiso: The vulnerability of the built heritage because of catastrophes—A case study of Serrano Street. *ICOMOS Global Case Study Project on Reconstruction.* https://issuu.com/icomos/docs/kaplan_paulina_valparaiso_final_201/1

Kasmo, R., & Kutiefan, L. (2021). Post-war recovery of the Old City of Aleppo: The rehabilitation of Suq al-Saqatiyya as a pilot project. ICOMOS and ICCROM Sharjah, *Analysis of Case Studies in Recovery and Reconstruction, 2*, 90–115.

Martinez de Arbulo, A. (2018). Sencho-ji Temple main hall. *ICOMOS Global Case Study Project on Reconstruction.* https://issuu.com/icomos/docs/2018.03.31_sensho-ji___images/19

Nsubuga, J. (2019). The Kasubi Tombs, Uganda. *ICOMOS Global Case Study Project on Reconstruction.* https://issuu.com/icomos/docs/nsubuga_jonathan_kasubi_tombs_01-20

Ohs, A., Forbes, C., Clark, W., & Wykes, F. (2021). Christchurch: recovery from the canterbury earthquakes. *ICOMOS and ICCROM Sharjah, Analysis of Case Studies in Recovery and Reconstruction, 1*, 112–273.

Pullan, W. (2018). Case study in Jerusalem: Damascus Gate and the adjacent areas in the Old City, East and West Jerusalem. *ICOMOS Global Case Study Project on Reconstruction.* https://issuu.com/icomos/docs/pullan-damacus_gate-icomos_global_c/2

Schimek, M. (2021). Flood protection provisions in the world heritage cultural landscape Wachau, Following the Flood of 2002. *ICOMOS and ICCROM Sharjah, Analysis of Case Studies in Recovery and Reconstruction, 2*, 152–183.

Schneider, R. (2021). Reconstruction of the symbolic and physical space of the Temple of Nuestra Señora de la Asunci6n of Santa María Acapulco, San Luis Potosí, México'. ICOMOS and ICCROM Sharjah, *Analysis of Case Studies in Recovery and Reconstruction* 2, 184–215.

(The) Venice Charter for the Conservation and Restoration of Monuments and Sites. (1964).

(The) World Heritage Convention concerning the Protection of the World Cultural and Natural Heritage. (1972).

(The) Athens Charter for the Restoration of Historic Monuments. (1931).

UNESCO. (2022). *UNESCO commits to completing rehabilitation works at Kasubi Tombs in 2022.* https://www.unesco.org/en/articles/unesco-commits-completing-rehabilitation-works-kasubi-tombs-2022

UNESCO World Heritage Convention. (1986). *Ancient City of Aleppo.* https://whc.unesco.org/en/list/21/

UNESCO World Heritage Convention. (2001). *Tombs of Buganda Kings at Kasubi.* https://whc.unesco.org/en/list/1022/

UNESCO Silk Roads Programme, *Ancient City of Aleppo.* https://en.unesco.org/silkroad/silk-road-themes/world-heritage-sites/ancient-city-aleppo

Loughlin Kealy Professor Emeritus in Architecture, University College Dublin, Ireland studied at UCD (philosophy, then architecture) and University of California, Berkeley; practiced architecture in London and Dublin; active in community development, environmental research and education with the Irish Foundation for Human Development; consultant to the Energy Research Group UCD; taught at School of Architecture UCD from 1973 (research: architectural inventory and technology transfer), Director of Conservation Studies 1989–2005; Chair, Scientific Committee, Urban Institute Ireland; Head of School of Architecture UCD; retired from university 2007; Retired Fellow, the Royal Institute of the Architects of Ireland; leading contributor, Irish Government Policies on Architecture, 2002–2005, 2009–2015; currently co-coordinator, Conservation Network of the European Association for Architectural Education; Advisor to State Party on World Heritage Site, Sceilg Mhichil (Ireland) and to ICOMOS International Secretariat (post-trauma recovery and reconstruction); Chair, South Tipperary Arts Centre; editor, contributor to journals, books and conferences.

Trevor H. J. Marchand Emeritus Professor of Social Anthropology at the School of Oriental and African Studies, London, UK. Recipient of the Royal Anthropological Institute's Rivers Memorial Medal (2014). He studied architecture (McGill), received a PhD in anthropology (SOAS), and qualified as a fine woodworker at London's Building Crafts College (2007). Marchand has published extensively. His books include The Pursuit of Pleasurable Work: craftwork in twenty-first century England (2021), Architectural Heritage of Yemen (2017), Craftwork as Problem Solving (2016), The Masons of Djenné (2009, winner of three international prizes), and Minaret Building and Apprenticeship in Yemen (2001). Marchand produces and directs documentary films on architecture and craftwork, and has curated exhibitions for the Brunei Gallery in London, Museum of Oriental Art in Turin, Pergamon Museum in Berlin, Royal Institute of British Architects, and the Smithsonian's National Museum of Natural History. He is an independent advisor on World Heritage for the International Council on Monuments and Sites (ICOMOS) and an advisor on the international experts panel for the Endangered Wooden Architecture Programme at Oxford Brookes University.

Chapter 11
Community and the Reconstruction Process After the Kumamoto Earthquake

Eisuke Tanaka

Abstract In recent years, the frequent occurrence of large-scale natural disasters has led to the development of disaster legislation. However, the preservation of cultural heritage damaged by disasters has not been positioned in the disaster legislation. Focusing on local responses towards the reconstruction of damaged historical buildings in the case of the 2016 Kumamoto Earthquake, this paper explores what is required to position the preservation of damaged cultural heritage in disaster legislation. It demonstrates the importance of human networks between the owners of damaged historic buildings and experts and municipalities. It also suggests the importance of coordination between different support systems to enable the owners to make use of these systems according to their circumstances, with the help of experts.

Keywords Reconstruction process · Human network · Community · Cultural heritage · Kumamoto earthquake · Japan

11.1 Introduction

In general, the administrative act of designation of cultural properties by the national or local government and the process of the inscription on the UNESCO World Heritage List is an opportunity for us to recognize the value of cultural heritage for the targeted properties through news reports in newspapers, television, and the Internet. However, what is considered cultural heritage is not limited to designated cultural properties, world heritage, whose value has been officially recognized. The value of 'heritage' is also found in undesignated historical buildings and long-lasting customs.

One of the triggers for awareness of the value of 'heritage' is disasters. When major disasters occur, such as floods caused by typhoons, torrential rains, or earthquakes, the damage to cultural heritage is widely reported and often becomes a symbol of the magnitude of the damage. An emergency caused by a disaster interrupts the

E. Tanaka (✉)
Research Faculty of Media and Communication, Hokkaido University, Sapporo, Japan
e-mail: eisuket233@imc.hokudai.ac.jp

T. Kono and J. Okahashi (eds.), *Post-Trauma and the Recovery Governance of Cultural Heritage*, https://doi.org/10.1007/978-981-19-6041-3_11

continuity of daily life and brings to the surface the latent distortions in the area. In the process, the value of the tangible and intangible cultural 'heritage' of the affected community is recognized.[1]

In recent years, large-scale natural disasters such as floods and earthquakes have frequently hit Japan, which, at the same time, has entailed the development of disaster laws and regulations. In addition, since the Great Hanshin-Awaji Earthquake in January 1995, a system to support the preservation of cultural heritage damaged by large-scale disasters has been developed. In March 2003, the Cabinet Office, the Ministry of Land, Infrastructure, Transport and Tourism, the Fire and Disaster Management Agency, and the Agency for Cultural Affairs jointly formed the "Committee for Protecting Cultural Heritage and Local Communities from Disasters" to study the roles of various parties involved in cultural heritage (property owners/managers, residents, and government) in the face of earthquake disasters, the concept of disaster prevention planning for cultural heritage in local communities, and specific methods. The basic concept of the plan is to protect cultural heritage from natural disasters. The basic ideas were summarized in the report entitled "Measures to protect cultural heritage and local communities from the earthquake disaster." In response to the Great East Japan Earthquake, which occurred on 11 March 2011, specialized institutions, such as universities, museums, and related expert organizations, formed cooperative relationships nationwide and conducted systematic rescue activities. Since then, efforts have been made to build a network of these institutions for the purpose of disaster prevention and rescue of cultural heritage in the event of a large-scale disaster.

Because cultural heritage is in danger of disappearing as a result of a disaster, its value as 'heritage,' whether designated or undesignated, is recognized, and the question of how it should be preserved is raised. The frequent occurrence of large-scale disasters has led to discussions in various fields on the rescue and conservation of cultural heritage in the event of a large-scale disaster as well as discussions on the importance of disaster prevention. These discussions suggest that while new cultural heritage protection mechanisms, such as efforts to build networks among governments, related organizations, and experts, are being implemented, many cultural heritage sites are disappearing due to disaster. However, it is important to note that these efforts are based on legislation for the protection of cultural heritage during normal times, and the preservation of damaged cultural heritage is not positioned within disaster legislation. In previous studies, the discussion of disaster legislation has been limited.

Based on the report published by the Japan ICOMOS National Committee ("The 2016 Kumamoto Earthquake Report on Damages to the cultural properties and Recommendation for their restoration and rehabilitation") and the results of interviews with related parties including owners, this paper explores how undesignated cultural heritage was protected as the value of 'heritage' was recognized through

---

[1] In recent years, studies on cultural heritage have not only looked at cultural heritage as an object of protection and preservation but also as a social process in which the value of 'heritage' is recognized among various actors involved in tangible and intangible culture (see Harrison 2013; Smith 2006).

disasters. It examines what is required to include the preservation of damaged cultural heritage in disaster legislation. Focusing on the Kumamoto earthquake that occurred in April 2016 as a case study, it analyzes how owners and heritage experts attempted to repair undesignated historical buildings damaged by the earthquake were preserved.

In response to the question of what separated the cultural heritage that was lost through the disaster from the preserved cultural heritage, many previous studies have discussed the problems with existing systems that lead to the loss of cultural heritage. In addition, these discussions have assumed the preservation of the damaged cultural heritage. In order to consider the conservation of damaged cultural heritage with an eye to the post-disaster reconstruction process, it is necessary to examine this premise itself critically. In order to incorporate cultural heritage preservation into disaster legislation and provide a framework for any cultural heritage protection in the reconstruction process, this paper explores what role existing reconstruction support systems play in preserving damaged cultural heritage at the time of the disaster, and how people affected by the disaster use the existing support systems.

First, this paper reviews the recent jurisprudential discussion on the conservation of cultural heritage at the time of the disaster and points out what is missing in the current disaster legislation. Focusing on historical buildings damaged by earthquakes in Japan, it also examines what efforts were made by heritage experts to preserve cultural heritage in the event of a major disaster. Next, the paper overviews the damage situations of the 2016 Kumamoto Earthquake and efforts to preserve the damaged cultural heritage, especially in the Shinmachi and Furumachi areas of Kumamoto City. Then, based on interviews with owners who chose to restore their undesignated historical buildings, this paper considers what is required to restore and preserve cultural heritage in the disaster legislation. Through this, it suggests the importance of a human network to orient owners toward restoration and the importance of coordination among support systems to enable owners to utilize support systems and choose restoration flexibly.

11.2 Cultural Heritage Protection as a Challenge for Current Disaster Legislation in Japan

This section examines the protection of cultural heritage as an issue in the current disaster legislation. It points out that the discussion on the preservation of cultural heritage damaged in disaster recovery legislation is limited (Chapter by Yatsunami for a detailed discussion of disaster legislation and cultural heritage protection, Chapter by Nishi for a detailed discussion of the Cultural Heritage Protection Law and disasters).

11.2.1 Restoration and Conservation of Damaged Cultural Heritage Missing from Disaster Countermeasures

In Japan, specific disaster prevention plans are formulated at the level of each ministry and agency and each local municipality, based on the Disaster Countermeasures Basic Act, a law enacted in 1963. In addition, laws on special measures (Act on Special Measures against Large-Scale Earthquakes and Act on Special Measures against Earthquake Disaster Prevention) have been enacted for earthquake countermeasures and disaster prevention support (Adachi 2014, p. 408). However, since the Great East Japan Earthquake, which is said to be the largest of its kind in the postwar period, there has been a growing interest in the legal system related to major disasters and various issues related to disaster legislation, such as support for evacuees, protection of personal information, and the response of disaster response personnel, have been pointed out, not only in academic books but also in general books (e.g. Tsukui, 2012).

In particular, analyzing the legal needs of disaster victims by analyzing information on free legal consultations that had been provided since immediately after the Great East Japan Earthquake, Tadashi Okamoto (2014, 2018a, 2018b) advocates the systematization of disaster recovery jurisprudence for the designing and operating systems and verifying them during disaster response and recovery based on post-disaster legal needs. Okamoto that the current Basic Act on Disaster Control Measures, Disaster Relief Act, and Disaster Victims' Livelihood Reconstruction Support Act only cover a small number of issues related to the reconstruction of the lives of disaster victims and the economic recovery of companies. He also points out that the areas related to disaster recovery span all fields of public and private law, including existing civil law, land and tenant law, compartmentalized ownership law, bankruptcy law, and personal information protection law, making it difficult to discuss within the framework of conventional public and private law (Okamoto, 2018b, p. 2). Therefore, he argues that disaster recovery jurisprudence should be positioned as a platform for the continuous exploration of cross-disciplinary legal issues.

In his book "Disaster recovery and reconstruction law," published in 2014, Okamoto (2014, p. 7) summarizes the results of free legal consultations following the Great East Japan Earthquake into the twenty four main types of cases. These categories are diverse, including ownership of real estate, cars, boats, etc., lease of the real estate (land and house), liability for structures, neighborly relations (exclusion of disturbance, prevention, compensation for damages), liquid assets such as deposits and stocks, insurance, reconstruction, loans and leases, taxes, divorce, relatives, wills and inheritance, and labor issues. Specific explanations are provided for each category. Okamoto explains each category but does not discuss them from the perspective of damage to cultural heritage. In "Disaster recovery and reconstruction law II," published in 2018 as a sequel to his previous book, he introduces new systems and issues that emerged from the lessons of the Great East Japan Earthquake from the perspectives of housing, family life, and community and information (Okamoto,

2018a). However, there is no direct reference to the treatment of damaged cultural heritage here either.

On the other hand, Shoji Sasaki (2017) proposes an integrated approach to disaster prevention and reconstruction, including disaster prevention, emergency response, emergency measures, and reconstruction and recovery measures.[2] Specifically, he suggests the need to integrate disaster management from the following three perspectives (Sasaki, 2017, pp. 1–3).

1. Integrated response and mutual coordination of disaster prevention, emergency response, emergency measures, and recovery and reconstruction measures.
2. Consolidate policies to strengthen cooperation between the government and the private sector.
3. Breaking down the stove-piping among administrative staff in the field and strengthening substantive cooperation.

The first point is about an effort to create a system that will enable government officials to deal with disaster prevention, emergency and first-aid measures, and disaster recovery and reconstruction projects in an integrated manner, which have traditionally been handled separately (Sasaki, 2017, p. 2). Secondly, the cooperation of the private sector in terms of utilizing private facilities as well as securing human resources is essential for the appropriate and smooth implementation of emergency measures, such as the operation of evacuation centers and the issuance of disaster victim certificates after a disaster. Sasaki argues that integrating policies is necessary to strengthen such cooperation between the government and the private sector (Sasaki, 2017, p. 2). Finally, in the event of a large-scale disaster, a chain of command from the national government to local municipalities is established according to the relevant ministries and agencies of the national government. However, in urgent situations, such as saving lives and maintaining the living environment of disaster victims, municipalities close to the disaster site need to support each other's operations to the extent that the vertical chain of command is not hindered. It is also important to support each other at the municipal level (Sasaki, 2017, pp. 2–3). Thus, Sasaki argues that the necessity of strengthening cooperation among administrative staff in the field should transcend vertical divisions. However, in his discussion, there is no mention of cultural heritage damaged by the disaster.

In the event of a large-scale disaster, there is a wide range of issues that need to be addressed. Notably, previous studies on disaster legislation have pointed out the importance of mutual coordination and cooperation beyond the framework of government and the private sector for an integrated response from the disaster prevention stage during normal times to the emergency and response stage immediately after the disaster, and to the recovery and reconstruction stage after the disaster. At the same time, however, there has been limited attention paid to issues related to the

[2] When the Great East Japan Earthquake occurred, Sasaki was involved in the planning of the reconstruction system for the earthquake. He later became Deputy Director-General for Disaster Management in the Cabinet Office and worked on the planning of a permanent disaster prevention and reconstruction system.

restoration and conservation of damaged cultural heritage from the perspective of disaster legislation.

11.2.2 The Law for the Protection of Cultural Properties and Disasters

The need to respond to disasters was the driving force behind the enactment of the Law Concerning the Protection of Cultural Properties in Japan (Hisasue, 2020, p. 1). On 26 January 1946, a fire broke out in the Golden Hall of Horyu-ji Temple, the oldest existing wooden structure in the world, destroying most of the murals in the hall, which were considered to be representative of ancient Buddhist paintings. In addition to this incident, there were a series of other incidents in which historical buildings, such as the castle tower of Matsumae Castle, were lost due to fires. This heightened social interest in the need to protect cultural heritage from disasters. Consequently, the Law for the Protection of Cultural Properties was enacted in 1950.

Under the Law for the Protection of Cultural Properties, there are two levels of designation by the national government, especially for tangible cultural properties and monuments, depending on the level of importance. Priority is given to the protection of particularly important objects (Hisasue, 2020, p. 9). The law also stipulates specific repair methods using traditional methods, restoration work for large-scale disasters, and special projects that are carried out separately from general repair projects because they require a long repair period and a large amount of money (Articles 34 to 43 of the Law for Protection of Cultural Properties). The law also deals with state compensation for national treasures and important cultural properties as a provision for damages under special laws. Provisions for damage caused by natural disasters are built into Articles 136 and 140 (Hisasue, 2020, p. 10).

Examining legislation for the protection of cultural properties in the event of a disaster in a modern city, Yayoi Hisasue (2020) discusses the limitation of the current Law for the Protection of Cultural Properties. Concerning the provisions on state-funded compensation for damage caused by natural disasters, she points out that the targeted cultural properties are limited and do not assume urban disasters (Hisasue, 2020, p. 10). In particular, she discusses that the existing classification of cultural properties under the Law for the Protection of Cultural Properties, which assumes damage to tangible objects, should be updated to include damage to intangible cultural heritage such as folk materials. She also argues that it is necessary to supplement the current legislation by developing a legal system to rescue damaged cultural heritage as an after-the-fact response to extreme natural disasters (Hisasue, 2020, p. 12).

According to the Law for the Protection of Cultural Properties, national and local governments are to ensure that all tangible cultural properties are properly preserved, regardless of whether they are designated or not (Hisasue, 2020, p. 10). As mentioned in the Introduction, efforts to preserve damaged cultural heritage since the beginning of the 2000s have assumed that cultural heritage to be preserved in the event of a large-scale disaster includes nationally designated cultural properties and undesignated cultural heritage. In the above-mentioned "Measures to protect cultural heritage and local communities from earthquake disaster," it is stated that 'cultural heritage includes not only cultural properties as defined by law but also, in a broader sense, spatial properties such as historical landscapes and townscapes' (Committee for Protecting Cultural Heritage & Local Communities from Disasters, 2003, p. 3). The fact that designated and undesignated cultural heritage is considered to represent the identity of the region in which they are located means that the utilization and inheritance of rescued damaged cultural heritage is also linked to future disaster prevention and mitigation (e.g. Okumura, 2014b, p. 29; Hidaka, 2019, p. 52). Nevertheless, while designated cultural properties are positioned as common social property with a legal basis under the National Law for the Protection of Cultural Properties and the cultural property protection ordinances of local governments, undesignated historical buildings do not have such legal status (Adachi, 2014, p. 407).[3] Therefore, the restoration cost burden on the owner is greater for undesignated buildings than for designated historical buildings. Hiroshi Adachi (2014, p. 408) points out that the difference in public support depending on whether a building is designated cultural property or not is a significant factor leading to the dismantling of damaged cultural heritage.

The Law for the Protection of Cultural Properties was revised in June 2018. Its purpose was to prevent the loss or destruction of cultural properties due to depopulation and the aging of society, and to promote the inheritance of cultural heritage, including undesignated cultural properties, while utilizing them for urban development. Hisasue evaluates this amendment as a step forward in terms of countermeasures against urban disasters (Hisasue, 2020, pp. 13–15). For example, as for the comprehensive conservation and utilization of cultural properties in the region, which is the purpose of the amendment, she argues that the revised law leads to the promotion of the inheritance of undesignated cultural properties. She points out that the background of this is that the damage to undesignated cultural properties in urban disasters is remarkable (Hisasue, 2020, p. 14). Furthermore, since the new provisions in the 2018 amendment include more references to disaster prevention, Hisasue (2020, p. 15) sees this revision as the beginning of a cultural property protection law system in Japan that assumes urban disasters.

11.2.3 Issues Related to Field-Level Responses

So far, this paper has pointed out that the current disaster legislation and the legal framework of cultural heritage protection have limitations in dealing with cultural heritage damaged by disasters. In light of this, this section looks at what efforts are being made to preserve cultural heritage in the event of a large-scale disaster and what

[3] However, in recent years, not a few municipalities have included undesignated cultural properties in the regional plan for the utilization and conservation of cultural properties.

issues cultural heritage experts have identified in the field. Since this paper looks at a case study of the restoration of undesignated historical buildings damaged in the Kumamoto earthquake, it will mainly focus on the issues of damaged buildings.

First of all, since the Great Hanshin-Awaji Earthquake in 1995, establishing a network to support the conservation of cultural heritage in the event of a large-scale disaster has been in full swing among experts dealing with cultural heritage (Okumura, 2014b, p. 14). At the same time, there has been an accumulation of research on the safeguarding of tangible and intangible cultural heritage in the event of a large-scale natural disaster in related fields such as architecture, conservation science, cultural anthropology, and folklore studies. In particular, there have been many reports on the rescue of damaged historical documents and the damage of intangible cultural heritage in the earthquakes and disasters that have occurred in the 2000s and 2010s, such as the Great East Japan Earthquake in 2011, the Western Tottori Earthquake in 2000, the Northern Miyagi Earthquake in 2003, the Niigata Chuetsu Earthquake in 2004, and the Fukuoka Earthquake in 2005. Many scholars have reported efforts to rescue damaged historical materials and damage to intangible folk cultural properties in earthquake disasters that have occurred in the past two decades (Okumura, 2014a; Kibe, 2015a; Society for Cultural Property Restoration, 2007; Morii et al., 2018; Takakura & Takizawa, 2014 etc.). These studies, which deal with both response to the damage to cultural heritage in disaster and efforts in areas where no specific disaster has occurred, discuss how cultural heritage should be preserved in the reconstruction process before, during and after a disaster and how the required network of government and experts should be built. However, as Nobuko Kibe (2015b, p. ii) notes, accumulated previous studies have shown that 'human cultures are diverse, and this has led to a variety of conservation activities during disasters'.

In the case of movable cultural properties, examining the issues of cultural property rescue in the Great East Japan Earthquake, Shingo Hidaka (2019, pp. 50–51) argues that the goal of cultural property rescue should not be limited to the treatment of the damage of the disaster. He points out that it should also include how the rescued cultural properties should be used and passed on in the community afterwards. Similarly, Satoshi Shirouzu, who was involved in the rescue of cultural properties in the Northern Nagano Earthquake that occurred the day after the 2011 Great East Japan Earthquake, emphasizes the importance of post-rescue care in cultural property conservation activities and the significance of passing on culture as a living thing (Shirouzu, 2014, p. 310).

Furthermore, Saori Maekawa, who worked as a curator at Tono Culture Research Center in Tono, northeast Japan, discusses the importance of human networks in the event of a disaster (Maekawa, 2019, p. 77). When the Great East Japan Earthquake struck, she was involved in rescuing cultural properties doing her best to use the public and private networks she had built up (Maekawa, 2019, pp. 79–82). She utilized the network she built through this experience in the subsequent floods caused by a typhoon that hit Tono in 2016 (Maekawa, 2019, pp. 88–91). Based on her own experience, Maekawa suggests that building a human network for the conservation of cultural heritage should be considered not only at the time of a large-scale disaster but also from a long-term perspective, including pre-disaster efforts and the maintenance of relationships after the disaster.

For professionals involved in the preservation of cultural heritage, 'a disaster is a situation that interrupts the continuity of daily life' and 'exposes the incompleteness and inadequacy of measures that should have been taken in advance' (Adachi, 2014, p. 406). Similarly, owners of undesignated old buildings affected by a disaster are forced to decide whether to repair or demolish their properties. However, such a situation also means an opportunity for the owners to reevaluate the historical value of their damaged building and their future relationship.

What are the assumptions behind the discovery of the value of old buildings as 'heritage' in the wake of disasters? Above mentioned previous studies have pointed out that while there is great significance in passing on cultural heritage to future generations, the premise of the discussion is that once lost, it becomes challenging to restore cultural heritage. For example, Hidaka discusses that cultural heritage rescue in disaster areas will lead to the recovery of memories of the living culture of the disaster areas, from the standpoint that 'preserving cultural heritage for the future is the foundation for building a prosperous society' (Hidaka, 2015, p. 180). Adachi argues that the loss of the historical environment will lead to the loss of individuality of the town, which in turn will lead to the crisis of survival of the town. He discusses how to take measures before and after the disaster to minimize the damage (Adachi, 2014, pp. 407–408).

National and local governments also share this premise. As an example of intangible folk cultural properties, Hiroki Takakura, who was the principal investigator of the "Survey of Folk Cultural Properties Damaged by the Great East Japan Earthquake" commissioned by Miyagi Prefecture, points out that in the post-earthquake reconstruction administration, there was an assumption that intangible folk cultural properties could play a certain role in rebuilding local communities (Takakura, 2014, pp. 293–297).

In response to why some cultural heritage disappeared after a disaster while other cultural heritage was preserved, many previous studies, from the standpoint of cultural heritage experts, have considered the preservation of cultural heritage as a necessary condition for disaster recovery. They have discussed problems with existing systems that lead to the loss of cultural heritage. In other words, the preservation of cultural heritage was a prerequisite, and the discussion focused on why its preservation was unsuccessful. However, in considering the desirable way of preserving cultural heritage after the disaster, it is necessary to pay more attention to why it disappeared, why it was preserved, and what kind of actions led to its preservation.

11.3 Efforts to Preserve Cultural Heritage Damaged by the Kumamoto Earthquake in the Shinmachi and Furumachi Areas of Kumamoto City

The Kumamoto earthquake that occurred in April 2016 was considered the largest inland earthquake to hit Japan since the end of World War II. The earthquake destroyed 6,090 houses, half destroyed 20,219, and partially damaged 85,635. In addition, 1,042 non-residential dwellings were damaged (Japan ICOMOS National Committee, 2019, p. 3). At the end of May 2016, damage to cultural heritage was reported in 6 Prefectures in Kyushu, including 96 nationally designated and registered cultural properties and 54 designated cultural properties designated by prefectures, two thirds of which were found in Kumamoto Prefecture, the epicenter of the earthquake (Morii et al., 2018, p. 181; Japan ICOMOS National Committee, 2019, p. 4). Notably, damage to Kumamoto Castle, a special historic site, and the tower gate of Aso Shrine, a nationally designated important cultural property, were widely covered in the media, making a nationwide impression of the magnitude of the damage caused by the Kumamoto earthquake.

In this section, this paper examines the movements toward the damaged cultural heritage after the Kumamoto earthquake, the support systems involved, and the issues involved. In particular, it focuses on the restoration of undesignated historical buildings in the Shinmachi and Furumachi areas of Kumamoto City as a case study.

11.3.1 Response to the Cultural Heritage Affected by the Kumamoto Earthquake

Actions to preserve cultural heritage damaged by the Kumamoto earthquake began immediately after the quake. Concerning historical buildings, the Architectural Institute of Japan, the Japan Institute of Architects, the Japan Federation of Architects, the Japan Society of Civil Engineers, and other related organizations discussed how to deal with the situation at the Agency for Cultural Affairs for approximately one week after the main quake on16th April. As a result, they decided to set up a committee to implement a project to support the restoration of cultural properties damaged by the Kumamoto earthquake (hereinafter referred to as the "Dispatch of Cultural Property Doctors Project"). The Agency for Cultural Affairs commissioned this project with the Federation of Architectural Institute of Japan as the secretariat (Japan ICOMOS National Committee, 2019, pp. 81–83).

In the "Dispatch of Cultural Property Doctors Project", experts with skills in surveying and restoring historical buildings called "heritage managers" were dispatched to survey the damage to historical buildings, both designated and undesignated, based on the "Historical Building Inventory Database" prepared by the Architectural Institute of Japan (Japan ICOMOS National Committee, 2019, p. 81). This survey was twofold: the first survey aimed to assess the external appearance of the damaged building from the exterior; the second survey included a more detailed survey of the interior of the selected buildings. The first survey, which started in June 2016, covered 1,687 historical buildings in Kumamoto and Oita prefectures. In particular, priority was given to the survey of buildings with official statuses, such as nationally registered cultural properties, those designated by the prefecture or municipality, those designated as Structures of Landscape Importance, and Important Structure for City Scenery Formation. As for undesignated buildings, the survey focused on those located in historical districts (Japan ICOMOS National Committee, 2019, p. 81). The second survey was a detailed investigation that included an internal survey, preparation of drawings necessary for technical support, and interviews. It focused on the 435 buildings whose owners had requested further investigation.

Although the details will be discussed in the next section, Kumamoto Prefecture decided to implement a project to support the restoration of historical buildings, including those that had not yet been designated, by using the fund to restore and reconstruct damaged cultural properties. The target of this project is those buildings for which the second survey of the "Dispatch of Cultural Property Doctors Project" was conducted (Japan ICOMOS National Committee, 2019, p. 82).

In the fiscal year of 2017, the "Dispatch of Cultural Property Doctors Project" commissioned by the Agency for Cultural Affairs was continued, focusing on technical advice to property owners for the use of the reconstruction fund of Kumamoto Prefecture (Japan ICOMOS National Committee, 2019, p. 82, see below). The specific targets of the support were 114 buildings that were the subject of the second survey and needed further support and 45 more properties that were not included in the previous year's dispatch project survey but were recommended by the local municipalities (Japan ICOMOS National Committee, 2019, p. 82). The experts individually visited the owners of these 159 buildings to inform them of the subsidy system, discuss the problems they were facing, and confirm their intention to preserve them. The project's purpose was to provide practical support for receiving subsidies for restoration support, such as presenting restoration methods and calculating costs. This initiative is regarded as the third survey of the "Dispatch of Cultural Property Doctors Project" (Japan ICOMOS National Committee, 2019, p. 83).

Private organizations in Japan and abroad also carried out support activities to restore the damaged historical buildings. One notable example was the Kumamoto Machinami Trust (hereinafter referred to as KMT), which has engaged in the preservation and utilization of modern architecture in the historic quarter of Kumamoto City. Immediately after the Kumamoto earthquake, KMT supported a survey of the damage to historical buildings conducted by the Japan ICOMOS National Committee. Many of the heritage managers involved in the above-mentioned "Dispatch of Cultural Property Doctors Project" also participated in the activities organized by KMT (Japan ICOMOS National Committee, 2019, pp. 86–91). The case of the 2016 Kumamoto Earthquake suggests that the restoration support activities were based on the human network between the government and private sector that had been established before the earthquake.

11.3.2 Support Systems for Disaster Recovery and Conservation of Damaged Cultural Heritage and Their Problems

In Japan, historical buildings damaged in a large-scale disaster receive a variety of support related to disaster recovery measures. However, immediately after a disaster strikes, the owners and users of historical buildings, who are also affected by the disaster, may have to rebuild their lives first, and the measures for livelihood rehabilitation are not necessarily aimed at preserving of their historical buildings. In this section, this paper will discuss the following systems that influenced the decision to preserve or demolish historical buildings damaged by the Kumamoto earthquake.

1. Emergency Safety Evaluation of Damaged Buildings
2. Determination of Disaster Victim Certificate
3. The support system of dismantlement at public expense
4. Small and Medium Enterprise Association Disaster Recovery Project (subsidy for groups of small and medium-sized enterprises.)
5. Subsidies from the Fund for Restoration and Rehabilitation of Damaged Cultural Properties.

First of all, Emergency Safety Evaluation of Damaged Buildings (hereinafter referred to as "emergency safety evaluation") is an emergency risk survey of the damage to buildings conducted by each municipality in order to prevent secondary disasters caused by damaged buildings due to aftershocks and to ensure the safety of residents (Japan ICOMOS National Committee, 2019, p. 72). Immediately after the main quake, the survey starts with the most urgent areas, and stickers will be put up in different colors: red for "Dangerous", yellow for "Caution", and green for "Surveyed". The purpose of the emergency safety evaluation is to provide information on the danger of the building to the owner and people passing by, not to issue a disaster certificate (Japan ICOMOS National Committee, 2019, p. 72).

However, the report of the Japan ICOMOS National Committee pointed out that the problem was that the victims were not thoroughly informed about the purpose of the emergency safety evaluation. In particular, when a red "Dangerous" sticker (commonly known as "Red Paper") is attached to a building to warn that the building is off-limits, it can lead to misunderstandings by the owner, such as 'I can no longer live in that building' or 'I will lose my property value.' The owners sometimes chose to demolish their buildings (Japan ICOMOS National Committee, 2019, p. 107). KMT members also pointed this out in the interviews.

Secondly, determining a Disaster Victim Certificate based on the survey of damage to buildings played an important role in receiving public aid for the restoration or demolition of buildings. Depending on the category, such as "totally destroyed," "mostly destroyed," and "partially destroyed," victims can receive relief money and support for rebuilding their lives. In particular, the category of "totally destroyed" provides more support for each household (Japan ICOMOS National Committee,

2019, pp. 72–74). In the case of the Kumamoto earthquake, this point significantly impacted the demolition of the damaged houses at public expense.

As for the demolition of damaged houses, in May 2016, one month after the earthquake, it became possible that the houses that were judged as "totally destroyed," "mostly destroyed," or "partially destroyed" were dismantled at public expense as part of the disaster waste disposal project conducted by the municipal government with the owner's consent. However, this system led to the dismantling of damaged historical buildings judged as "mostly destroyed" and "partially destroyed" because households with "mostly destroyed" and "partially destroyed" ratings and opted for demolition received the same amount of support as those households as households with a "totally destroyed" rating (Japan ICOMOS National Committee, 2019, p. 107).

Between October and December 2020, 5 years after the earthquake, the Historical Buildings Committee of the Kumamoto Prefecture Association of Architects & Building Engineers surveyed on the current situation of historical buildings damaged by the Kumamoto Earthquake (Historical Buildings Committee, 2021).[4] The survey mainly focused on the 435 historical buildings investigated in the "Dispatch of Cultural Property Doctors Project" in 2016. The overall trend is that about 70% of the buildings have been restored, about 15% have been demolished, and less than half have been rebuilt. The remaining 15% were either left as emergency measures or had not yet been taken. In the case of privately owned buildings, 22.1% were not restored to their original state, such as demolished or rebuilt, while only 9.9% of public buildings and religious facilities that were not privately owned were not restored to their original state (Historical Buildings Committee, 2021). Because public funds cover the cost of demolition, whereas the restoration of privately owned buildings requires self-financing, the survey results are consistent with the point made above that the support system of dismantlement at public expense has encouraged the demolition of privately owned historical buildings.

On the other hand, there is a support system that does not directly aim at preserving and restoring damaged historical buildings but, as a consequence, has contributed to their relief. One such program is the Small and Medium Enterprise Association Disaster Recovery Project (hereinafter referred to as Group Subsidy), which was established in the wake of the 2011 Great East Japan Earthquake. The Group Subsidy is a subsidy system for small and medium-sized enterprises affected by the disaster to continue their business. It is strictly limited to business facilities, and 75% of the estimated cost of the restoration work is subsidized (Japan ICOMOS National Committee, 2019, pp. 77–78). In the case of the Kumamoto Earthquake, the program started calling for applications in June 2016, two months after the earthquake and started accepting applications in September (Japan ICOMOS National Committee, 2019, p. 78). Although the scheme only covers the cost for parts of the buildings

[4] This survey was commissioned by Prof. Toshiyuki Kono, the Graduate School of Law, Kyushu University, as part of the "International Joint Research for the Development of an Integrated Governance Methodology for Cultural Heritage Protection" (Research Representative: Toshiyuki Kono), an international research project funded under the scheme of the JSPS "Project for the Promotion of Leading Humanities and Social Sciences Research through the Setting of Challenges" (Global Development Program).

for business use, the system motivated owners to consider restoration instead of demolition according to their needs (Japan ICOMOS National Committee, 2019, p. 78).

Finally, as a support system for the conservation of cultural heritage, while there is a public subsidy system for the restoration of cultural properties that are designated by the government, for privately owned properties, even if they are designated as cultural properties, a high percentage of the burden is borne by the owner, which makes the progress of restoration slow down. In addition, in the case of undesignated properties, there was concern that some owners would have no choice but to demolish them at public expense due to the lack of existing subsidy systems (Japan ICOMOS National Committee, 2019, p. 79). In the case of Kumamoto Earthquake, thanks to the efforts of the "Liaison Council of Affected Cultural Heritage Owners", which was formed by owners of undesignated historical buildings (see below), Kumamoto Prefecture has established a new subsidy system (hereinafter referred to as "Cultural Heritage Subsidy") using the "2016 Kumamoto Earthquake Affected Cultural Properties Reconstruction Fund."[5] Japan ICOMOS National Committee points out that establishing this framework, which can financially support the restoration of undesignated cultural properties as well as designated cultural properties and registered tangible cultural properties, was a significant breakthrough (Japan ICOMOS National Committee, 2019, p. 109). In the framework of "Cultural Heritage Subsidy", the government subsidized half of the cost of restoration, design and management of registered tangible cultural properties. As for registered tangible cultural properties and undesignated cultural properties (historical buildings and movable cultural properties) for which there was no public subsidy system until then, the government subsidized up to two thirds of the owner's share of the construction costs (Japan ICOMOS National Committee, 2019, p. 109, see Fig. 11.1). This subsidy system started accepting applications in April 2017, and the decision to grant the subsidy was made in November 2017.

Japan ICOMOS National Committee (2019, p. 109) points out that the timing of the implementation of these public policies that affected the dismantling and restoration of historical buildings damaged by the Kumamoto earthquake differed from each other, and this was a factor that made owners of undesignated historical buildings decide to choose to dismantle them at public expense. In particular, while the call for applications for dismantlement at public expense began immediately after the Kumamoto earthquake and the work would be completed by the end of the fiscal year of 2017, the establishment of the "Cultural Heritage Subsidy" and the start of accepting applications came in the second half of 2017. Since the demolition of the damaged building funded by the dismantlement at public expense program was to be completed in time for the end of the fiscal year of 2017 (March 2018), some owners could not wait for the decision of the "Cultural Heritage Subsidy" (Japan ICOMOS National Committee, 2019, p. 78).

---

[5] The "2016 Kumamoto Earthquake Affected Cultural Properties Reconstruction Fund" was based on the reconstruction fund given by the government and donations from the private sector.

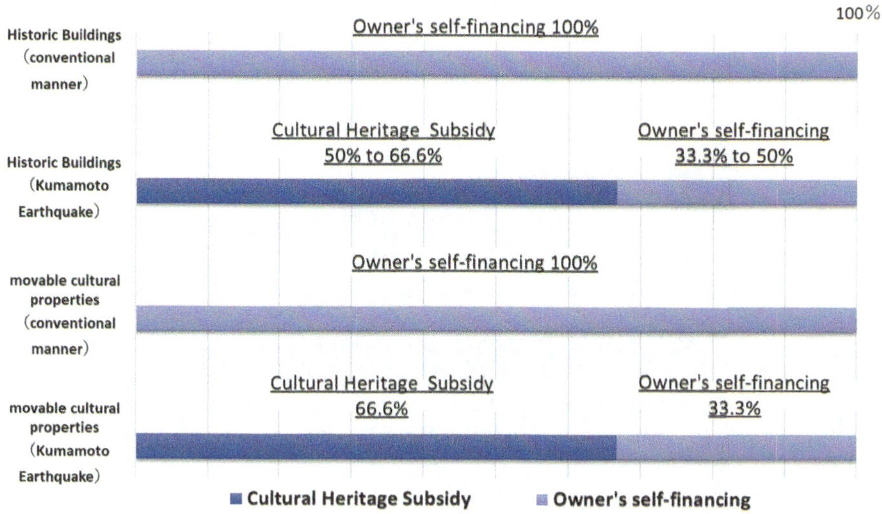

Fig. 11.1 Subsidy system for undesignated cultural heritage damaged by the disaster (Japan ICOMOS National Committee, 2019, p. 80)

As we have seen, various public support systems were in place for the Kumamoto earthquake. However, there was a time lag in the establishment of these systems. Considering the gap in the timing of the support systems and their financial circumstances, the owners of the affected historical buildings decided whether to restore or dismantle their buildings.

11.3.3 Case Studies of the Reconstruction Process of Damaged Historical Townhouses in the Shinmachi and Furumachi Areas, Kumamoto City

The Shinmachi and Furumachi districts in the center of Kumamoto City formed as the castle town of Kumamoto Castle in the seventeenth century. Although the areas were destroyed by fire in the Civil War after the Meiji Restoration, they continued to develop by inheriting the town layout during the Edo Era. According to a survey conducted by KMT in 2008, there were still 447 old houses called "machiya" found in these areas, which had been rebuilt after the Civil War (Japan ICOMOS National Committee, 2019, p. 50). However, KMT conducted another survey immediately after the Kumamoto Earthquake, which shows that the number of historical townhouses had decreased to 357(Japan ICOMOS National Committee, 2019, p. 78). The Kumamoto earthquake further accelerated the demolition of these buildings in the area, which had progressed slowly before the earthquake. By 2018, the number of historical townhouses decreased only to 201 (Japan ICOMOS National Committee,

Fig. 11.2 A restored historic house in the Shinmachi and Furumachi Areas (Photo by Author)

2019, p. 50). Nevertheless, according to the results of the "Survey on Historical Buildings Damaged by the Kumamoto Earthquake" mentioned above, the historical townhouses in the Shinmachi and Furumachi areas have been restored at a higher rate than those in Chuo Ward, where building reconstruction through redevelopment projects is underway, and Higashi Ward, which is close to Mashiki Town that was severely damaged by the earthquake (Historical Buildings Committee, 2021; Figs. 11.2 and 11.3). Before examining individual cases of how owners of damaged historical buildings have chosen to restore their historical buildings, this paper will briefly contextualize the post-disaster activities in the Shinmachi and Furumachi districts.

Established in 1997, KMT has played a significant role in preserving undesignated historical buildings in the Shinmachi and Furumachi areas. Immediately after the Kumamoto Earthquake, KMT was involved in surveying the damaged townhouses and modern buildings in the Shinmachi and Furumachi areas. Moreover, KMT members were stationed in these areas to consult with owners of undesignated historical buildings that were particularly affected by the earthquake about repairing them and applying for support programs (Japan ICOMOS National Committee, 2019, pp. 86–87).

Notably, KMT supported the establishment of the "Liaison Council of Owners of Cultural Heritage Affected by the Earthquake" (hereinafter the Liaison Council) in

Fig. 11.3 A restored shop in the Shinmachi and Furumachi Areas (Photo by Author)

November 2016 and served as its secretariat. Consisting of owners of historical buildings in the Shinmachi, Furumachi, and Kawajiri areas,[6] the Liaison Council aims to urge the government to provide financial support for the restoration of undesignated historical buildings damaged by the Kumamoto Earthquake. Through their urging, Kumamoto Prefecture established the "Cultural Heritage Subsidy" (Japan ICOMOS National Committee, 2019, pp. 86–87). In addition, in the summer of 2017, the Council signed a partnership agreement with the World Monument Foundation (WMF) and obtained financial support from WMF for a project to restore 5 historical buildings along the Tojin-machi street in the Shinmachi and Furumachi areas (Japan ICOMOS National Committee, 2019, pp. 89–91).

As shown in the following two cases, KMT's activities in the Shinmachi and Furumachi areas, such as helping owners obtain public support and external funding, were also deciding factors for owners to choose restoration over demolition.[7]

[6] Eight kilometers south of the city center of Kumamoto, there are many historic houses in the Kawajiri area as it flourished as a port of Kumamoto Castle Town during the Edo Era.

[7] The interviews with the owners of the damaged historical houses in the Shinmachi and Furumachi areas were conducted in April 2021.

11.3.3.1 Case Study 1: Store a, Household Goods Sales

Store A, a merchant house, was built in 1887 after the Civil War, consisting of the main building, a storehouse, and other buildings.[8] The building complex had not been designated cultural property at the time of the Kumamoto Earthquake. The owner said that the local government had asked him to designate the house as Structures of Landscape Importance, but he refused. The building was already over 120 years old before the earthquake, and in any case, he thought that repairs to the house were necessary.

Although the house did not collapse in the Kumamoto earthquake, all the buildings were damaged. The judgement of the emergency safety evaluation was "red (Dangerous)," and the Disaster Victim Certificate was judged as "totally destroyed." At first, the owner thought to apply for the support system of dismantlement at public expense to demolish his damaged old house and rebuild it because, given the extent of the damage and an estimate of the cost of repairs, he realized that it would be difficult to repair the buildings at his own expense.

However, the owner could communicate with KMT members stationed in the Shinmachi and Furumachi areas. He began to consider the possibility of restoring the buildings while considering the option of demolishing them at public expense. He joined the Liaison Council, and urged the local government to establish a subsidy for undesignated cultural heritage damaged by the earthquake. As a result, the Cultural Heritage Subsidy was established to support the restoration of undesignated cultural properties. In addition, through the partnership with WMF, Store A became one of the historical buildings for KMT's restoration project. With the combination of the group subsidy, Cultural Heritage Subsidy, and the support from WMF, the owner was able to secure funding for the restoration of the house, and he decided to withdraw his application for the support system of dismantlement at public expense in December 2017. His decision was made at the last minute because the demolition of the damaged building with financial support from the dismantlement at public expense program had to be completed by the end of March 2018. Although some of the severely damaged buildings had to be demolished, the restoration of the main building and a storehouse, which started in the spring of 2018, was completed in March 2020.

11.3.3.2 Case Study 2: Store B, Production and Sales of Herbal Medicines

The first proprietor of Store B moved from Nagasaki to Kumamoto in the first half of the nineteenth century and developed their business with great success in manufacturing and selling herbal medicines. Today, Store B consists of 13 buildings (including the main building, a teahouse, a pharmaceutical building, and storehouses) and gardens built after the Civil War to the end of the Meiji era. However, the mansion

[8] The owner's family has been running a shop since the mid-Edo period.

was rarely opened to the public due to the importance of protecting the family business. For this reason, although Shore B was designated as Structures of Landscape Importance by Kumamoto City in September 1995, there was no move to designate it as cultural property before the Kumamoto Earthquake.

All buildings in the compound were damaged during the earthquake. The emergency safety evaluation" was "Red (Dangerous)," and the Disaster Victim Certificate was judged as "mostly destroyed." The cost of repairing all the buildings would be enormous, and raising all the money on their own was difficult. However, the owner said that she could not think of demolishing the building because she wanted to protect her family business. In addition, the Group Subsidy program started calling for applications in June 2016. Fortunately, since the machinery used to manufacture the family's herbal medicines was not damaged by the earthquake, the owner thought that there was a prospect that she would be able to continue the business using the Group Subsidy to repair the buildings. In this way, she came to think that she could (and wanted to) do something to protect the mansion inherited from her ancestors. In addition, like the owner of Store A, she also joined the Liaison Council through KMT, which she said was a great way to share her concerns with other owners to feel that she was not alone.

In the case of Store B, the restoration work was to be funded by the Group Subsidy for the store and pharmaceutical building, while the residential part was to be supported by Cultural Heritage Subsidy. In addition, discussing with KMT members about the house's restoration, the owner of Store B started to consider future designation as a cultural property. It was necessary to avoid losing the building's historical value through hasty repairs. Therefore, under the supervision of the KMT's experts, the focus was on temporary reinforcement and seismic countermeasures to maintain the current state of the building until full-scale repair in the future.

As mentioned in the introduction, disasters are an opportunity for owners to reaffirm the significance of their historical buildings as 'heritage,' which significantly influences whether to restore or demolish their houses. The owner of Store B said that the earthquake made her realize that her purpose in life was to protect her family business and home. That is why demolishing her house using the scheme of dismantlement at public expense was 'unthinkable.' She also said that the sympathy and encouragement he received from her neighbors and customers made her feel that '(the family business and house) is not just my personal property.'

11.4 Requirements for Locating the Restoration and Preservation of Damaged Cultural Heritage in Disaster Legislation

In the previous section, I have reviewed the damage caused by the Kumamoto earthquake and the support system for cultural heritage damaged by the earthquake. I have also demonstrated how undesignated cultural heritage damaged in the Shinmachi and Furumachi areas of Kumamoto City was restored, focusing on the actions of the owners and intermediate support groups. This paper suggests three requirements below for restoring and preserving damaged cultural heritage in disaster legislation. This section explores each of these requirements in detail.

1. Development of a support system for the conservation and restoration of undesignated cultural heritage
2. Coordination among different support systems to enable "juggling" of support
3. Building a human network to connect owners, experts, and government.

11.4.1 Development of Support System for the Conservation and Restoration of Undesignated Cultural Heritage

In both the cases of Store A and Store B, at issue was how to raise the cost of restoring undesignated historical buildings. In the case of Store A, the problem was that the owner could not choose between demolition and restoration immediately after the disaster according to his needs. The owner wanted to rebuild the house and continue to live in the same place even if he demolished the original house. Even if he wanted to demolish the house and build a new one, he would have to pay for the reconstruction, which he could do at his own expense. However, over time, the establishment of the Cultural Heritage Subsidy and financial support from the WMF made it possible to restore the house as much as he could at his own expense. The owner said that this encouraged him to choose restoration instead of demolition.

On the other hand, in the case of Store B, the owner sought restoration immediately after the disaster. The Group Subsidies funded the restoration work for the store and factory part, but the Cultural Heritage Subsidy funded the residential part. However, even with public support, the scope of repairs was so enormous that it was difficult for the owner to carry out all the repairs she wanted to do with the money she could afford. The owner of Store B also said, 'It is difficult to give a percentage of how much I could repair my house.'

Before the Kumamoto Earthquake, in the case of undesignated cultural heritage compared to designated cultural heritage, the share of the burden on the owner for post-disaster restoration was greater. In addition, owners tended to choose to dismantle their historical buildings when judged to be "mostly destroyed" or "partially destroyed" in emergency safety evaluation of damaged buildings. Given the limitations of their self-financing, some owners have no choice but to demolish their buildings using the system of dismantlement at public expense. On the other hand, if the restoration of damaged historical buildings as a cultural property, even if not yet designated as such, will reduce the financial burden on their owners, then their owners will have the option of restoring instead of demolishing them. That is why the establishment of a subsidy that supports the restoration of undesignated historical buildings after the Kumamoto earthquake was so revolutionary. In fact, like the owner of Store A, restoring the damaged building became an option. Although there are issues to be considered, such as securing the source of funds for subsidies, reducing the financial burden on owners of cultural heritage, particularly undesignated cultural heritage, is crucial. Increasing owners' options by expanding the support system in disaster legislation will save damaged cultural heritage at risk of demolishing.

11.4.2 Coordination Among Different Support Systems to Enable "Juggling" of Support

Since the Kumamoto Earthquake, various public support frameworks have been prepared for the demolition and recovery of cultural heritage damaged by the earthquake. However, there was a time lag in setting up these public support frameworks, which consequently promoted the demolition of undesignated historical buildings. As the case study of Store A shows, owners who applied for the dismantlement at public expense had to complete the demolition of their damaged buildings by the end of March 2018. The owners were forced to make a decision on whether to restore or demolish the building while keeping an eye on the timing.

Moreover, even when owners chose restoration, their decision differed. The restoration using the public support system also differed depending on the owners' circumstances. Some public support programs, such as the Group Subsidy, which was initially intended for business continuity, were used to help restore the damaged historical buildings. Both stores A and B chose to restore their buildings by applying for the Group Subsidy. However, the Group Subsidy could be a constraint on the restoration of cultural heritage. In another interview survey conducted in the Shinmachi and Furumachi areas, some owners chose to use the Cultural Heritage Subsidy instead of the Group Subsidy to restore their buildings more carefully, even if some parts of the buildings were used as stores. In other words, the owners of the affected historical buildings could 'juggle' these support systems according to their own circumstances.

The case studies of Shinmachi and Furumachi areas suggest that it is necessary to make it easier to 'juggle' various support systems to include the preservation of damaged cultural heritage in disaster legislation. In particular, in the case of undesignated historical buildings, which are often their owners' living and working places, it is not easy to assume that they should be protected as cultural heritage to assume that they should be protected as cultural heritage. If the framework of the public support system is set up in an intermittent style, owners have to keep an eye on the timing of the deadline. Such a situation would consequently promote the demolition of undesignated historical buildings. In order to avoid this, developing a system in disaster legislation that allows different public support systems for disaster recovery to coordinate with each other through cooperation among related parties (national and governments, experts, and owners) is necessary. The number of cultural heritage sites that can be saved will increase by positioning the preservation of damaged cultural heritage as part of the coordination and integrated response required in disaster legislation and by creating an environment in which various types of support can be 'juggled.'

11.4.3 Building a Human Network to Connect Owners, Experts, and Government

The interviews revealed that the owners restored their houses with a combination of Group Subsidy and Cultural Heritage Subsidy according to their financial circumstances. In the case of the Kumamoto Earthquake, a list of historical buildings prepared before the disaster helped cultural heritage experts conduct surveys of damage to these buildings. In the form of damage surveys, the owners had the opportunity to connect with experts. Furthermore, in the case of the Shinmachi and Furumachi areas, KMT, an intermediary support organization with expertise, played an essential role in advising owners on how to select and use various public support systems, and also acted as the secretariat of the "Council of Owners of Affected Cultural Heritage" to connect owners. The 'juggling' of public support systems was made possible through the communication between the experts in the private intermediary support organizations and the owners.

Even if the owner chooses to restore the building, it is also important to have a specialist with skills in surveying and restoring historical buildings, who check the current situation of the damaged building and advise future restoration plans in order to restore without diminishing its historical value. In the first place, it is not easy for an individual owner to know what public support systems are available and what can be done in an earthquake emergency and proceed with the procedures.

For example, in the case of Store B, even though the owner and her family decided to restore the building, they were still very anxious because they did not know what to repair and to what extent. They had to start with collecting data on the building. Therefore, it took a long time to estimate the costs necessary to carry out repairs that could be done on our own. In addition, it became very complicated to calculate the proposed portions of the building to be repaired under which support system. The policy for repairs under the Group Subsidy, which was not intended for the conservation of cultural heritage, was different from the policy for repairs under the Cultural Heritage Subsidy. Intermediate support organizations like KMT, which have good knowledge of different support systems (especially their merits and demerits) as well as the preservation and restoration of cultural heritage, play a significant role in connecting the owners with cultural heritage experts and the government.

In addition, the owners of stores A and B participated in the Liaison Council, of which KMT supported the establishment. The fact that they could consult with the KMT members and other owners at the weekly meetings of the Liaison Council also helped them to feel relaxed and think that they might be able to manage the restoration option. In choosing restoration, the activities of the Liaison Council created horizontal connections among the owners, prevented them from being isolated, and allowed them to share their problems. The council also played a role in conveying the owners' voices to the government, which led to the creation of Cultural Heritage Subsidy. In other words, the connections among people in the local community, created mainly by private intermediary support organizations, became a major driving force for the owners to choose restoration.

As we have seen, human networks between owners, the government, and experts play a significant role in preserving cultural heritage damaged by disasters by 'juggling' various support systems. Strengthening the cooperation between the government and the private sector is also an issue that must be addressed in future disaster legislation. In order to protect damaged cultural heritage from loss, it is important to include the preservation of cultural heritage as part of the cooperation between government and the private sector in disaster legislation.

11.5 Conclusion

This paper has shown that the current disaster legislation has a limited perspective on the conservation of damaged cultural heritage, and that the legislation for protecting cultural properties is also inadequate in dealing with disasters. Then, using the 2016 Kumamoto Earthquake as a case study, it has examined the requirements for placing the preservation of damaged cultural heritage in disaster legislation, focusing on how damaged historical buildings were restored and the movements of the actors involved in the choice between restoration and demolition, such as owners and experts.

In the case of the Kumamoto Earthquake, the establishment of a subsidy system for the restoration of undesignated cultural heritage was a breakthrough. At the same time, public support systems, such as the Group Subsidy, whose original purpose was not the restoration of cultural properties, were also used to restore undesignated cultural heritage damaged by the disaster. Undesignated cultural heritage is easily affected by the financial situation of its owners. It is crucial to create an environment where the owners can efficiently 'juggle' various support systems according to their financial circumstances and choose conservation. The role of experts and intermediary support organizations that support owners and act as a bridge to the government is also essential in enabling the 'juggling' of these various support systems. Strengthening cooperation between the government and the private sector is also required to facilitate the functioning of this network after a disaster, while building a human network before the disaster. This paper has attempted to show that these requirements for placing the restoration and preservation of damaged cultural heritage in disaster legislation, overlap with the integrated response to disaster prevention and recovery, including prevention, emergency response, emergency measures, and reconstruction and recovery measures, which have been identified as issues for disaster legislation. Linking cultural heritage to disaster legislation will help fill in the gaps in the discussion of previous studies.

As stated in the purpose of the amendment of the Law Concerning the Protection of Cultural Properties in 2018, cultural heritage, including undesignated cultural heritage, can be said to be the core of a region's identity. In the case of undesignated cultural heritage, which is often the place where the owner lives and makes a living, it is difficult to assume that it should be protected as cultural property. Also, even if the significance of protecting cultural heritage is shared, what it means to preserve cultural heritage varies depending on each individual's position. For the owner of Store B, the Kumamoto Earthquake was an opportunity to recognize the public value of her mansion, a place for her daily life, as a cultural heritage for her customers and neighbors. Even if saving lives and restoring lifelines are the top priorities at the time of a disaster, cultural heritage plays a significant role in the reconstruction of the community. In this sense, it is crucial to explicitly articulate the restoration of damaged cultural heritage in disaster legislation and orient it so that its preservation is chosen.

References

Adachi, Y. (2014). Protecting the historical environment from disasters: Building an emergency system. In H. Okumura (Ed.), *Protecting history and culture from catastrophic disasters: Building local historical material studies* (pp. 403–422). University of Tokyo Press.

Committee for Protecting Cultural Heritage and Local Communities from Disasters. (2003). *Measures to protect cultural heritage and local communities from earthquake disaster*. https://www.bousai.go.jp/kohou/oshirase/h16/pdf/arikata.pdf. Accessed 10 June 2022.

Harrison, R. (2013). *Heritage: Critical approaches*. Routledge.

Hidaka, S. (2019). Issues with cultural asset rescue in large-scale disasters: From the experience of cultural asset rescue in the Great East Japan Earthquake Disaster. *Bulletin of the National Museum of Japanese History., 214*, 47–61.

Hidaka, S. (2015). Reclaiming the memory of living culture: From the field of cultural heritage rescue. In N. Kibe (Ed.), *Learning from disasters: Conservation and revitalization of cultural resources* (pp. 175–199). Bensei Shuppan.

Hisasue, Y. (2020). *Urban disaster and cultural heritage protection legislation*. Seibundo.

Historical Buildings Committee. (2021). *Report on the current status of historical buildings affected by the Kumamoto Earthquake*. Kumamoto Prefecture Association of Architects and Building Engineers.

Japan ICOMOS National Committee. (2019). *The 2016 Kumamoto Earthquake: Report on damages to the cultural properties and recommendations for their restoration and reconstruction*. https://kumamoto-machinami-trust.org/wp-content/uploads/2019/05/IcomosReport_20190507.pdf. Accessed on 10 June 2022.

Kibe, N. (Ed.) (2015a). *Learning from disasters: Conservation and revitalization of cultural resources*. Bensei Shuppan.

Kibe, N. (2015b). Foreword. In N. Kibe (Ed.), *Learning from disasters: Conservation and revitalization of cultural resources* (pp. i–vi). Bensei Shuppan.

Maekawa, S. (2019). Tono City and the cultural property rescue network: In the no man's land between volunteer work and civil service, and between being affected by and aiding in a disaster. *Bulletin of the National Museum of Japanese History, 214*, 77–93.

Morii, M., Naito, Y., Manno, K., & Okada, K. (2018). [Report] rescue of cultural properties after the direct subduction earthquake from the Report of Rescue Activities for Cultural Properties Affected by the 2016 Kumamoto Earthquake. *Conservation Science, 57*, 181–188.

Okamoto, T. (2014). *Disaster recovery and reconstruction law*. Keio University Press.

Okamoto, T. (2018a). *Disaster recovery and reconstruction law II*. Keio University Press.

Okamoto, T. (2018b). *System of disaster recovery and reconstruction law: Legal needs and reconstruction policy trajectories*. Keiso Shobo.
Okumura, H. (Ed.). (2014a). *Protecting history and culture from catastrophic disasters: Building local historical material studies*. University of Tokyo Press.
Okumura, H. (2014b). Reasons why we raise the issue of local historical material studies: Large-scale disasters and historiography. In H. Okumura (Ed.), *Protecting history and culture from catastrophic disasters: Building local historical material studies* (pp. 3–31). University of Tokyo Press.
Sasaki, S. (2017). *Disaster prevention and recovery legislation: Commentary on disaster prevention, emergency, recovery, and reconstruction systems based on the Great East Japan Earthquake*. Daiichi Hoki.
Shirouzu, S. (2014). In order not to make the term "cultural property" an unsubstantial word: Sakae Village's quest to utilize rescued cultural properties. In H. Okumura (Ed.), *Protecting history and culture from catastrophic disasters: Building local historical material studies* (pp.300–311). University of Tokyo Press.
Smith, L. (2006). *Uses of heritage*. Routledge.
Society for Cultural Property Restoration (Ed.). (2007). *Save our cultural properties! Confronting disaster*. KUBAPRO.
Takakura, H. (2014). Conclusion: The significance of involvement in the research project on intangible folk cultural properties and anthropology for the Great East Japan Earthquake. In H. Takakura & K. Takizawa (Eds.), *Intangible folk cultural properties in disaster: The Great East Japan Earthquake and the ethnography of Miyagi Prefecture coastal communities* (pp.290–311). Shinsensha.
Takakura, H., & Takizawa, K. (Eds.). (2014). *Intangible folk cultural properties in disaster: The Great East Japan Earthquake and the ethnography of Miyagi Prefecture coastal communities*. Shinsensha.
Tsukui, S. (2012). *Great disasters and the law*. Iwanami Shoten.

Eisuke Tanaka (Professor at the Research Faculty of Media and Communication, Hokkaido University, Sapporo, Japan) Since his Ph.D., Eisuke has studied issues of ownership of cultural heritage, focusing on the cases from Turkey (e.g. the role of cultural heritage in modern Turkish nationalism, illicit antiquities trade, and the destruction of heritage sites through the development projects). He is currently working on how ruins become heritage in heritage tourism and how the ideas of protection and destruction are differentiated in heritage tourism. He also considers how the idea of heritage constitutes the relationship between different stakeholders in the case of the post-disaster reconstruction process in Japan. His recent publications include 'Heritage Destruction in Context: the Case of the Roman Mosaics from Zeugma, Turkey' (International Journal of Heritage Studies 21 (4), 2015) and Who owns cultural heritage?: Ownership and Protection of the Remains of the Ancient Anatolian Civilizations in Turkey (in Japanese, Shumpu-sha, 2017).

Chapter 12
Impacts to Society Around Cultural Heritage in Post-trauma Situations: Reactions of Different Stakeholders in the Reconstruction Process in the Cases of Shuri-jō Castle and Wangduephodrang Dzong

Junko Mukai

Abstract This section takes up two post-disaster reconstruction projects, the State Hall of Shuri-jō Castle in Okinawa, Japan, and Wangduephodrang Dzong in Bhutan. These two fortresses were destroyed by fire in 2019 and 2012 respectively, but the decision of rebuilding was made immediately after the fires due to their cultural significance. Due to their legal or institutional situation, it was not mandated to reconstruct them true to their original form, materials, and techniques. In the case of Shuri-jō Castle, the State Hall was not included in the category of the cultural heritage building, as it was reconstructed only in 1992 after the Second World War. Wangduephodrang Dzong built in 1638, is of high cultural heritage value, but heritage protection in Bhutan cannot stay away from the traditional notion that Dzong, temples, and monasteries can be modified better in use and design. Yet in both cases, the plans were, in principle, to reproduce them to their pre-fire state. How were those decisions taken? What controversies have arisen in the decision-making process or later? Where has attention been focused? Those are worth considering when thinking about community participation in the cultural heritage process and how their voices should be understood.

Keywords Wangduephodrang Dzong · Bhutan · Shuri-jō Castle · Okinawa · Cultural heritage · Reconstruction

12.1 Introduction

On October 30, 2019, still reeling from the shock of the Notre Dame de Paris fire, Shuri-jō Castle in Okinawa, Japan, was destroyed by fire. Shuri-jō Castle was a fortified structure that was built around the fifteenth century and reigned as the center

J. Mukai (✉)
Rimo Associates, Naha City, Okinawa, Japan
e-mail: rimoassoc@ymail.ne.jp

T. Kono and J. Okahashi (eds.), *Post-Trauma and the Recovery Governance of Cultural Heritage*, https://doi.org/10.1007/978-981-19-6041-3_12

of administration, diplomacy, culture, and religion of the Ryukyu Kingdom until the end of the nineteenth century. The Castle had gone through several extensions, reconstructions, and repairs over time. After the annexation of Ryukyu to Japan and the establishment of Okinawa Prefecture, the State Hall of Shuri-jō Castle was designated as a cultural property by the government of Japan in the name of the "Okinawa Shrine Worship Hall". However, during the Battle of Okinawa at the end of the Second World War, the buildings including the State Hall were flattened and the ramparts were severely destroyed. The State Hall and adjacent buildings which were turned into ash in 2019 were those buildings that were reconstructed at their original location as a national park project. This postwar reconstruction was carried out with a strong motivation to faithfully recreate the Shuri-jō Castle of the Ryukyu Kingdom based on detailed research and archaeological excavations. The Shuri-jō Castle Ruins, where the reconstructed State Hall stands, is a designated national historic site and a World Heritage site. Even though the reconstructed State Hall is not included in the category of cultural heritage, there is no doubt that it is an important structure for the history and culture of Okinawa.

It is hard not to be reminded of Wangduephodrang Dzong in Bhutan, which was destroyed by fire on June 24, 2012, as Shuri-jō Castle billows smoke. Wangduephodrang Dzong is a fortress that Zhabrung Ngawang Namgyal (Zhabdrung), who unified what is now Bhutan, founded in 1638. The citadel, which functioned as both a ruling center and a monastery, was expanded by his successors, and although it had undergone frequent repairs and alterations since then, much of the seventeenth century building had remained. There is no doubt that Wangduephodrang Dzong is one of Bhutan's most important cultural heritage buildings, but the structure is not designated as a heritage site nor protected by unshakable rules. Bhutan has never ranked temples and monasteries according to their historical or artistic value from the religious viewpoint, and there is no law in force to dictate procedures to preserve cultural heritage buildings to date.

The decision was made to rebuild both of these fortresses soon after the fires. In both cases, the plan was to reproduce them basically to their pre-fire state. However, it was not compulsory to make them with their original form, materials, and techniques,[1] as they were not included in the category of cultural heritage building, or not dictated to do so within a rigorous protection system.

This paper will begin with a section on cultural heritage protection in Bhutan, as it may help to understand the case of Wangduephodrang Dzong. Then, after providing the history and architecture of Wangduephodrang Dzong, it will be examined how the people perceived the fire, and where their attention was directed in the process of decision-making for the reconstruction. It will also be examined how those emotions and perspectives have influenced decisions and the process of the reconstruction. The same topics will be discussed for Shuri-jō Castle, about history, architecture, peoples'

[1] In April 2020, "the Standards for the reconstruction of historical buildings at historic sites" was issued by the Council for Cultural Affairs under the Ministry of Education, Culture, Sports, Science and Technology (MEXT), which defines the basic principles for reconstruction of lost heritage buildings. It states that the building to be reconstructed shall have high probability of size, structural type, and form.

emotions and attention. Then, it will be examined the background of such attention. These two cases may suggest something for the participation of local residents in the preservation of cultural heritage, which has been the focus of much attention in recent years.

The description about Bhutan's cultural heritage protection and Wangduephodrang Dzong in this paper is based mainly on the author's experiences and observations while working for the Division for Conservation of Heritage Site under the Department of Culture in Bhutan. As for Shuri-jō Castle, it is based on information acquired while the author was living in Okinawa Prefecture, for the purpose of developing a Dzong disaster risk management plan, and later on producing the web exhibition "Notre Dame de Paris and Shuri-jō Castle" at the initiative of Prof. Toshiyuki Kono.

12.2 Cultural Heritage Protection in Bhutan

His Majesty Jigme Singye Wangchuck, the fourth King of Bhutan (reigned 1972–2006), is known to have declared at the beginning of his reign that he would strive to build a country by increasing "Gross National Happiness (GNH)" rather than GNP. GNH later became a guiding philosophy for the Bhutanese government, the essence of which is to promote sustainable development by taking a good balance between spiritual attainment and material fulfillment. Recently, various indicators have been proposed to measure GNH, and scientific and economic approaches have become prominent, but the basic concept is expressed in the four pillars that support GNH. They are (1) sustainable socioeconomic development, (2) preservation and promotion of culture and tradition, (3) conservation of the natural environment, and (4) good governance.

It is not hard to agree that culture and tradition are important for the balance between spiritual attainment and material fulfillment that GNH advocates. What, then, is "Bhutanese culture and tradition"? It is generally accepted that much of what is considered "Bhutanese tradition and culture" was established by Zhabdrung. Thus, it is based on Buddhist values[2] and its preservation and promotion is perceived as a common good.[3]

[2] However, even within the Buddhist appearance, one can observe a mixture of animist rituals and belief in indigenous deities, the shades of which vary from region to region. When Buddhism was revived in Tibet and new schools emerged one after another, the schools spread their influence to Bhutan and competed for supremacy. Biographies of high priests from this period tell the story of how they subdued local deities and made them their protective deities through the power of the Dharma. It can be seen that the Buddhist culture expanded while adopting the indigenous culture. Another point which should not be overlooked is that Bhutan also has citizens who belong to different cultural spheres, such as those with roots in Nepal.

[3] This is clearly reflected in the fact that in the Penal Code of Bhutan, the larceny of a tensum (Buddhist treasure) or vandalizing a choeten (stupa) is considered a first-degree felony and carries a life imprisonment as same as murder, treason, and terrorism.

We also must not forget that cultural uniqueness has been regarded as a guarantee of its independence in Bhutan, which is a small country located between two giant countries. As modern Bhutan's ties with India deepened, tradition and culture that express Bhutanese distinctiveness became indispensable for the national identity. When Zhabdung is said to have established a unique culture, it had to be distinguished from Tibetan culture. At that time the situation was such that Zhabdrung who fled from political strife in Tibet, and his successors, were subjected to repeated military invasions by the Tibetan central regime,[4] and later on to political interventions. Hence, people in national dresses and buildings incorporating Bhutanese designs which are the popular subjects in photographs of Bhutan are the manifestations of the cultural policy of the government.[5]

This section summarizes the cultural heritage administration in Bhutan from its early days to the present. It also seeks to clarify the perceptions and attitudes of the government, the monastic community, and the general public toward cultural heritage and its protection.

12.2.1 History of Cultural Heritage[6] Administration

The year 1985 is earmarked as the beginning of cultural heritage administration in Bhutan, when the Special Commission for Cultural Affairs was established by royal decree of the fourth King of Bhutan. The background for the establishment was a sense of crisis over the changing values that modernization had been bringing since the 1960s. The modern development in Bhutan began with the first Five-Year Plan in 1961, which was hastened as a result of the Tibetan uprising. His Majesty Jigme Dorji Wangchuck, the 3rd King of Bhutan (reigned 1952–1972) implemented a series of reforms including emancipation of serfs, establishment of the National Assembly, and reforms related to taxation and land ownership. It is said that he was aiming for

[4] In the beginning, it was invaded by Tsang Desi, who was the political rival of Zhabdrung, and after 1642 by the Gelug Ganden Phodrang, which had conquered Tsang.

[5] On the other hand, there is criticism that these policies gave rise to the refugee in the 1990s. Many people with Nepalese roots live in southern Bhutan. Policies such as the mandatory wearing of Bhutanese national dress and the removal of Nepali-medium curricula in school education exacerbated the discontent of these people, leading to armed clashes between activist groups and government forces. As a result, thousands to tens of thousands of the citizens of Nepalese origin have fled to refugee camps set up by the UNHRC and the Red Cross.

[6] The English words "Cultural Heritage" and "Heritage Conservation" are widely used as they are, instead of using Dzongkha, the official language of Bhutan, which has limited vocabulary available to describe modern objects, things, and concepts. Some newly coined Dzongkha words for "Cultural Heritage" and "Heritage Conservation" are not familiar to most of people. Dzongkha was originally spoken in western Bhutan, where most of the administrative centers since Zhabdrung have been located, and it is believed that this language became the dominant language. It was originally an unlettered language, and thus documents had been written in archaic Tibetan. It became an official language in the 1960s when a spelling and grammar system was developed by using the Tibetan script. Against this background, not many people are perfect in Dzongkha.

development that was carefully implemented by Bhutanese officials who would be well trained in a modern education system he was introducing. However, the situation changed drastically in September 1958, when India's first Prime Minister, Jawaharlal Nehru, visited Bhutan. At that time, China was invading Tibet, which had been a buffer zone for India against the communist state of China. Nehru saw Bhutan's significant value as the next and last buffer zone, and proposed economic aid to promote modernization and development in Bhutan. Soon after, the Ganden Phodrang defected to India, and a security crisis was imminent for Bhutan. Bhutan finally decided to accept Nehru's proposal, which resulted in relying heavily on India's financial and technical support. Thus, infrastructure developments were undertaken, beginning with the construction of Bhutan's first motor road connecting the capital city of Thimphu with a town on the Indian border. While the rapid influx of goods and information through this new corridor was observed, it was seen as a major concern that would eliminate Bhutan's traditional values and threaten its identity. Bhutan's sense of impending crisis was further heightened by the annexation of the neighboring Kingdom of Sikkim to India in 1975. The Kingdom of Sikkim was a small kingdom of Tibetan Buddhist culture, like Bhutan. However, a parliamentary vote and a national referendum favored its incorporation into India. At that time, it is said that more than 70% of the population of Sikkim was of Nepalese descent, which had migrated in large numbers as labor since the end of the nineteenth century.

Special Commission for Cultural Affairs to the Department of Culture

The mission of the Special Commission for Cultural Affairs (Special Commission), created under the above-mentioned circumstances, is to curb the negative effects of modernization by preserving and promoting culture and tradition, as stated in the Special Commission's brochure.[7]

In 1995, the Special Commission was reconstituted with 15 members who were well versed in tradition and culture, and from 1998, the Minister for Home Affairs was appointed chairman of the Commission. The Secretariat was established to implement the decisions of the Commission. It should be noted that in 2000, there was a widely held misconception that the Secretariat of the Special Committee was a part of the Central Monk Body.[8] It may have happened because the position of Secretary of the Special Commission was concurrently held by the Secretary of the Central Monk Body's Supreme Council secretariat. However, another reason that may be

[7] This recognition can also be found in a number of government documents. A representative example is "Bhutan2020" prepared by the then Planning Commission in 1999, which states "it is the culture and tradition … that can protect us from some of the negative and indiscriminate forces of modernization.

[8] The Central Monk Body dates back to a Sangha of Drukpa-Kagyu school founded in the seventeenth century by Zhabdrung, who unified to rule Bhutan under the Drukpa-Kagyu teaching. Currently, there are more than 7000 monks in the Central Monk Body, many of whom are registered with District Monk Bodies in different districts. They receive annual funds and other facilities from the State. The Supreme Council of the Central Monk Body consists of Je Khenpo as a chairman, five high priests, and the Secretary of the Supreme Council secretariat who is a civil servant. Article 3 of the Constitution of the Kingdom of Bhutan specifies the status of Je Khenpo and the Supreme Council. The District Monk Bodies are headed by a chief priest appointed by the Council.

rather worth noting is that the people perceive culture and Buddhism in the same sphere.

In 2003, the Special Commission secretariat was merged with the then Ministry of Home Affairs to form the Department of Culture of the Ministry of Home and Cultural Affairs. Currently, the headquarters of the Department of Culture includes the Division for Cultural Properties and the Division for Conservation of Heritage Sites (DCHS). The Division for Cultural Properties is responsible for Buddhist treasures whose inventory was being developed prior to the establishment of the Special Commission. On the other hand, the predecessor organization of DCHS was originally established for the repair of temples and monasteries. As to be described, the origins of these two organizations reflect the philosophy behind the protection of Buddhist treasures and temples and monasteries.

One more division in the headquarters is the Driglam Division, which has jurisdiction over ceremonial protocol and traditional etiquette. It provides guidance for national ceremonies, as well as training for government officials and newly graduated young people in traditional manners and etiquette. Three museums,[9] the National Library and Achieves of Bhutan,[10] and the Royal Academy of Performing Arts are also under the Department of Culture. The National Institute for Zorig chusum, which teaches traditional arts and crafts, used to be under the umbrella of the Special Commission before being transferred to the new Ministry of Labor and Human Resources which is in charge of vocational training. The Director of the Department of Culture is also the Member Secretary of the Commission for Religious Organisation, which was created in 2009 and consists of representatives of Buddhist and Hindu institutions in the country.

Establishment of the Division for Cultural Properties

Around 1983, prior to the establishment of the Special Commission, an inventory of Buddhist treasures held by Dzongs, temples, and monasteries across the country began to be compiled by order of the fourth King. Persons with knowledge of history and culture were selected as surveyors, and the survey team was dispatched to each administrative district. The names and characteristics of each of the treasures housed in the shrines of Dzongs, temples, and monasteries were listed in the inventory. Buddhist treasures are collectively called tensum, and they are divided into three categories of body, speech, and mind. Specifically, they are: body treasures such as Buddhist statues, paintings, and murals; speech treasures such as sutras, woodblocks, and stones carved with sutras; and mind treasures such as stupas containing relics, precious stones, and the remains of high priests. The background of this project seems to be that at that time, claims of vandalism of stupas, larceny and illegal trafficking of tensum to neighboring countries were beginning to occur. Through this inventory project, it came to be known that there are some 2000 Dzongs, temples,

[9] The National Museum of Bhutan was opened in 1968 by the 3rd King of Bhutan who collected Buddhist treasures in the watch tower of Paro Dzong.

[10] The National Library and Achieves of Bhutan are the origin of a small collection of old scripts founded in 1967 by the second Queen of Bhutan in a room in Tashichho Dzong.

and monasteries in the country, and consequently it also served as the basis for the inventory of heritage buildings.

With the establishment of the Special Commission in 1985, the inventory project was taken over by the Commission. The Division for Cultural Properties was established to maintain and update the inventory and database, provide training and support on fire and crime prevention to caretakers, and conduct studies regarding tensum and history upon inquiries from the government. When the Commission's secretariat was reorganized as the Department of Culture, the Cultural Properties Division remained and continued to perform the above duties.

The high level of interest in the protection of tensum is evidenced also by the fact that the only law enacted to date pertaining to cultural heritage is the Movable Cultural Property Act of Bhutan. There was an urgent need for national law in order to track and recover stolen and illicitly trafficked cultural properties in cooperation with Interpol and other international organizations. It was enacted in 2005 after deliberation by the Parliament, which at that time included two high priests of the Central Monk Body as members of the Parliament. It is noteworthy that the articles are divided into four chapters according to the type of ownership, and each chapter stipulates different management and procedures. The four types of ownership are: (1) owned by the Central Monk Body, (2) owned by the state (museum, etc.), (3) owned by the reincarnated linage or community, (4) owned by an individual. This shows a trace of negotiations between the Central Monk Body, the prideful custodian of tensum over the centuries, and the heritage administration which wants power for protective intervention over national treasures.

In contrast to the general attitude toward heritage buildings discussed next, tensum emphasizes their originality. Buddhist statues formed from the remains of high priests by their dharma power, statues and paintings that are said to have expressed their intentions by changing the direction of their bodies or uttering words, and ritual implements, paintings, and statues created by high priests have irreplaceable value and power in their existence. On the other hand, the tensum inventory does not omit not only antiquities but also newly created Buddhist statues and implements. In this way, the similarity is found within the concept behind the cultural heritage designation system, which has not yet been adopted for temples and monasteries.

Establishment of the Division for Conservation of Heritage Sites (DCHS)

DCHS was formerly the Restoration Unit of the Special Commission secretariat. The role of the Restoration Unit, consisting of a few engineers and draft persons, was to issue technical sanctions and provide technical assistance for the restoration of temples and monasteries as well as the construction of auxiliary facilities, in response to requests from the government or district administrative offices. Temples and monasteries here include not only old temples and monasteries but also those newly built just a few decades ago. In principle, the owner or caretaker of a temple or monastery must submit a request to the district administrative office where the temple or monastery was located for restoration work. After confirming lawful land ownership and necessity of the work proposed, the chief administrator submitted the cost estimate and drawings, these were often simple sketches hand-drawn by the monk, to the Special Commission secretariat. The documents were reviewed by the Restoration Unit, and if deemed appropriate, the Director of the Special Commission issued a technical sanction. The national treasury allocated the budget for the work to the district administrative office, and in most cases, the engineering unit of the district administration implemented the work.

These procedures indicate the strong commitment that the state protects temples and monasteries. One more notable point is that what the state support was intended to protect were their functions from a religious standpoint, which is understood from the fact that the above-mentioned procedure includes all temples and monasteries, regardless of their historicity, and also includes the construction of new facilities of temples and monasteries. With this reasoning, the government has not introduced a cultural heritage designation system that would differentiate some buildings based on their historical or artistic value.

The main focus of the review for technical sanction was whether traditional techniques and designs were used, and whether the cost estimate, or budget request, was reasonable. If the drawings were deemed inadequate, a draftsperson from the Restoration Unit would often redraw them on behalf of the applicant. Inadequate in this case meant that the building did not look like traditional Bhutanese architecture, was too humble as a temple or monastery, was not beautiful, or required functional improvement.

Thus, restoration work on temples and monasteries at that time was not intended to respect the original design and materials. Temples and monasteries were symbols/icons of sacred sites, shelters of tensum, and systems for sustaining traditional functions and value systems. What is generally considered to be the "protection" of cultural heritage is that once the opportunity for restoration was given, it should be embellished and improved upon (Fig. 12.1).

In 2003, after the transition to the Department of Culture, the Restoration Unit was upgraded to the Division for Conservation of Heritage Sites. This promotion was the result of the Restoration Unit's lobbying efforts with the chairman of the Special Commission and the Royal Civil Service Commission. It was the result of the enthusiasm of architect Dorji Yangki, who was assigned to the Restoration Unit in the late 1990s. She had studied architecture at a university abroad and was knowledgeable about architectural heritage. At the same time, the Restoration Unit was the focal point for overseas institutions related to architectural heritage, and thus, had opportunities to communicate with UNESCO, the Japanese Agency for Cultural Affairs, and others. DCHS has since been gradually expanded with newly appointed architect Nagtsho Dorji as its chief, to start various initiatives to protect Dzongs, temples, and monasteries based on their cultural values, and also to protect rural houses and landscapes as cultural heritage sites.

On the other hand, restoration work on Dzong was managed by engineers under the Ministry of Home Affairs, under the direction of a high-ranking government official Dasho Zepon Wangchuk, who was with a deep knowledge of traditional architecture. The reason why the Ministry of Home Affairs was responsible for the maintenance and restoration of Dzongs was that each Dzong is used by a district administrative office along with a district Monk Body. Since the Ministry of Home

Fig. 12.1 A monastery built in the eighteenth century by a high priest who recognized the place as the land of Perfect Bliss and extracted hidden sutras from the rock. After the photo was taken, the building was restored in 2005 and the site has been developed as a monastic institute for higher studies (© Junko Mukai)

Affairs was in charge of the district administrative system, it was also in charge of facilities for district administration. After the Special Commission was merged with the Ministry of Home Affairs to form the Department of Culture, the engineers of the Ministry of Home Affairs were transferred to the Department of Culture, and the protection of Dzongs, along with temples and monasteries, were placed under the jurisdiction of the Department of Culture.

12.2.2 Current Heritage Site Legislation

It has been widely recognized by the people of Bhutan that the protection of cultural heritage, including Dzongs, temples, and monasteries, is a duty of the state, and the Constitution of the Kingdom of Bhutan, promulgated in July 2008, states in the Article 4,[11] Section 1 that "The State shall endeavor to preserve, protect and promote

[11] The emphasis given to culture is also seen on that "Culture" comes the fourth Article, out of its 35 articles of the Constitution, following the Articles the first on Kingdom of Bhutan, the second on the institution of Monarchy, and the third on spiritual heritage.

the cultural heritage of the country, including monuments, places and objects of artistic or historic interest, Dzongs, Lhakhangs (temples), Goendeys (monasteries), Ten-sum, Nyes (holly sites), language, literature, music, visual arts and religion to enrich society and the cultural life of the citizens."

However, as mentioned at the beginning, there is no law in Bhutan to date that dictates a protection system for Dzongs, temples, monasteries, or other structures as cultural heritage. This is not because the protection of cultural heritage is given less priority, but rather because administrative laws have generally been underdeveloped.[12] Apart from the penal codes, the prototype of which can already be found in the pre-modernization period, and the acts on citizenship, security, land, etc., which were developed relatively early in the modernization period, those acts in practical needs, such as the aforementioned Movable Cultural Property Act were developed from around the beginning of 2000, but there are not many of these laws.

Therefore, administrative actions in each sector needed to be carried out according to good common sense and customary practices. This meant that each sector was to work with wisdom to achieve the goals set forth by the king's discernment, and to respond to them in the best possible manner. Based on this understanding, interventions that amounted to little more than administrative advice had a certain degree of effectiveness.

However, the Constitution of the Kingdom of Bhutan was promulgated in July 2008, completing the transition to a constitutional monarchy based on parliamentary democracy that had been gradually implemented over several decades. This also marked a major shift in the perception of administrative action as proceeding on the basis of common sense and customary practices. The legislation was drafted at an accelerated pace, with each sector seeking a basis for the authority it exercised. Numerous bills were prepared one after another, and many are awaiting Parliament deliberation.

A Cultural Heritage Bill was also prepared by 2016. The article on heritage buildings and sites is mainly a codification of the efforts of the DCHS, but it has not yet been discussed in the Parliament, because further coordination with the relevant agencies was found to be required. Meanwhile, as it has been done, the DCHS is reviewing restoration applications and monitoring works in accordance with the Basic Guidelines for conservation of heritage sites in Bhutan 2004 (Basic Guidelines 2004) that has been compiled by the DCHS. At the same time, it is carrying out preparative work to introduce the procedures proposed in the Cultural Heritage Bill, as it is able to do so.

Internationally, Bhutan ratified the World Heritage Convention in 2003, and in March 2012, submitted a Tentative List of four cultural, three natural, and one mixed heritage sites to the World Heritage Center. The preparation of the Tentative List of cultural heritage sites originated from an exercise carried out in the DCHS for capacity

[12] To cite just one example, there are no acts on construction or development activities to date. The Ministry of Works and Human Settlement has established ministerial ordinances and guidelines to regulate height, building-to-land ratio, setbacks, structural calculations, and other necessary regulations, but no act has yet been passed by the Parliament that would provide a basis for enforcement.

development purposes.[13] The exercise was to select representative cultural heritage buildings and define Outstanding Universal Values for each, reflecting traditional Bhutanese values and concepts. The outputs of this exercise were further brushed up and recompiled into four tentative lists, and submitted along with the Ministry of Agriculture and Forest's proposal for natural and mixed heritage sites after the Cabinet approval. Wangduephodrang Dzong is one of the five Dzongs in a single Tentative List.[14]

12.2.3 Current Heritage Site Administration

DCHS is considered responsible for the protection of Dzongs, temples and monasteries in the country. As we have seen, this is based on: (1) a widespread public understanding that the preservation and promotion of culture and tradition is one of the four pillars that support the country's development philosophy of GNH; (2) the Constitution of the Kingdom of Bhutan that clearly states that the protection of cultural heritage is a national responsibility; and (3) DCHS's work experience since the time of the Special Commission.

Currently, restoration work on Dzongs, temples, and monasteries and new construction in their premise, as well as new temple and monastery construction, require approval from the Director of the Department of Culture. An owner or caretaker of the site[15] must first submit drawings and cost estimates for the restoration work to the district administrative office, and then submit them to the Department of Culture, along with documents confirming that the district administrative office has given its consent. If the DCHS determines that the proposal submitted is appropriate, it will submit it to the Director of the Department of Culture, who will in turn grant approval. In other words, the procedural flow is largely unchanged from the time of the Special Commission. However, as mentioned in Sect. 12.2.1, during the time of the Special Commission, the purpose of the review was mainly to confirm the appropriateness of the use of the national budget, and the Bhutan-like designs and materials, and then, if appropriate, to grant technical sanction. Today, under the concept of value-based protection, changes to the status quo are carefully judged,

---

[13] DCHS has been cautious about moving toward a nomination process, even though it takes up the World Heritage theme for educational purposes. In addition, around 2008 and 2018, the higher authorities examined regarding nominations to the World Heritage List, but resolved not rushing a nomination for reasons that emphasized Bhutanese values and culture.

[14] "Dzongs: the centre of temporal and religious authorities (Punakha Dzong, Wangdue Phodrang Dzong, Paro Dzong, Trongsa Dzong and Dagana Dzong)".

[15] In the case of Dzongs, temples, and monasteries under the custody of the Central Monk Body, caretakers, school principals or teachers are assigned to the temples and monasteries. Restoration of the temples and monasteries are normally initiated by those monks, and the necessary procedures are born by those monks. In case of the temples and monasteries that are the seat of reincarnations, community temples, or temples owned by individuals, an owner of the temple or monastery, or a representative of a follower's group is responsible for the procedure for the work. Often, follower's groups are organized among villagers or close associates to support the work.

although coming to some compromise with the owner/caretaker's demands. Specifically, in the case of a temple or monastery with high historical value, the DCHS team visits the site and conducts on-site measurements and surveys. Approval is then issued, but in most cases, it is accompanied by written instructions to change the proposed plans or a proviso requesting that the material and design be preserved. Often, it leads to endless negotiations with the applicants who are unable to agree on the instructions.

In recent years, the DCHS has established a strategy of selectively allocating limited financial and human resources to heritage buildings of high historical value. The old mission of reviewing the restoration and construction of all temples and monasteries throughout the country has been revised, and preparative works for the introduction of a registration and designation system are being carried out, including the preparation of a list of candidate buildings for designation. For designated buildings, heritage site management plans are to be prepared, in order to develop guiding principles on conservation and management. It aims to promote understanding of the value-based protection among its owner and caretaker, before they embark on specific plans for significant alterations as a "good deed". As a start, a Punakha Dzong heritage site management plan was developed in consultation with stakeholders, including the Central Monk Body and Punakha district administrative office, and was approved by a Cabinet meeting and came into effect in 2019. This will be followed by the preparation of management plans for different types of heritage buildings, such as a small temple, a large monastery, a local palace and a rural settlement. These pilot plans will be referred to as a template for the sequential development of management plans for other designated buildings. Simultaneously, a disaster risk management plan is to be prepared for a designated heritage building. It should be noted that the lessons learned from the response to Wangduephodrang Dzong fire are reflected in Punakha Dzong disaster risk management plan.

12.3 Overview of Wangduephodrang Dzong

Before describing Wangduephodrang Dzong, it may be useful to briefly mention Zhabdrung Ngawang Namgyal (1594–1651), who founded Wangduephodrang Dzong, as well as his Monk Body.

Zhabdrung Ngawang Namgyal (Zhabdrung) was born in Tibet in 1594, as the prince abbot of Drukpa Kagyu School, a Tibetan Buddhist school founded in Ralung by Tsangpa Gyarey Yeshi Dorji (1161–1211). Zhabdrung was also recognized as the reincarnation of Padma Karpo who was in the successive lineage of reincarnations of Tsangpa Gyarey. However, the ruler of Tsang region supported Pagsam Wangpo who also claimed to be the reincarnation of Padma Karpo. In 1616, Zhabdrung and some thirty monks fled to the south[16] from an imminent danger stemming from the

[16] At that time, the region which is present-day Bhutan was called "Lho-yul" or "Lho-Mon", which means a southern country or a southern country of Monpa. Stories in the early centuries implicate

conflict, and were received by the local patrons.[17] Zhabdrung consolidated Drukpa Kagyu's rule in the region, which at the time the different Buddhist schools had competitively established footholds for their rule.[18]

Punakha Dzong, which construction began in 1637, became the center of Drukpa rule for the next 270 years. After Zhabdrung's demise in Punakha Dzong in 1651, his authority was divided into two; one for religion and the other for ruling, known as the "dual system of the government". The two tasks were presided over by Je Khenpo or chief abbot, and Druk Desi or regent respectively, who were appointed by a council of high priests. While Druk Desi was abolished before the enthronement of the first king in 1907, the lineage of Je Khenpo continues to the present day, with the 70th Je Khenpo His Holiness Ngawang Jigme Choedra heading the Central Monk Body today.

12.3.1 Establishment of Wangduephodrang Dzong

Zhabdrung founded Wangduephodrang Dzong in 1638, at the height of the construction of Punakha Dzong. Fifteen km down the Punatsang-chhu River from Punakha Dzong, the Dang-chhu River joins the Punatsang-chhu River. Wangduephodrang Dzong was built on the edge of a steep hillside located between these two rivers. The mythical story that describes how the Dzong was named implies the significance of the location. Zhabdrung, as per a prophecy to build a Dzong at this place, sent his attendants to check the site. They saw four ravens on the ridge, and when they approached, the ravens flew away in four directions. Upon this being reported, Zhabdrung understood that this is the place from where he would subjugate the county. Thus the Dzong was named the palace (phodrang) of subjugation (wangdue).[19] As indicated in this story, the construction of Wangduephodrang Dzong was essential for the unification of Druk-yul (Drukpa's country) (Fig. 12.2).

12.3.2 Architecture of Wangduephodrang Dzong

Wangduephodrang Dzong is a long fortified structure, 200 m north to south along a ridge, consisting of a series of buildings surrounding three courtyards. A steep

a relationship between Tibet and Bhutan. For instance, two of the 12 temples built by the king of Tibet in the seventh century are located in Bhutan, and in the eighth and ninth centuries, the princes of Tibet fled political strife and came to Bhutan to become the founders of noble clans.

[17] Several power bases had formed in the region by the descendants of Phajo Drukgom Zhigpo, who first introduced the Drukpa-Kagyu teachings to Lho-yul in the early thirteenth century.

[18] As Buddhism was revived and new schools established in Tibet, these schools began to extend their influence to the south. From around the twelfth century, they competed for power in present-day western and central Bhutan.

[19] Phuntsho (2013).

Fig. 12.2 Wangduephodrang Dzong seen from the Punatsang-chhu River before the fire (© Junko Mukai)

wooden staircase on the northernmost façade leads up to the main entrance, which opens into the first courtyard. The first courtyard which is much larger than the other two courtyards is surrounded by two or three stories of buildings on the east and west. Across the courtyard, 70 m away, is a tower-like building on the north side of the next courtyard. After passing through a gateway of the tower-like building, one will be in the second courtyard narrowly enclosed by the east and west buildings of two-stories excluding the attic space under a roof. Towards the third courtyard, one ascends 20 or so stone steps at the southern end of the second courtyard, and then enters a door on a three-story building that enshrines protective deities on the upper floors. Another dozen or so stone steps lead one into a narrow, dark space. Standing in front of it is another tower-like building called an utse, the center of Dzong. After passing through a shoulder-width passageway with the utse to the right, one comes to the third courtyard, measuring about 15 m from north to south and 8 m from east to west. At the end of the courtyard is a kuenray (congregation hall), which is the southernmost building of the Dzong.

The exterior of the Dzong is characterized by massive stone masonry walls. Because the courtyard is built at the level of the ridge, the exterior walls are built on steep slopes that drop down to the east and west. As a result, the east–west buildings have a two-storied space below the courtyard. These lower-level rooms were used

Fig. 12.3 Overview of Wangduephodrang Dzong before the fire (© Junko Mukai)

as warehouses for the grain that was paid as taxes or for prisons before the modernization, but most of them were not used after that. Above the courtyard level, these buildings are two or three stories high. In other words, exterior walls rise four to five stories high from the steep sided ground. The upper portion of the exterior wall has a small number of window openings, but the lower portion is completely solid, except for a few small, gaping openings. The interior walls facing the courtyard are attached by a series of painted wooden balconies, creating an open spatial composition. The roof frame is supported by struts erected on long beams of more than 300 mm in height, that are lifted up by thick struts which stood on the attic floor. The gabled roof was thatched with split pine shingles and boulders were put on the shingles. While other Dzongs replaced the thatch with Corrugated Galvanized Iron (CGI) sheets, only Wangduephodrang Dzong had maintained the traditional split shingle roofing (Figs. 12.3 and 12.4).

Use of the Dzong

The first courtyard area accommodated the district administrative office,[20] while the second and third courtyard areas were occupied by the District Monk Body. Each of the rooms surrounding the first courtyard was occupied by different sectors of the district administrative office. In the sector, officials dispatched from the ministries worked under the supervision of a chief administrator appointed by the central government. The larger room was used as a conference hall for local elected leaders. The east and west buildings of the second and third courtyard were used as monks' residential quarters and offices. One-hundred and fifty monks resided in the Dzong,

[20] There are 20 administrative districts throughout the country.

Fig. 12.4 View of the first courtyard before the fire: the three-storied building of the main entrance and the east and west buildings accommodating the district administration office (© Junko Mukai)

of the 300 or so monks registered in Wangduephodrang Dzong.[21] They are headed by a chief priest appointed by the Central Monk Body. Fifty senior monks are assigned different responsibilities[22] and the other monks perform rituals. Such a use pattern, in which the administrative office occupies the courtyard area near the main entrance and the District Monk Body occupies the courtyard area at the back, is common to most other Dzongs, that originate the "dual system of the government" introduced in the mid-seventeenth century, when the religious and ruling authorities were bifurcated.

Zhabdrung's Dzong and the Changes That Followed

An architectural survey conducted before the fire revealed that the original Wangduephodrang Dzong constructed by Zhabdrung in 1638 is the area around the third courtyard. Thus, the door opened on the ground floor of the three-story building enshrining the protective deities used to be an original entrance of Zhandrung's

[21] Apart from the monks residing in the Dzong, the District Monk Body assigns monks to temples and monasteries in the Wangduephodrang district as caretakers, teachers, or students.

[22] For instance, those responsible for maintaining the monastic disciplines, presiding over the rituals, preserving tensums, taking care of each shrine, and clerical work, and also teachers of philosophy, arts and crafts, ritual music and dance.

Dzong. The utse was built on the highest point of the ridge which was the reference of the courtyard level. The original entrance building was located on the steep slope that drops down to the north—that is why, since the second courtyard has been developed, climbing up 30 or so steps is needed to access this building. Thus, the original Dzong was pretty small in scale, but highly defensive in its strategic use of terrain. Later, Zhabdrung's Dzong was expanded to have the first and second courtyard areas. The utse was also enlarged toward the east as well as upward. The architectural survey indicates that the original utse was two stories lower in height and a quarter narrower in width. Because of the reason that the original part of Zhabdrung's Dzong was distinguishable, Wangduephodrang Dzong was an exceptional example out of other Dzongs supposedly built by Zhabdrung (Fig. 12.5).

It is said that Gyalsay Tenzin Rabgay, the Zhabdrung's successor, expanded Wangduephodrang Dzong in 1683. It is not certain whether the first and second courtyard areas were built by Tenzin Rabgay at the same time. There is a little over a 6 m gap between the two areas, which was connected by a wooden bridge (later replaced by a reinforced concrete bridge). What is clear is that all parts were completed by 1783 at the latest. In that year, Warren Hastings, Governor-General of Bengal, sent a mission

Fig. 12.5 View of the second courtyard before the fire: the narrow courtyard is surrounded by the east and west buildings accommodating monk's residence. The three-storied building in front is supposedly an original entrance of Zhabdrung's Dzong, and the utse is seen behind (© Junko Mukai)

led by Captain Samuel Turner to Bhutan.[23] Lieutenant Samuel Davis, who accompanied the mission as a surveyor, drew a few sketches of Wangduephodrang Dzong.[24] One of these sketches, which depicts the Dzong from the main entrance side, shows the front facade in detail. The north-facing masonry wall is clearly identical to the wall in this sketch, although changes have been made around the openings.

According to biographies of high priests and other sources, Wangduephodrang Dzong underwent at least three major renovations in the eighteenth and nineteenth centuries: the renovation including expansion of a gateway in 1767,[25] the restoration after the fire in 1837, and the restoration after the 1897 earthquake.[26] In the twentieth century, two renovations were executed. The 1952 renovation was carried out by order of the Second King, which was prompted by the crumbling of the outer wall of kuenray in the third courtyard. The 1983 renovation was mainly of the buildings surrounding the second and third courtyards. The changes in the buildings over time can be analyzed by comparison with Samuel Davis' 1783 sketch, photographs taken by John C White (Political Officer in Sikkim) in 1905, and the existing building before the fire. In addition, the architectural survey conducted prior to the fire and the survey of the remaining structures after the fire revealed numerous traces of past alterations, including the enlargement or reduction of the buildings and changes in the height of the floors.

12.3.3 Wangduephodrang Dzong Conservation Project in the Tenth Five-Year Plan

The Wangduephodrang Dzong conservation project was implemented during the 10th Five Year Plan (2008–2013). What was this project to contribute to the history of the Dzong, if the fire didn't occur?

The Wangduephodrang Dzong conservation project included restoration of the Dzong as well as facility improvement. The restoration work consists of repairing stone masonry walls that have become loose or bulged by partial dismantling and reconstruction, and replacing weathered wood with new timbers. Weathering of wood is severe in Bhutan, where the altitude is high and dry. At the same time, it is important to plan for the construction of new facilities, as all Dzongs are unusually overcrowded, with large numbers of monks residing in them. Improving their living conditions and allowing more appropriate use of the space helps to not only sustain its historical function but also reduce the burden on the historical building.

---

[23] Hastings sent multiple missions to Bhutan to resolve the dispute between Cooch Behar and Bhutan over possession of West Bengal.

[24] Aris (1982).

[25] The biography of Penchen Tenzin Choegyal that was compiled by Je Yonten Thaye mentions the restoration executed by Dzongzin Sonam Lhendrup in 1767.

[26] "Sikkim and Bhutan" written by J. C. White (Political Officer in Sikkim) who visited Wangduephodrang Dzong in 1905 describes damages caused by the 1897 earthquake.

In this restoration work, the original forms were respected to some extent when the window frames and balconies were replaced with new wood. However, when the original form was found too humble and inappropriate for the Dzong, it was often changed to an embellished style. Project manager Leki Wangchuk described his thought-evoking view that preservation could begin from the point of time when this restoration project was completed with the suitable structure that future generations would be proud of.

The following is an overview of the project implementation and activities. The project was interrupted by the fire, but in retrospect, it played a role in the post-disaster response and the smooth transition to the reconstruction project.

Framework of the Project

The pioneering large-scale restoration project for Dzong was the Punakha Dzong restoration project, which was triggered by a fire in February 1986. The damage to the buildings caused by the fire was limited to the area only around the fire, but the restoration work led to an expansion of the scope of the project, which eventually led to the restoration of the entire Dzong. The consecration ceremony was held in 2004, which means that it took 18 years to complete the work.[27] In 1999, the Trongsa Dzong restoration project was initiated. Engineers from the Ministry of Home Affairs were engaged in managing these two projects.

From the viewpoint of financial sources, the Semtokha Dzong conservation project marked a turning point: It is the first Dzong project that was carried out with foreign funds.[28] During the Ninth Five-Year Plan (2002–2008), an Indian government fund was earmarked for the project. The Wangduephodrang Dzong conservation project was one of the four Dzong conservation projects implemented by the project-tied assistance grant of the government of India during the subsequent Tenth Five Year Plan (2008–2013).

As in other major projects of Dzongs and temples/monasteries of national importance,[29] a steering committee was constituted as a decision-making body of the Wangduephodrang Dzong conservation project. The committee was chaired by the secretary of the Ministry of Home and Cultural Affairs and vice-chaired by the chief administrator of the Wangduephodrang district, and consisted of the administrative officer of the District Monk Body, representatives from the GNH Commission and the Ministry of Finance, the director of the Department of Culture and the head of the DCHS. Steering committee meetings were held about twice a year to discuss the approval of the plan, budget execution, reconciling different opinions between the

[27] Another remarkable project for Dzong is the reconstruction of Tashichho Dzong in the 1960s.

[28] Until then, restorations of Dzong, temples, and monasteries were supposedly carried out with the state budget. In addition, villages used to provide paid labors for such work, but this practice, which was no longer popular among village people due to unattractive daily wage, was in principle abolished with the Semtokha Dzong conservation project.

[29] Most of the restoration projects on temples and monasteries is carried out by the engineering units of the district administrative offices where they are located, but for temples and monasteries of national importance, the DCHS implements.

stakeholders, and coordination with agencies concerned such as the Department of Forest which manages the natural resources.[30]

Project Management

The site office, located near the Dzong, was staffed by a project manager, a junior engineer, an account officer, an accountant, and a storekeeper. The DCHS's engineer Leki Wangchuk was appointed as a project manager. The account officer and the accountant were dispatched for this project from the Ministry of Finance. Temporary housing units for these staff members were constructed in a nearby area. Two-hundred to 300 workers, including craftspeople in various skills, are directly employed in the project. Thus, the project begins by temporarily building up labor camps near the site where they live with their families. The project manager is not only responsible for providing necessities for the work, but also should be expected to take care of all aspects of their lives, from helping their children with school transfer procedures to mediating quarrels and disputes among them. Many of the traditional craftspeople, such as carpenters and masons, are old acquaintances as they work across Dzongs and temples on restoration work. The conservation project is carried out within the context of such close relationships among the people involved.

Restoration and Facility Development

Prior to the restoration work, the DCHS first conducted a survey of the Dzong in order to prepare measured drawings, and identify characteristics of the structure and any evidences to show past changes on the structure. Carrying out studies on literature and interviews helps to analyze the different states of the Dzong over the course of time. Based on the survey findings, a restoration plan is developed.

For the facility development, it is necessary to first understand in detail the use of the space, especially those of the monks' residences. Based on the survey of rooms, the appropriate number of monks in the Dzong was determined in the manner of considering the ranks and roles of the monks in consultation with the Central Monk Body. The number of monks to reside in Wangduephodrang Dzong, which used to house 150 monks, was analyzed to be 60. Within the project, three new building complexes were built on the ridge between the Dzong and an ancient temple located 300 m north of the Dzong. First, near the ancient temple, a school complex with classrooms and residential rooms for 35 monks was built to provide a better educational environment for young monks, then a residential complex with a capacity

[30] In Bhutan, timber harvesting is strictly controlled, and the Constitution of the Kingdom of Bhutan mandates that at least 60% of the country's land be maintained as forest. Acquisition of large volumes of timber or timber of substandard dimensions requires the permission of and coordination with the Department of Forest under the Ministry of Agriculture and Forest and the Natural Resources Development Corporation Limited (NRDCL). NRDCL was formerly the Logging Division established in 1979 under the Department of Forest, following the nationalization of logging operations for the purpose of sustainable forest resource management. During the restructuring, it was entrusted with commercial mandates adding to its initial social mandates. In 2007, it was again restructured as the NRDCL, and since then, it has been responsible for the management of sand, stone, and other natural resources in addition to timber.

Fig. 12.6 Young monks studying in the school complex newly built in the Wangduephodrang Dzong conservation project. They used to reside in the Dzong but moved to the complex before the fire (© Junko Mukai)

of 100 monks, and finally a dining hall near the Dzong where monks from the Dzong and the new residential complex can gather together for meals.

By October 2011, the school complex and the monks' residential complex were completed, and the monks, except for those who were necessary to stay back in the Dzong, were moved to these two newly built complexes, and the restoration work on the Dzong finally began in 2012. Six months later when the fire occurred, these complexes served as a place to enshrine the rescued tensum and conduct daily rituals, and as a residence for the monks in the Dzong (Fig. 12.6).

After the fire, the conservation project switched its tasks to building facilities to sustain the function of the district administrative office and the District Monk Body. The project also appropriated the remaining budget for procurement of materials—logs and stones to be needed in reconstruction of the Dzong.

12.4 Loss of Wangduephodrang Dzong

Wangduephodrang Dzong was destroyed by fire in June 2012. This section traces the chronology of the fire and the response to it. It will also focus on the people's feelings and perceptions toward the Dzong and their mixed emotions in the post-disaster situation.

12.4.1 Fire and Response

On Sunday, June 24, 2012, at around 4:00 p.m., a fire broke out on the second floor of the east building in the first courtyard; a police investigation report released in early July indicated that a sudden power surge may have been the cause. On the afternoon of that day, the residents in the Dzong as well as nearby houses had noticed a burning smell and smoke coming out of their electronic appliances and witnessed ceiling fans rotating at an unusual speed. The district officials and monks contacted the Bhutan Power Cooperation (BPC), and the branch manager and electrician apparently inspected the situation. Eventually, the people noticed the thick smoke coming from a corner of the first courtyard area and informed police duties stationed in the Dzong. The initial response was unsuccessful, partly due to no key to open the room where the fire started and a malfunctioning fire hydrant, and the fire quickly spread, driven by the strong winds famous in this area. The fire truck deployed in the Dzong and another fire truck rushed from the hydroelectric power plant construction project downstream and sprayed water from the north face, but they could not compete with the firestorm. The drizzle that had been falling for some time wasn't helpful to them. What the fire showed us was, that when initial firefighting fails, no measures of firefighting will be left, due to the steep slopes on three sides and the defensive features of the Dzong's architecture. The photos taken by the conservation project show that two hours after the fire started, the buildings of the third courtyard area were already ablaze. By 7 p.m., the wood portion of the superstructure was almost completely consumed. On the other hand, looking inside the exterior walls from the openings, it was still full of red flames even after 11 pm. It is assumed that the joists and planks of each floor, which were covered with a thick layer of soil, did not burn down easily. What we saw in the morning through a cloud of smoke was masonry walls that sustained severe damage specifically around window and door openings, but had not collapsed and retained the outline of the Dzong. At its foot was a thick pile of burnt wood and crumbled stone, and this debris was still emitting high heat even a month later (Figs. 12.7 and 12.8).

It was fortunate that there were no human casualties. Since the day of the fire was Sunday, the district administrative office was closed, and most of the monks were gathered in the residential complex, which had been newly constructed eight months earlier. The few monks who were in the Dzong at the time bravely climbed onto the rooftop of the tower-like building on the north side of the second courtyard to remove roof shingles to prevent the fire from spreading from the first courtyard buildings, but they were no match for the flames which were fanned by the strong winds. All of the high value tensums enshrined in different shrines in the Dzong were reported to have been rescued. Important tensums were kept in steel safes placed in each shrine. These safes were lowered through the windows onto the cactus-covered

Fig. 12.7 Utse engulfed in flames at 18:20 (© Wangduephodrang Dzong conservation project)

Fig. 12.8 The morning after the fire. The people engaged in the recovery work are seen on the southern slope. The building blocks seen in the north is the monk's residential complex built in the Wangduephodrang Dzong conservation project (© Junko Mukai)

ground with the help of army personnel and volunteers called desuup.[31] They were retrieved before dawn and enshrined in the hall of the monks' residential complex.

[31] Desuups are the volunteers who have completed the three to four week-long program of Desuung Training, which began in 2011 to train people to be active in disaster relief and community service

This series of emergency operations had not been planned in advance, but it was an instinctive response by the people who rushed onto the spot, out of a natural sense of duty to protect tensums. On the other hand, almost all the other items besides tensum, such as important documents of the district administrative office, were lost.

Upon receiving the report about the fire, His Majesty the King Jigme Khesar Namgyel Wangchuck arrived at the scene, and His Majesty the fourth King also moved to Punakha that day. In the same evening, government head and officials concerned rushed to the scene, including the prime minister in-charge, the minister for Home and Cultural Affairs, the cabinet secretary, the chief operations officer of the Royal Bhutan Army, the deputy chief of the Royal Bhutan Police, the members of Parliament from the Wangduephodrang constituencies, the secretary and Department heads of the Ministry of Home and Cultural Affairs, and the secretary and directors of the Central Monk Body.

On the 27th of June, the masonry walls that were about to collapse were brought down by jets of water for safety reasons. The police conducted the fire investigation, and recovery work had begun. Since the beginning of the month of July, the army personnel were engaged in clearing debris, and salvaging the tensums and other items from the debris. After coordinating with the progress of this recovery work, entry was allowed for the first time on July 5th in order to carry out a survey of the remaining structures. For a while after the fire, the Dzong had been kept strictly cordoned off by the police stationed in front of the Dzong's entrance. On every entry and exit, name and frisking were mandatory.

The district administration resumed normal operations on July 2nd, after temporarily renting the newly completed BPC office and receiving equipment and supplies from other district offices. Later, the district administration vacated the BPC office and moved to Moenlam-chenmo Chhoekhang (a large hall for Great Prayer where thousands of devotees gather) in Bajo town, a new town built less than 3 km away from the Dzong. This building was under construction in the center of Bajo town, and then the Wangduephodrang Dzong conservation project took over to expedite the completion. The new monk's residential complex provided space for the District Monk Body, after the conservation project built up partition walls and necessary settings.

12.4.2 *Perceptions of the Loss*

The incident that destroyed Wangduephodrang Dzong shocked the government and citizens of Bhutan. One of the most striking reactions to the fire was the government's declaration of June 25th, the day after the fire, as a "Day of National Mourning". All offices and schools across the country were closed. On this day, His Majesty the King entered the Dzong after the crumbling masonry walls around the main entrance were

activities. As of today, nearly 28,000 completed the training, including more than 10,000 women. Desuung means "Guardians of Peace".

brought down. Standing alone in front of the collapsed entrance in prayer, he stepped into the Dzong and did not come out for a while. What occupied people's minds after the fire was not simply the loss of an important historical building, but rather the touch of insecurity. The Dzong, which was supposed to be full of the power that came from Zhabdrung Ngawang Namgyal and his successors was gone. That is why, the first person who had to enter the Dzong after the fire was the King himself, who is responsible for the country united by Zhabdrung. On that day, all the ministers also paid their condolences at the site. The Central Monk Body conducted a purification rite in the monks' residential complex, led by Je Khenpo. Regular ritual services also started with tensums rescued, which were sheltered in the complex.

Prime Minister Jigmi Y. Thinley toured the Dzong on June 28th, the day after his return from an official overseas trip, and then met the residents of Wangduephodrang. He emphasized the government's commitment to rebuilding the Dzong, that the reconstructed Dzong would be more glorious and magnificent than ever, and that this disaster would provide an opportunity for the people to accumulate great merit through this reconstruction. The expressions of relief and anticipation on the faces of the residents, who filled the packed hall to overflowing, were impressive. What was passionately said at the briefing was summarized in a message from the prime minister published in the Kuensel newspaper on June 26th[32] prior to the meeting. "What we must remember is that it was rebuilt and it always stood as the Dzong that Zhabdrung Ngawang Namgyal built until the day before. We the people of Bhutan have not lost but gained another opportunity to renew and further enrich our proud heritage" and "we must seize the opportunity to build a stronger, more durable and glorious Dzong in the name of Zhabdrung Ngawang Namgyal…" His message reflects his conviction on the restoration of cultural heritage buildings—restoration work should be considered in the course of the history of a heritage building, which has been damaged and restored repeatedly in the past.

The reconstruction of Wangduephodrang Dzong was of great interest not only to the Wangduephodrang residents, but also to many citizens throughout the country. The new Dzong was often a topic over their chats, and many expressed their desire for the Dzong that would be more beautiful and larger than it was before the fire.

The business community in Wangduephodrang and neighboring districts, including shops, restaurants, and hotels, began voluntarily providing free lunch and dinner for the personnel engaged in recovery work in the Dzong, and this continued until the beginning of July. After the start of the reconstruction project, individuals and groups have been seen offering food to all the construction workers from time to time. Citizens also sent donations toward the reconstruction of the Dzong, and those who did not have cash brought in gold jewelry, precious stones, and other items that they had put on. By the end of October of that year, citizens' donations totaled more than 86 million Ngultrum.

[32] Thinley (2012), June 26.

12.5 Process of Decision-Making and Where People's Interests Lie

Moves toward reconstruction began immediately after the fire. At the public meeting in Wangduephodrang on June 28th, the prime minister promised to rebuild the Dzong as soon as possible, along with the prospect of securing funds for the project. On June 26th, the day after the fire, the Indian Ambassador to Bhutan visited the scene and expressed support for the reconstruction project. The reconstruction budget had to be included in the 11th Five Year Plan (2013–2018), which began a year later.

There were two main concerns of the government as to what kind of building the reconstructed Dzong would be. One was how to improve its resilience to disasters. The second was whether to restore the remaining stone walls and rebuild on top of them, or whether to completely rebuild anew after dismantling all the remaining walls.

Initially, it was also unclear which agency within the government would be engaged in the planning of the reconstruction work. This was because the Ministry of Works and Human Settlement could have been in charge of the project, if the Dzong would be rebuilt using reinforced concrete to increase disaster resilience. However, the consideration was that the reconstruction should be based on traditional materials and techniques but incorporate new technologies as necessary, the Department of Culture was put in charge of the planning. Once the 11th Five-Year Plan began, a steering committee was instituted as a decision-making body for the reconstruction project. The 1st steering committee meeting was held on November 20, 2013, and had been held twice a year since then. The steering committee was chaired by the Minister for Home and Cultural Affairs and vice-chaired by the minister for Health elected from Wangduephodrang constituency, and its members included the representative of the King's office, the high priest of the Central Monk Body, the secretary of the GNH Commission, and the chairman of the district council. In addition, the aforementioned official who supervised the Dzong restoration projects including those of Punakha Dzong, was appointed as a member. Thus, the committee members were of a higher level compared with other Dzong projects, and the various representatives of the Wangduephodrang community were included. Kinley Wangchuk, an engineer from the DCHS was appointed as a project manager.

This section will examine how the decision on whether or not to reuse the remaining walls was taken and what was decided for disaster resilience, under the above-mentioned project framework. And through such decisions, what was achieved or not from the perspective of the cultural heritage value-based approach?

12.5.1 Reuse of the Remaining Masonry Walls

In the "Assessment Report; Wangduephodrang Dzong structure post June 24, 2012 fire" discussed below, the DCHS recommended that the masonry walls below the courtyard level be restored and reused. The intention was, of course, to preserve as much of the original wall as possible, but moreover, a decision to preserve those walls was the key to lead the project to reconstruct the pre-fire Dzong. There is a general desire to restore Dzongs, temples, and monasteries to a more spacious, higher, and more magnificent state, and this attitude was also observed in the case of Wangduephodrang Dzong, as mentioned in the Sect. 12.4.2. If all the walls are to be dismantled and rebuilt from the ground, a new Dzong would be designed from scratch. However, if the superstructure were to be reconstructed on the remaining walls, there would be almost no room for changes in the layout, and also in height, as any upward expansion would increase the building load, which was undesirable from the standpoint of structural stability.

It took a long time for the decision to be made. This section will trace the steps involved in the survey of the remaining structures, the preparation of proposals for policy directives, and the study of the bearing capacity of the remaining walls, and at last, will examine what ultimately led to the decision to reuse the remaining walls.

Survey of the Remaining Structure

The survey of the remaining structure[33] was conducted in three phases in coordination with the police and army recovery operations: July 5–9 in the first courtyard, July 24–25 in the second courtyard, and then, August 20–23 in the third courtyard which was the most congested with debris. The survey, which was conducted while the army was still carrying out recovery work, was made possible by the prime minister's instruction during his site visit on June 28 that the DCHS should conduct a detailed survey of the remaining structure.

The survey was conducted for two purposes: to visually assess the damages to each remaining masonry wall, and to evaluate the cultural heritage value of each wall. More than 80% of the floors of the rooms at the courtyard level had not collapsed, and therefore most of the masonry walls below this level could be expected to be sound. The report summarizing the survey findings recommends that the masonry below the courtyard level be restored and utilized. Other historically important walls, such as the masonry walls of the utse, the central structure of Dzong, and the walls of the ground floor, where various historical traces have been found, were also proposed to be retained, but were ultimately demolished because the strength of the walls exposed to high heat could not be estimated.

Proposals for Policy Directives

The 146th Cabinet meeting on November 13, 2012, after reviewing the assessment report, instructed the Ministry of Home and Cultural Affairs to present the pros and cons of the different proposals for the reconstruction of the Dzong, in order for them to provide informed policy directives.

The document prepared by the DCHS begins by citing sections from various policy documents pertaining to the protection of heritage buildings. The citation includes

---

[33] Mukai et al. (2013).

the aforementioned Article 4 of the Constitution, the Chapter 5 of Bhutan2020[34] (a document issued in 1999 by the then Planning Commission setting forth the goals to be achieved by the government by 2020), the Tenth Five-Year Plan main document, and the Basic Guidelines 2004 prepared by the DCHS. At that time in the government, there were various views about reconstruction, which include opinions that the Dzong should be rebuilt with reinforced concrete to make it stronger, or that the flammable wooden parts should be replaced with stones. The above-mentioned citations would have reminded the fundamental principles that it was the duty of the government to preserve and protect cultural heritage, and that traditional architectural styles and designs should be promoted.

The following pages are an overview of the restoration and reconstruction works that have been carried out on Dzongs, temples, and monasteries throughout Bhutan, and they pointed out the trends toward standardization by adopting the design that was generally considered "the finest" example in the process of restoration work.

After the two preliminaries, the following three proposals for reconstruction are presented. One is to rebuild on the remaining masonry walls using the same materials and traditional technique as before the fire, the other is to rebuild on the remaining walls but using modern materials and technology, and the third is to dismantle the remaining walls and rebuild on a foundation built with modern technology—namely a reinforced concrete foundation. A matrix is presented that compares each of these proposals in terms of Strengths, Weaknesses, Opportunities, and Threats. Weaknesses of the two proposals using the remaining wall include the resilience issue that the stability of the wall cannot be guaranteed. In fact, major views which emerged indicated that the stability of the remaining wall should be guaranteed if a new wall is to be built on top of it.

Stability Studies of the Remaining Wall

In May 2013, at the request of the Department of Culture, ICOMOS arranged to send the US/ICOMOS team to assess of and propose a strategy for the treatment of the remaining walls. In July 2014, the Ministry of Works and Human Settlement, after a visual inspection, reported that the remaining walls were in dilapidated condition and cannot be used as structural load-bearing walls. In August, the DCHS conducted plate loading tests on the remaining wall employing equipment limitedly available, and came to the tentative result that the wall had bearing capacity against the upper load as it had before the fire. In January 2015, the DCHS held an international workshop on structural issues related to traditional Bhutanese buildings especially Dzongs, inviting researchers from the UK, Switzerland, Portugal, India, and Germany, for the purpose of discussing appropriate methods to understand the strength of the remaining wall and measures to reinforce and stabilize it. All of the outputs of these studies were reported to the steering committee, but eventually they didn't fully convince the committee.

---

34 Planning Commission (1999).

Use of the Remaining Wall

Ultimately, the decision to use the remaining walls below the courtyard level was settled not because of the scientifically proven bearing capacity of the walls, but rather because of the technical challenge of building a reinforced concrete foundation on the steep slope of the hill made of riverbank deposits and the enormous cost expected for it. But there was another reason worth noting. In contrast to the general tendency to desire changes in the superstructure, there was an emphasis on originality when it came to the foundation. The people associated the foundation of the Dzong with the foundation of Buddhism or the foundation of the nation laid by Zhabdrung. Hence, it can be said that such perception of the people eventually led to the restorative reconstruction of the Dzong.

There were persistent requests for major changes to the status quo from viewpoints of function or prestige, such as expanding the perimeter of the utse and increasing the height of the kuenray by 3 m. Even after construction began, these requests were repeatedly brought up in the Steering Committee meeting, but due to the physical and structural limitations of the building on the remaining wall, those requests could not materialize.

12.5.2 *Improvements in Disaster Resilience*

So, what discussions and decisions have been made on improving resilience to disasters?

Immediately after the fire, there were voices from government officials, media, and the general public for the Dzong to be more fire resilient. It wasn't only about improving fire alarms and fighting systems. As a result of witnessing the situation where firefighting was desperately limited due to the Dzong's defensive structure and settings, such ideas emerged to rebuild the Dzong with reinforced concrete, to replace the wooden structure with stone, and even to construct a motor road around the perimeter of the Dzong, despite the Dzong being on a three-sided cliff.

In the end, the Dzong to be built on the remaining wall was decided, in principle, of a traditional Dzong of random stone masonry with mud mortar and wooden frames such as joists, windows and doors, and balconies. The decision reflected the people's faith and confidence in traditional construction methods and craftspeople.

Having decided to reconstruct the Dzong of stone and wood, the challenge to reduce the fire vulnerability remained. In addition to upgrading the fire alarms and fighting systems, a service-tunnel running north–south under the three courtyards was constructed to ensure emergency access. For another disaster of great concern in Bhutan—earthquake, some extensive measures were adopted, including seismic isolation of the utse. It is highly exceptional that Swiss engineering experts were employed and materials and equipment were imported to adopt the measures[35]—the high-profile reconstruction project was seen as an opportunity to broaden the technological horizon. However, it should also be noted that the introduction of those new technologies was met with considerable opposition from craftspeople and community representatives. Again, people have a high level of faith and appreciation in their traditional skills.

12.5.3 *Insights from the Policy-Making Process*

As we have seen, the general view about Dzongs, temples, and monasteries is that they should be made better than before, whether for restoration or reconstruction, whenever the opportunity arises. Doing so contributes to the promotion of Buddhism and is considered to be a meritorious deed. In such an environment, it is not easy to implement the work under the policy of "value-based protection," which emphasizes historical value as well as religious value, in the manner of restoration being prudent to change the status quo, or reconstruction bringing the building back to its original state.

In the case of Wangduephodrang Dzong reconstruction, the lower part of the remaining masonry wall has been retained and new walls are built over it, except in the case of the partial collapse of the base wall in the process of demolishing the upper wall that led to rebuilding from the ground up. In this way, there was almost no room for change in the layout, and vertical extension was also avoided so as not to overload the old walls with extra height. Thus, the Dzong has become neither larger nor taller—the pre-fire contours were followed. The decision to retain the remaining walls in place was not only due to the difficulty of constructing a new reinforced concrete foundation, but also the emphasis on the originality of the base masonry. Such emphasis on the originality is reasoned out that the foundation of the building was considered in relation to the foundation of Buddhism or the nation.

There was little support for the idea of rebuilding with reinforced concrete or other foreign materials and techniques. It has shown a high level of faith and appreciation in traditional materials and techniques. For the same reason, the adoption of new technology for earthquake resistance was met with strong opposition from craftspeople and the community.

By this time, the reconstruction work is almost complete, the Dzong, while maintaining the pre-fire contours and skyline, looks more magnificent than before the fire, within the traditional architectural style. For instance, the windows and balconies are more embellished and beautiful, adorned with wood carvings. Of course, they are also better equipped for disaster resilience and improved for better living and working standards.

[35] These expenses were paid separately from the national treasury.

12.6 Overview of Shuri-jō Castle

Shuri-jō Castle is located in Okinawa Prefecture, Japan. Okinawa Prefecture is an island prefecture with 160 islands (47 of which are inhabited) scattered over an area of approximately 1000 km from east to west and 400 km from north to south. Naha City, where Shuri-jō Castle is located, is 660 km across the East China Sea from the capital of Kagoshima Prefecture, the nearest neighboring prefecture. Okinawa Prefecture was a kingdom called Ryukyu until it was annexed by Japan in the late nineteenth century, and Shuri-jō Castle was the castle of its royal capital, Shuri. Before describing Shuri-jō Castle, It may be necessary to briefly touch on the history of Ryukyu and Okinawa.

On the main island of Okinawa, the largest of the Ryukyu Islands, after the transition from a hunter-gatherer society to an agrarian economy in the twelfth century, the local rulers, or "aji," rose to power in various regions and built fortresses called gusuku[36] to compete for power. The emergence and development of gusukus, characterized by their unique flowing masonry ramparts, suggests the active movement of people and transmission of technology during this period. In the gusuku period, local rulers were united and separated, and it is said that the island had been unified into three countries. From among the three countries, Chu-zan (country of center) gained supremacy, and the Ryukyu Kingdom was established in 1429. The Ryukyu Kingdom became a tributary state to the Ming Dynasty, China, and from the 14th to sixteenth centuries, it prospered through intermediate trade with China, Japan, Korea, and Southeast Asian countries such as Siam and Malacca.[37] By the fifteenth century, neighboring islands from Amami to Yaeyama were also under Ryukyu rule. In the early seventeenth century, the Satsuma domain (present-day Kagoshima Prefecture, Japan), the most southwesterly federal domain under then Tokugawa shōgunate,[38] invaded Ryukyu and brought it under its rule. However, the Ryukyu Kingdom sustained royal rule as a tributary state of the Ming and then Qing dynasties,[39] and Shuri-jō Castle remained the center of diplomatic ceremonies. The Meiji

[36] The origins and character of gusuku are diverse. It is not only the word for fortress, but some places of worship and defensive settlements are also named gusuku.

[37] With the Ming Dynasty's sea ban policy to crack down on piracy and smuggling (later banned private trade as well) issued in 1371, Ryukyus were favored as an alternative player to Chinese merchants in trade. Ryukyus were initially allowed to make an unlimited number of entries to the trade port, later annually or biennially (Japan in the Muromachi period made one entry every ten years). When the sea ban was lifted in 1567, Ryukyu's intermediate trade declined.

[38] A feudal system of rule by the Tokugawa shogunate in Edo (present-day Tokyo) and its vassal clans, in the period from 1603 to 1867.

[39] Sustenance of Ryukyu as a tributary state was favorable for the Shogunate and the Satsuma domain for the purpose of trade and intelligence under their isolation policy. In addition, they had taken advantage of exhibiting the unique culture of Ryukyu to visualize their power of ruling a foreign nation. The old illustrations of the Ryukyuan delegation to the Shogunate depicts the exotic customs.

government[40] overthrew the Tokugawa shōgunate in the late nineteenth century, abolished the Ryukyu King,[41] and designated Ryukyu as Okinawa Prefecture (Ryukyu Disposition). By the late nineteenth century, Okinawa had been rapidly assimilating into Japan. In April 1945, at the end of the Pacific War, U.S. forces landed on Okinawa. By that time, the Japanese Army had turned Okinawa into a military base and mobilized the residents, including boys and girls, to continue a war of attrition. In June, when Japanese defeat became clear, the Army commander committed suicide and the organized fighting ended. However, individual troops and soldiers continued guerrilla warfare to buy time to delay the battle on the Japanese mainland, and as a result, many residents were killed or forced to commit mass suicide. A death toll is estimated at 25% of the prefecture's population, and most of the cultural properties, including Shuri-jō Castle, were lost in the war. Okinawa remained under U.S. Army occupation after the war.[42] After 27 years of "America-yu (American reign)", Okinawa returned to Japan in 1972, but the vast bases were maintained. Even today, 70% of the U.S. Army bases in Japan are concentrated in Okinawa Prefecture, which accounts for 15% of the area of the main island of Okinawa. Densely populated urban areas border the base fences, a situation that is still fraught with danger.

Now, let us look at the history of Shuri-jō Castle as it went through the transition from the Ryukyu Kingdom to the "Yamato-yu (Japanese reign)" and from the "America-yu" to the "Yamato yu" again.

12.6.1 History of Shuri-jō Castle

Shuri-jō Castle, built on a hill of Ryukyuan limestone blessed with springs and overlooking all directions, reigned as the royal court of the Ryukyu Kingdom from 1429 to 1879. Shuri-jō Castle once comprised the State Hall and other government buildings, the royal residence, and a forest and 10 utaki (sacred sites) where the rituals of the kingdom would take place. Shuri-jō Castle is thought to have been established in the late 14th or early fifteenth century.

By the mid-fourteenth century, the powerful clans known as 'aji', who were spread across the main island of Okinawa, were said to have consolidated into the three countries of Chu-zan in the center, Hoku-zan in the north, and Nan-zan in the south as they competed for power. In 1350, Satto dynasty of Chu-zan was established in Urasoe as its capital, and in 1372, adopted the tribute system of the Ming Dynasty. It is said that the capital was moved from Urasoe to Shuri around this time. Buney, who succeeded Satto, was destroyed by Shō Hashi in 1406. In 1429, Shō Hashi, the

[40] Four clans, including the Satsuma clan, overthrew the Shogunate and the new government was established. It was a centralized state with the emperor as head of state that adopted Western systems and technology and promoted modernization reforms.

[41] The last king Shō Tai was bestowed as a noble and ordered to reside in Tokyo.

[42] Japan regained administrative authority in 1951 with the signing of the San Francisco Treaty, but Okinawa remained under U.S. rule until 1972.

King of Chu-zan, unified the three countries and established the Ryukyu Kingdom. The inscription on the "Ankokuzan Jukabokunoki" stone monument erected in 1427 says that Ryutan Pond was dug as part of the outer garden of Shuri-jō Castle, whose soil was heaped up to build Ankokuzan Mountain where flowers and trees were planted. This inscription indicates that Shuri-jō Castle was built around this time, and developed as a suitable royal court.

In 1470, the first Shō dynasty was taken over by Shō En[43] who ascended to the throne to begin the second Shō dynasty. Under the reign of King Shō Shin (reigned 1477–1527), a son of Shō En, the central authority had been strengthened. The local lords had been kept back in Shuri, official classification had been developed, and district administration had been reformed. Shuri-jō Castle developed into a highly organized government office.[44] During the reign of King Shō Shin and his son King Shō Sei (reigned 1527–1555), the outer ramparts and several gates including Shurei-mon Gate were built, and the North Hall was constructed. In this way, the castle took on a form similar to that of the present-day Shuri-jō Castle. By this time, the Ryukyu Kingdom also ruled over neighboring islands such as Amami, Miyako, and Yaeyama. Until the end of the sixteenth century, the Ryukyu Kingdom prospered by playing the main actor in the intermediate trade in a wide area of East and Southeast Asia, as indicated by various foreign goods excavated from the Shuri-jō Castle area. Shuri-jō Castle was elaborated with a unique architectural style that blended diverse cultures (Fig. 12.9).

However, the Ryukyu Kingdom was invaded by the Satsuma domain in 1609, and thereafter the Ryukyu Kingdom was ruled by them. The Satsuma domain imposed on Ryukyu heavy taxes and kept the tribute trade under their control, while sustaining the kingdom as a tributary state of the Ming and Qing dynasties. Thus, even under the Satsuma's rule, the State Hall of Shuri-jō Castle had been the scene for diplomatic ceremonies and was repeatedly reconstructed and restored. Around Shuri-jō Castle, there had been sake breweries concentrated to control the production, the workshop to create the finest arts and crafts, and the institute to promote performing arts.

The new Meiji government, established in 1868, overthrew the Tokugawa shōgunate and established Okinawa Prefecture in 1879. Here, the 450-year history of the Ryukyu Kingdom came to an end and was replaced by the "Yamato-yu". The Shuri ward office decided to dismantle the State Hall of Shuri-jō Castle due to its disparate condition, and set out to work in 1923. However, owing to the efforts of

[43] He rose to prominence in the service of King Shō Taikyu. It is said that he was promoted to the throne in order to re-unify the country that had been in chaos since the death of Shō Taikyu.

[44] Meanwhile, many of the gusukus in different regions, which had been the residence and administrative center of the local lords, fell into decline.

Fig. 12.9 The flowing lines of outer ramparts and one of the gates of Shuri-jō Castle, which have been restored and reconstructed in the postwar project (© Junko Mukai)

Yoshitaro Kamakura[45] and Chuta Ito,[46] it was barely saved from demolition. Two years later, in 1925, the State Hall was put under the state's protection as a specially protected building in the Ancient Temples and Shrines Preservation Law. This Law, enacted by the Meiji government in 1897, designated buildings and treasures owned by shrines and temples as specially protected buildings or national treasures, and provided government subsidies to cover the costs of their preservation. Since buildings under other types of ownership like castles and palaces were not included in this category, the State Hall was renamed "Okinawa Shrine Worship Hall",[47] in order to

[45] Yoshitaro Kamakura was assigned to Okinawa Prefectural Girls Normal School and Okinawa Prefectural High School for Girls as an art teacher for two years from 1921, where he took a deep interest in Ryukyuan culture and conducted research on cultural assets. In 1924, he again came back to Okinawa to conduct a grant-funded survey of Ryukyuan art until 1927. His research records and photographs have played tremendously important roles in the revival of Ryukyuan movable and immovable cultural heritage, including the postwar reconstruction of Shuri-jō Castle. "Sunpo-ki" discussed later was found in his collection.

[46] Chuta Ito was a Japanese architect, and well-known as the founder of the history of Japanese architecture and a pioneer in the preservation of old buildings from an artistic point of view. He served as a member of the Society for the Ancient Shrines and Temples Preservation under the Ministry of Home Affairs.

[47] The idea of building an Okinawa Shrine on the site of the State Hall had been conceived even since 1910, as part of the imperialization policy.

make it eligible for protection. The Okinawa Shrine Worship Hall was next designated a National Treasure under the National Treasures Preservation Law of 1929[48], and underwent major restorations between 1928 and 1935, saving it from imminent risk of collapse. Many buildings in the Shuri-jō Castle area, including temples, royal residences, gates, and mausoleums, were also designated as national treasures.

Towards the end of the Second World War, Okinawa was fortified as a military base for the purpose of defending the Japanese mainland. The Japanese army established its headquarters in tunnels dug under the hard limestone on which Shuri-jō stands, and fought a war of attrition. In the spring of 1945, U.S. forces aiming to capture the Shuri frontline launched a naval barrage and air raids that pulverized Shuri-jō and burned the State Hall to the ground. The war destroyed almost all Okinawa's cultural assets.

12.6.2 Changes in the State Hall in the Kingdom

The Shuri-jō Castle, built on a hill overlooking Naha Port, has beautifully curved Ryukyu limestone walls that follow the terrain. By the mid of sixteenth century, it was almost complete in its present form. The center of the royal court was the State Hall with the throne, the courtyard in front of it, and a group of buildings surrounding the courtyard. The State Hall boasts a unique architectural beauty, incorporating Japanese architecture[49] and the architectural style of the Chinese court, while the direction of the State Hall facing the west[50] reveals the ancient Ryukyuan belief in the god of the Sun and respect for the east. The State Hall burned down three times during the Kingdom's reign, and was rebuilt each time. The last fire occurred in 1709, and the State Hall was rebuilt in 1712, which was the State Hall later destroyed during the Battle of Okinawa. The transitions of the State Hall through reconstructions and restorations are known through the records of drifting Koreans, the reports of the Chinese envoys, and the documents of the royal court of Shuri, which are as follows.[51]

The earliest record of the State Hall is that of Koreans who drifted to Ryukyu in 1450. The State Hall was a three-story building, with the king seated on the upper floor and his attendants dressed in formal attire worshipping him from the courtyard.

The State Hall is said to have been burnt down in 1453 during the Shilo-Furi War,[52] but it appears to have been rebuilt soon afterward. According to Koreans who

[48] With the enactment of the National Treasures Preservation Law, the scope of designation and subsidies was expanded to include buildings and treasures owned by private individuals like old families and companies other than shrines and temples.

[49] In the mid-fifteenth century, a Japanese Zen monk of the Rinzai School, Kaiin Shohko came to Ryukyu and served for the kings. He built many temples including Engakuji, the temple for the Royal family.

[50] According to Chinese concepts, the Emperor shall face south.

[51] Asato (1998).

[52] A civil war in which the fifth king's son and brother split the kingdom in two over the throne.

drifted to Ryukyu in 1456 and 1460, the State Hall was a three-story building painted in vermilion with a shingled roof. Chen Kan, the Chinese envoy in 1534 reported that the State Hall faced the west, and was seven kens on the south façade and seven kens on the west façade (a ken is equivalent to about six feet).

After the fire in 1660, it was rebuilt with a tiled roof, but the floor layout followed the same, having seven kens on each facade, according to a record written by Wang Ji, the Chinese envoy in 1683. During the renovation work in 1682, a five-color dragon head decoration was installed on the roof ridge of the State Hall.

The State Hall was again destroyed by fire in 1709, and rebuilt in 1712. The Ryukyu-koku Yuraiki[53] notes that the State Hall had a kohai (a roof built over the steps) and karahafu (cusped gable) on its front facade. For this construction, 19,525 pieces of lumber were sent from Satsuma. "Chu-zan Denshinroku" written by Xu Baoguang, the Chinese envoy in 1719 describes that the State Hall was of nine kens, which indicates that the width of the State Hall was extended during the 1712 reconstruction.

Sai Wen, who assumed the position of Prime Minister in 1728, greatly revolutionized the ritual rites of the royal court, which is assumed to have influenced the subsequent restorations of Shuri-jō Castle. During the renovation work in 1729, the throne, which had previously been located to the south, was moved to the center of the State Hall.[54] "Ryukyu-kokushiryaku" compiled by Chou Huang, the Chinese envoy in 1756 states that the State Hall was nine kens, with narrow chambers on either side. This floor layout corresponds to the illustration in the "Momourazoeudun Fushinnitsuki Miezu narabini Ozaimoku Sunpo-ki (Sunpo-ki)",[55] a record of the restoration work in 1768. During this restoration, a five-ken-wide overhanging eaves in the center of the front facade and a three-ken-wide overhanging kohai with karahafu were built.

The State Hall was also restored in 1811 and 1846, and the restoration work in 1846 is described in detail in four books[56] of the so-called "Shō-family documents".[57]

---

[53] The first official geography of Ryukyu, compiled by the Shuri Royal Government in 1713.

[54] Iyori (1997).

[55] It was found among the research records compiled by Yoshitaro Kamakura, which has been contributed to the Okinawa Prefectural University of Arts upon its opening in 1986. Sunpo-ki has provided irreplaceable information to the postwar reconstruction project.

[56] "Momourazoeudun Gofushin Nikki", "Momourazoe Gofushin Nikki", "Momourazoe Gofushin Nikki Ataihou", and "Momourazoe Gofushin Ezucho".

[57] The "Shō-family documents" escaped the Battle of Okinawa because Kanjun Higashionna, who was given responsibility to compile a biography of Shō Tai, the last king of Ryukyu, had transported some of the royal documents from Nakagusuku palace in Shuri to Tokyo in 1910. Of the other records of the royal government, the documents seized by the Meiji government at the disposal of Ryukyu were lost in the Great Kanto Earthquake, and those left at Nakagusuku palace were destroyed by fire during the Battle of Okinawa. Over 1300 items of the documents that belonged to the Shō-family were donated to Naha City in 1995 by Mr. Shō Hiroshi, the 22nd head of the Shō-family. The 85 items of arts and crafts were also donated. These documents, arts and crafts were designated as a national treasure in 2006 as "Materials Related to the Shō-family of the King of Ryukyu". Currently, they are preserved in the Naha City Museum of History.

Fig. 12.10 The postwar reconstructed State Hall and the courtyard in front, before the fire (© Junko Mukai)

The "Ukansen-no-Toki Gozagamae-no-Zu", which was made to receive the Chinese envoy in 1866, contains many illustrations showing the setup for the ceremonies at different places in the Shuri-jō Castle, which gives a vivid picture of the Shuri-jō Castle in its former days. Although it is impossible to know at this time, this was the last Chinese envoy dispatched to the Ryukyu Kingdom.

The transition of the State Hall is also imprinted in its remains. Excavations in the State Hall area were conducted by the Cultural Properties Division of the Okinawa Prefectural Education Agency from 1985 to 1987.[58] Researchers are divided as to which of the six rows of excavated stone foundations remain on the front (west) side of the building belong to each of the reconstruction and restoration works mentioned in the literature.[59] However, the rows of masonry foundations tell us of the overwhelming presence of the State Hall, which was continuously solemnized and renewed as a center of diplomatic and cultural power for the royal court (Figs. 12.10 and 12.11).

[58] Okinawa Prefectural Centre for Buried Cultural Properties (2016).

[59] Asato (1998).

Fig. 12.11 View of the second floor of the State Hall, before the fire. The throne is seen in the center (© Junko Mukai)

12.6.3 Postwar Reconstruction

The postwar reconstruction of Shuri-jō Castle had already been proposed by the Committee for Cultural Properties Protection in the Ryukyu Government in 1970, when Okinawa was still under US rule. The movement of reconstruction gained momentum with the return of Okinawa to Japan in 1972, and in 1973, the Shurijo Fukugen Kiseikai (Association for Shuri-jō Castle Reconstruction) was established.[60] The decision to relocate the University of the Ryukyus, which had been built on the Shuri-jō Castle site shortly after the war, made the reconstruction of Shuri-jō Castle a reality, and in 1984 the LDP Subcommittee on the Reconstruction of Okinawa's War Lost Cultural Properties announced a proposal to develop the

60 Editorial Committee for Yomigaeru Shuri-jo - rekishi to fukugen (1993).

Shuri-jō Castle site as a national park, and in 1986 the cabinet approved a national park project.[61] The State Hall was to be rebuilt as part of this project.[62]

The Shuri-jō Castle State Hall Design Committee,[63] established in 1986, decided that "The State Hall has undergone various changes in form and scale since its construction until it was destroyed by fire during the Battle of Okinawa, and that the reconstruction shall be based on related documents and materials and in the principle of restoring the State Hall, which was rebuilt in 1712 and designated a national treasure in 1925." The committee brought together experts in architecture, history, archaeology, sculpture, landscape architecture, and other fields from within and outside of the prefecture to make the decisions on design principles and policies, design plans, detailed specifications, and other matters. Under the committee, four specialized subcommittees on wood construction, roof tiles, coloring, and sculpture were established to examine specific technical issues.[64]

When the design for the reconstruction of State Hall was first started, the related materials available were limited to a set of drawings prepared during the 1930s restoration work of the Okinawa Shrine worship hall, which was owned by the Agency for Cultural Affairs. There was a definite lack of specifications on the interior partitioning, coloring, the shape of the throne, etc., that would allow the team to understand what it was like when it was used as a royal court. More than 100 years after the disposal of Ryukyu, the memory of the Ryukyuan reign has been severed, and many valuable related materials were lost in the Battle of Okinawa and the Tokyo Air Raid. However, through a combination of various fortuitous circumstances, the "Sunpo-ki" was found among the collection of Yoshitaro Kamakura, which had just been donated to the Prefectural University of Arts, followed by the four volumes of the "Shō-family documents" which had been kept in the strict custody of the descendants of the last king.[65]

These two sets of documents were the key basis for the reconstruction of State Hall as a royal court. The detailed records of the renovation of the State Hall in 1768 and 1846 provide a picture of the palace as it used to be when the king sat there and ceremonies and rituals were performed. Various documents were analyzed, photographs were collected, and detailed information was collected. Clues were also obtained from surveys of similar buildings in Japan, China, and Korea, as well as from interviews with Shuri elders, and the colors, patterns, and techniques of the detailed design were determined in detail.[66]

[61] As part of a project to commemorate Okinawa's reversion to Japan, approximately 4.7 hectares of the former Shuri Castle site was developed. The reconstruction of the main hall was placed under the jurisdiction of the Okinawa General Bureau's Okinawa Memorial Park Office, while the development of the buildings and gardens within the national park area, excluding the main hall, was placed under the jurisdiction of the Housing and Urban Development Corporation (now the Urban Renaissance Agency).

[62] National Okinawa Memorial Park Office (1995).

[63] Inaugurated under the auspices of the Okinawa Development Agency.

[64] Takara, et al. (2003).

[65] Takara, et al. (2003).

[66] Takara, et al. (2003).

The exact location and ground level of the State Hall were confirmed from the remains of the basement excavated in the State Hall area of the Shuri-jō Castle Ruins. The excavated building parts also provided information for reconstruction.[67] For example, the Yamato-style tiles and Ming-style tiles excavated from around the foundation at different periods, as well as the foundations from which no tiles were excavated, led the team to identify the transition of the roofing material of the State Hall. Stone fragments that were excavated such as balustrades, foundations, and plinths were good references for the sculptures.

Meanwhile, the traditional techniques necessary for reconstruction were being lost. One hundred years after the Ryukyu deposition and more than 40 years after the loss of Shuri-jō Castle to war, the craft techniques that once supported the kingdom's culture had fallen into disuse, and many buildings and artifacts from the kingdom period had been lost. The State Hall reconstruction provided the perfect opportunity for researchers and craftspeople from mainland Japan and Okinawa to work together to revive carpentry techniques, lacquering and coloring, roof tiles, stone carvings, and more.[68]

The reconstruction of the State Hall began in 1989 and was completed in 1992. Along with the State Hall, the buildings surrounding the courtyard and several gates were also reconstructed, and Shuri-jō Park was opened. Subsequent reconstructions of the back palace, ritual spaces, and other buildings followed, and the entire park was opened in February 2019.

12.6.4 Management of Shuri-jō Castle

After the Battle of Okinawa, the ruins of Shuri-jō Castle were designated as a historic site by the Ryukyu government in 1955. After the reversion to Japan, it was designated as a historic site under the Law of Cultural Properties Protection. The reconstructed State Hall and other buildings are not subject to protection under the Law of Cultural Properties Protection. The State Hall is exempted from the Building Standards Law as a building that reproduces the original form of a building that was designated as a national treasure.[69] Therefore, the fireproofing provisions of the Law do not apply to the State Hall. As for the installation of firefighting and evacuation equipment, the report[70] concludes that the rules defined in the Fire Defense Law had been complied. The Shuri-jō Castle Ruins have been operated and managed by the National Okinawa Memorial Park Office (Park Office), Okinawa General Bureau, Cabinet Office, as part of the National Okinawa Memorial Park. In the area, the outer ramparts and their gates have been maintained by the Okinawa Prefectural Board of Education, while

[67] Okinawa Prefectural Centre for Buried Cultural Properties (2016).

[68] Takara, et al. (2003).

[69] Falls under Article 3, Item 4 of the Building Standards Law.

[70] According to the report of the Committee for the Prevention of Recurrence of the Shuri Castle Fire in March 2021.

the inner ramparts and architectural facilities, including the State Hall, have been maintained by the Park Office. The area around Shuri-jō Castle, which is outside the national park, is designated as the Okinawa Prefectural Shuri-jō Park as an area that forms an integrated historical atmosphere with Shuri-jō Castle.

In 2000, the Shuri-jō Castle Ruins were inscribed on the World Heritage List as "Gusuku and Related Properties of the Ryukyu Kingdom," together with eight other components representing the history of Ryukyu during the twelfth to seventeenth centuries. The sites demonstrate the role of the Ryukyus as a key player in trade and cultural exchange linking East and Southeast Asia, and are highly regarded as a group of heritage sites representing the unique culture created by this wide-ranging exchange. Of Shuri-jō Castle, the ramparts and the State Hall foundation ruins are the components inscribed, while the reconstructed State Hall isn't. Yet the report prepared by ICOMOS, an advisory body to UNESCO, in response to the nomination evaluates the reconstruction of the Shuri-jō Castle State Hall as highly accurate and evidence-based work, and a symbol of the Okinawan people's pride.

12.7 Loss of Shuri-jō Castle

A fire in October 2019 destroyed the State Hall and a group of adjacent buildings that had been reconstructed after the war. In this section, let's look back at the fire situation and see how the loss was perceived by the people of Okinawa.

12.7.1 Fire and Response

At 2:34 a.m. on October 30, 2019, a motion sensor of the security system of the State Hall was triggered. The fire is believed to have started in the northeast part of the State Hall. Security guards immediately rushed to the scene, but the area was already filled with black smoke. When the fire brigade finally started to spray water, after getting over the blockages by the multiple ramparts and locked gates, 30 min had passed since the sensor was triggered. The interior of the State Hall was already ablaze, flames gushing from the openings, and the State Hall collapsed before 4:30 a.m. A total of 219 firefighters and 60 fire trucks fought to extinguish the fire, but the fire was driven by winds from the northeast, which also destroyed six adjacent buildings, including the north and south halls. The fire was brought under control at 11:00 a.m., and by the time it was extinguished, it was 1:30 p.m. Many of the exhibits were destroyed by the fire, and some of the artifacts and historical materials stored in the two storage rooms in the building were damaged by the radiant heat and water. As a result, 395 of the 1,524 artifacts and materials were lost, including those designated as cultural properties by the prefecture (Fig. 12.12).

Chief Cabinet Secretary Yoshihide Suga announced at a press conference held in the morning on the day of the fire that he would work on the reconstruction

Fig. 12.12 Shuri-jō Castle during fire-fighting seen over Ryutan Pond, around 10:30 (© Junko Mukai)

of Shuri-jō Castle as soon as possible. Okinawa Governor Denny Tamaki returned from an official trip to South Korea and at 2:30 p.m. on the day of the fire, he set up a Headquarter Conference for the Shuri-jō Castle Fire Response with a view to rebuilding Shuri-jō Castle.

12.7.2 Perception of the Loss

The loss of Shuri-jō Castle seems to have shocked many Okinawans. After the fire, two local newspapers carried articles with detaild information about the fire and reconstruction. Not a day went by without a mention of Shuri-jō Castle in the readers' columns. From time to time, special feature articles were published, conveying the voices of people, experts and ordinary citizens. What stands out among them is the number of people who say they realized that Shuri-jō Castle was a symbol of Okinawa just after it was destroyed by fire. Some of these include young people who have never set foot in Shuri-jō Castle.

The previous reconstruction of Shuri-jō Castle was actually of little interest to many ordinary citizens of the prefecture. It took 47 years after the loss of almost all monuments from the Ryukyu reign, including Shuri-jō Castle, during the

Battle of Okinawa, for the bright red lacquered State Hall to suddenly appear. For many people, it was an unfamiliar monument. However, the magnificent State Hall, which was reconstructed as faithfully as possible, was a significant manifestation of Ryukyuan architecture, which until then existed only in small black-and-white photographs. Twenty-seven years after its completion, Shuri-jō Castle became a symbol of Okinawan identity when it was destroyed by fire.

There are also people in other parts of the world who felt they had lost a symbol of their identity when Shuri-jō Castle burned down. Okinawa Prefecture is known as one of Japan's leading immigrant-sending prefectures since 1899 when it sent out immigrants to Hawaii. It is estimated that more than 400,000 people who have their roots in Okinawa live around the world. It is said that the first to send relief supplies to the devastated postwar Okinawa were those immigrants who themselves were forced to live in harsh conditions, but who still cared about their distant homeland. And this time, too, the people of Okinawan descent from all over the world sent their donations and encouragement with hopes for the reconstruction of Shuri-jō Castle.

12.8 Reconstruction Policy and Where People's Interests Lie

The principle of following the postwar reconstruction approach to rebuilding the State Hall, which was destroyed by the 2019 fire, was announced at an early stage. The informative materials that were the basis of the postwar reconstruction are available, and it would certainly be most rational to rebuild based on these materials in order to realize an early reconstruction. Architects and historians who were deeply involved in the postwar reconstruction play a central role in this reconstruction. There would be no reason or room to consider any other policy other than to reproduce the State Hall, which was reconstructed based on the old documents and archaeological data, aiming at the State Hall of the Ryukyu reign. If any changes would be considered, the reason is to seek a higher degree of authenticity based on the research findings acquired after the previous reconstruction.

In this section, after reviewing the policies of the central and prefectural governments regarding the reconstruction, one matter that is of particular concern to the people of Okinawa will be discussed. That issue is the policy of facing the dragon-pillars in the same direction as the previous reconstruction, and the criticism of that policy. Why is this issue of particular interest of the people?

12.8.1 Reconstruction Policy

At the 3rd Ministerial Conference for the Reconstruction of Shuri-jō Castle on December 11, 2019, the government decided the basic policy,[71] which is "to restore Shuri-jō Castle by following the basic idea of the previous reconstruction based on the detailed chronological study. In other words, the State Hall of Shuri-jō Castle will be reconstructed in principle to the original building, which was rebuilt in 1712 and designated a national treasure in 1925.", and "to reflect the findings discovered after the postwar reconstruction and shifts in the condition of material procurement, and to strengthen fire prevention measures in consideration of the possibility of future fires." It was also decided to set up a forum for technical study in the Okinawa General Bureau of the Cabinet Office, which includes Okinawan experts involved in the postwar reconstruction. Thus, the first meeting of the "Technical Committee for the Reconstruction of Shuri-jō Castle" was held on the 27th of the same month. The Committee was chaired by Kurayoshi Takara, Professor Emeritus at Ryukyu University, who served as a member of the Shuri-jō State Hall Design Committee for the postwar reconstruction and contributed to the evidence-based reconstruction as a historian of Ryukyus. The other 10 members include experts in Ryukyu history, architectural history, and cultural studies, and also in architecture and urban planning, disaster prevention, and cultural property restoration. The Committee established three working groups on the State Hall reconstruction: disaster prevention, wood and roof tiles, and coloring and sculpture. Based on the research that has continued since the postwar reconstruction and the re-analysis of the historical documents and materials, the Committee has been studying the coloring, carvings, raw materials for painting, roof-tile patterns, and decoration of the throne in order to achieve a more accurate reconstruction.

Meanwhile, Okinawa Prefecture compiled seven "Basic Ideas" in December 2019, and based on them, announced the "Shuri-jō Castle Reconstruction Basic Policies" in April 2020. The "Basic Policies" include promoting the use of the Okinawan craftspeople, use of building materials produced in the prefecture, public display and exhibition of the reconstruction work, and prevention of recurrence of fires, in cooperation with the national government. It also includes the development of the surrounding area and the rehabilitation and awareness rising out of Ryukyuan culture and traditional techniques. In March 2021, the "Shuri-jō Castle Reconstruction Basic Plan" was published to provide specific direction and facilitate well-planned implementation of the measures outlined in the "Basic Policies". In February 2020, Okinawa Prefecture also established a Committee to Study the Prevention of Recurrence of the Shuri-jō Castle fire, consisting of five members from within and outside the prefecture who specialize in law, cultural property disaster prevention, and park planning. The committee released an interim report in September of the same year and a final report on measures to prevent recurrence in March 2021.

In this project, both the national and prefectural governments aim to actively publicize the reconstruction process, and through such public access and organizing

[71] https://www.kantei.go.jp/jp/singi/shurijo_fukugen/knj_dai3/gijisidai.html.

Fig. 12.13 Shuri-jō Castle overviewed from the east end after the fire. The Naha Port is behind it. The small prefabricated shed (the left side of the photo) has been built on where the State Hall was, to protect and display the rows of the stone foundation (© Junko Mukai)

related events, contribute to community development. The reconstruction of the State Hall is scheduled for completion in 2026 (Fig. 12.13).

12.8.2 What People Are Interested In?

After the fire was extinguished, a pair of great dragon pillars in front of the stone platform on which the State Hall stood attracted the public's attention. They are approximately three meters high, made of fine-grained sandstone, and have the shape of dragons with their bodies stretched out straight. The pillars were damaged by high heat, but they remained standing without collapsing, leaving a strong impression on people. The fragile dragon pillars were carefully moved to a safe place and repaired for cracks and peeling. The repair work was completed in November 2020. Those repaired pillars will be preserved as an archive and a pair of new dragon pillars will be made in the State Hall reconstruction project (Figs. 12.14 and 12.15).

The dragon pillars are of great interest to the people of Okinawa for another reason. The debate is whether the two paired dragon pillars should face each other or face forward. Since both Sunpo-ki and the Shō-family documents, which were the

Fig. 12.14 The scene after the fire. In the center, only the State Hall's stone platform and a pair of the great dragon pillars remained. The children are looking at the scene from outside the ramparts (© Junko Mukai)

primary sources for the State Hall reconstruction, depict the two dragon pillars facing each other, the dragon pillars made for the postwar reconstruction of the State Hall were installed facing each other.[72] In contrast, some civic groups and researchers have argued that the dragon pillars should be installed facing the front in the current reconstruction project.[73] In fact, the same argument was raised during the postwar reconstruction, but in this time, because of the great interest people are showing in the reconstruction itself, the dragon pillar issue is also attracting more attention from the people. In the old paintings depicting Shuri-jō Castle by royal painters, town painters, and Chinese envoys, some are facing the front, and others facing each other.[74]

---

[72] Takara (1994).

[73] Starting with a petition submitted to the prefectural assembly in September 2020 by Dai-Ryuchu wo Kangaerukai (the Association for examining the Great Dragon Pillars), several civic groups which advocates a frontal orientation, including Shuri-jō Saikou Kenkyukai (the Shuri-jō Restoration Research Society), have held lectures and symposiums. Local newspapers have also taken up the debate, featuring commentary articles from researchers taking both sides of the issue.

[74] For instance, Ryukyusen to Shuri Naha wo Egaita Kaiga Shiryo Kenkyukai (2019).

Fig. 12.15 The fire damaged great dragon pillars are being repaired. The repair work was on display for the public (© Junko Mukai)

What We Know About the Dragon Pillar

The first dragon pillar was made in 1509, and new ones were made after the fires of 1660 and 1709, respectively. Based on the drawn images and fragments of old pillars preserved in museums, it is suspected that in the older period the dragon pillars faced the front in such a way that their backs were connected to the stone balustrades of the steps leading up to the State Hall. By the time of the 1768 restoration work documented in Sunpo-ki, for some reason, they were placed on pedestals facing each other, and even in the 1846 restoration work documented in the Shō-family document, they were facing each other. However, the next source, which is a photograph of the State Hall showing one of the soldiers of the Meiji government stationed at Shuri-jō Castle from 1879 to 1896, shows it facing the front. A measured drawing prepared before the 1930s restoration also shows it facing the front. However, the short length of one of the dragon pillars in the photograph and the drawing suggests that the dragon pillar has been altered in some way, and the genuineness of the orientation has been questioned. In the 1930s restoration, the pillar's orientation was changed to facing each other as seen in the project drawings, and they had stood in that orientation until the war destroyed them. The reason why the restoration project changed orientation is not known. As per a record, interviews were conducted with an elderly person to assess the old state of the State Hall, but whether the dragon pillar orientation was discussed in the interview is not known. Instead, a story spoken among people speculates that the two dragons were placed facing each other in order to follow the usual orientation of a pair of komainu, a mythical creature that looks like a lion, standing in front of Japanese shrines.[75] This interpretation argues that the State Hall was unjustifiably changed, not only in name but also in form, into a Japanese shrine which was a symbol of assimilation in Japan, in contrast to another aspect of the re-naming in order to protect the dilapidated State Hall under the contemporary law as mentioned in the Sect. 12.6.1.

There are some research findings to suggest the reason for the change from the front facing in the old days to the facing each other in the eighteenth century. Tsutomu Iyori, Professor Emeritus at Kyoto University cites as the reason that the original axis of the State Hall has become noticeably misaligned with the axis of the courtyard and surrounding buildings such as the main gate and the south hall which were later developed in accordance with newly introduced manners of rituals.[76]

Firstly, it should be pointed out that the State Hall has faced west-southwest instead of true west. Further, as mentioned above, until 1718 when it was moved to the center of the State Hall, the throne had been located on the south side of the State Hall. The old Ryukyuan sense of direction and right-sided dominance was replaced by a format that emphasized true north direction and a central axis. For instance, according to "Kyu-yoh",[77] in 1712, the New Year's Day ritual in the courtyard, which had previously been performed facing east-northeast, thus facing the State Hall was changed to a form of worship facing due north, the direction of the Chinese Forbidden City. Another change was on a path in the center of the courtyard meant for palanquins to pass through. It is known from the remains of the State Hall platform that in the old days, this path was orthogonal to the State Hall platform. However, it was later realigned, an inspection conducted by the minister in 1713 pointed out that the path in the center of the courtyard followed the true east–west axis and was not aligned with the central axis of the State Hall. In other words, the dragon pillar facing the front would have been slightly turned away if viewed straight along the path.

In order to camouflage the misalignment between the central axis of the State Hall and the east–west axes of the gate, the courtyard path, and the south hall, the State Hall's kohai was widened and the stone steps leading up to it were made wider at the lower step during the 1768 restoration work. The parallel railings were thus made in the shape of the letter "V", and the connection between the oblique railings and the front-facing dragon pillars became unnatural. Hence, it is assumed that the dragon pillars were made to face each other in order to make the misalignment of the axis less noticeable and to eliminate the unnatural connection between the railings and dragon pillars.

The dragon pillars installed in the postwar reconstruction were placed facing each other. The reason is explained that when the integrity with the State Hall is

[75] Nishimura (2020) September 22, and 23.

[76] Iyori (1997).

[77] An official history of Ryukyu written from 1743 until 1876.

emphasized, the dragon pillars should face as indicated by the "Sunpo-ki", the central basis for the reconstruction. While the "Sunpo-ki" provides the richest information on the room layout, interior partitions, coloring, and carvings of the Ryukyu reign, there are no sufficient data to make it possible to reconstruct the State Halls of the older period, when the dragon pillars faced the front.

A Photograph Taken in the Late Ryukyu Reign

However, in November 2020, at a symposium of the Association of Comprehensive Studies for Independence of the Lew Chewans, Atsushi Shiitada, Associate Professor at Kanagawa University, presented a photograph.[78] The photo, allegedly taken by a French naval officer in 1877,[79] shows a pair of dragon pillars facing the front. The Technical Committee also confirmed the year when the photo was taken, from old documents stipulating that the French delegation visited Shuri-jō in 1877, confirming that this photo was taken in the late Kingdom reign. This means that the aforementioned front-facing dragon pillars, shown with Japanese soldiers, were not turned around when one of the pillars was shortened as it had been presumed.

Sadao Nishimura, Professor Emeritus at the University of the Ryukyus, who created the great dragon pillars in the postwar reconstruction, speculates, based on an investigation of the fragments of the old dragon pillars, that the dragon pillars were connected to the "V" shaped railing, but was damaged in the 1770 earthquake and placed on a pedestal that was installed as a tentative measure. He also assumes that the dragon pillars in the "Sunpo-ki" and "Shō-family documents" were not drawn realistically and there are even some mistakes in the illustrations, and thus, it is not adequate material to determine the orientation.[80] Civic groups and researchers who support this claim have gained further confidence in their assertion with the photograph from the late Kingdom reign. They are urging the Technical Committee to clarify why the dragon pillars were photographed facing the front some 30 years later from the year of 1846, if they had been facing each other as per the "Shō-family documents", and otherwise, the dragon pillars should be reconstructed facing forward this time.[81]

12.8.3 Background of the Interest

In December 2021, the Technical Committee announced as a tentative conclusion that the orientation of the dragon pillars would follow the postwar reconstruction in this

[78] Taken by Ensign Jules Revertegat, a crew member of a French Navy cruiser. The existence of this photograph has been known for some time, as its etching is included in Revertegat's "Ryukyu Islands Travels".

[79] Later, through the intermediary of Professor Tsutomu Iyori, the image was donated to the Okinawa Prefectural Library and the Okinawa Prefectural Archives by Mr. Hervé Bernard, the owner of the original.

[80] Nishimura (2020) September 22, and 23.

[81] Shiitada, et al. (2021).

project as well. The reason is to maintain the consistency with the exterior and interior details of the State Hall, that follow the "Sunpo-ki" as in the postwar reconstruction, while the French naval photo only informs of the external appearance. The Committee reported that "the orientation of the dragon-pillars was changed during the 30 years from the "Gofushin Ezucho[82]" (1846) to the French naval photo (1877)," but "no clear description was found in the documents to indicate that the orientation was changed". Therefore, "the decision will be reconsidered, if new evidence is discovered in the future, which specifies historical context or reason how or why the dragon pillar's orientation was altered."

In response to this conclusion, three civic groups issued a protest statement, and in the following month sent an open letter of inquiry to the Okinawa General Bureau and the Technical Committee. The Okinawa General Bureau and the Technical Committee held a debriefing session for the general public in January 2022, where Kurayoshi Takara, chairman of the committee, explained how they reached their tentative conclusion. Susumu Asato, Professor Emeritus at the Okinawa Prefectural University of Arts, presented a report that verified and refuted Prof. Nishimura's claims about the connection between the dragon pillars and the stone railing, as well as his doubt on the realism of the "Sunpo-ki" iconography.[83] The next day, local newspapers carried comments and articles by the civic groups and others who were not satisfied with this conclusion.

The focus in this section should be on the impression that many people in Okinawa are somewhat in favor of the frontal orientation, and their interest lies elsewhere than in a stringent examination of chronological consistency as deliberated among the researchers. Rather, people's interest is more likely in the matter of how the dragon pillars primarily have been, and what they should be as a symbol of Ryukyuan/Okinawan culture.

12.9 Conclusion

Cultural heritage in Bhutan is not preserved through legal and institutional enhancement. In restoration and reconstruction of Dzongs, temples and monasteries, facing squarely the various opinions about how they should be, a better path toward "value-based protection" is being explored case by case. Every experience and its outcomes, including that of Wangduephodrang Dzong, contribute to the progressive development of the heritage protection system in Bhutan.

In Japan, perhaps due to a general impression that cultural properties are protected by an unchanged system—although it is not correct as explained in the other chapter—not much public attention would be raised to the theme of how heritage buildings should be restored. In the process of evidence-based reconstruction of

[82] One of the volumes of the "Shō-family documents".

[83] Asato (2020).

Shuri-jō Castle, which is outside the ordinal system of cultural property buildings, the dragon pillars have found space in the civic controversy.

In recent years, the importance of community participation in the cultural heritage process has been emphasized. From the cultural heritage community's perspective, this may mean a gradual opening up of the traditional expert-driven approach to people and community. However, in our two cases, the principles and methodologies that are taken for granted in the cultural heritage community have not been taken as the default, and people's views have been placed on an equal footing with these principles and methods. Therefore, these two cases should be worth examining when thinking about community participation in the cultural heritage process and how we should face their voices.

References

Wangduephodrang Dzong

Aris, M. (1982). *Views of medieval Bhutan—The diary and drawings of Samuel Davis 1783.* Smithsonian Institution Press and Serindia Publications.

Mukai, J., et al. (2013). *Assessment report: Wangduephodrang Dzong structures post June 24, 2012 Fire, Department of Culture.* Royal Government of Bhutan.

Mukai, J., Wangchuk, L., et al. (2013). *Project report for Wangduephodrang Dzong conservation project (2008–2013).* Department of Culture, Royal Government of Bhutan.

Phuntsho, K. (2013). *The history of Bhutan.* Random House India.

Planning Commission. (1999). *Bhutan 2020—A vision for peace, prosperity and happiness.* Planning Commission.

Thinley J. Y. (2012, June 26). *Prime Minister Jigme Y Thinley's Message to Fellow Citizens.* Kuensel.

Shuri-jō

Asato, S. (1998). *Gusuku, Kyodotai, Mura (Gusukus, communities, and villages).* Yoju Shorin.

Asato, S. (2020). *Heisei Fukugen no Kensho (Verification of the postwar reconstruction)*, Handouts for the Briefing of Technical Committee for the Reconstruction of Shuri-jō Castle. National Okinawa Memorial Park Office.

Editorial Committee for Yomigaeru Shuri-jō – rekishi to fukugen. (1993). Yomigaeru Shuri-jō – rekisi to fukugen (Reviving Shuri-jō – History and Reconstruction). Shuri-jō Fukugen Kiseikai.

Iyori, T. (1997). Shuri-jō Seiden Karahafu no Kigen to Sono Kaishu ni tsuite (About the origin and alterations of the cusped gable of the Shuri-jō State Hall). In: Shirijo Kenkyu-kai (Ed.), *Shuri-jō Kenkyu (Studies on Shuri-jō)* No. 3. Shuri-jō Tomo no kai.

National Okinawa Memorial Park Office. (1995). *Kokuei Okinawa Kinenkouen Shuri-jō Chiku-Keikaku & Sekkei no Kiroku (National Okinawa Memorial Park Shuri-jō Area – Records on the Planning & Designing).* National Okinawa Memorial Park Office.

Nishimura, S. (2020, September 22 and 23). Shuri-jō Saiken wo Kangaeru (Thinking the reconstruction of Shuri-jō). *Okinawa Times.*

Okinawa Prefectural Centre for Buried Cultural Properties. (2016). *Shuri-jō Seiden Chiku Hakkutsu Chosa Houkokusho (Report on the excavation and research of the State Hall Area of Shuri-jō)*. Okinawa Prefecture.

Ryukyusen to Shuri Naha wo Egaita Kaiga Shiryo Kenkyukai. (2019). *Ryukyusen to Shuri Naha wo Egaita Kaiga Shiryo Kenkyu (Research on painted historical documents depicting Ryukyuan ships and Shuri-Naha)*. Shibunkaku.

Shiitada, A., et al. (2021). Shuri-jō Saikou – Dairyuchu Shomenmuki – Kenmin no Koe (Restoration of Shuri-jō—Front-Facing Great Dragon Pillars—Voices of Okinawan Citizens). In: N27 Editorial Committee (Ed.) (pp. 2–32). N27.

Takara, K. (1994). Shuri-jō Seiden no Dairyuchu no Mukini tsuiteno Oboegaki (Memorandum on the orientation of Great Dragon Pillars of the Shuri-jō State Hall). In Shirijo Kenkyu-kai (Ed.), *Shuri-jō Kenkyu (Studies on Shuri-jō)* No1. Shuri-jō Tomo no kai.

Takara, K., Fukushima, K., Taira, H., et al. (2003). *Shuri-jō no Fukugen – Seiden Fukugen no Kangaekata, Konkyo wo Tyushin ni (Reconstruction of Shuri-jō – focusing on Policies and Basis for Reconstruction of the State Hall)*. Ocean Expo Commemorative Park Management Foundation.

Junko Mukai (Heritage Architect) She works in development of institutional and legal frameworks and human resource to protect cultural heritage of Bhutan since 2001 in the Ministry of Home and Cultural Affairs of the Government of Bhutan and later as consultant. Currently engaged in collaborative research project to improve seismic resilience of Bhutan's traditional house in Nagoya City University, Japan. She is a member of the Scientific Committee of the Web exhibition Notre-Dame de Paris Cathedral and Shuri-jo Castle (https://www.notredame-shurijo.com/eng/index.shtml). Her selected publications include: Mukai Junko (2016), "Heritage Sites Protection work profile (2001–till date)." Department of Culture of Bhutan; Mukai Junko et al. (2018), "The Cultural Landscape and Important Cultural Sites—Bhutan's approach to protect space and life from cultural heritage viewpoint." Final Technical Report—Support South Asian Cultural Landscape Initiatives; Experience in Bhutan. UNESCO Japan-FIT Support South Asian Cultural Landscape project; Mukai Junko (2012). "Assessment Report; Wangduephodrang Dzong structures post June 24, 2012 fire." Department of Culture of Bhutan.

Chapter 13
Social Aspects of the Cultural Heritage and the Process of Recovery—Notre-Dame de Paris Cathedral and Shuri-jô Castle

Toshiyuki Kono

Abstract In 2005, the Operational Guidelines of the World Heritage Convention expanded the list of factors that may be considered in the authenticity test. The factors such as "use and function; traditions, spirit, feeling, and other internal factors" on this list represent social aspects. Notre-Dame de Paris Cathedral and the State Hall of Shuri-jô Castle suggest that such factors play a significant role in the recovery of the cultural heritage beyond the World Heritage system. More discussions will clarify the roles of communities in the context of recovery of the cultural heritage.

Keywords Notre-Dame de Paris Cathedral · Shuri-jô Castle · Authenticity · Intangible aspects · Social aspect · Community

13.1 Introduction

2019 was a shocking year for those involved in the conservation of cultural heritage. Notre-Dame de Paris Cathedral was heavily damaged by fire, followed six months later by the loss of the State Hall of Shuri-jô Castle also by fire. The former is a prime example of Gothic architecture, an essential component of the World Heritage Site along with Paris, Banks of the Seine, and one of the world's most prominent cultural heritage buildings. It has been protected under French law since the nineteenth century. The fire destroyed both the nineteenth century spire and the medieval truss, and its collapse severely damaged the vault. The entire building lost its balance, and the parts that did not burn were in danger of collapsing. On the other hand, the Seiden, the State Hall of Shuri-jô Castle, was a national treasure designated in 1925. That was destroyed by fire during WW II and reconstructed in 1992. The reconstructed Seiden was not designated as a cultural property. Hence the building itself was not legally protected. Although located within Shuri-jô Castle, a component of Gusuku Sites and Related Heritage Sites in the Kingdom of Ryukyu, the World Heritage Site, the Seiden itself was not a component of the World Heritage Site.

T. Kono (✉)
Kyushu University, Fukuoka, Japan
e-mail: konoto@law.kyushu-u.ac.jp

T. Kono and J. Okahashi (eds.), *Post-Trauma and the Recovery Governance of Cultural Heritage*, https://doi.org/10.1007/978-981-19-6041-3_13

These two monuments with very different histories, materials, and legal statuses, however, provoked very similar social reactions after the disaster. In both cases, the locals were sad, and many voices of lamentation came from abroad. Domestic and international offers of donations poured in, and politicians responded immediately, pledging their recovery support.

13.2 Authenticity and Social Aspect of the Cultural Heritage

The authenticity of cultural heritage has been one of the most critical concerns for heritage professionals. Since the second international conference in Athens in 1931, experts have discussed monuments' significance and public nature. The Venice Charter, adopted in 1964 by experts from all over the world, declared that the "monumental works of peoples" and "human values" are considered a common heritage for which humanity is jointly responsible for safeguarding, in all the richness of their authenticity.[1]

The authenticity test has been a core in evaluating the World Heritage Convention of 1972. From 1978 until 2004, authenticity was tested based on the following four factors, design, materials, workmanship, and setting.[2] In 2005, the list of the factors was expanded. It includes now form and design; materials and substance; use and function; traditions, techniques and management systems; location and setting; language, and other forms of intangible heritage; spirit and feeling; and other internal and external factors.[3] The factors such as "use and function; traditions, spirit, feeling, and other internal factors" clearly represent social aspects of the World Heritage. These factors can be applied to other heritage sites than the World Heritage.

---

[1] The preamble of the Venice Charter (1964). https://www.icomos.org/charters/venice_e.pdf.

[2] The Operational Guidelines (1978), para. 9: In addition, the property should meet the test of authenticity in design, materials, workmanship, and setting; authenticity does not limit consideration to original form and structure but includes all subsequent modifications and additions over the course of time, which in themselves possess artistic or historical values.

[3] The Operational Guidelines (2005), para 79: Properties nominated under criteria (i) to (vi) must meet the conditions of authenticity. Annex 4, which includes the Nara Document on Authenticity, provides a practical basis for examining the authenticity of such properties and is summarized below.

Para.82: Depending on the type of cultural heritage and its cultural context, properties may be understood to meet the conditions of authenticity if their cultural value (as recognized in the nomination criteria proposed) are truthfully and credibly expressed through a variety of attributes including: form and design; materials and substance; use and function; traditions, techniques and management systems; location and setting; language, and other forms of intangible heritage; spirit and feeling; and other internal and external factors.

For instance, the earthquakes heavily damaged Knox Presbyterian Church in Christchurch in 2010 and 2011.[4] This church building was listed in 1984 as Category 2 Historic Place in Christchurch City before the earthquake. However, the building was so heavily damaged that it had to be demolished to secure the safety of visitors. The Presbyterian church decided to stay in the same setting, continuing its service, and dismissed the idea of relocation. The Knox Presbyterian Church retains its "social and spiritual significance" and continues to contribute to "the social fabric of the community".[5] The Knox Church did not lose its status as a Category 2 Historic Place. However, the assessment has been revised to focus on the value of the interior of the building.[6] The material authenticity of the building was lost because of its demolition. However, the new building continues to serve in the same venue as the place of spiritual activities of local communities.

This evaluation of the social aspects of the building is related to the debate on the authenticity of Notre-Dame de Paris Cathedral. Notre-Dame de Paris Cathedral is so famous as a representative monument of Gothic architecture that religious and social aspects of the building may not attract due attention. However, it has a lot of intangible heritage aspects, for instance, religious importance,[7] the long tradition of chants by its chorus,[8] and various national ceremonial events[9] and social prestige. The acoustic of the Cathedral[10] is related to the architecture, but it is more linked to religious activities, music lives, and visitors' senses. The roles of such various intangible aspects in the authenticity test have not been fully elaborated so far, even in the practice of the World Heritage Convention.

In the case of the Seiden, the State Hall of Shuri-jô Castle, its social functions are more limited than Notre-Dame de Paris Cathedral because, before the fire, the building was an exhibition hall and did not have any religious function. However, the building was used as the venue for ceremonial opportunities, which include the G7 summit meeting in 2000. In addition, the reconstruction project, which was completed

---

[4] See my contribution on Christchurch to this volume.

[5] Catherine Forbs (2021), Knox Presbyterian Church, Christchurch, ICOMOS/ICCROM, Analysis of Case Studies in Recovery and Reconstruction, Case Studies, Vol. 1, p. 216.

[6] Ibid., p. 221.

[7] The cathedral is, by definition, the church of the bishop, the spiritual leader of the community of Christians within the boundaries of the diocese, the region over which the authority of this ecclesiastical dignitary invested by the Pope is exercised. Cathedral comes from the Latin name cathedra, which refers to the throne where the bishop sits in the choir. The Cathedral is considered the mother church (mater ecclesia) of the entire diocese, whose hundreds of churches, with rare exceptions, are considered daughters, in a strictly hierarchical relationship. See Prologue, What is the Cathedral? https://www.Notre-DamedeParis-shurijo.com/eng/index.shtml.

[8] Isabelle Chave (2022), Chap. 3, The Choir of Notre-Dame de Paris, https://www.Notre-DamedeParis-shurijo.com/eng/html/readmore-Notre-DamedeParis05-rm04/.

[9] Yann Potin (2022), Chap. 1. Chapter 1, In the Great Hours of History https://www.Notre-DamedeParis-shurijo.com/eng/html/readmore-Notre-DamedeParis03-rm08/.

[10] Brian Katz (2022), Chap. 1, Restoring acoustics and soundscape. https://www.Notre-DamedeParis-shurijo.com/eng/html/readmore-Notre-DamedeParis05-rm04/.

in 1992, revived essential traditional craft techniques in Okinawa.[11] Although not all Okinawan people had supported the reconstruction at that time, when the reconstructed State Hall was burnt down on October 31, 2019, only twenty-seven years after its reconstruction, many residents in Naha felt that they had lost something significant for them. A scientific committee has been established to prepare for its "re-reconstruction". The to-be-reconstructed State Hall of Shuri-jô Castle will be a new reconstruction so that it will not immediately obtain the formal status as cultural property under Japanese law. However, a subjective link of the local people to the monument is a basis of the cultural heritage.

The restoration of Notre-Dame de Paris Cathedral incentivized experts in France to investigate its intangible aspects comprehensively.[12] More dialogues based on scientific analysis will enrich the debates on authenticity on a global scale. In order to approach tangible and intangible aspects of two different monuments with similar social reactions, purely academic articles would not present the issues sufficiently. Using many visual materials and combining easy-to-understand explanations with scholarly essays will encourage more constructive dialogues.

13.3 Conclusion

The social reactions after the incidents at Notre-Dame de Paris Cathedral and Shuri-jô Castle incentivized to organize the virtual exhibition: Notre-Dame de Paris Cathedral and Shuri-jô Castle - Reconstruct and Restore their Cultural Value - Beyond the Fire of 2019.[13] Two monuments with differences brought similar social reactions and phenomena. Intangible aspects of cultural heritage seem to be a key to understanding them. The exhibition would contribute to stimulating more scientific dialogues. This small article illustrates why this exhibition should be organized as an invitation to visit the exhibition (Fig. 13.1).

[11] "Almost 100 years after the abolition of the Ryukyu Kingdom and 40 years after the end of the war, the traditional skills and techniques required for reconstruction were in danger of being lost. The revival of these techniques and crafts that had once supported the kingdom, including carpentry, lacquering of walls and the application of gorgeous colors, the manufacture of roof tiles, and stone carving, was vital if a faithful reconstruction was to be achieved. The reconstruction of the State Hall provided the best opportunity for researchers and artisans around Japan and Okinawa to come together to revive such techniques and skills." Room 2, Permanence and Transformation, Revival of Techniques and Crafts at https://www.Notre-DamedeParis-shurijo.com/eng/index.shtml.

[12] https://www.Notre-DamedeParis-shurijo.com/eng/html/readmore-Notre-DamedeParis05-rm04/.

[13] https://www.Notre-DamedeParis-shurijo.com/eng/index.shtml.

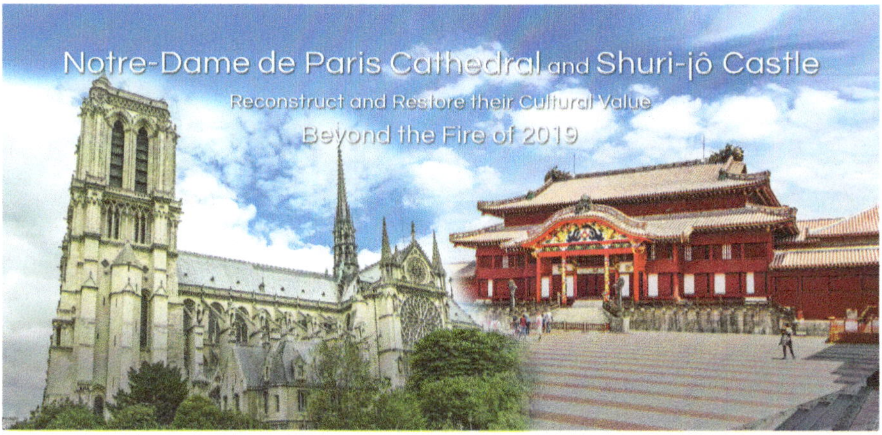

Fig. 13.1 The Virtual Exhibition: Notre-Dame de Paris Cathedral and Shuri-jô Castle—Reconstruct and Restore their cultural value—Beyond the Fire of 2019. https://www.notredame-shurijo.com/eng/index.shtml

Reference

The Virtual Exhibition: Notre-Dame de Paris Cathedral and Shuri-jô Castle—Reconstruct and Restore their Cultural Value—Beyond the Fire of 2019. (2019). https://www.notredame-shurijo.com/eng/index.shtml

Toshiyuki Kono Distinguished professor, Kyushu University, Japan. Toshiyuki Kono was born in Osaka, Japan, in 1958. After graduating from the Faculty of Law, Kyoto University, he went on to obtain his LL.M. from the Graduate School of Law, Kyoto University. He is a specialist in private international law, international civil procedure law, and international cultural heritage law. He was a member of UNESCO's Expert Groups for the drafting of the Convention for the Safeguarding of the Intangible Cultural Heritage (2003) and the Convention on the Protection and Promotion of the Diversity of Cultural Expressions (2005). He was appointed as a member of the Executive Committee of the International Council on Monuments and Sites (ICOMOS) in 2011. After working as vice president, he was elected as the 8th president of ICOMOS in 2017. As the former president, he continues as an honorary president of ICOMOS. He is the series editor of Springer's book series Perspectives in Law, Business and Innovation.

The manufacturer's authorised representative in the EU is Springer Nature Customer Service Centre GmbH, Europaplatz 3, 69115 Heidelberg, Germany. If you have any concerns regarding our products, please contact ProductSafety@springernature.com

Printed and bound by CPI Group (UK) Ltd, Croydon, CR0 4YY
30/09/2026
02225244-0006